THE NORTH AFRICAN STONES SPEAK

Djemila, Severan forum and arch

THE NORTH AFRICAN
STONES SPEAK

PAUL MacKENDRICK

THE UNIVERSITY OF NORTH CAROLINA PRESS

CHAPEL HILL

© 1980 The University of North Carolina Press

All rights reserved

Manufactured in the United States of America

ISBN 0-8078-1414-8

Library of Congress Catalog Card Number 79-18534

Library of Congress Cataloging in Publication Data
MacKendrick, Paul Lachlan, 1914–
  The north African stones speak.

  Bibliography: p.
  Includes index.
  1. Africa, North—Antiquities. 2. Africa, North—
History—To 647. I. Title.
DT191.M28 939'.7 79-18534
ISBN 0-8078-1414-8

CONTENTS

PART 2: LIBYA

PART 3: ALGERIA

ILLUSTRATIONS

PREFACE

In this book, the seventh in a series, I have tried once more to use archaeology to write cultural history. Its predecessors, to which cross-references will appear in the text, are *The Mute Stones Speak* (*MSS*), *The Greek Stones Speak* (*GSS*), *The Iberian Stones Speak* (*ISS*), *Romans on the Rhine* (*RoR*), *Roman France* (*RF*), and *The Dacian Stones Speak* (*DSS*). References to the many valuable scholarly works consulted in the preparation of the present manuscript are contained in the chapter bibliographies that appear at the end of this book. Arabic names have been transliterated throughout the text according to French conventions, except in chapters 5 and 6.

The book is in part the fruit of extensive travel in the Maghreb: in 1944, and (with my wife, who took many of the photographs that appear here) in 1966, 1974, and 1975. It also owes much to the photographs and information supplied by Michel Janon, of the Centre Camille Jullian, Université de Provence, Aix. It is a pleasure once again to thank my colleague Emmett L. Bennett, Jr., for a critical reading of my manuscript; he is responsible for improvements; the remaining flaws are mine. Susan Stevens and Laura Ward, *doctae sermones utriusque linguae*, served above and beyond the call of duty as research assistants. As always, I am indebted to various institutions for material support: the Research Committee of the University of Wisconsin Graduate School; the Department of Classics of the University of Florida; the Rockefeller Foundation, which made available to me the unforgettable amenities of the Villa Serbelloni at Bellagio; the Winston Churchill Foundation of the United States; and the Master and Fellows of Churchill College, Cambridge. It seems to me singularly appropriate that a book about what was on the whole a successful exercise in imperialism should have been written in large part in a college dedicated to the memory of a great defender of another great empire.

ACKNOWLEDGMENTS

Aix-en-Provence, France
  M. Euzennat: 3.4; 7.5
  M. Janon: 8.4, 6, 7, 9, 10, 12, 14; 9.2, 6, 7; 10.2, 8, 9,
    10, 11; 11.2, 3, 4, 5, 6, 10, 11, 13, 15, 18, 19, 20
Algiers, Algeria
  Ministère de l'Information et de la Culture: 7.4; 9.5
Ann Arbor, Michigan
  John Humphrey: 1.5
Berlin, West Germany
  Propyläen Verlag: 11.1
Bristol, England
  B. H. Warmington: 2.1; 4.5
Brussels, Belgium
  Collection Latomus: 8.1
Cambridge, England
  C. R. Whittaker: 8.2
Chicago, Illinois
  R. Schoder, SJ: 6.11
Cologne, West Germany
  DuMont Buchverlag: 7.3
Cyrene, Libya
  Controller of Antiquities: 5.1, 9, 11, 13
Florence, Italy
  Centro degli Studi: 5.18; 6.2, 9, 10
Las Palmas, Canary Islands, Spain
  Adolf Hakkert: 1.8
London, England
  G. Bell & Sons: 2.2
  British Museum: 5.3

Evans Brothers: 1.1 [from *Rome in Africa*, by Susan Raven]
D. B. Harden: 1.6
Journal of Hellenic Studies: 5.15
Journal of Roman Studies: 6.14; 9.4
Roger Wood: frontispiece; 6.6
Madison, Wisconsin
  Dorothy MacKendrick: 1.2, 7, 9; 2.9, 11, 13; 3.3, 5, 6,
    8, 12, 15; 4.1, 6, 8, 15, 16; 5.4, 5, 6, 7, 10, 12, 14;
    6.3, 7, 12; 7.6, 7; 8.3, 5, 8, 11, 15, 16; 9.3, 8; 10.4, 5,
    6, 7; 11.9
Oxford, England
  Oxford University Press: 10.1
Paris, France
  Annales: Economies, Sociétés, Civilisations: 2.4
  Cabinet de Médailles: 5.2
  Doin Editeurs: 7.1
  N. Duval: 4.12; 6.13
  Guides Bleus: 7.2
Philadelphia, Pennsylvania
  Donald White: 5.8
Rabat, Morocco
  Service d'Archéologie: 11.7
Ravenna, Italy
  Longo Editore: 4.13; 5.17
Rome, Italy
  Bretschneider Editore: 3.11; 5.16, 20
  British School at Rome: 6.5
  Deutsches Archäologisches Institut: 2.6, 7, 8, 10, 12;
    3.2, 9 [model owned by INAA, Tunis], 10, 16; 4.4; 5.19;
    6.4, 8; 10.3
  Ecole Française de Rome: 3.1
  Enciclopedia dell'arte antica classica: 4.10
  Fototeca Unione: 3.7; 9.1
  Università degli Studi: 11.1
  J. B. Ward Perkins: 8.13
San Francisco, California
  The Fine Arts Museums: 2.5
Talence, France
  R. Etienne: 11.12, 17

Tripoli, Libya
  Department of Antiquities: 6.1, 15
Tunis, Tunisia
  Bardo Museum: 3.13, 14, 17; 4.2, 3, 7, 14
  Institut National d'Archéologie et d'Art (INAA): 1.3, 4;
    2.3; 3.7; 4.9, 11

PART 1: TUNISIA

1. THE CARTHAGINIAN AREA IN PREHISTORIC AND PUNIC TIMES

At Capsa (modern Gafsa; see map, fig. 1.1) in southern Tunisia, the people, at a carbon 14 date of about 6000 B.C., were very fond of snails, so much so that the shell heaps they left behind them, called *escargotières*, sometimes measure twenty-five meters long, as many wide, and three meters thick. Such a deposit, from what has come to be called the Capsian culture, would require, according to one calculation, twenty-five hundred years to accumulate. We call the descendants of these late Paleolithic snail-eaters Berbers. Nowadays there are many more of them east of Gafsa, in Tripolitania, and west, in Algeria and Morocco, than in Tunisia itself, and their ancestors' most interesting material remains—the Sahara cave-paintings and engravings—come from southern Algeria, and will be described, together with their religious and burial practices, in chapter 7. In historic times the Greeks and Romans called them Garamantes or Gaetulians if they lived in the Libyan desert; Libyans if they were nominally subject to Carthage; Numidians if they dwelt in eastern Algeria; and Moors if their habitat was Mauretania (Morocco). They lived in the open, in small groups; made and used stone tools—burins, blades, and scrapers; and, when the Sahara was cooler and more humid than now, hunted the zebra, antelope, lion, panther, hyena, jackal, bear, and stag, in forests of pine, cedar, cypress, oak, ash, wild olive, poplar, or elm. The Neolithic Revolution seems to have come to them later than to dwellers on the other side of the Mediterranean, perhaps about 3000 B.C. By then they knew the hoe and the plow, and Neolithic sites have yielded spelt, sorghum, millet, barley, beans, peas, turnips, almonds, figs, grapes, and dates.

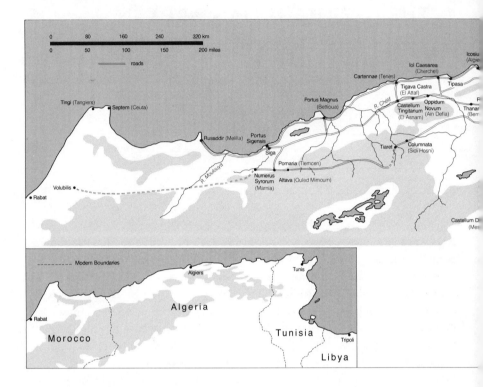

FIGURE I.I *Roman North Africa, map*

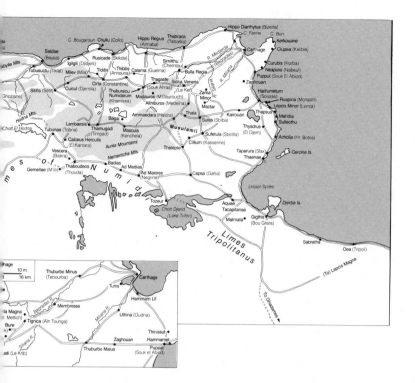

These were the natives with whom Phoenician sailors made contact on their way to exploit the rich metals of Spain, according to tradition, about 1100 B.C. This is the date assigned by literary sources to Utica, some twenty-five kilometers northwest of Carthage, and, as a Phoenician port of call, halfway between Tyre and Cadiz. If the literary sources are trustworthy, Utica is nearly three centuries older than Carthage, and Carthage, whose name means "New Town," is new by comparison with Utica. But there is a discrepancy at Utica between the literary and the archaeological evidence; the earliest of the latter dates only from the eighth century. If the earlier date is a historical fact, the gap may be explained by assuming that contact began with sporadic trade, centered on what was then a sheltered harbor. (The site now lies about eight kilometers inland.) Native resistance may have restricted territorial expansion, but the back country was fertile and attractive, and burials show that Phoenician families were settled here by the eighth century. One of the earliest vases contained the ashes of an infant; a special type of vase was reserved for this use, for the western Phoenicians notoriously sacrificed their firstborn to the god Ba'al—Moloch is the word for the sacrifice, not the god. They covered the faces of the little victims with a laughing mask. Slave babies were substituted when their parents could be persuaded or coerced. The practice continued until the second century B.C., when the god apparently began to find small animals or birds acceptable.

The Punic level at Utica (fig. 1.2) lies far (six meters) below the Roman, and below the modern water table. One large monolithic sarcophagus had, carved inside, a stone pillow, a footrest, and a bridge amidships to keep the friable stone from breaking. A chalcedony scarab with a kneeling archer dates the burial in the sixth century and is one of many evidences of contact with Egypt, including a jasper scarab of the hawk-god Horus, seated among lotus blossoms, and one of the goddess Isis, with a solar boat. She has spread wings, and the sacred uraeus (asp's head, symbol of sovereignty) above. The heavy sarcophagus-covers have cuttings in them for the ropes by which they were let down into the grave. The pottery buried with the corpses included oil flasks whose flat disc-like tops could be rubbed on the skin. One grave was apparently a criminal's; in it was found a skeleton whose hands had been bound behind its back, and its head severed. A sixth-century B.C. child's grave contained feeding bottles and amulets. One monolithic sarcophagus was so perfectly sealed that one could upon first opening it see the outline of the skeleton, with a shroud up to its chin. The contents included a poly-

FIGURE 1.2 *Utica, Punic burials, eighth century* B.C.

chrome glass vial which crumbled to dust on contact with air, and a gold ring with a device of a god—perhaps Ba'al—seated on a throne with winged sphinxes for arms; his scepter is topped with a wheat-ear.

Contacts with Greece as well as Egypt are proved by a grave dated to the seventh century B.C. by a proto-Corinthian pyxis, a round, flat-bottomed, covered box for cosmetics. The Greek painted pottery shows scenes from the Trojan War: Achilles saying farewell to his mother, Thetis; Laodamia's parting with her bridegroom, Protesilaus, destined to be the first to die upon the beach at Troy.

On the whole the imported pottery shows enough differences from that found at Carthage to suggest different mother cities—for example, Tyre for the one and Sidon for the other. Utica, always to some degree the rival of Carthage, opposed her in the Third Punic War (149–146 B.C.) and was rewarded by being made the capital of the Roman province of Africa; her later history, as archaeology reveals it, is more conveniently told in the next chapter, in a Roman context.

With Carthage, as with Utica, there is a discrepancy between the historical and the archaeological dates. The traditional date of its founding is 814 B.C., and its alleged founder, Tyrian Dido, was a real person, the

niece of the notorious Jezebel in the Bible, who died in 843. But there is
no archaeological evidence earlier than the early or mid–eighth century,
which is the pottery date of the level called Tanit I, in the so-called tophet
(place of human sacrifice) of Salammbô near the seashore about one
hundred meters west of the rectangular commercial harbor. This is a
necropolis, incompletely excavated (fig. 1.3), where thousands of children, from two to twelve years old, were immolated to the Phoenician
high god Ba'al, and in later, fifth-century phases, to the mother-goddess
Tanit, called "face of Ba'al" and probably regarded as his consort. The
ceremonies were held at night before a bronze statue of the god, with a
trench before it and a brazier below. The relatives of the small victim
were in attendance; there was music, and dancers, wearing masks. The
priest placed the infant in the arms of the statue; it rolled into the flames.
Music of fifes, tambourines, and lyres, and wild dancing averted attention from the grief of the parents, who were forbidden to express their
sorrow audibly. In the earliest phase of the cemetery, dated by pottery
from 800 B.C. to the early seventh century, cremation urns, with milk-
teeth among the ashes, were found under cairns standing on bedrock.

Tanit I is separated from Tanit II by a thin level of viscous yellow clay,
of a sort which was laid down whenever a tophet needed reorganization.
Tanit II dates from the early seventh to the late fourth century B.C. At this
level the cremation urns were placed in groups under grave-stelae on
either side of a pathway. On one of the stelae was incised the figure of a
bonneted priest carrying in the crook of his arm an infant for sacrifice.
Another stele records the priesthood of Tanit as handed down in one
family for seventeen generations. In Tanit III, which runs from the late
fourth century to the Roman destruction of Carthage in 146 B.C., the
cremation urns were found loose in the earth and scattered by later construction. From the lowest to the highest level the incidence of sacrifice of
the newborn decreases from 55 percent to 22 percent.

Other burial places, not all of children, have been excavated on the
inward side of slopes surrounding the ancient city (plan, fig. 1.4): on the
Byrsa hill, crowned by the preternaturally ugly nineteenth-century ex-
cathedral; on the Hill of Juno, northeast of the Byrsa; in the Dermech
quarter behind the Antonine Baths (this area has been transformed into a
shady archaeological park); at Ard et-Touibi, east of Dermech; in the
Ancona district, north of the baths; and around the odeon and theater.
The richest graves are inhumations from before 480 B.C.; the defeat in
that year by the Sicilian Greeks of a Carthaginian armada off Himera, on
the north coast of Sicily, ushered in a period of depression. Among the

FIGURE 1.3 *Carthage, Salammbô tophet, eighth century* B.C.

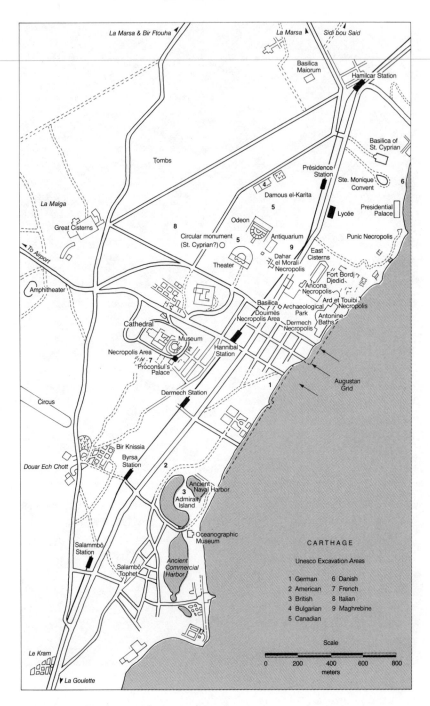

FIGURE 1.4 *Carthage and necropoleis, plan*

grave goods from the prosperous years were found, for instance, in the Dermech area, gold and filigree jewelry, scarabs, ostrich eggs, ivories, coral, scallop shells (for holding cosmetics), and toy furniture. On the Hill of Juno (seventh to fifth centuries) some of the pottery comes from Corinth, some is glossy black Etruscan bucchero ware; a Carthaginian treaty with the Etruscans is dated 509 B.C. From here, too, come silver signet rings, inset with scarabs, and ornaments in onyx and alabaster. Many of the finds are irretrievable in the Bardo Museum storerooms, which have been described by a Frenchman as the most important dig in Tunisia.

Interest in these finds is inspired in part by the fascination of the tragic and romantic figure of Dido, the legendary foundress of Carthage. Daughter of the king of Tyre, she fled, according to the legend, to the African coast from her bloodthirsty brother Pygmalion, who had murdered her husband. She bought from a native chief, Iarbas, as much land as could be covered with a bull's hide (*byrsa* in Greek). Prompted by her native Phoenician cunning to cut the hide into strips, she acquired all the land the strips encircled, but did not enjoy it long, for she built a pyre and committed suicide to avoid the unwelcome advances of Iarbas. Vergil's version of the story, in which Dido's suicide is motivated by unrequited love for Aeneas, who abandons her at Jupiter's command to found a new Troy in Italy, has captured the imagination of readers from Saint Augustine, who in his *Confessions* scolds himself "because I wept for Dido, who killed herself for love," to Harvard undergraduates, who, sympathizing with the jilted queen, voted Aeneas "the epic hero least likely to succeed."

Dido's city prospered from trade and was until 480 dominant in the western Mediterranean. The archaeological evidence for this is the two harbors (fig. 1.5), one circular, for naval vessels, and one rectangular, for merchant ships. The outlines of these harbors survive today between the Salammbô tophet and the sea. Scuba diving has failed to reveal alleged traces of a harbor to the south of the rectangular port. The harbors intercommunicated and had a common entrance from the sea, seventy feet wide, which could be closed with chains. Sediment from excavation in

FIGURE 1.5 *Carthage, naval and commercial harbors (stone-built phase, fourth century* B.C.*)*

FIGURE 1.6 *Hanno's periplus (before 480 B.C.), map*

the harbor has yielded evidence of Carthaginian diet in fruit and nuts: pomegranate (*malum punicum*, "Punic apple"), fig, grape, olive, peach, plum, melon, lotus, almond, pistachio, filbert. Recent British excavation, sponsored by UNESCO, has revealed three Punic levels on the island in the middle of the circular harbor, with two phases—the first in timber,[1] the second (fourth century B.C.) in stone—of the 220 shipsheds mentioned as being there by Appian, writing in Rome in the mid-second century A.D. Also of the fourth century B.C. is an amphora-sherd pavement, the date guaranteed by south Italian black-glaze fragments. These improvements bespeak the prosperity of a city revived after the depression that followed the defeat of Carthage at the battle of Himera (480 B.C.). The Punic city's wall, thirteen meters high and nine meters thick, triple on the landward side, with a four-story tower every fifty-nine meters, and stalls in casemates for three hundred elephants and four thousand horses, was twenty-one Roman miles around. The population was between 300,000 and 400,000. At its apogee in the sixth century B.C. it was the world's most powerful state, the first city-state to try to rule an empire. It controlled the North African coast from the Altars of the Philaeni, on the Libyan coast, to the Atlantic, though its influence inland did not extend much beyond the boundaries of present-day Tunisia.

Its maritime supremacy is symbolized by the expedition of Hanno (before 480 B.C.; fig. 1.6) through the Pillars of Hercules (Straits of Gibraltar) and down the West African coast perhaps as far south as Sierra Leone. The ancient source states that the expedition was state-sponsored, to found cities, and that Hanno commanded sixty fifty-oared ships bearing thirty thousand passengers of both sexes—an implausible number. They saw elephants, troglodytes, inhospitable savages wearing animal skins; crocodiles, hippos, a volcano, and gorillas, of whom they caught and flayed three females and brought their skins back to Carthage. Perhaps the gorillas appear in myth as Gorgons. Hanno's story contains so many puzzles and so many fearsome wonders that some scholars think it was deliberately intended to put Carthage's rivals off the scent and scare them away.

---

1. The latest excavators emphasize that there is no archaeological evidence relating these harbors to the original Phoenician colony.

Expansion brought the Carthaginians into contact with Sicilian Greek culture and religion, so that early in the fourth century we find them worshiping the Greek vegetation-goddess Ceres (but in the plural, Cereres). They came to the attention of Aristotle, who in his *Politics* (1272b24–1273b27) describes their constitution as it was about 335 B.C., the only non-Greek constitution so honored. The population of the Carthaginian *territorium* was (according to Newman) seven hundred thousand; the government, Aristotle says, was oligarchic at home, monarchic in the field—either way stable, unlikely to degenerate into tyranny. There was a council of 104, unpaid, not chosen by lot. The highest office, that of *suffete*, was reserved for the rich, and purchasable. As a safety valve for political unrest, the Carthaginians sent out a part of the common people into colonies.

Perhaps Aristotle had in mind the ports of call along the coast at regular intervals, westward to the Atlantic, or he might have been thinking of towns in what is now Tunisia: Gigthis, Tacapae (Gabès), Thaenae, Acholla, Thysdrus (El Djem), Thapsus, Lepcis Minor, Ruspina (Monastir), Hadrumetum (Sousse), Neapolis (Nabeul), Kerkouane, Utica, Hippo Diarrhytus (Bizerte), Thabraca (Tabarka), and others on into Algeria. At many of these there are Punic necropoleis. One at Thapsus proved particularly rich, yielding a wooden catafalque, a gleaming Greek black-glaze lamp of Hellenistic date, water jars, incense burners, and a mother-of-pearl ointment box with silver hinges. Some of the sites will be described below in later phases as revealed by archaeology. Generally the Carthaginians allowed these towns home rule, as being less trouble—a practice largely followed later by the Romans in North Africa, and for the same reason.

Carthaginian economic power is reflected in the Etruscan treaty of 509, which guarantees a Punic mercantile monopoly in the western Mediterranean; and a Carthaginian colony in Etruria is probably to be inferred from three inscribed early fifth-century gold plaques, one in Punic, two in Etruscan, found in 1964 at Pyrgi, the port of Caere in southern Tuscany, and recording a dedication to Uni-Astarte by the ruler of Caere.

Rivalry between Carthaginians and Greeks in Sicily led in 310 B.C. to an invasion of Carthaginian territory by the Syracusan tyrant Agathocles, who with fourteen thousand men from sixty ships landed on Cape Bon, burnt his boats (thus originating a proverb), and from a base at Clupea (modern Kelibia) took two hundred "cities," and nearly captured Carthage, though he failed at last and withdrew to Sicily. The Sicilian historian Diodorus, who wrote in the middle third of the first century B.C., describes the prosperity of Carthaginian territory at the time of Agathocles' invasion: market gardens, vineyards, orchards, irrigation channels, stuccoed villas, teeming barns, flocks of sheep and herds of cattle, and horses.

Archaeology has revealed the mute remains of a unique site that felt the force of Agathocles' invasion: this is Kerkouane (Dar Essafi) on Cape Bon, near Kelibia, the most complete Carthaginian inhabited site yet excavated. Its original settlers may have been refugees from Nebuchadnezzar's taking of Tyre in 574. Its walls enclosed some fifty hectares; it had wide streets and a regular plan. The houses were constructed of poor materials, but handsomely stuccoed over, the stucco painted gray or red. The house walls, of earth pressed between boards, were strengthened by cut stone inset upright, in a technique that, though called *opus Africanum*, was thought to be Roman until Kerkouane was discovered. The house plans resemble closely those of Tunisia today, sometimes, but not always, built round a central court paved with a pink cement called *opus signinum*, made waterproof by adding ground-up potsherds to the mixture. Inset into these floors are bits of black, greenish, or dark blue glass paste, often forming the Tanit sign (a triangle with arms) flanked by dolphins, to ward off ill luck.

The House of the Sphinx, in the center of the town, its outside door angled to balk the curiosity of passers-by, has ten rooms, of which one measures a sizable ten by seven-and-a-half meters, its roof once supported by two columns. The open court, which is not central, contained an oven, a handmill for grinding grain, and (fig. 1.7) a shoe-shaped hip bath. (Claims that these, a number of which were found on the site, were vats used for mixing purple dye have proved to be without foundation, though a thick layer of shells of the murex—the mollusc from which the dye is derived—has been found outside the walls.) One room was used as a glass-blower's workshop, and in the room adjoining was found the mold for a winged uraeus. In one corner was a chapel that contained a skull and the terra-cotta altar with a sphinx after which the house is named. There is a reception room frescoed to imitate marble, in what is irreverently called the fried-egg pattern. The dining room has a Dionysiac frieze and a blue and white mosaic floor. The reception room had a pebble-mosaic of a griffin attacking a stag. The women's and children's quarters were above; one of the finds was a nursing bottle fallen from an upper floor. Pits containing the remains of sacrifices have led to the conjecture that in at least one of its three phases (dated from 500 to 150 B.C.) a part of the house was in use as a temple. No public religious buildings—nor for that matter civil ones—have yet been found. Kilns prove that pottery was locally made. A small terra-cotta plaque from a private house, showing a bearded figure in a cylindrical cap, riding a sea horse, perhaps represents the Phoenician sea-god Yam, equated with Greek Poseidon, Roman Neptune. The discovery of a number of hooks and weights for nets shows that fishing was important.

Located about a kilometer and a half northwest of the walled city, its necropolis included four chamber-tombs and one grave. The grave goods (fourth–third centuries B.C.; Kerkouane, rebuilt after Agathocles' depredations, was destroyed again, by the Roman Regulus, in 256) included pottery, mostly local, fish and animal bones, eggs, bronze coins (unidentified by the excavators), razors, earrings, a Greek signet ring with the device of an armed warrior, and a scarab in jasper representing an animal-headed Egyptian god. The most interesting find, however, was a wooden sarcophagus painted red (now in the Utica site museum) with an anthropoid cover in the shape of a clothed female figure (the goddess Astarte or a worshiper), her left hand carved separately and placed across her breast. Her hair is parted in the middle, and she wears the headdress, rather like a chef's hat, that the Greeks call a *polos* (still worn by Greek Orthodox priests). She is coated with plaster painted red, blue, and yellow. The Tunisian press, when she was discovered, was quick to name her "the princess of Kerkouane."

Just before World War II the French excavated sixteen tombs at Djebel Mlezza, also on Cape Bon, one of which had unique wall paintings depicting a mausoleum, an altar, and a walled town with seventeen houses and a cock, but no human figures. This mural is dated by coins that show Demeter (Ceres in Latin), palm, and horse (Dido found a horse's head on the Byrsa), and by Italian black-glaze ware, to a time just

FIGURE 1.7 Kerkouane, purple-dye vats (sixth century B.C.)

before Agathocles' landing. There were wooden coffins and traces of a shroud, and also many Egyptian amulets, including a Horus and the squat comic god Bes, but deformed hieroglyphs suggest copies, not understood.

Though most of the towns in Carthaginian territory speak to us most eloquently in their Roman phase, Hadrumetum (Sousse), a seaport 141 kilometers by road south of Tunis, is a Punic foundation earlier than Carthage, with a population in its prime of perhaps ten thousand, where has been excavated a Punic sanctuary in use from the seventh–sixth century B.C. to sometime in the first Christian century. Six levels have been distinguished, strongly reminiscent of the Salammbô tophet. Here, too, the presence of milk-teeth in the ash urns betrays infant sacrifice. The finds in the lowest level included amber, coral, and carnelian jewelry, ostrich eggs, a silver earring, beads, and a mask in glass paste. Level II from the bottom (fourth–third century B.C., a period in which Hadrumetum was sacked by Agathocles) yielded some interesting stelae. One represents a seated god, wrapped like a mummy; Ba'al in a tiara, seated on a griffin, greeted by a minuscule worshiper; a seated divinity holding an orb, facing a stand with another orb, with a crescent above, horns downward; an altar bearing three trapezoidal pillars, called betyls, characteristic symbols of Ba'al worship; and a winged Isis, perhaps to be identified with Tanit. Level II was separated from Level III (third–second century B.C.) by a layer of golden sand. Level III is dated by coins showing the new Greek influence upon Carthage; the coin device has the Greek goddess of agriculture, Demeter, on the obverse, and the usual Carthaginian palm tree on the reverse. In Level IV (second–first century B.C., including the year of Carthage's fall, 146), the ash urns sometimes contain the bones of animals or birds instead of those of children. From names on the stelae it is possible to construct a family tree of six generations, stretching from the end of the third century down to 50 B.C. Level V embraces the first half of the first century of our era. Motifs include a betyl like a large egg, seated on a throne, and several scenes of worshipers sacrificing. There were no human bones in Level V urns. Finally, Level VI (late first century A.D.) rests on concrete, sealing in all below. It yielded stelae with crude representations of animals. The later history of Hadrumetum, and especially the remarkable flowering of a school of mosaicists there, are best discussed when we deal with the high Roman period in chapter 3.

At El Kenissia, six kilometers south of Hadrumetum, excavation has revealed a typical Punic sanctuary: an open court with a cistern under it, a portico, an altar on a High Place that is reached by steps, chapels containing statues, and a burial place for the bones of sacred animals.

The prosperity revealed by so many of the graves and sanctuaries was brought about not only by maritime trade but also by expert capital farming. One of the most famous agricultural handbooks of the ancient world was written by the Carthaginian Mago in the third century B.C. Translated into Latin after Rome's destruction of Carthage in 146, it contributed to the development of Italian wines, for of its twenty-eight books (of which sixty-six fragments survive) ten were devoted to viticulture. Another ten were on the raising of horses and cattle, and there were four on beekeeping.

A state this prosperous could only be looked upon with suspicion and fear by the rising power of Rome; the clash came in Sicily, in 264 B.C., the date of the beginning of the first of three Punic wars, which occupied 54 of the 118 years between 264 and 146. Here we must confine our attention to the impact of the wars upon North Africa. In 256 the Roman general M. Atilius Regulus landed, like Agathocles a half-century before, on Cape Bon, with allegedly 140,000 men in 330 ships, but was defeated and captured. Later, the Romans made of him a secular saint and martyr, extolling the courage which prompted him, having been sent back to Rome by his captors to urge peace, to advise the contrary and then, having given his word to return, pluckily to go back to Carthage, well knowing what the "barbarian torturer" had in store for him. The most refined punishment recorded was cutting off his eyelids and exposing him to a strong light.

Since for this history no Carthaginian sources survive, the Romans' enemy suffers from an unrefuted reputation for cruelty. One of their own kings, we are told, paid for subversion by being flogged and blinded; his limbs were broken, and his subjects crucified his lifeless corpse. Cruel and overweening in prosperity, they were abject, Appian tells us, in adversity; and Plutarch, with anti-Semitism rare in antiquity, generalizes about the Phoenicians: they are bitter, surly, tyrannical, fierce, fanatical, stern, humorless, and unkindly. One other memorable tale survives from the First Punic War: of the Roman admiral P. Claudius Pulcher, aboard whose flagship the sacred chickens refused to eat before a battle. "If they will not eat, then let them drink," he cried, throwing them into the sea. Of course he lost the battle (the date was 249 B.C.), but the Romans did not lose the war. In 241 the Carthaginians sued for peace, which involved their evacuating Sicily and paying, over a ten-year period, an indemnity of 3,200 talents (£3,840,000 uninflated).[2]

The defeat of Carthage meant that she could not pay her mercenaries. The story of their revolt is immortally told in Flaubert's *Salammbô*. Their leader Matho, a Libyan giant unkindly described by a contemporary of Flaubert as "an opera tenor in a barbarous poem," loves Salammbô, priestess of Tanit and elder sister of the future war hero Hannibal. Matho steals the sacred veil of Tanit; Salammbô sacrifices her honor to get it back, and falls in love with Matho. The mercenaries are defeated, Matho is tortured to death, and Salammbô, grieving, dies. The book evokes a voluptuous, gorgeous, exotic picture, meticulously exact, the fruit of a fifty-day visit to Carthage and ten years of reading and revising; Flaubert would rewrite a single passage as many as fourteen times. Few men have to better purpose used archaeology to write history—in Flaubert's case more nearly an epic poem.

The Second Punic War (218–201) belongs to Hannibal Barca (the family name means "Thunderbolt"), that hero of a lost cause admired by all who nourish a sympathy for the underdog. The story of the oath of eternal enmity to the Romans, exacted by his father Hamilcar when the boy was nine years old, and of his epic crossing of the Alps and ravaging of Italy, which the south of that country has not even yet got over, is too familiar to need retelling and falls outside the scope of this book. But connoisseurs of romance would not want to see omitted the story of the Carthaginian princess Sophonisba (or Sophoniba), who married the Numidian prince Syphax and converted him to the Carthaginian cause. When he was overthrown, his rival Masinissa gave her poison to save her from captivity at Rome.

Our main concern, however, is with Hannibal's return to Africa and his confrontation with "a greater than Napoleon," Scipio Africanus the Elder, at the battle of Zama (202 B.C.). Hannibal, whose family, the Barcids, had estates near Hadrumetum, landed there from Italy and used

2. I.e., calculating twenty cents to the gold franc, the 1914 rate of exchange.

it as his base. A good deal of ink has been spilt over the site of the battle. The question is complicated by the existence of more than one Zama (see map, fig. 1.8) and the problem of whether Zama Maior and Zama Regia are two names for the same town. Most scholars identify Zama Regia with Sebaa Biar. In any case, Zama was the site of Hannibal's camp, not of the battle. The plain of Draa el-Metnan, west of Sebaa Biar and southwest of Sicca Veneria (Le Kef, perhaps founded from the Sanctuary of Venus at Eryx in western Sicily; the basis for the conjecture is temple prostitution in both places, but in Sicca this may have been derived from native Berber practice) is a likely spot for the battle, since it affords space for the eighty thousand infantry, ten thousand cavalry, and eighty-three elephants that were involved. Hannibal, defeated, counseled peace, according to the terms of which Carthage gave up her navy and the lands Hannibal's father had won in Spain, and retained her territory in what is now Tunisia, but became a satellite state to Rome, which exacted an indemnity of ten thousand talents, payable over fifty years. After a term as *suffete* (chief magistrate) of Carthage, Hannibal was forced into exile by his political enemies, fled to Asia, and finally committed suicide (183 or 182 B.C.), allegedly by drinking bull's blood, to avoid falling into Roman hands. So died antiquity's noblest failure. If Hannibal had won, Gibbon's culture-bound nightmare of the Koran taught to circumcised Oxonians might have become reality—as indeed it yet may. But he lost, and Rome was dominant in the western Mediterranean for nearly seven hundred years.

Rome would not have won the Second Punic War without the help of the Numidian king Masinissa (reigned 203–148), one of the most remarkable native personalities that North Africa ever produced. His reign will be more appropriately discussed in chapter 7; here suffice it to say that his expropriation of Carthaginian territory—Carthage in 172 complained to Rome that he had seized seventy towns and forts—goaded Carthage into retaliating, in violation of the peace treaty of 201, and thus gave Rome an excuse for the Third Punic War and the total destruction of Carthage. Among the places with which we shall later be concerned that fell into Masinissa's hands were Tacapae (Gabès), the oasis city, later the terminus of a Roman military road; the whole north coastal area from Thabraca westward; the rich farmland round Souk el-Khmis, later to form part of vast Roman imperial estates (*saltus*); and Thugga (Dougga), where a famous and nearly perfectly restored mausoleum (fig. 1.9) was perhaps a cenotaph erected in Masinissa's honor. It is dated 139, and is twenty-one meters high. Approached by rock-cut steps, it is

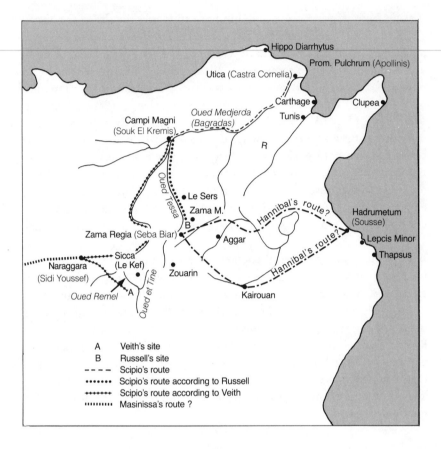

FIGURE 1.8 *Battle of Zama, 202 B.C., plan*

FIGURE 1.9 *Thugga, Punic mausoleum, 139 B.C.*

built in three levels capped by a pyramid. The first level contained the tomb, with one window on the north and false windows on the other three sides. It has Aeolic capitals with lotus motifs. The second level is of the Ionic order; the third is Aeolic again, with a relief of a four-horse chariot. At the corners of the pyramid are Sirens holding the sphere of heaven; a lion, symbolizing the sun, tops all. The architecture mingles Greek with Egyptian–Near Eastern motifs. Also into Masinissa's hands fell the area around Bulla Regia (later famous for its rich underground apartments; its epithet suggests the residence of a king) and Mactar, one of whose citizens, the "Mactar Reaper," a third of a millennium later, would typify the local boy who makes good.

Meanwhile in Rome the old puritan Cato the Elder was revolted at what he saw as Carthaginian loose morals. His prejudice was reflected in our time by King, the classics master in Kipling's short story "Regulus," who is made to refer to Carthage as "a god-forsaken nigger Brummagem." Cato was also perhaps impressed at Masinissa's "cry wolf" diplomacy. At all events he displayed to his fellow senators ripe figs gathered in Carthage only three days before, to dramatize the fertility of Carthaginian soil and the closeness of the alleged Carthaginian menace; and thereafter, as every schoolboy used to know, he ended every speech, whatever the subject, with the words "Karthago delenda est" (Carthage must be destroyed). In 149 Rome declared war on Carthage; eighty thousand Roman infantry, four thousand cavalry, and fifty quinqueremes formed the expeditionary force. Many cities in Carthage's territory—

Utica, Hadrumetum, Thapsus, Lepcis Minor, Acholla—went over to Rome; only Hippo Diarrhytus, Neferis, Tunis, Clupea, and Neapolis remained loyal. Though the Carthaginians gave three hundred hostages, the Roman general Scipio Aemilianus, adoptive grandson of the victor of Zama, inexorably set about starving the city out. The citizens had been moved to a heroic last-ditch struggle by a Roman demand that they abandon their city and settle elsewhere. With the fever of despair they set about manufacturing armaments; the women gave their springy hair for use in catapults. Scipio set up an earthwork counterwall, traces of which were found in 1949, together with his camp, now under the Carthage airport. In town, near the present BP station, was found a stock of nearly 3,000 clay sling-bullets, and on the coast 150 meters north of the naval harbor, 2,500 stone ballista balls, ranging in diameter from ten to thirty centimeters; 222 of them bear twelve different Punic signs. He was to build just such a counterwall thirteen years later at Numantia in Spain (see *ISS*, fig. 5.6), with the same intent: to keep the besieged from breaking out or supplies from coming in. He blockaded the naval harbor with a mole containing 12,000 to 18,000 cubic meters of material; the defenders scorched the earth around it. There was house-to-house fighting for six days and nights, from the harbor to the Byrsa hill; finally, the fifty-five thousand in the citadel surrendered. The Romans set fire to the city; a burnt stratum two feet thick on the west side of the hill of Saint Louis testifies to how thoroughly they did their work. The blaze raged unchecked for ten days. Noncombatants were burned alive. The historian Polybius, who was with Scipio at the end, reports that the victor quoted Homer on the fall of Troy and wept at the thought that Rome, too, would one day suffer a like fate. But he licensed the soldiers to plunder, the male inhabitants were sold into slavery, the buildings of the city were leveled to the ground, the site plowed over, salt sown in the furrows, and a ritual curse pronounced. Carthage was not to rise again for a hundred years.

Many scholars think that Rome destroyed the city to keep it out of the hands of Masinissa's Numidians. The old king had hoped to be given Carthage as a present; instead, he died two years before she fell. (Cato, too, did not live to gloat over the fallen enemy.) All Masinissa's heirs got out of the Third Punic War was Carthage's library—a symbol of how thoroughly Punicized Masinissa's Numidia had become. The cities that had been loyal to Carthage were destroyed; the rest were freed, and their territory enlarged. Utica became the capital of Rome's new province of Africa. Carthaginian civilization and political forms survived in Numidian territory.

Meanwhile, Rome learned from Carthage how to exploit conquered territory, and Roman moralists connected the destruction of Carthage with the beginning of the century of violence called the Roman Revolution. The large estates (*latifundia*) in the fertile Tunisian hinterland were run according to the precepts of Mago, whose agricultural treatise, as we saw, was now translated into Latin. The estates produced pomegranates ("Punic apples"), olives, and honey. The Romans learned from their African subjects how to lay cut-marble floors (*opus sectile*), to weather-proof beehives with clay, to tan the soft leather we now call "morocco"; perhaps to make *garum* (fish sauce), appreciated by ancient gourmets; and to keep monopolies by limiting the growing of vines. Carthaginian war prisoners, enslaved, worked the latifundia, and perhaps the use of *coloni*, free laborers tied to the land, derived from the Carthaginians' practice of demanding free labor from natives in their territory.

2. FROM THE CONQUEST THROUGH NERVA, 146 B.C.–A.D. 98

Not all the sons of Carthage perished or were enslaved in the debacle of 146. One Hasdrubal, a philosopher who had migrated to Athens and changed his name to Clitomachus, addressed to the survivors his *Consolation*, which mourned their city's fall, and lived to become (127 B.C.) head of the Academic school, which Plato had founded.

Out of the most fertile part of the Carthaginian territory—about five thousand square miles in the northeast corner of modern Tunisia—the Romans made their new province of Africa, governed from Utica. Scipio's engineers traced a frontier line, the Fossa Regia (see map, fig. 2.1), running irregularly from Thabraca to south of Taparura (Sfax) and dividing Roman territory from Numidia, which fell under the rule of Masinissa's heirs. In 122 B.C. the Roman tribune Gaius Gracchus, ignoring the curse that had been pronounced upon Carthage, led thither a draft of six thousand colonists and named the new foundation Junonia. (Juno, consort of Jupiter the Best and Greatest, was the Roman equivalent of Carthaginian Tanit.) Each colonist was allotted two hundred *iugera* of land (a *iugerum*, a quarter of a hectare, is what a yoke—*iugum*—of oxen can plow in a day). The allotments were laid out on a rectangular grid; the Romans called the process centuriation. The surveyors marked the intersections of the grid with stakes, which one night were systematically pulled up by wolves. Scholarly opinion is virtually unanimous that the wolves were two-legged, perhaps reactionaries who were against distribution of land to the landless, but more likely natives resentful of the loss of their land. So the colony died, but the allotments were sold to investors; this led to

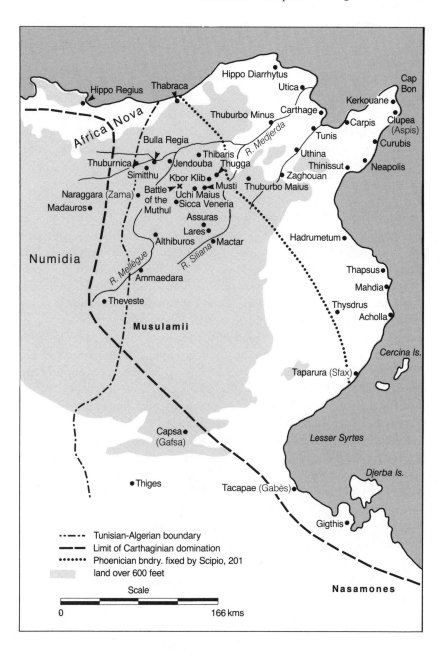

FIGURE 2.1 *Africa Proconsularis, map*

the rise of *latifundia*, usually run by bailiffs for absentee landlords. The less valuable land was assigned to native communities on lease subject to revocation.

Air photographs, taken in an oblique light in the dry season, have revealed (fig. 2.2) hundreds of square miles of centuriation seldom visible on the ground. Not all of it is Gracchan, and not all of it is oriented in the same direction. In Carthage itself two orientations are visible (fig. 2.3), one for the city proper, another for the countryside. The city plan centers on the crossing of the Cardo Maximus (main north-south street) and the Decumanus Maximus (main east-west street). The city blocks, called by the Romans *insulae* (islands), were rectangular, measuring 120 by 480 Roman feet. The intersection mentioned above falls within the walls of the ex-cathedral, on the Byrsa hill, which was the citadel of Dido's Carthage and perhaps the forum of the Roman city (the seaside location of the forum on the map is controversial). The weight of scholarly opinion inclines to date the city plan of Carthage to the foundation of the Augustan colony (29 B.C.). We are privileged to have a poeticized account of the founding in Vergil's *Aeneid* (1.418–438): the description of the bustle attending the building of Dido's new city, as Aeneas sees it for the first time. He marvels at the massive buildings, once mere huts (the word Vergil uses, *magalia*, survives in the name of La Malga, a suburb of Carthage, the site of massive Roman cisterns); at the gates, at the din, the paved streets, the industrious activity, compared by the poet to the labor of bees: building the circuit wall, rearing the citadel, rolling up stones by hand, drawing the ritual furrow around the new colony, digging harbors, laying the foundations of the theater, quarrying columns for it. Vergil may have attributed to his patron Augustus the responsibility for some of the building that must have gone on when Julius Caesar decreed the revival of Carthage in 46 B.C., just a century after its destruction. Caesar's is probably the centuriation differently oriented, seen at a slant on the plan. This in turn may have followed the lines laid down by Gaius Gracchus' surveyors in 122.

The difficulty with dating comes about because one cannot date surveyors' ditches by looking at air photographs; there have to be ground reconnaissances and datable potsherds, and very little of this sort of work has been done in Tunisia. However, five different orientations have been distinguished countrywide; this is the largest centuriated area ever

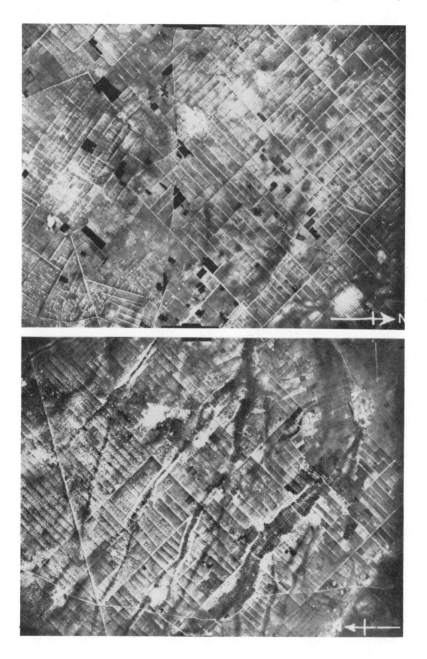

FIGURE 2.2 *Proconsularis, centuriation, air view*

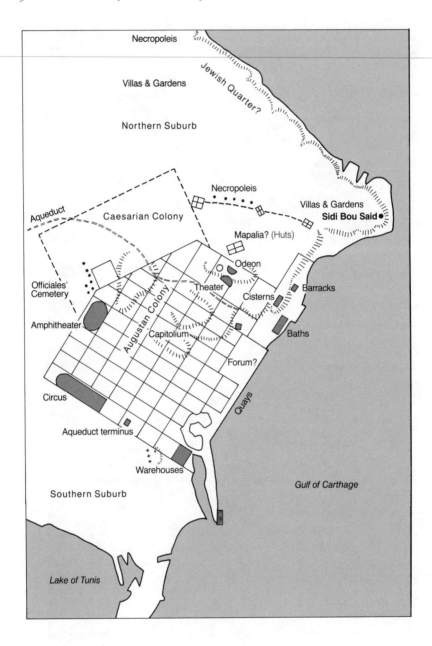

FIGURE 2.3 *Carthage, centuriation*

made available for study through air photographs. A northern group (fig. 2.4) extends from Bizerte to Enfida and from Cape Bon to Teboursouk; it measures 150 by 180 kilometers and is oriented 32° off true north. It is possible that it was laid down early, perhaps for the Gracchan colonists, perhaps in connection with the agrarian law of 111, which put public land up for sale to private owners. An east-central group, oriented 42°, stretches from Sousse to Chebba, a coastal strip of 120 kilometers long by 30 wide; this corresponds to the territory of Caesar's *civitates liberae*, cities whose land was confiscated because they had chosen the losing side in his war with Pompey. The area around Thysdrus (El Djem) is differently oriented (37°), the surveyors' *limites* (guidelines) marked by white pebbles. The date could be anywhere between Gracchus' time and the reign of Tiberius (A.D. 14–37). The southeast group centers round Acholla, and is oriented 32°; it is dated after Caesar was active there, which was in 46 B.C. West of Tacapae (Gabès) a number of boundary stones of centuriated areas have been found, dating from A.D. 29; the work was done by the Legio III Augusta, a sort of Foreign Legion stationed for centuries in North Africa. Nearby runs the Tacapae-Capsa-Ammaedara military road, dated by milestones to A.D. 14. A fifth and final group is oriented 28°. It lies west of the Fossa Regia, where Marius, victorious Roman general in the war (112–105 B.C.) against the Numidian prince Jugurtha, Masinissa's illegitimate grandson, settled some of his veterans. An inscription of Marian date has been found at Ghardimaou, in this district.

After the Legio III Augusta left Ammaedara for Theveste, about A.D. 75, the area vacated by the troops was centuriated on the Roman government's initiative. The district contained many private estates, some owned by Italian absentee landlords, some by native aristocrats. Both needed, and some exploited, native labor, slave and free. The free laborers, the *coloni*, came more and more to be tied to the land, like medieval serfs; we shall be exploring more of their story in chapter 3. Meanwhile, centuriation made many nomads sedentary and brought the natives what they needed to civilize themselves. In modern Tunisia, buildings, roads, railroads, and town sites are based on Roman centuriation.

Scipio Aemilianus, as hereditary patron of the Numidian royal house, encouraged the pretensions of Jugurtha, which involved Rome in squabbles over the division of the kingdom. The murder of some Roman

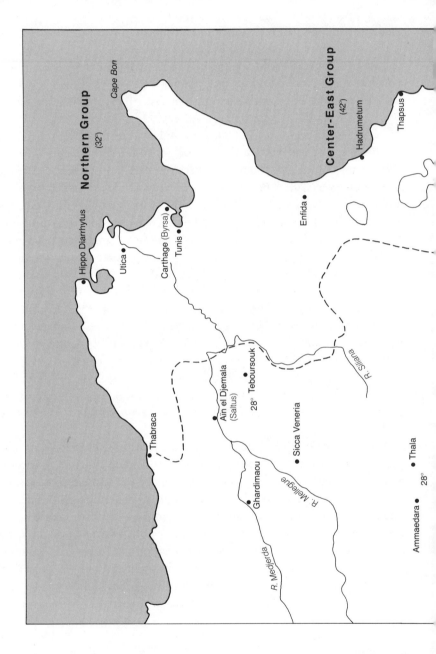

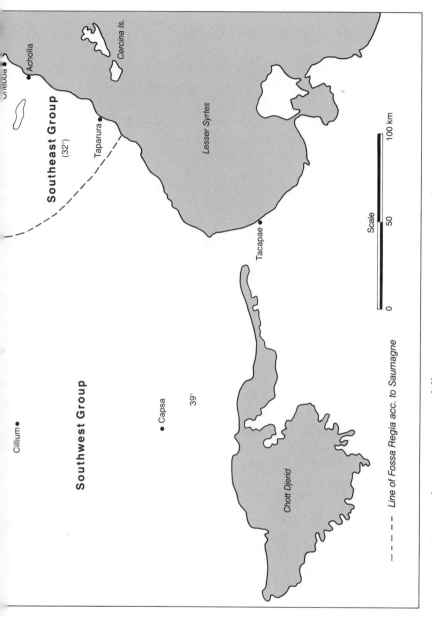

Cillium ●

Southwest Group

● Capsa

39°

Chott Djerid

Oreona ●
Acholla ●

Southeast Group

(32°)

Taparura ●

Cercina Is.

Lesser Syrtes

Tacapae ●

Scale

0   50   100 km

– – – – – Line of Fossa Regia acc. to Saumagne

FIGURE 2.4 *Proconsularis, centuriation, different orientations*

businessmen in Cirta, the Numidian capital, caused anger and bellicosity in Rome. The story of the Jugurthine War is told in a surviving monograph by the historian Sallust; it is an exciting tale of guerilla warfare, scorched earth, poisoned wells, raids, and ambushes, and also much graft and for a time incompetence on the Roman side. Jugurtha, though poorly qualified to take a moral line, called Rome a city up for sale, if only she could find a buyer. The Roman general Q. Caecilius Metellus, who led the forces against Jugurtha, was a nabob whose family counted six consuls, four censors, and five generals who won the honor of a triumph. Like the Carthaginian Clitomachus, he had been a pupil of the skeptic philosopher Carneades. His lieutenant P. Rutilius Rufus had philosophic training also, under the Stoic Panaetius, who belonged to the circle of Scipio Aemilianus and Polybius. Rutilius' memoirs were a major source for Sallust's monograph. Sallust is not much help to the archaeologist, for his interest in topography is scanty, and he never saw Numidia until fifty years after the Jugurthine War, when he fought in Caesar's African campaign and was rewarded by being appointed the first governor of Africa Nova. Nor, for lack of excavation, does archaeology shed much light on Sallust's text. But at least some work has been done, on the site of the battle of the Muthul, where Metellus and Rutilius won a major victory (109 B.C.). The Muthul has been identified as the Oued Tessa, in the territory of the Musulamii, a native tribe to which Tacfarinas, a later resistance hero, belonged. The battle site was probably a point twenty-five kilometers southeast of Bulla Regia.

A by-product of the research in this connection has been a more precise knowledge of the tortuous course of the Fossa Regia from east of Thabraca to south of Taparura (Sfax). The area left outside the Fossa includes native cities later to prosper under Rome: Bulla Regia, Vaga (Béja), Thugga, Sicca Veneria, Simitthu (Chemtou, noted for quarries of the prized yellow Numidian marble), Althiburos (Médeïna), and Ammaedara (Haïdra), which will be discussed later in other connections. In them Punic or Numidian political and religious institutions largely survived; Roman rule tended to be tolerant as long as the subject peoples behaved and paid their taxes.

Though Metellus won a triumph for his Numidian victories, he lost his command when he lost the consulship to his former lieutenant C. Marius in 107 B.C. Marius, a self-made man with aristocratic connections, took and burned Capsa, and finished the war in Africa with the help of his lieutenant P. Cornelius Sulla. Jugurtha was betrayed (105), taken to Rome, displayed in Marius' triumph (along with 3,065 pounds of gold and 5,775 of silver), and strangled (104). Marius, who like his successors in North African affairs, Caesar (his nephew by marriage) and Octavian (later to be called Augustus, Caesar's grandnephew and heir), knew the political value of rewarding the loyalty of his troops, settled some informally on African soil—for example, at Clupea and Thabraca (not formally colonized till the reigns of Caesar and Octavian respectively), Thibaris (where excellent red wine is still made), Thuburnica (Sidi Ali Belkacem), and Uchi Maius (Henchir Douemis). Thuburnica has yielded Libyan, neo-Punic, and Greek, as well as Latin inscriptions, one of which mentions Marius. When political circumstances forced Marius to flee from Italy in 88 B.C., he naturally turned to Africa, where he could count on the loyalty of his veterans. John Vanderlyn's painting of 1817, *Marius amid the Ruins of Carthage* (fig. 2.5), both underlines the classical influence on federalist America and with its striking evocation of frustrated ambition alludes to the abortive career of Vanderlyn's patron, Aaron Burr.

The presence of Marian veterans in Numidian territory guaranteed the friendship of the Numidian kings. Their settlement, however informal—the initiative was Marius', not the government's, and they had an independent political structure—has been accurately described as a revolutionary act with widely consequential political, economic, and legal results. As a by-product of the unrest in Italy of the 80s, a colony from Chiusi, calling themselves "Dardanians," settled at Zaghouan in 83/82 B.C., thus reversing in a small way the process allegedly begun by Aeneas. But Roman government of the African province did not always run smoothly: in 82 the pro-Marian proconsul C. Fabius Hadrianus was roasted alive by irate Romans in Utica, perhaps because he protected the natives from the tender mercies of Roman free enterprise.

Roman moralists, as is well known, dated the beginning of the decline and fall of the Roman Republic from the sack of Carthage and the equally ruthless destruction of Corinth in the same year. One of the alleged signs of decadence was the cultivation of a taste for luxury goods. A whole cargo of these was found by Greek sponge-divers in 1907, in thirty-nine meters of water about five kilometers off Mahdia, in the shoal

FIGURE 2.5 *John Vanderlyn,* Marius amid the Ruins of Carthage *(ca. 1817)*

water called in antiquity the Lesser Syrtes. The find illustrates the point that the Mediterranean seabed may be the world's richest museum. The ship measured forty meters long by ten meters beam. On her middle deck she carried sixty-five quarry-fresh columns weighing two hundred tons, the bulk of the cargo. They were neatly arranged in seven rows; the sponge-divers thought they were cannon. There are also column capitals of all three Greek architectural orders, Doric, Ionic, and Corinthian. The Ionic capital is still mint-fresh, with the struts left on to prevent the fragile volutes from breaking off. The rest of the cargo, now on display in the Bardo Museum in Tunis, consisted of objects of art or interior decoration, in bronze or marble. Some inscriptions, of the fourth century B.C., are unhelpful for dating, but they all come from Athens' port, the Piraeus, and guarantee the Attic provenience of the cargo. There are a bronze Eros and a Hermes, both signed by Boethius of Chalcedon, who was at work between 130 and 120 B.C. The Eros is an androgynous adolescent, with a bow and detachable wings, a copy of a fourth-century original by Lysippus or Praxiteles. A set of three dancing dwarfs, all in bronze and all from the same workshop, perhaps Boethius', have rings in their backs for hanging; they were intended to swing in the air. The female, thirty centimeters high (fig. 2.6), clacks castanets. Her male partner, also with castanets, has a huge phallus and is hydrocephalic and blind in one eye.

FIGURE 2.6 *Mahdia wreck, early first century* B.C., *dancing dwarf, in Bardo Museum, Tunis*

His other eye and his nipples are inset in silver. There are also bronze statuettes of Hermes as orator, of a satyr about to pounce upon an unsuspecting nymph, and of another Eros, with a torch. He has a hole in his head and was intended for use as a lamp. Other bronze pieces include four bedsteads; a comic actor perched on an altar for protection against his master's wrath; the mask of a prostitute, a stock character in Greek New Comedy; reliefs of Bacchus and Ariadne, and of Athena and Nike; and a recumbent dog.

The marble pieces have all suffered from the depredations of a sea creature who bores into marble as a termite burrows into wood. The Pan (fig. 2.7), to whom a protective father would certainly not entrust his

FIGURE 2.7 *Mahdia, Pan, in Bardo*

daughter, is, like Boethius' Eros, from a fourth-century original. The Aphrodite (fig. 2.8), perhaps from a Praxitelean original, is very like a well-known fourth-century head from Chios in the Boston Museum of Fine Arts. There is a female satyr who resembles one signed by Boethius in the Lateran collection in Rome. There is a seated boy, related, so it is claimed, to Boethius' famous Boy with Goose, and a grave-relief that represents Hades and Persephone and a pair of what in Renaissance art criticism would be called "donors," and a funeral banquet; another funerary relief shows a boy carrying a pig for sacrifice, and another banquet. Both are fourth-century, and both were taken from a Piraeus cemetery. There is a number of marble *craterae*, or mixing bowls, which

FIGURE 2.8 *Mahdia, Aphrodite, in Bardo*

Roman nabobs' wives liked to use for flowers. The bowls bear reliefs connected with the worship of the wine-god Dionysus: a thiasos, or Dionysiac procession, with a dancing maenad; another maenad with castanets; Dionysus and Ariadne, with a lyre; and a drunken Silenus supported by a young satyr. Another crater shows the god's entrance into the house of Icarius. Pleased with Icarius' hospitality, Dionysus made him a present of Attica's first grapevine. The effect of sampling the first vintage made the neighbors assume they had been poisoned. They killed Icarius, who became the constellation Boötes. A set of twelve marble "candelabras," on triangular bases, with baroque decoration, was intended to serve as incense burners. The ship's gear included a couple of anchors, weighing six hundred or seven hundred kilograms each, the remains of food (bones of hare, mutton, and pig), and a human skeleton, to prove that disaster was sudden. Cooking pots and a clay lamp are dated about 100 B.C., and Virginia Grace, expert on stamped amphora handles, dates the examples from the wreck in the second century B.C.

This raises the vexed question of the date of the wreck and the purpose of the cargo. The proposals are that the cargo was (1) a consignment for Juba II, a Roman-educated Numidian prince of dilettante tastes, who married Selene, Cleopatra's daughter by Mark Antony; or (2) booty taken by Sulla when he sacked Athens in 87 B.C.; or (3) a miscellaneous lot being brought to Rome on speculation by an art dealer. The first of these possibilities may be excluded because Juba II, who was a babe in arms in 46 B.C., when he was carried in Caesar's triumph, is too late for the pottery. The second is tempting: the miscellany of the cargo suggests the indiscriminate nature of Sulla's sack; the dwarfs accord with his known tastes; the capitals may have been intended for his veteran colony at Pompeii, and the columns for the Capitoline temple in Rome, which was burnt in 83. If the cargo was loaded in 87, Sulla on this point showed remarkable prescience. But if the dates for the pottery and lamps are right, a Sullan date is too late for the cargo, and we must fall back on the third possible explanation and plump for an unidentified art dealer as entrepreneur.

The years from 82 to 47 B.C. are nearly blank in the archaeological history of Tunisia. The record comes to life again with the arrival of Julius Caesar late in December 47 in pursuit of the remnants of the

Pompeian forces, which he defeated in battle at Thapsus in 46. His propaganda for himself as a clement ruler is borne out in Africa: it was he who started the revival of Carthage (and, incidentally, of Corinth as well) after a century of devastation, and he contented himself with fining pro-Pompeian towns in money or in kind instead of consigning them to fire and sword. Loyal towns he rewarded with immunity from taxes. The question of which colonial foundations in Tunisia are Caesar's is complicated, because the epithet "Julia," which many colonies bear, can apply equally well to Caesar or to his adopted son Octavian, later Augustus. But there seems to be pretty general agreement that the following are Caesar's: Carpis, Carthage, Clupea, Curubis (Korba), Hadrumetum, Hippo Diarrhytus, Musti (*municipium*, not colony), Neapolis, Thapsus, and Thysdrus (a free town, not a colony). *Municipia* consisted of Roman citizens living under peregrine (local) law, with magistrates of Roman type, subject to the provincial governor and paying taxes. *Coloniae* consisted of Roman citizens (*coloniae Romanae*) or noncitizens with magistrates who were Roman citizens (*coloniae Latinae*), autonomous under their own magistrates and sometimes tax-exempt. *Civitates* (like Thysdrus) consisted of noncitizens living under peregrine law and non-Roman magistrates, but subject to the proconsul; they paid tribute.

Natives took Roman names on becoming Roman citizens. The generosity of Julius Caesar and Augustus in granting citizenship is statistically attested: of 1,903 names on inscriptions from our area, 316 are Julii. At Sicca Veneria, one in six is a Julius; at Simitthu, one in eight; at Thuburnica, one in nine; at Thabraca, one in fourteen; 53 percent of the governing class in the municipalities were native Africans. The involvement of indigenes in the process of Romanization meant that the Romans could control the area and assure a steady grain supply for Rome without the need for an army of occupation larger than the single Legio III Augusta (maximum strength, six thousand men), plus auxiliary units.

Sallust, and four generations later Silius Italicus, in his epic on the Second Punic War, give us some idea what the unassimilated natives were like. The Romans called the Numidians *semihomines*, that is, "half-men," and our word *nomad* comes from "Numidian." They were fierce, polygamous, promiscuous, skin-clad, with no fixed houses, traveling by wagon, gypsy-like; they lived in portable huts, called by a Punic term, *mapalia*, which Sallust says looked like overturned dories. Juba I, the last independent Numidian king, comes down to us as cruel and arrogant. He joined Pompey's side but aimed at gaining Roman Africa for himself.

Defeated at Thapsus, he was rejected by his own people, who refused to admit him within the walls of Zama. He committed suicide, and Numidia became a Roman puppet-state.

The Romans were tolerant of local religion as well as politics. At Thinissut, near Siagu on the Bay of Hammamet, a coin of a Pompeian general allows us to date to 45 B.C. a sanctuary (its contents may be later) of Ba'al and Tanit consisting essentially of three courts preceded by a terrace. A pair of footprints in the pavement, intended to indicate a spot for removing shoes or for praying, is matched in the sanctuary of Saturn at Thugga, discussed in chapter 3. Among the finds now in the Bardo is a splendid terra-cotta statue of Tanit as a lioness (fig. 2.9), which guarded the entrance. She wears a fixed smile—as though she came from Cheshire—is feathered, and has vulture wings. There are holes in the back, for venting in the kiln, for carrying, or for the insertion of offerings. She is one of five such figures found in the sanctuary, all of different sizes. Much smaller is the Ba'al (fig. 2.10), seated between sphinxes and wearing a plumed crown.

But however tolerant the Romans were in matters of religion, they let their subjects know in no uncertain terms who was supreme militarily. At Kbor Klib, near Mactar, a monument fifteen meters square and now six meters high, though once much higher, celebrates the triumph of Caesar over his enemies foreign (in Gaul) and domestic (the Pompeians, at Alexandria and Thapsus). It would not have been good manners to erect the monument at Thapsus: it was considered bad form to gloat in Roman territory over a victory in a civil war. But Kbor Klib was in Barbary. The monument's frieze figures trophies: a cuirass on pikes, and shields with devices such as Artemis (a Macedonian device—Caesar had just won at Alexandria, where the Ptolemaic dynasty was descended from members of the general staff of Alexander the Great, of the royal line of Macedon). In 46, the year of his triumph, Caesar also placed trophies on his coins. And a huge trophy from Hippo Regius (Annaba in Algeria) will be described in chapter 8.

Caesar's murder in 44 left his work in Africa unfinished, but Octavian (later called Augustus) carried on his tradition as a prolific colonizer. Pretty certainly Augustan are Assuras (Zanfour), which eventually pros-

FIGURE 2.9 *Thinissut, cat-goddess,*
first century A.D., *in Bardo*

FIGURE 2.10 *Thinissut, seated Ba'al,*
first century A.D., *in Bardo*

pered to the point of having three monumental arches and an amphitheater; Carthage itself, which began a new system of dating, by priests of Ceres, in 39/38, early in the period of Octavian's rise to power; Sicca Veneria; Simitthu, the marble center; and Thabraca and Uthina (Oudna), of which the former certainly, the latter possibly, had Augustus' colleague M. Aemilius Lepidus for patron; Thuburbo Maius, to be discussed in the next chapter; Thuburbo Minus, a colony for time-expired veterans (it, too, like Assuras, had an amphitheater); and finally, a new draft of colonists for Thuburnica. Augustus' policy involved three things: first, security, at the ports and against nomads; second, politics—alliances with native princes, and settlement of veterans, as reward and as riddance; third, economic and social policy, to favor Romanization and keep natives in their place. For example, he made few grants of citizenship to *peregrini* (noncitizen freemen), and while he allowed autonomous coinage, Carthage now minted, instead of her traditional horse and palm, the head of the empress Livia, and a wheatsheaf, to emphasize the importance of North Africa to Rome's grain supply (the *annona*). The net result, for five hundred years, was widespread peace, urbanization, and Romanization, brought about not so much by the Legio III Augusta as by the political and civilizing influence of Roman cities.

Utica, for instance, was made a municipium in 36 B.C. It had a theater before that; after all, it had been provincial capital since 146; a block of Roman houses southeast of the Punic necropolis—House of the Cascade, of the Figured Capitals, of the Coin Hoard—is partly Flavian (A.D. 69–96) in date, including possibly but not certainly some of the mosaics (fig. 2.11).

Colonization went on apace. A series of triumphs celebrated by Augustan generals in 34, 33, 28, 21, and 19, and then, with a long gap, in A.D. 3 and 6, is taken by leftist historians as evidence of heroic native resistance; by pro-Romans, as implying necessary defense against nomads. However heroic the resistance, the Romans sent a draft of three thousand colonists to Carthage in 29. Perhaps from this time dates the Roman quay of the Carthage harbor, built from the debris of Punic buildings; roadmaking in connection with the new draft may have occasioned the milestone from Lares (Lorbeus), fifteen kilometers southeast of Sicca Veneria (Le Kef), reported in 1965. In 27 Augustus consolidated the two provinces of Africa Nova and Vetus into one, Africa Proconsularis, whose governor, resident in Carthage, also commanded the Legio III Augusta. The date coincides with the first salutation of Octavian as Augustus by the Senate.

At a later date—how long after is controversial—must be placed the altar to Augustus' *gens* (clan) found in 1916 on the Byrsa hill, close to the religious center of Augustan Carthage. In theme it corresponds closely with Augustus' Altar of Peace in Rome (13 B.C.); in artistic quality it is so inferior that many scholars think it must be an imitation, later, perhaps much later, in date. Its four panels connect Augustus with the gods and the founding of Rome. One panel shows Apollo, god of poetry and prophecy, with lyre and tripod. Another shows the goddess Roma, very

FIGURE 2.11 *Utica, House of the Cascade, mosaic, perhaps Flavian*

close stylistically to the corresponding panel on the Altar of Peace. She is represented as an Amazon, with lion-skin boots, a crested helmet, a sword in her right hand, and in her left a miniature pillar supporting both a shield like the one with the cardinal virtues set up at the door of Augustus' house on the Palatine in Rome, and a winged Victory. Nearby are a sword, cuirass, helmet, two shields, and a trumpet. To fill the rest of the space the sculptor has carved a stele with an orb, a caduceus (a winged staff with entwined snakes), and a horn of plenty filled with the same fruits and grain depicted on the inside of the precinct wall of the Altar of Peace in Rome: pinecone, pomegranate, an ear of wheat, grapes. The third panel shows Aeneas (fig. 2.12), with his old father Anchises perched on his arm. In a basket, Anchises carries the Penates, household gods of

FIGURE 2.12 *Carthage, altar, Aeneas and Anchises panel, perhaps Augustan*

Troy; they recur on a panel of the Roman altar. Aeneas' son Ascanius, in a Phrygian cap, symbol of liberty, holds his father's hand. An oak tree with a bull's skull (another motif on the Roman altar) in its fork symbolizes the forests of Mount Ida, near Troy. The fourth panel depicts sacrifice. The sacrificer is Augustus; attending him are two *camilli* (acolytes; also on the Roman altar) carrying incense boxes, a flute-player, and a servant with a mallet (which will be used to stun the bull), represented wearing a leather bib. A pair of volutes (scrolls), with eagles and serpents, crowns the altar. An inscription bears the dedication and the name of the dedicator, P. Perelius Hedulius, an entrepreneur whose name also appears on tile-stamps; he profited from the rise of Augustan Carthage. The altar and the temple that went with it—also mentioned in the inscription—presumably confirm the removal from Carthage of Scipio's curse.

The spread of Roman power produced at various times resistance heroes in many provinces: Viriathus in Portugal, Vercingetorix in Gaul, Arminius in Germany, Decebalus in Romania, and Tacfarinas in North Africa. His revolt (A.D. 17–24) was the most important North African event in Tiberius' reign. Tacfarinas was a native ex-officer in an auxiliary unit, who deserted to lead, with the discipline he had learned from the Romans, his people's revolt against the Romans' cutting off their age-old right of transhumance, that is, the seasonal movement of their livestock from mountain to lowland pasture, which was being interfered with by the Roman policy of encouraging the nomads to settle down on border farms. The archaeological evidence for the revolt, like the revolt itself, transcends the bounds of Tunisia. There are the *castella* (blockhouses) along the northern edge of the Sahara, best treated in chapter 9, on Algeria, where they have been best studied. There is an inscription of thanksgiving by the proconsul who finally, after three others had tried and failed, defeated and killed Tacfarinas at Auzia in Algeria. The victor was P. Cornelius Dolabella; the stone was found in Lepcis Magna, in Libya. But Tunisia plays its part in Tacfarinas' story: Tacapae was one of his bases, Thala was one of the settlements he besieged, and Ammaedara was a Roman base for the campaigns of 21/22. The Romans at first proved able to win battles but not the war. In fact, the proconsul Q. Junius Blaesus, uncle of the notorious Sejanus, Tiberius' then favorite, was personally acclaimed *imperator* by his troops. This entitled him to a triumph. He was the last to receive this honor, henceforth reserved for the emperor alone. It was not granted to Dolabella, for example.

The pertinent events of the reigns of Caligula (37–41) and Claudius (41–54) can be rapidly summarized. Caligula, equally pathological in his fear and in his practice of violence, separated, in 37, the civil from the military powers of the governor of Africa Proconsularis, giving the latter to a new legate of Numidia, responsible to the emperor himself. Nevertheless, several governors of Africa Proconsularis, whose proconsular status entitled them to senior rank among senators, later took the throne by violence: these were Galba, Vitellius, and Vespasian.

Under Claudius, an inscription of Thugga (A.D. 48) proves that Punic institutions still survived there: the *portae* (Latin translation of the name of a Punic deliberative body) honors a distinguished native who has a Roman wife. A Claudian coin dates a phase of the necropolis of Thysdrus, where imports betoken prosperity if not taste: there are statuettes of a monkey-faced man, and of a horse having intercourse with a woman. The prosperity came from grain. Thysdrus produced three hundred thousand bushels in 46, which is 2.5 percent of the total Tunisian export in 1955; it would require a production area of seven thousand hectares. This rather affluent period may have seen the construction of a small amphitheater that predates the famous one of 238.

After Nero had engineered the murder of the six most extensive landowners in Africa (about A.D. 60), the crown acquired the estates; some important inscriptions, discussed in chapter 3, give some interesting facts about how they were run.

The unrest in Rome in the "year of the four emperors" (68/69) was reflected in North Africa, where Galba, Vitellius, and Vespasian each arranged the murder of a hostile Roman official. But daily life in the towns and cities seems to have remained stable and relatively prosperous. Ammaedara and Bulla Regia, both Flavian foundations, are most conveniently discussed in later chapters, but mention may be made here of the theater at Cillium (Kasserine; fig. 2.13), pronounced by its excavator to be of Flavian date. Its diameter—fifty-three meters—makes it smaller than the theater at Timgad and about the same size as the one at Herculaneum. It would hold from 2,000 to 2,500 spectators. It is worth men-

FIGURE 2.13 *Cillium theater, Flavian (?)*

tioning that Pliny the Elder was probably procurator of Africa under Vespasian, about 70–72. From these years, too, dates the founding of the imperial cult with the institution of the *flamen Augusti*. Held by local dignitaries, the flaminate became a potent instrument of Romanization.

From the Flavian age dates the remarkable cemetery of imperial slave and freedman functionaries (*officiales*) on the western outskirts of Carthage. The number of persons involved, with their age at death, makes mortality statistics possible: the average male longevity was 33.4 years; female was 30.33. Here mortality had nothing to do with class: death struck indiscriminately. Though the age at death was higher in Carthage than in Rome, it was higher still in Numidia: 46 in Cirta, 60.2 in Celtianis. These latter figures, as Hopkins has shown, should be discounted to allow for the tendency of the very old to exaggerate their age. But the figures for officiales seem reasonable.

At Tigisis, west of Capsa, a frontier blockhouse protected a settlement of Flavian date (83), which covered some twenty hectares; it was discovered from air photographs. A revolt of Nasamones about this time (85/86) may have been sparked by resentment at the expansion of centuriation.

Because the proconsul in Carthage no longer had his legion, he was assigned a detachment from the urban cohort (essentially a police force) in Rome; in 86 he sent it to Mauretania to put down an uprising there.

Finally, archaeologists date to Nerva's reign (96–98) the founding of Gigthis (Bou-Ghara), discussion of which is also best postponed to the next chapter.

3. THE HIGH EMPIRE:
TRAJAN THROUGH ALEXANDER
SEVERUS, A.D. 98–235

"If a man were called," wrote Gibbon in a famous passage, "to fix the period in the history of the world during which the condition of the human race was most happy and prosperous, he would, without hesitation, name that which elapsed from the death of Domitian to the reign of Commodus." In Roman North Africa this golden age lasted longer, down at least to the end of the Severan dynasty, and the wealth of archaeological material is such that this chapter must be rigorously selective.

We begin with four inscriptions defining relations between landowner and tenant on imperial estates in the Bagradas (Medjerda) valley (fig. 3.1). The first, Trajanic (116/17), comes from Henchir Mettich; the second, Hadrianic, from Aïn Djemala; the third, Commodan (182), from Souk el-Khmis; and the fourth, Severan (209–212), from Aïn Oussel. These estates (*saltus*), inherited or confiscated, were run by *procuratores*—often freedmen, with staffs of slaves—who usually leased acreage to *conductores*, who in turn sublet to *coloni* (freeborn tenants). When manpower became short, the emperors began to offer inducements to the coloni; for instance, if they faithfully worked waste or abandoned land (*subseciva*; literally "oddments"), they were granted all rights of ownership in it except the right to sell and were allowed to occupy it rent-free for five years if the crop was figs or vines, seven years for fruit trees, or ten years for the slow-growing olive. On the whole, the system worked, and created stability, since a colonus would be loath to leave rent-free land, but as generations of coloni passed their holdings on to their heirs, they came to be regarded as tied to the land, like medieval serfs.

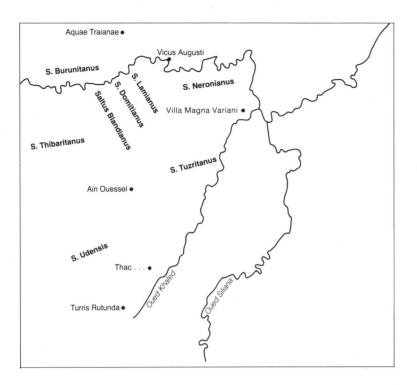

FIGURE 3.1 *Proconsularis, imperial saltus, A.D. 116–212, map*

The Henchir Mettich inscription is an altar, dedicated to Trajan. It begins with the names of the representatives of the coloni. They are indigenous names—Odilo, Annobal, Birzil. Two procurators are listed, one a bourgeois (*eques*), the other a freedman. Given the age-long rivalry between emperors and aristocrats, it was obviously in the emperor's interest to employ nonaristocrats in potentially powerful posts, which to a senator would seem beneath his dignity. The tenants themselves are sharecroppers: from regularly allotted land (as opposed to "oddments") they owe to the procurators or conductores one-third of the crop (brought to market) of wheat, barley, wine, and oil; one-fourth of the beans; about a pint of honey per hive; and all the hay. There is a nominal per capita tax on livestock. The penalty for theft or destruction of crops—double the value—falls on the tenant. If a tenant abandons an oddment, it reverts to the conductor after two years. The tenant is held to owe a *corvée*—two days a year each of plowing, harvesting, and cultivating. The Aïn Djemala and Aïn Ouessel inscriptions grant to would-be cultivators of swampy and wooded lands the right to cultivate olives and vines thereon, under the usual terms as to exemptions and shares owed. The Souk el-Khmis (Saltus Burunitanus) text is a protest to Commodus against oppressive procurators who call in soldiers to torture, fetter, and cudgel tenants in retaliation for their daring to appeal to the emperor for redress and who illegally increase the percentage of shares and the days of corvée normally required. In reply the emperor orders the procurators to conform. Presumably they did so; otherwise the document would not have been published.

Africa Proconsularis in its prime was alive with cities, and even today, the opulence and extent of the ruins excite the wonder of the traveler. Gigthis (Bou Ghara), in south Tunisia, connected by a causeway with the island of Djerba, traditionally the land of the carefree Lotus Eaters, is a provincial small town, unpretentious but typical in its amenities, mostly the gifts of prosperous townsmen: a forum (fig. 3.2) set about with temples and secular buildings, a monumental arch, the aerarium (town treasury), a market, a porticoed street leading to the harbor, two sets of baths, and comfortable surburban villas. Though the larger provincial cities often vied with one another and with Rome in the size and décor of their places for public entertainment, excavation at Gigthis has not revealed a theater, circus, or amphitheater. Sixty years ago, Gigthis was an exotic spot:

the excavators reported flamingoes on the beach. Its prosperity came from agriculture; it sent grain direct to Rome's port of Ostia. Inscriptions mention emperors from Nerva (96–98) to Caracalla (212–217). Antoninus Pius (138–161) made the place a *municipium*; it survived

FIGURE 3.2 *Gigthis, forum, Hadrianic and later*

until the Vandals came (439), after which there clustered around the forum hovels built of secondhand stone from more impressive earlier buildings. And in the sixth century the Byzantines and Justinian's general Solomon built a fort sixty meters square on the sea cliff to the north.

The forum of Gigthis measures sixty by forty meters; its open space was surrounded by a portico with nineteen columns on the long sides, eleven on the others; they are in unfluted reddish limestone with pinkish-white marble bases and Corinthian capitals. On the forum's west side rose a temple with columns in gray, violet-grained marble on the facade, engaged pilasters on the other three sides, and the outer walls stuccoed in white. This economical way of covering inferior stone was in use also at Sabratha in Tripolitania (see chapter 6). The presence of a sundial beside the temple steps suggested—dubiously—to the excavator a connection with the Greco-Egyptian deity Sarapis, equated with the sun-god Helios. The forum's south side faced a shrine to the Genius (indwelling spirit) of Augustus and the speakers' rostra. The east side contained the civil basilica (lawcourt and covered market), an arch, and another temple, to Liber Pater (Shadrach, a conflation of the Punic and Roman wine-gods). The temple portico had twenty-eight monolithic columns in yellow limestone, and Ionic capitals. It is Antonine in date (161–180). On the forum's north side is a temple to Hercules (Punic Melqart), an unidentified temple, and a sanctuary of Concord, which may have been used as the curia, for meetings of the town council; then comes a gate, then a sanctuary of Apollo, then the aerarium, made secure by double-thick walls. Between the forum and the sea rose, in a portico, another unidentified temple, differently oriented; cater-cornered to it, a porticoed square; opposite, a small temple to Aesculapius, the god of healing, identified by his snake-twined staff. Both these temples are oriented with the forum, and, on the same orientation, with the monumental entrance, flanked by oil and wine stores, to the porticoed street leading to the harbor. The harbor was protected by a porticoed jetty, 17 meters wide and 140 long, with a rounded end.

Gigthis had two sets of baths, one south of the forum, one west; the former yielded mosaics, the latter had a circular exercise ground attached. The market, 150 meters south-southwest of the forum, had a square central building and shops in a hemicycle, as at Timgad (see chapter 9). Nearby was an inn; scratched on its floor was a board-game with a legend in Greek. The suburban villas had hypocaust (radiant) heating, geometric mosaic floors, stuccoed peristyles, frescoed walls; one fresco, in a florist's house, portrays him bearded and with a bouquet and bears the legend VENDE FELICI. A suburban temple, 300 meters south of the market, was dedicated to Mercury, the god of commerce, at a caravan-halt. The precinct measured 34.5 by 22 meters, with an Ionic portico, its columns fluted in stucco. The cella had a coffered ceiling like the peristyle of the temple of Bacchus at Baalbek (*GSS*, 403–4). An inscription records a gift to the god of a silver candelabrum and a gold statue. Chapels to Minerva and Fortuna (Lady Luck) flank the temple to the north and south.

Houses with luxurious underground rooms make Bulla Regia one of the most interesting sites not only in Tunisia but in the entire Roman world. One of the most remarkable if lugubrious finds, from as long ago as 1906, was an iron collar riveted around the neck of a female skeleton. It was inscribed ADULTERA MERETRIX: TENE ME QVIA FVGAVI A BVLLA REGIA—"Adulterous prostitute: hold me, because I have run away from Bulla Regia." Bulla Regia's name shows that it was used by Numidian kings; its oldest datable building is Tiberian (34/35); it was a municipium by 110–112, perhaps even by the time of Vespasian (69–79), for there was a colossal statue of him in the forum. Hadrian, whose portrait bust was found in the southwest corner of the forum, raised the town to colonial status, and it survived into Byzantine times, when its theater was transformed into a fort.

The forum, measuring forty by twenty-six meters, had a temple of Apollo on the north, a capitolium (temple to Jupiter, Juno, and Minerva) on the west, and an apsed basilica on the east. The theater, picturesque, sixty meters in diameter and built on vaults in the Roman fashion, not into a slope in the Greek way (the site is flat), dates from Marcus Aurelius. The orchestra is paved with yellow Simitthu (Chemtou) marble, the prized *giallo antico*, as the Italians call it, and has inset into its center a mosaic of a bear. Among the numerous statues found here were several of empresses represented as Cereres (fertility goddesses, part Greek, part descendants of Tanit).

The massive baths are dated at the end of the second century. Their vaults display a feature characteristic of Bulla Regia: the use along the groins of interlocking tubes of terra-cotta, shaped like containers for Hollands gin, but striated to make mortar stick. These made scaffolding unnecessary, in an area where there was little wood. The tubes were also used in the remarkable underground living rooms; eight houses with this feature have been excavated, and twelve more are known. Since Bulla Regia is in the part of Tunisia that is hottest in summer, these shady, vaulted dining and sleeping rooms, with their fountains and their cool mosaic floors, must have been delightful places of refuge. The oldest datable dwelling, Hadrianic, is the House of the Fishing Motifs (more gracefully described by the French as the Maison de la Pêche), where the summer rooms are eighteen steps (six meters) down. The house is named from its mosaics of Cupids fishing, or riding a dolphin and playing the lyre like the minstrel Arion in Herodotus' story, who was saved by a dolphin from the designs of piratical sailors (for a mosaic of this from Piazza Armerina in Sicily, see *MSS*, 335). In this house, eighteen air vents, for relieving humidity, pierce the vaults. The House of Amphitrite (Antonine; A.D. 138–193) is twenty-three steps down; it boasts a mosaic of the hero Perseus saving the Ethiopian princess Andromeda from a dragon; it has an underground fountain, and facing it, a mosaic of the Triumph (and Toilet) of Venus. She wears a halo and rides a sea horse. Cupids hold a crown above her; others ride dolphins and carry her jewel box and mirror. The House of the Hunt is dated 225–250. Hexagons cut out of the concrete relieve the weight on the columns of the rooms below (fig. 3.3). There are twenty-two steps down. The triple-bay dining room is vaulted—with tubes—and is slightly off-center in the plan, to give a perspective view of the peristyle.

The many inscriptions of Bulla Regia show that many of its most prosperous citizens, who would be likely to live in these houses, bear Roman cognomina that reveal Punic origins: Concessus, Donatus, Rogatus, Saturninus, Felix, Fortunatus, Honoratus, Januarius, Victor. This possibility of luxurious living for native Africans is one of the things Romanization meant.

Far to the south was nomad country. Though at first the Romans ignored the nomads, as centuriation proves, they later became realistic and maintained seminomads as soldier-farmers around settled centers along the Limes Tripolitanus, less a frontier barrier than a contact zone fifty to a hundred kilometers deep, with defensive works in echelon and an astonishing proliferation of devices for irrigating. Along this line there were military camps every fifteen to thirty kilometers and fortified farms between. A French team has inventoried the sites, of which the following are second-century: Turris Tamalleni (Telmine), which is Hadrianic;

FIGURE 3.3 *Bulla Regia, House of the Hunt,* A.D. 225–250, *underground room*

Bezereos (Bir Rhezan), a Commodan fort of playing-card shape, measuring fifty by sixty-five meters, reinforced under the Severi (193–235); native settlements (*canabae*) adjoin. The curious troglodyte community of Matmata, where families lived underground long before the founding of Bulla Regia—and still do—is nearby. A Commodan advanced base is Tisavar (Ksar Rhilene), a blockhouse of forty by thirty meters. A major fort (137 by 124 meters) of Antonine or Hadrianic date is Tillibar (Remada), also with canabae. The desire to change from a flexible to a fixed and stabilized line of fortification does not manifest itself before 238, when the Legio III Augusta was temporarily disbanded. Perhaps as late as that is the *clausura* (rampart) of Bir Oum Ali (fig. 3.4), not unlike Hadrian's Wall in Britain. It runs for seventeen kilometers, sixty kilometers southeast of Gafsa; the allies used it in 1943 to outflank the German Mareth Line. The strategic nature of the ground in another sense is shown by its use nowadays for an oil pipeline.

One of the more picturesque communities protected by the Limes Tripolitanus was Sufetula (Sbeïtla), at a strategic crossroads in south-central Tunisia. It is noteworthy, among other things, for being an open city, with no circuit wall. Though its earliest inscriptions, and perhaps its grid

FIGURE 3.4 *Bir Oum Ali, Tripolitanian limes, wall, perhaps ca.* A.D. *238*

of streets, date from Vespasian, its most interesting feature is its colonnaded forum, dated by the inscription on its three-bay entrance arch
to early (139) in the reign of Antoninus Pius. The forum, larger than
Gigthis' (sixty-seven by forty meters overall), surrounded on three sides
by shops, had against the wall opposite the arch a unique set of three
temples (fig. 3.5) connected by low arches, forming together a capitolium
complex. The worship of the Capitoline triad in three separate buildings
is extremely unusual. The tetrastyle (four-column façade) temples stand
on high podia and have columns of the composite order, the most ornate,
combining the acanthus-leaves of the Corinthian with the volutes of the

FIGURE 3.5 *Sufetula, capitolia, viewed through forum entrance arch,* A.D. *139*

Ionic. The importance of the central temple, which must be Jupiter's, is signalized by its having engaged half-columns on its other three sides, while the other temples have merely engaged pilasters. The curia (council house) in the left rear corner has a red and white marble pavement and a statue-niche. Sufetula also had baths (Antonine), a theater, and an amphitheater. The history of its Indian summer, which saw the building of an arch of Diocletian and a remarkable number of Christian churches, is postponed to the next chapter.

Carthage under the high empire was the third largest city in the Roman world, after Rome and Alexandria. The African novelist and rhetorician Apuleius, born about 123, has left us (*Florida* 18) a description of Carthage's Hadrianic theater, its size, its standing-room-only audiences, its marble paving, the multistoried, multicolumned architectural backdrop of its stage, the golden gleam of the coffered stage ceiling, the huge semicircle of seats—all this reflecting the city's wealth. The theater, restored, survives; Apuleius did not exaggerate: it had spiral as well as fluted columns, of marble, granite, porphyry, onyx, the yellow of Simitthu, the green of Sparta. Winston Churchill addressed the Allied troops there in June 1943. The odeon, or covered theater for musical events, the largest in the Roman world, adjoins the theater to the north-northeast; its date is Severan (207). The amphitheater, oriented to the Augustan grid, measured 156 by 128 meters, of which the arena accounted for 65 by 70, which equates it in size with Verona's. The circus (Flavian, or a little later), near the south circuit wall, is 516 meters long, about the same length as the Circus of Maxentius in Rome, or the El Djem amphitheater—for which see the next chapter. The Circus Maximus in Rome is over 80 meters larger; that at Lepcis Magna (see chapter 6), 66 meters shorter. Because Carthage has been so much built over—especially for summer villas since World War II—disappointingly little of the Roman city survives, though international salvage operations sponsored by UNESCO have begun to reveal many new facts about its latest phase.

But at the moment the most impressive surviving Roman building is the Antonine Baths (fig. 3.6), dated by an inscription to 145 and finished, according to another, in 162. Its area, 17,850 square meters, places it fourth in size among Roman baths; those of Diocletian, Caracalla, and Nero, in Rome itself, outranked it. Some comparisons with the Baths of

FIGURE 3.6 *Carthage, Antonine Baths, A.D. 145–162*

Caracalla in Rome, as being the best known, may be illuminating: at Rome, the cold pool measures 24 by 56 meters, the exercise ground 29 by 66; at Carthage the former is 22 by 47, the latter 37.4 by 37. The plan is symmetrical, with identical facilities in each half, perhaps one set for each sex. What is exposed to view is simply the massive foundations (fig. 3.6), not now open to the public because of the danger of falling masses of concrete. The plan is centered on an octagonal hot room and a central room for strolling; the baths face the sea, roughly east. A pair of cold pools, nearly square, lies to the north and south; other pools adjoin them. The semicircular rooms at the northwest and southwest corners were latrines. The ordinary routine of bathing involved, after undressing in the *vestibularium*, anointing oneself with oil in the *unctarium*, working out on the *palaestra* (wrestling ground), scraping oneself down in the *destrictarium*, enjoying dry heat in the *sudarium* or *laconicum*, then a warm plunge, then a cold, then a warm again. The routine was so attractive that it was found necessary at closing time to throw darnel seed in the braziers to smoke the patrons out. An inscription from the Antonine Baths mentions a victory of Marcus Aurelius' colleague Lucius Verus over the Parthians in 163. With this victory is to be connected a likeness in marble relief of a three-dimensional bronze trophy (fig. 3.7) once on display in the Musée Lavigérie in Carthage. It consists of a helmet with thunderbolts on the cheekpieces; a cuirass with a Gorgon's head, and griffins heraldically facing; three shields, one an Amazonian—and therefore barbarian—crescent-shaped pelta; a pair of javelins, a saber, and bow, arrows, and quiver—the Parthians were famous bowmen.

The water for the Antonine Baths was supplied by an aqueduct with an estimated capacity of 32 million liters per day, which fed into the Bordj el-Djedid cistern, three blocks north, one of the largest in the ancient world, now inaccessible on presidential property. It held 25,000 to 30,000 cubic meters of water, over twice as much as the huge and famous Piscina Mirabilis near Baiae in Italy. The aqueduct had a source at Zaghouan, 56 airline kilometers south; but following contours it covers 132. Some impressive stretches survive near Uthina (Oudna; fig. 3.8); they were built in sectors distinguished by military masons' marks. The source, a spring 289 meters above sea level, at the cliff foot of Djebel Zaghouan (1,300 meters), determined the siting of the cella of the water sanctuary shown in the model (fig. 3.9). The water was piped under a U-

FIGURE 3.7 *Carthage, trophy, after* A.D. *163, cast*

shaped court to emerge in a peanut-shaped settling basin formed by two
intersecting three-quarter circles: the shape induced a whirl. From either
side of the basin two semicircular flights of stairs rose to the porticoed
court, whose dimensions are interesting. The court, measured to where
its apsidal end begins, is exactly 72 Roman feet (21 meters) square. The
radius of the apsidal curve is exactly half that. The cella is 24 Roman feet
long; its apse 12 feet deep and 12 feet wide, its door 12 feet high. The
portico is 18 feet wide, a quarter the width of the open court. This is a
symmetry which expressed and satisfied the Roman love of order. The
masonry, which is perfect, was wrought, however, by local workmen; the
module for the ashlar blocks is the Punic ell, or cubit, of 51.4 centimeters.

The portico had a mosaic floor and was roofed with intersecting barrel
vaults, coffered and stuccoed; octagons with molded surrounds marked
the intersections. In alternate intercolumniations were niches topped by
half-domes. The cella was revetted (veneered) with polychrome marble.
The style points to a date of about 160–170, when the décor of the
Carthage baths was being finished. The Roman water commissioner

Frontinus, who wrote a book about aqueducts in about A.D. 100, is quite naturally impressed by those thoroughly Roman works of engineering, which he compares favorably to the "useless" pyramids of the Egyptians and the "famous but inert" works of the Greeks. Modern engineers, as we shall see in chapter 9, can find matter for criticism in Roman engineering techniques, but there can be no doubt that the Zaghouan water sanctuary exemplifies the truth of Peter von Blanckenhagen's statement that Roman architecture is not novel or independent; rather, it uses, changes, and gives new meaning to a legacy, in this case from such sanctuaries as those of Pisidian Antioch or Xanthos, in the Greek East.

Uthina, a Julian colony on the line of the Zaghouan-Carthage aqueduct, flourished in the high empire: it had a theater, amphitheater, and baths, which have yielded a number of sculptures; eleven luxurious houses have been excavated, which have produced no fewer than sixty-seven examples of that African specialty, mosaics, aptly described by an Italian expert as "polychrome petrified carpets." Those at Uthina range in date from the first to the fourth Christian century. The richest house, that of the Laberii, is forty meters square, with forty rooms, a twenty-by-fourteen-meter peristyle, and in its atrium a justly famous mosaic (fig. 3.10) showing scenes of farm life, expertly dated to the reign of Marcus Aurelius. The scene centers on a farmhouse with a plow parked in front

FIGURE 3.8 *Uthina, stretch of Carthage aqueduct, Antonine*

FIGURE 3.9 *Zaghouan, water sanctuary,* A.D. *160–170, model*

FIGURE 3.10 *Uthina, House of the Laberii,* A.D. *161–180, mosaic*

of it. A shepherd with a crook reviews his flock of goats and fat-tailed sheep—Herodotus says they needed little carts trailing behind them to carry their tails. In front of the farmhouse is a slave's hut, and a drinking trough fed by a well with balance and bucket. A horse drinks; another is tied nearby; two dogs bounce after game, and a slave whips a mule to market. At the top, a plowman with an ox-team; at right angles to this scene, on the right of the mosaic, are a herdsman with his goats, a shepherd-fowler, and a shepherd with a flute. At the bottom, Molossian hounds attack a boar and a hunter spears him; a peasant disguised as a goat drives partridges into a trap; on the left two mounted men spear a lioness; another gallops away.

Thugga (Dougga) is the best-preserved Roman city in Tunisia. Though racially and constitutionally it was Punic, it had an important and active *pagus* (settlement: Italian *paese*) of Roman citizens. It covers twenty-five hectares; its estimated population in its prime was five thousand. Its history of building in Roman times goes back to Tiberius (A.D. 36); it was rebuilt under the Antonines, with a porticoed piazza of red-veined marble Corinthian columns, and marble-revetted walls. The market, apsidal with lateral shops, is Claudian. At Thugga more, and more varied, cults and religious buildings are known than from anywhere else in Tunisia. Especially interesting is the Hadrianic (128–138) complex of three temples—to Concord, Frugifer (the town's tutelary deity), and Liber Pater—built on the slope southeast of the forum; they were the gift of a philanthropic local family, the Gabinii (plan, fig. 3.11). The temple of Concord (A) is approached by a column-flanked side entrance to an open court. At right angles to the entrance a steep flight of nine steps led up through a four-columned portal to a curious vestibule or narthex with an apse only at its east end; the temple itself had a single, square cella. The temple of Liber Pater (B) is strikingly like Vespasian's Forum of Peace in Rome (*MSS*, 225–30): at the back of an almost square peristyle—eight columns by seven—opened a three-apsed room with flanking chambers which in the Roman case were libraries. Abutting the peristyle to the southeast, and to the right of the shrine of Frugifer (C), was a theatral area (compare the Temple of Cybele at Vienne, *RF*, 83), with some thirty rows of seats arranged in a curve, where some sort of religious pageant was presented—Liber Pater was, as we saw, the wine-god, Punic Shadrach. Adjoining this area to the south was a curious horseshoe-shaped annex whose closest parallel is the Aesculapius complex at Lambaesis in Algeria (see chapter 8).

From Marcus Aurelius' reign dates the capitolium (166–169), also the gift of a rich citizen. It is Corinthian, tetrastyle, of modest size (thirteen by fourteen meters), on a high podium, with a crypt below and three statue-niches at the back. Adjoining the capitolium was built in

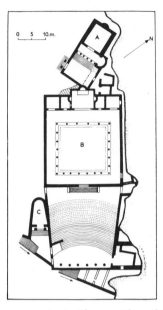

FIGURE 3.11 *Thugga, plan of temples of Concordia, Frugifer, Liber Pater;* Hadrianic

Commodus' time a temple of Mercury, flanked by apsidal rooms, and facing Windrose Square, so-called from a compass-rose engraved on its pavement in the third century, with the Latin names for the winds. Clockwise from north, they are Septentrio, Aquilo, Euraquilo, Vulturnus, Eurus, Leuconotus, Auster, Libonotus, Africus, Favonius, Argestes, and Circius. Contemporary with the capitolium and to the northeast of it is the theater, in a sense a religious building, since theaters were dedicated to the wine-god. Its site at the top of the city slope commands an impressive view and enabled it to be built into the hillside, less expensively than if the nineteen rows of seats—for 3,000 to 3,500 spectators—had to be supported by vaults. Its diameter is 63.5 meters, about the size of Timgad's, larger than Djemila's; the stage is typically Roman, long and narrow: 36.75 by 5.5 meters. By the stage is what may be either a prompter's box or a special arrangement for the curtain, which in Roman theaters rolled down into a slot to open the performance. Like the Concord complex and the capitolium, the theater was the gift of a rich citizen. Wealthy Africans sometimes spent their money in more philanthropic causes: a nabob from Sicca Veneria (Le Kef) between 169 and 180 left an endowment to educate three hundred boys and two hundred girls.

In 195 yet another benefactor built the temple of Saturn, on a High Place north of the theater, over a temple to Saturn's forerunner, the Punic Ba'al. It had three vaulted apsidal cellae with geometric mosaic floors (in an early excavation dynamite was used on the vaults): the left one contained a statue of the Genius of the town, the center a colossal seated Saturn; the dedicatee of the third is unknown. In front of the cellae stretched a spacious courtyard (26.37 by 16.5 meters), surrounded by a peristyle of eight by eleven Corinthian columns. In the stylobate of the peristyle, in front of the central cella, is, as at Thinissut, a pair of footprints in the pavement, indicating places either to pray or for the worshiper to remove his shoes. Cisterns in the courtyard and the colonnade supplied the water for ritual ablutions, as in a mosque. West of the forum in the Severan age rose the temple of Caelestis, Roman Juno, equated with Punic Tanit, goddess of the crescent moon. Her temple is set in a unique crescent-shaped hemicycle, fifty meters wide, strikingly handsome even in its ruined state, lying in the midst of shimmering olive groves; the grass, flower-spangled in spring, grazed over by sheep and goats tended by Bedouin children sadly in need of ablution, ritual or other. An inscription records the gift of a silver statue worth 30,000 sesterces ($6,000 uninflated).

Thugga boasts two arches of Severan date, one of Septimius, the other of Severus Alexander. The houses, built on a slope, are often split-level; the House of the Trifolium, for example, is entered from its second story (first story, by European reckoning), and, as at Bulla Regia, it is twenty-one steps down to the lower level. The best-known house, that of Dionysus and Ulysses (named after its mosaic of the wine-god turning Tyrrhenian pirates into dolphins, and the man of many devices lashed to the mast, listening to the Sirens' song—fig. 4.2) is dated 250–275. Of the same date are the Licinius Baths, comparable in symmetry of the plan to the Antonine Baths of Carthage.

Sixty kilometers east of Thugga, inside the Fossa Regia, in Carthage's territorium, lies Thuburbo Maius. Under Hadrian it was a municipium, under Commodus (161–180) a colony. Its area, thirty-five hectares, may have held a population of seven thousand. Its paved and porticoed forum is forty-eight meters square; its open space, of about fourteen hundred square meters, is about the same as Sbeïtla's; or Tipasa's or Djemila's in Algeria (see chapter 8). It dates from 161, early in Marcus Aurelius'

FIGURE 3.12 *Thuburbo Maius, Pegasus relief from curia, perhaps Antonine*

reign. Facing its northwest side is the capitolium, dated by an inscription
to 167/68. It contained a colossal statue of Jupiter, whose fragments—
head 1.35 meters high, foot 1.15 meters long—mean that it was originally seven meters high. Vaults below housed the town treasury, the site,
in the years of decline, of an oil press. Diagonally across the forum, on
its north side, was the small but richly decorated curia (12.3 by 9.25
meters), perhaps Antonine, from which comes the charming little relief,
only sixty centimeters high, of Pegasus, worth illustrating (fig. 3.12)
because he was the mascot of the Legio III Augusta. About the same size
as those of Sbeïtla, Timgad, Madauros, Djemila, and Tipasa, the curia
yielded dedications to Peace and Concord. Fragments of its luxurious
ceiling-coffers with acanthus decoration lie strewn about on the ground.
The temple of Mercury—Caracallan, of 211—opening on to the forum's
south side, is a curiosity, because of its circular, columned forecourt with
four semicircular niches. The southeast corner of the forum touches the
northwest corner of the market, nineteen meters square, colonnaded, and
surrounded by shops.

The Portico of the Petronii, a hundred meters south of the forum, named from the inscription in monumental letters of its architrave, which lies on the ground beside it, is striking, with its black, gold-flecked marble columns. It was the palaestra of the summer baths. Adjoining it on the southeast was a sanctuary of the healing god Aesculapius (Punic Eshmoun) which has yielded an inscription prescribing ritual purity for three days before consulting the god: the worshiper must not have had his hair cut, nor have bathed, nor had intercourse, nor eaten pork or beans, and he must enter the sanctuary barefoot. Mention should also be made of the amphitheater, the winter baths, which are late (361), and the Temple of Baʿalit-Caelestis, with its U-shaped peristyle.

We have noticed the persistence of native cults in these more or less Romanized centers. A description of the site of Bou Kourneïn, "The Two-horned Mountain," 550 meters above sea level, rising above the wine-rich plain of Mornag, twenty kilometers east and south of Tunis, will afford an opportunity to discuss the Saturn cult at greater length. Of 118 attested sites of the Saturn cult in Africa Proconsularis, only 10 have been dug; of these the richest, Aïn Tounga, yielded 538 stelae, the most important single concentration in Roman Africa. Archaeologists have at last count recorded 2,828 Saturn stelae, of which the latest publication reproduces 233. Votaries worshiped Saturn as master of the sky, the fruitful earth, and the Beyond. They describe him as "the God, the Holy, who places the braziers of the heavens in the firmament, the Prince of Days." His priests worshiped him with veiled head and unshod feet; they wore a headband, knotted sash, fringed cape, and crescent pendant. The worshipers, warned by the god in a dream, vowed a sacrifice. The victim, a bull or a ram (never, after the Roman conquest, a child), was solemnly offered and consecrated—"life for life, breath for breath, blood for blood"—then slain, and the remains disposed of. One scholar believes the aim of the sacrifice was to get a child: hence favorite names like Donatus, Concessus, Restitutus, Datus, Impetratus—that is, Vouchsafed, Granted, Restored, Given, Answer-to-Prayer.

The Bou Kourneïn sanctuary, where Saturn is called Balcaranensis, is typical as being in the open air—even the Thugga temple is largely hypaethral—and on a High Place, now the site of a television tower: it commands a view for fifty kilometers around. The footings for the precinct wall were cut in the living rock; there was an altar but no temple. Excavators discovered 365 fragments of inscribed and figured stelae here; they show Saturn bearded, veiled, wearing a radiate crown, carrying a whip and *patera* (sacrificial saucer). The inscriptions are dated between

139 and 215. Most of the dedicants bear the praenomen, nomen, and cognomen of the Roman citizen, but the Roman names are translations from the Punic. Some of the worshipers, as we have seen elsewhere, were rich enough to dedicate whole sanctuaries, but many belonged to the indigenous Berber lower class, and while it is probably exceeding the evidence to see in Saturn worship—it persisted till 323—a symbol of overt resistance to Roman rule, the cult unquestionably stiffened Berber particularism. The symbols on the stelae are Berber-Punic fetishes: disc, crescent, star, palm, caduceus, sickle, scimitar. The triad Saturn-Sun-Moon is often represented. The animal victim often wears a festive ribbon around its stomach. The Saturn stele illustrated here (fig. 3.13), the Boglio stele from Siliana, about forty kilometers south-southeast of Thugga, though later than our period—it is dated 175–200—is a splendid example of its type. In the pediment is an eagle; in the second register, the god in a niche, with a sickle, Victories above; next below, the dedicant and his family sacrificing, his wife in a huge turban, his daughters with baskets; finally, two registers of farm prosperity: plowing with oxen, reaping, loading sheaves onto a wagon.

A collection of mosaics from near the forum at Acholla, forty kilometers north of Taparura (Sfax) has the virtue of being closely datable. The earliest are from the Baths of Trajan, east of the forum. They are dated 110–120. The central theme is the Triumph of Dionysus, symbolizing Trajan's victory over the Parthians. The god appears as an adolescent, wearing a fawnskin, an ivy crown, and a *mitra* (turban) of cloth-of-gold, and holding a gold *cantharus* (wine bowl). A wind-blown veil floats above his head. He rides in a chariot drawn by two centaurs, one old, one young. The main mosaic is flanked by medallions of winter—holding a mattock—and summer—crowned with grain-ears—the whole framed by a cortège of sea monsters. The House of Asinius Rufinus contains the most precisely dated mosaic of all, for Rufinus was consul in 184, in the reign of Commodus, and the mosaic portrays the Labors of Hercules, whom Commodus adopted as his patron deity. The Labors include the rescue of Theseus from the underworld, the fetching of the apples of the Hesperides, and various killings: the Cerynaean stag, Lernaean hydra, triple-bodied Geryon, Calydonian boar, Nemaean lion, and Stymphalian birds. The peristyle House of the Triumph of Neptune measures thirty-five by thirty-two meters (1,120 square meters). It had twenty-four to

FIGURE 3.13 *Siliana, Boglio stele, A.D. 175–200, in Bardo*

thirty rooms, of which thirteen had mosaics. The mosaic that gives the house its name is in the *oecus-triclinium* (main dining room). Neptune rides in a chariot drawn by two sea horses; the central panel is surrounded by medallions of generally marine inspiration (these were seaside villas): Nereids, sea horses, Cupids on dolphins. Another smaller dining room has gourmet items as the mosaic motif: mussel, hen, rabbit, cucumber, zucchini, quinces, apples, pears, figs, and grapes. A reception room in its medallions mingles Bacchic and gastronomic motifs: a bacchante, a couple of Sileni (companions of Bacchus, usually drunk), together with artichokes, cucumbers, eggplant, a partridge, a pheasant, a lemon, a pomegranate, and a basket of roses. Lozenge-shaped medallions portray animals: wild ass, panther, tiger, lion, gazelle, antelope, stag, goat. The whole complex is dated 170–180.

These mosaics are classicizing; a relief found in 1947 near Vaga (Béja), thirty kilometers north of Thugga, gives some insight into Berber gods revered in the third century A.D. by Roman citizens, perhaps naturalized Berbers. Seven gods are represented (fig. 3.14) and labeled—could they be days of the week? The ones on each end are accompanied by miniature horses, and may be equated with the Greco-Roman Castor and Pollux, the Great Twin Brethren. The one on the left is labeled MACVRTAM and carries a bucket and a lantern (Castor and Pollux, as patrons of sailors, are identified with Saint Elmo's fire). Next comes MACVRGUM; he wears a Phrygian bonnet and a midi-tunic, and carries a scroll, a staff, and a snake, attributes like those of Greco-Roman Asklepios-Aesculapius. Obviously a midwife, VIHINAM carries a pair of forceps and has a child at her feet. The central figure, BONCHOR, carries a scepter, and VARISSIMA wears a feather cap. A standing figure, MATILAM, wears a long-sleeved tunic and carries an incense-burner; beside her a small figure sacrifices a ram at an altar; IVNAM, on the far right, completes the group. Two of the figures carry tambourines. The local name for their findspot means "the seven sleepers." Obviously they come from a small rustic sanctuary frequented by simple folk, but elsewhere (twenty-one other examples are known) they are cultivated by, among others, a petty officer, an officer of auxiliary troops, a procurator, two admirals, a priest of Caelestis, and a provincial governor. The epithets by which these mysterious figures are addressed are highly respectful: Immortal, August, Holy, Saviors. Many of those who invoked them have naturalized Roman names like Exora-

FIGURE 3.14 *Vaga, Di Mauri stele, third century* A.D., *in Bardo*

tus, Impetratus, Donatus, Saturninus, Donatianus; the rest probably petitioned them just to be on the safe side.

One of the Roman sites where Punic culture long survived is Mactar, on the High Tell ninety kilometers south of Béja. Beside the arch called Aïn el-Bab were excavated a Punic tophet and eighty-five stelae, now in tbe Bardo Museum in Tunis. Traces of the old Numidian circuit wall, destroyed by the Romans about A.D. 30, are visible south of the Basilica Iuvenum, a clubhouse, dated A.D. 88 by an important inscription, of a paramilitary group of young men of good Romanized Punic local family, rather like Athenian ephebes. Their meeting room was later made over into a church. The central one of the clubrooms, on two sides of a porticoed court, was an apsidal chapel with mosaic. The inscription that dates the building contains a number of Romanized Punic names: many of the young men had Punic fathers. The names are the usual telltale translations: Rogatus, Fortunatus (son of an Arsaces), Saturninus, Optatus, Victor (son of Balsamon), Felix, Datus.

A relief of the late first or early second century, dedicated to the Cereres Punicae, shows all the attributes of Demeter worship at Eleusis, near

Athens: an ear of grain, torches, a basket containing the holy mysteries, a winnowing fan. Under Trajan were built an arch (dated 116) and a new forum, but under Hadrian an inscription of the extramural temple of Apollo still bears Punic names. Mactar built itself a capitolium in 169, and was made a colony between 176 and 180; the period from 150 to 225 was one of intense Romanization. The famous symbol of this, the verse inscription of a local boy who made good, the "Mactar Reaper," is in the Louvre. He came, he says, from a poor, unpropertied family, worked unceasingly under unrelentingly tropical conditions, from infancy, as an itinerant, and reaping his own crops. He rose to foreman, acquired a house and land, was elected to the town council, and rose from hayseed (*rusticulus*) to censor. In peace, high reputation, and honor, he watches his children and grandchildren grow up. The moral he urges is, "Keep your skirts clean." Though this harmless inscriptional boast of blameless social mobility is admittedly unique, the Punic names on lists of benefactors show that this rags-to-riches story could be multiplied.

The second-century temple of Hathor Miskar at Mactar yielded the longest Punic inscription in Tunisia. In forty-seven lines, set out in ten columns, it inventories the building and its contents, including statues, and lists thirty-two members of a *mizrach* (collective). Another inscription mentions thirty-six contributors to repairs, including three *suffetes* (Punic chief magistrates).

In the old forum, which remained in use, the fullers (clothes-cleaners) dedicated before 180 a temple to the Romano-Punic Liber Pater, with a double crypt. But by far the handsomest building in Mactar is the Great Baths of 199 (fig. 3.15), modeled on Carthage, with the same symmetry and doubling of facilities. The reerected arcades of the porticoed court are uniquely beautiful. Near the apse of the Hathor Miskar temple recent excavations (1970–73) have revealed Mactar's largest (five hundred square meters) and richest house, that of Venus, whose bedchamber has a (late) bird mosaic—peacocks, guinea hens (such as run about today at Mactar), pigeons—and frescoes with flower buds and a meander pattern. The main mosaic is in an apse; the dining room has a marine motif, in which, for example, an octopus fights a lobster.

Hadrumetum (Sousse) became in the high empire one of the most prosperous cities in the province. One of its most famous sons was the jurist Salvius Julianus, proconsul of Africa from 166 to 169. It reached its peak

FIGURE 3.15 *Mactar, West Baths,* A.D. *199*

under the Severi; the evidence is over 250 mosaics, many on display in the local Casbah museum, some of the most famous in the Bardo in Tunis. Trajan made Hadrumetum a colony. From Hadrian's reign to the Severi it expanded, acquiring an amphitheater, circus, theater (110 meters in diameter, smaller than Carthage's, larger than Thugga's), and baths. From about 180 dates a mosaic from the House of the Ostrich, showing a beast-hunt in the amphitheater. One of the four hunters wears a sort of sweatshirt with a lion's head on it, another brandishes a scare-cloth like a matador's cloak. The mosaic swarms with fauna: antelope, ostrich, stag, wild horse, mountain goat. Another mosaic shows the notorious gladiator Neoterius beside a bleeding bear. Under the Severi a *nouveau riche* named Sorothus was quite a fancier of horseflesh; a mosaic from his house proudly portrays horses with his brand, and named Amor, Dominator, Adorandus, Crinitus (Cresty). A lead curse-tablet betrays the local mania for horse racing, calling down upon the horses of the rival stable paralysis, insomnia, and bad turns. (Women as well as horses were cursed: one tablet expresses a hope that a faithless mistress may suffer from insomnia and loss of all appetite for meat and drink—this a particularly potent one, for the Latin is written in Greek letters.)

A Nilotic scene from nearby El Alia, dated 200–225, is entertaining: a towered arcaded villa rises on the river bank amid lotus and papyrus;

there are also a peasant's hut, a tethered horse, a goat stubbornly re-
sisting sacrifice to Priapus, a slave after a crane, a hunter after a hippopotamus, another after a crocodile, a crocodile with an ass halfway down
its throat, a duck being walked on a leash. A well-known parallel to this
popular Nile motif comes from the Sanctuary of Fortune at Praeneste
in Italy (*MSS*, fig. 5.1). The House of the Masks, Hadrumetum, has a
Severan mosaic showing an actor, and a tragic poet with a scroll and
scrinium (scroll box). The masks are of satyrs, bacchantes, and characters
from comedy.

But the most famous mosaic from Hadrumetum is the Vergil in the
Bardo Museum (fig. 3.16), now dated 210. The poet is shown with
Melpomene and Calliope, muses of tragedy and epic. They dictate to
him; the scroll in his hand reads, "Musa, mihi causas memora," from the
first lines of the *Aeneid*. Calliope reads from the scroll; Melpomene,
holding a tragic mask, listens. The poet, looking dark and austere, sits

FIGURE 3.16 *Hadrumetum, Vergil mosaic, ca.* A.D. *210, in Bardo*

with his feet on a stool; he wears, inappropriately, ankleboots, associated in antiquity with comedy, but Vergil never cracked a joke. He is dressed in a white toga with a narrow stripe. The householder who commissioned this piece paraded his culture most appositely, because of the prominence in the poem of the tragic story of Dido of Carthage.

At Thysdrus (El Djem), chiefly famous for its amphitheater (see chapter 4), recent excavation of Roman houses has revealed a number of Severan mosaics. One of these, perhaps later in date, represents the seasons, and the months with their attributes: Spring is symbolized by an elephant, Summer by a wheatsheaf and sickle, Autumn by a satyr amid vine leaves; Winter, in a hood, is shown with a hare and ducks. In the sequence of months, March comes first in the very old Roman fashion, symbolized here by the Quinquatria, a festival of Mars; April (Aphrodite's month) is symbolized by Venus; May, by Mercury (his mother was Maia); June, by a thermopolium (hot-food shop); July, by a dance; August, by Diana (her birthday was the thirteenth); September, by grapes being trodden; October, by Severus Alexander; November, by Isis; December, by slaves celebrating the Saturnalia, the topsy-turvy festival in which they played the part of their masters; January, by the festival of the Penates (household gods), who are shown dancing; February, by women being whipped at the Lupercalia, a fertility festival. During the construction of some new houses in 1960, an Orpheus mosaic of Severan date was found. The bard wears a Phrygian cap, and gathered about him are the birds and animals he has charmed by his music: a peacock, sparrow, duck, lion, wild ass, tiger, stag, panther, and antelope. The odd Mosaic of the Fancy-Dress Banquet, dated 225–250 (fig. 3.17) shows a group of diners, perhaps entrepreneurs who supplied animals for the amphitheater, eating at a table made to look like an arena, looking out on a herd of Brahma cattle like those used in the amphitheater; the inscription reads, "Let the bulls sleep. . . ."

At Cincari, near Thuburbo Minus, the baths, excavated, revealed a room called in an inscription SEPTIZONIUM. This aroused interest because a controversial façade, now destroyed, of the Severan palace on the Palatine Hill in Rome bore the same name. The Tunisian one presented, in a series

FIGURE 3.17 *Thysdrus, DORMIANT TAVRI mosaic, A.D. 225–250, in Bardo*

of semicircular niches, the seven planets: Saturn, Jupiter, Mars, Sun, Venus, Mercury, Moon.

An interesting commentary on this prosperous period is provided in a speech put by Dio Cassius, historian, and suffect consul in 205, into the mouth of Augustus' mentor Maecenas, but in fact announcing Dio's own program of how the empire ought to be run. Maecenas is made to recommend special education for public service, abolition of tax-exempt status, and curbing of urban extravagance in buildings and festivals. But the Carthaginian Christian Tertullian (160–240) comments (*De anima* 30) on the vitality of the Africa he knew: the roads, the estates, the flocks and herds, the culture of cities, the conquest of desert, mountain, and fen.

4. FROM THE MILITARY ANARCHY
TO THE ARAB INVASION

The murder of Alexander, the last of the Severans, in 235 was followed by nearly fifty years of almost uninterrupted anarchy, which has been called "military dictatorship tempered by assassination." From this, however, on the archaeological evidence, North Africa suffered rather less than the rest of the empire. When in 238 at Thysdrus (El Djem) a group of young oil-rich conservatives revolted against the soldiery and set on the throne their proconsul, the aged senator Gordian I (possibly African), there was in the process of building in their city a huge amphitheater, the largest in North Africa, which still survives, looming thirty-six meters into the air (fig. 4.1) to dwarf the Arab village clustered about it. It ranked seventh in size in the Roman world, after the Colosseum at Rome and the amphitheaters of Capua, Puteoli, Milan, Autun, and Verona. Its perimeter, 427 meters, is 100 meters less than the Colosseum's; its arena measures 132 by 220 Roman feet, a proportion of three to five. Its area, 12,156 square meters, would hold 31,700 to the Colosseum's 50,000. It has three concentric corridors to the Colosseum's four, and four beast-elevators to the Colosseum's twelve. It boasts the largest column capital in Tunisia, six Roman feet in diameter. This is a very ambitious building for a town of 25,000 to 30,000, but of course it was planned to draw spectators from miles around. Thysdrus had also a circus, comparable in size (516 by 100 meters) to Maxentius' in Rome, and, as we saw, a smaller, unexcavated amphitheater adjoining the large one.

Just after mid-century Cyprian, bishop of Carthage and martyr, whose mausoleum may lie just west of the Carthage theater, and the site of whose basilica has now been used as an archaeological dump, wrote on the decadence of the times (*Ad Demetrianum* 3–4), complaining that mines were exhausted, produce diminished, the number of farmers less; that slaves

FIGURE 4.1 *Thysdrus, amphitheater, unfinished in* A.D. *238*

ran away, coloni deserted and became brigands; that the whole world was decrepit and near its end. That this pessimism is in part rhetorical—an antipagan polemic exacerbated by the persecutions of the emperor Decius—is suggested by various pieces of archaeological evidence that contradict it. At Ostia, oil amphoras bearing third-century stamps from Lepcis Minor and Hadrumetum show that North Africa continued to furnish Rome's grain supply (the *annona*), which certainly profited someone, though how far the prosperity filtered down is controversial.

At Simitthu the theater, richly decorated with local marble, is dated by a coin to the reign of an emperor who has been called "a Bedouin sheik," Philip the Arab (244–249). The theater is expensively built on vaults, its orchestra richly paved with polychrome marble: yellow, rose, red-orange, lilac, violet, dark blue.

At Thugga the House of Dionysus and Ulysses is dated to the reign of Gallienus (253–268). In the rich mosaics, Dionysus, as we saw, punishes pirates by turning them into dolphins; the viewer sees the metamorphosis in progress. Ulysses, lashed to the mast, as we also noted, satisfies, without risk to life or limb, his curiosity about what song the Sirens sang (fig. 4.2). The Sirens form a trio, one on the double flute, one on the lyre, and one a vocal soloist. Christianity is not yet dominant, which may go part way to explaining Cyprian's pessimism; the theater shows pagan plays or pantomime, the mosaics show pagan subjects.

A striking statue (late third century A.D.), the so-called Hercules Massicault (fig. 4.3), shows a pagan votary—of Ceres, on the evidence of the ears of grain and the poppies. The lined face is energetic, austere, and sad, with an aquiline nose and deepset eyes. The subject wears a belted tunic, and a lion-skin hat, like Hercules. The dog who looks up at him is perhaps an allusion to Cerberus, the dog of Hades, of which Ceres' daughter Proserpina is queen.

FIGURE 4.2 *Thugga, Ulysses and Sirens mosaic,* A.D. *253–268, in Bardo*

FIGURE 4.3 *Bordj el-Amri, Hercules Massicault,* A.D. *250–300, in Bardo*

FIGURE 4.4 *Althiburos, ship mosaic, A.D. 280–290, in Bardo*

Althiburos, on the military road from Carthage to Theveste, is most famous for a ship mosaic of 280–290, but its municipal history goes back to Hadrian, to whom the grateful townsfolk erected an arch. There are also a forum, capitolium, and theater. The mosaic portrays twenty-five types of ships, of which it names twenty-two. (A more recently discovered mosaic, from Themetra, gives better detail.) The house-owner who commissioned the Althiburos mosaic was perhaps a wealthy grain merchant. The craft represented are naval and commercial, seagoing and river boats (fig. 4.4), with a perhaps surprising number of pirate craft—sympathetic magic, or a confession, more or less defiant? These last include the *celes, myoparo, stlatta,* and *paro.* The *catascopiscus* was a naval despatch-boat, the *prosumia* was used for reconnaissance, the *hippago* was a horse transport, and the horses she carries are named: Ferox (Fearsome), Icarus, Cupido. The *actuaria* was a troop transport. Commercial vessels include the single-masted *corbita*; the *ponto,* a two-master, shown with a boat in tow; the *horeia,* a bluff-bowed freighter; and a ship whose name is lost, which carried a cargo of amphoras. The fishing boats include the *ratiaria* (dory); the *vegeiia,* a very large, long rowboat, and the *cydarum,* shown with two of its crew hauling in a teeming net. The function of the rest of the named ships is unknown. The fashion of naming horses—Leontius, Bracatus, Syriaca (a mare), Perdix, Plumeus, Miniatus, Cucia, Auspicator, Icarus again, Amor—turns up again, along with some named dogs and bitches—Spino, Pinnatus, Lecta, Polyphemus, Boia, Atalanta—on a newly published hunting mosaic of the same date from the shrine of Aesculapius on the forum. Perhaps the hunters and the proprietor of the ship mosaic belonged to a club of shipowners.

Diocletian (284–306), whose reforms ended the fifty years of anarchy, set apart southern Africa Proconsularis as the province of Byzacena (see map, fig. 4.5). From his reign date such diverse events as the conversion (295) to Christianity of the rhetorician Arnobius of Sicca, and the severe persecution of Christians (303–304), producing a rich crop of African martyrs, forerunners of the Donatist movement, further discussed in chapter 10. At Abitina, ten kilometers south of Membressa, thirty-one men, eighteen women, and a child were haled before the local magistrates and charged with unlawful assembly and possession of subversive books. Their scriptures were burned. They were then taken in chains to Carthage, singing psalms and hymns all the way. There, despite subjection to the most exquisite tortures (the *eculeus*, or "pony," whose saddle had a prong which rammed the victim up the anus; the *ungula*, or "claw," which tore his flesh) they remained steadfast, and indeed courted martyrdom. Food and drink sent in by relatives they refused, smashing the winejars and feeding the meat to dogs. Some were beheaded, others sent to the mines, or exiled.

Under Diocletian, considerable building went on. The Christian Lactantius says it ruined the cities, and some modern historians have echoed his sentiments, arguing that public building was economically unproductive. While conspicuous consumption and conspicuous waste were certainly involved, it is clear that the alternative of investment to *improve* agriculture or manufacturing never occurred to the ancient mind; priority went to investment in land.

In Diocletian's reign the theater at Ammaedara was repaired; at Sufetula an arch (fig. 4.6), imitated from Severus' at Ammaedara, was dedicated to Diocletian, and mosaics were laid in the Baths of the Months at Thaenae (Thina), twelve kilometers south of Taparura. The date derives from a coin hoard, ranging from the reign of Diocletian's colleague Maximian Herculeus to Maxentius, Constantine's erstwhile colleague (the latter dated 311/12), found *on*—not under—the mosaic in the caldarium. The months that survive in the mosaic are January, February,

FIGURE 4.5 *Diocletianic Africa, map*

FIGURE 4.6 *Sufetula, Arch of Diocletian*

April, and December. There are also the usual marine motifs: Nereids, Cupids on dolphins, a ship with a dog for figurehead. There are also some frescoes—which rarely survive—of girls holding grain-ears and dancing. The baths had snugly fitting windows of translucent gypsum. Thaenae had four sets of baths. A mosaic from a private house, showing in medallions Orpheus charming birds and animals—a tiger, dogs, a gazelle, a hoopoe, a stag—was wantonly destroyed in or shortly after World War II.

While Maxentius was struggling for power in Rome, the vicar (head of the diocese of Africa in Diocletian's reorganization), L. Domitius Alexander, stationed in Carthage, revolted (308–311). The archaeological evidence for this is the destruction of the port, which prevented grain shipments and caused famine in Rome.

Constantine's reign lasted from 306 to 337, that of his dynasty until 363. After the usurper Domitius was put down (311), there was a surge of rebuilding in Carthage. After Constantine's conversion in 324, Christianity became the established religion; the last datable Saturn stele is of 323. Though the dating of mosaics is still very far from being an exact science, two famous ones from Carthage may safely be placed in the period of the Constantinian dynasty: the Dominus Julius mosaic from the hill of Saint Louis, now in the Bardo, and the more recently discovered one with racehorses in panels, on display in the open outside the Carthage Antiquarium. The Dominus Julius mosaic (fig. 4.7) portrays in precious detail life on a prosperous manor near Carthage in the fourth century. In the left center, the master arrives at his estate, with pomp and a valet. Center right, he is off on horseback to hunt hares, with hounds. Below and above are the Seasons. At the lower left is Spring: the mistress leans on a truncated column in front of an armchair and a rosebush; in her diadem and embroidered silk dress, she is a human Venus. She is choosing jewels from a box held out by a uniformed maid, while a boy offers a basket of fish. Behind the armchair a footman, in uniform to match the maid's, holds a basket of flowers. A cypress tree separates this scene from Autumn, in which the master is seated in an orchard, on a stool with a footstool, beside an elm upon which is trained a grapevine. A barefoot slave brings two waterfowl; he carries a scroll inscribed DOMINO IVLIO, from which the mosaic is named. Julius is clean-shaven, and wears his hair short, with a fringe. He is dressed in a dalmatic, a wide-sleeved overgarment with slit sides, and wears pointed shoes. Behind him a slave with fruit in a backpack carries a hare by the legs. At the upper right is Summer, the crop higher than the peasant's hut. The bearded peasant has a watchdog, and is shearing a sheep. A lamb feeds under a tree. A servant offers a lamb to the mistress, who now appears, with a plate of pastry, fanning herself in a cypress wood. Under her bench is a hen in a coop. Chickens peck about, and on the left a servant brings a basket of plums. On the upper left is Winter: two peasant children, in hoods, beat the fruit out of olive trees with poles. A hooded huntsman, in garters, crowned with ears of wheat or reeds, holds a brace of duck: he is the Genius of the Season. (A set of mosaics from a villa at Thabraca shows agricultural estates still prospering in the fifth century, with highly efficient land use: there olive trees grow under palms, figs under olives, vines under the fig trees, and wheat between the vine rows.)

The Antiquarium horse mosaic is one of a set from a rich townhouse dated 300–360. In another of these, from the peristyle portico, children

FIGURE 4.7 *Carthage, Dominus Julius mosaic, fourth century* A.D., *in Bardo*

eight to ten years old cruelly hunt child-size animals. One lances a jerboa, another lassos a duck, a third spears a lion cub; other victims are a hare, a wildcat, a cock, and a goose. A similar scene from Piazza Armerina in Sicily (*MSS*, 339) is now dated 315–360. The main mosaic, which originally decorated the oecus, survives in sixty-three panels, of which all but five represent pairs of branded horses, accompanied by gods, mythological figures, or humans. The best guess on the interpretation of the panels is that they are puns on the names of horses, taken from gods' names, mythological characters, or human activities. Gods and demigods include Jupiter, Neptune, Mars, Mercury, Vulcan, Pan, Attis (castrated consort of the earth-mother Cybele), Victory, Lucifer with a torch, Minerva (who invented dice) with a dicer, Carthage personified as a goddess with a turreted crown, and Aion (Time personified). Two Roman myths appear: Romulus and Remus suckled by the she-wolf, and Aeneas fleeing Troy. All the others are Greek: Daedalus, Icarus (we have twice mentioned horses by this name), Hercules fighting the triple-bodied Geryon, Danaë, Lycurgus, king of Thrace, being strangled by a vine for attacking the wine-god Dionysus, Achilles' mother Thetis dipping him in the Styx, Orpheus, Narcissus, the Theban hero-brothers Eteocles and Polynices, an Amazon, Pelops, Ulysses, Sappho taking the lover's leap, the pretty Argonaut Hylas kidnapped by nymphs, Pan and a ram. The humans

FIGURE 4.8 *Carthage, Antiquarium mosaic, A.D. 300–360, detail*

include an enigmatic figure of a man in bed (fig. 4.8), hunters, fowlers, a shepherd with a lamb, a footracer, a boxer flexing his muscles, an athlete crowning himself, an orator or poet reciting, a comic poet or actor with masks, an augur (bird-diviner), a tax clerk with a ready reckoner (forty-two saucers lined up for coins), racetrack employees with megaphones. Among other puzzles are a man kneeling to draw water, a man with a sack on his back leaving an ailing giant (Ulysses and Polyphemus?), a child with baskets on a pole, running amid roses, and a robust seated figure with a cantharus or basket. The conjecture lies ready to hand that the house belonged to a man or club to whom racing was what Livy called in another connection a "tolerabilis insania." Carthage, we saw, had its own circus, and when the Vandals attacked in 439 the fans refused to leave the track.

To somewhere about the mid–fourth century may be assigned four complexes, three pagan and one Christian. The first is the fully developed phase of the baths of Djebel Oust, overlooking the Oued Miliana, about fifteen kilometers southwest of Uthina. This extraordinary complex has over 219 rooms (fig. 4.9). It was in use, at least sporadically, for five centuries: the evidence is coins from Hadrian (117–138) to Justinian (527–565). The water for the baths emerged from a grotto with a three-cella shrine to Aesculapius and Hygieia, goddess of health, which came to be used as a Christian basilica and baptistery. Attached to the baths were sleeping rooms, for this was a shrine of the god whose votaries spent the night—in a rite called *incubatio*—near him, and were healed in dreams. The baths contain room after room of mosaics, mostly geometric—intertwined knots, shields, ribbons, quatrefoils, lozenges—but some of *opus sectile* (cut marble), and Room 1d contained a motif of personified Seasons, dated about 350 (fig. 4.10). Winter is associated with olives, harvested in December; Autumn is pictured with grapes and a pruning hook, and Summer has a fan and a peacock feather. The baths are remarkable for the number of individual tubs, for marble-revetted walls, and for the use of stucco and fresco to hide poor materials.

Secondly, at Thuburbo Maius the Summer Baths were rebuilt in 361, the forum portico in 376, the Winter Baths between 395 and 408, at the

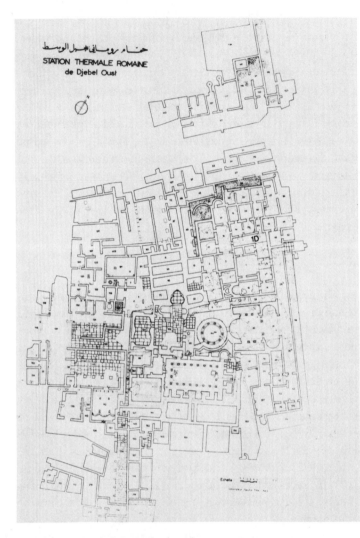

FIGURE 4.9 *Djebel Oust, baths, plan*

expense of local worthies, one a priest of the imperial cult, with an indigenous name. The Zaghouan-Carthage aqueduct still worked after the Vandals came. There was an amphitheater. The temple of Ceres was made over into a church; Thuburbo in the fourth century had two bishops, one Donatist, one Catholic. But there is evidence for slow material degradation in the oil presses, one, as we saw, installed in the capitolium basement, another in the Winter Baths.

FIGURE 4.10 *Djebel Oust, seasons mosaic, ca. A.D. 350*

In 1955 was published an Orpheus mosaic of about A.D. 350 from Sakiet es-Zit, seven kilometers north of Taparura, on the road to Thysdrus. The mosaic came from a house with private baths. The mythical bard is portrayed in front of an *aedicula* (small shrine). His face is destroyed. Christians at first adopted Orpheus as a symbol of immortality, and at Ptolemais in Cyrenaica he even has a halo. But later they defaced him, and a mosaic from Hadrumetum now in the Louvre shows him with the face of a monkey. Here he wears a green cloak with an expensive brooch at the shoulder, and trousers—sure sign of the barbarian. Facing him are some twenty birds and animals, charmed by his music; they include an ostrich, monkeys, cobra, marten, some sort of wading bird, a boar (who, exceptionally, does not appear to be particularly charmed), a tiger, jackal, griffin, hedgehog, squirrel or weasel, and bear (or perhaps lioness!), and also a horse, elephant, goat, scorpion, bull, and tortoise.

At La Skhira, about twenty-seven kilometers southwest of the Christian site of Macomades (later Iunca, nowadays Younga), the laying of an oil pipeline revealed four necropoleis and a large—thirty-four by twenty-one meters—basilica with baptistery, perhaps in its first phase to be dated in Constantine's reign, because that phase shows no human figures, which were prohibited in African Christian art until after his time. This phase has a nave, four aisles, two apses (one, a later addition, with a bench for the clergy), and a narthex with two trefoil columns. The floor is dark blue schist, the walls are stuccoed and painted, with marbled panels, or serpentine or scale patterns in yellow ocher, dark blue, red ocher, sky blue, green, and violet. The columns, a little over twelve meters high, had stuccoed Corinthian capitals. In the next phase, a century or two later, one apse was transformed into a funerary *exedra* (recess), and mosaics were added with such motifs as a dappled hart and a fat-tailed lamb. In Phase III (sixth century) there was a new burial and a new floor in the older apse, and also an altar table with sockets to keep the wine from spilling. The baptistery, which belongs with the latest phase, dated 540 by a coin of Justinian, lay off-center behind the older apse; it had side rooms with shelves for ritual gear. There were aisles on either side of the font, which is shaped like a Greek cross or four-leaf clover; it was originally roofed with a vaulted canopy. At the back of the room was a reserve water tank. At the front and sides of the font were elaborate mosaics, those in front in four panels: spotted harts above, panting after baptismal water (Psalm 42); below, spiral-fluted columns, linked by jeweled crosses with hanging chalices, aflame; in arches above the crosses, doves face each other heraldically. The smaller basilica, earlier than the other, and lying five hundred meters to the north, in the midst of a necropolis, was a funerary chapel, measuring only twenty by eleven meters; it has only two aisles. The necropoleis are dated by coins between Galerius (292–311; Necropolis B) and Julian the Apostate (361–363). They yielded amphoras, glass, lamps, pottery, metal, and poor jewelry.

Between 370 and 383 there lived in Carthage, first as student and then as professor of rhetoric, a young African who was to grow up to be recognized as the dominant personality of the church of his time, and the greatest thinker of Christian antiquity. This was Augustine of Thagaste in Numidia, later bishop of Hippo, saint, and Angelic Doctor. Augustine's Carthage was in its prime, and worth describing (see plan, fig. 1.4). He himself (*Confessions* 3.1) calls it, with an atrocious pun, "sartago flagitiosorum amorum" (a cartload of illicit loves), and speaks of seeing bacchantes dancing in the streets, Caelestis-parades, and Cybele-orgies. His Carthage had orderly streets and squares, planted with trees, and boasted not less than twelve churches, and a hypostyle hall on the Byrsa (a market basilica, not the proconsul's palace). The many Christian basilicas have had the misfortune to have been excavated in the last century by well-meaning but unscientific archaeologists, and more recently to have fallen victim to the exploitation of Carthage as a summer resort. For example, the so-called Saint Monica basilica, named after Augustine's mother, was reconstructed with modern walls and with columns chosen at random, and as we saw, the site is now covered with archaeological debris and in any case inaccessible in the grounds of the presidential palace. But we know that it measured seventy-one by thirty-six meters, had an atrium with cistern, and a nave and six aisles. From it 471 inscriptions have been published. It was built, probably in the fourth century, over a Christian cemetery, and dedicated to Saint Cyprian. It lasted tbrough the Vandal occupation into Byzantine times. From here comes the mosaic of the aristocratic "Lady of Carthage," with halo, diadem, and gesture of blessing (fig. 4.11), dated from her hairstyle in the late fourth or early fifth century; she symbolizes a reconsecration of the church. A mosaic discovered two hundred meters south of the Dermech railway station shows the capture of animals for the arena, in a technique identical with that of a similar mosaic from Piazza Armerina in Sicily (*MSS*, fig. 13.5) that has the same date (early fourth century A.D.).

The Basilica Majorum, a cemetery church—fifty-one by forty-one meters—with nave and six aisles, commemorates the martyrdom, in 203, of the aristocratic Perpetua and her slave Felicity. The vast basilica complex called Damous el-Karita (fig. 4.12), measuring overall two hundred by sixty meters, its church equipped with a nave and ten aisles, is the largest in Africa. It is built over a villa, which yielded a mosaic of the Triumph of Venus. Like the others, its site and orientation are suburban, for the pagan aristocracy long kept the Christians out of the central city. As the grandest church, it was probably the seat of the bishop; it has

FIGURE 4.11 *Carthage, "Lady of Carthage" mosaic, fourth–fifth century* A.D.

a baptistery and a subterranean rotunda with granite columns, and animal heads in the capitals. Perhaps there was a monastery attached. The UNESCO salvage project has assigned the further examination of Damous el-Karita to the Bulgarians, whose report is eagerly awaited. Probably here was the seat of the Council of Carthage, held in A.D. 411, which pronounced against the Donatist schism. In that year six dioceses, including Mactar, Thaenae, and Zama, had Donatist bishops only; nine, including Ammaedara, Thysdrus, Sufetula, and Hadrumetum, had both; three had Catholic bishops only.

The basilica called Dermech I, Byzantine in date, in the archaeological park behind the Antonine Baths, might, according to Frend, have been the Catholic cathedral, but it yielded a possible Donatist inscription, a quotation from Romans 8:31: "If the Lord is for us, who can be against

FIGURE 4.12 *Carthage, Damous el-Karita, from before* A.D. *411, air view*

us?" Behind an adjoining wall was concealed a whole museum of pagan statuary: Isis, Venus, Jupiter, Bacchus, Cupid, Silenus, Mithras, Ceres, an inscription to Jupiter Ammon, all intentionally hidden to circumvent Theodosius I's antipagan edict of 391. Bir Knissia, the only basilica in the southern part of the city, is a part of a complex of Vandal and Byzantine buildings, perhaps an episcopal group. Along the southern edge of the city runs a stretch of wall usually dated in the reign of Theodosius II (425). A late Roman or Byzantine inscription found near Le Kram records ferry fares across the Lake of Tunis: a camel without rider (*camellus levis*) traveled for three *folles*. Finally, Bir Ftouha, in the northwestern suburbs, has yielded a mosaic with a hart, as at La Skhira, and the four rivers of paradise flowing from eight chalices of Christ's blood.

Carthage also had a Jewish community. Results of excavations in their cemetery in Gammarth, which lies north of the city and was in use in 415, were published in 1895. There were two sets of seven and five rectangular rooms, each with seventeen compartments for burials opening off, a mosaic of the Menorah (seven-branched candlestick), and inscriptions in Hebrew. Another document of Judaism is a mosaic from a synagogue discovered in Hammam Lif, on the Gulf of Tunis. It shows the Menorah, and the separation of the sea and the dry land at the Creation. Frescoes with a similar theme, now at Yale, were found at Dura-Europus on the Euphrates (*GSS*, 440).

At Hadrumetum in 1903, incompetent but again well-intentioned excavation revealed an extensive series of catacombs, of which that of the Good Shepherd was in use at the beginning of the fourth Christian century. It had 105 tunnels, running for 1,500 meters, and nearly 5,000 *loculi* (burial places). The loculi are usually dug three high, and closed by tiles. The corpse is laid on and enclosed in plaster. Though most of the tomb furniture is poor and the names native—Felix, Saturninus, Restitutus, Dativa, Donata—one child was buried in garnet velvet and gold lamé. Symbols include a cruciform anchor, the dove of peace, the pelican (which allegedly sacrificed itself for its young), the fish, whose name in Greek is an anagram for Christ, son, savior, lord; also the chi-rho symbol (the first two letters of Christ's name in Greek), the palm, symbol of victory over death, and pithy Donatist inscriptions like BONIS BENE, "good luck to the good." The Catacombs of Hermes, named after a Christian occupant mentioned in a mosaic, had 2,500 loculi, and chapels very like those discovered under Saint Peter's at Rome (*MSS*, fig. 13.1), with vaults, slots for burials, painted stuccoed walls, and mosaic floors. One crypt had 184 burials in 165 loculi. One particularly pathetic inscription is of a baby who lived nine minutes. The Severus catacombs, also in use in the fourth century, had 1,767 meters of galleries, and 5,000 loculi, about a third of which were found intact. Many of the mosaics from here are still unpublished.

Christian mosaics may be crude and naive and lack perspective, but they are infinitely preferable to mediocre banality. A fifth-century example

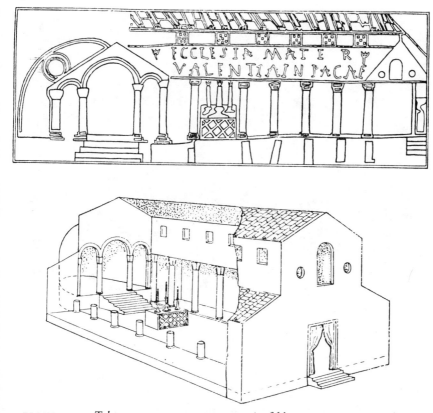

FIGURE 4.13 *Tabarca,* ECCLESIA MATER *mosaic, fifth century* A.D., *in Bardo*

from Thabraca (fig. 4.13) provides a case in point. It represents a church and bears the legend ECCLESIA MATER. Façade, side, and altar are all presented frontally, but from it a plausible reconstruction drawing has been made, showing nave, aisles, altar with carved front and candles, and steps up to the apse. The church at La Skhira must have looked very like this before its second apse was added. Another masterpiece of late Christian (sixth-century Byzantine) mosaic is the baptistery from Clupea (Kelibia) now reconstructed in the Bardo (fig. 4.14). On the sill are inscribed the words PAX, FIDES, CARITAS, "Peace, Faith, Charity"; an inscription dedicates it to Saint Cyprian. In the corners are *craterae* (wine bowls), grape clusters, and birds. Inscriptional thanks are given to God for *aqua perennis,* the ever-flowing water of baptism. Candles are represented at the intersections of the clover-leaves; in the curves, a dove with an olive branch, a fleur-de-lys, and the *labarum* (cross and crown) with alpha and omega, for Christ, the Beginning and the End. Another clover-

FIGURE 4.14 *Clupea, baptistery, sixth century* A.D., *in Bardo*

leaf has Noah's Ark, another a chalice. On the first step is a meander pattern and the trees (stylized) of Eden: fig, olive, palm, apple. An inscription emphasizes unity. The church from which this baptistery was taken contains fifty tomb mosaics—of priest, deacon, reader, laymen, women, and children—using the same symbols as those in the baptistery, but dating from the fourth and fifth centuries.

Careful excavation of seven Christian complexes at Sufetula shows that the town flourished right through the Vandal occupation—in fact the Vandals seem not to have vandalized as much as their bad press suggests. That building in the fifth century was generally in progress is shown by a mosaic from Ste-Marie-du-Zit that shows a basilica under construction: a stonemason is fashioning a column, a cart carries another, an architect gives orders; there are a square and a plumb-bob, plaster is being mixed—a veritable hive of activity. Though Sufetula had fortified buildings in Byzantine times—twenty meters square, with double walls and access only by ladder—it never seems to have felt the need for a circuit wall. Basilica I, of Bellator (fig. 4.15), is dated 313–400, and was the original cathedral. In its apse was buried Jucundus, martyred by the Arian Vandals in one of their more destructive moods. The arch of

FIGURE 4.15 *Sufetula, Bellator church,* A.D. *313–400, altar footings*

Diocletian, previously mentioned, is a testimony to renewed building activity under that emperor: the theater dates from after his founding of the province of Byzacena. Three monumental public fountains were presented to the town by a *vir clarissimus*—a senator of rank, after *spectabilis* and *illustris*—between 364 and 367. Basilica II, of Vitalis, became in Vandal times the new cathedral. It was carefully built of *opus mixtum*—a course or courses of brick inserted between courses of stone—and had sumptuous mosaics. Basilica III, of Servus, may have been Donatist. It was in use down into Justinian's reign, minus its porticoed façade, and with its cella collapsed, a baptistery in the midst of the ruins, and a cupolaed building behind. Basilica IV, built along the north wall of the forum, is of the late fourth or early fifth century, with later phases down into the seventh. It has a second apse and geometric mosaics. The church of Saints Gervais, Protais, and Tryphon, just west of a Byzantine fort, was in use until the tenth century, but an oil press in the street beside it proves that by then sophisticated urban life had ceased here. Basilica VI, of Sylvanus and Fortunatus, with cupola, Greek cross shape, and basket capitals, looks and is Byzantine. The Honorius Chapel (VII), named for a bishop, is of the fifth century.

The Vandals were Arians, and hard on Catholics. Their king Thrasamond banished the Catholic bishop, Fulgentius of Ruspe, to Sardinia; he was not finally recalled until 523. A fifth-century mosaic from Vaga, in the Bardo, has been interpreted as referring to this episode. It shows the centaur Chiron teaching the young Achilles to hunt. The centaur serves as both instructor and mount; he steadies his pupil with an encircling arm. The quarry is a dappled stag. Also present is a female Chimaera— amalgamated lioness, goat, and snake—breathing fire. Hanging between Chiron and the stag is a pair of sandals, a charm against the evil eye. The conjecture is that this is a piece of Christian symbolism: Achilles the Vandal king, the stag the Church, the Chimaera Satan. Is Chiron then Fulgentius?

The bishop had lived, before his elevation, for many years as a monk. His monastery was on Kneïs Island, near Macomades. Here on the mainland archaeologists have discovered several Christian basilicas. One, measuring thirty-two by eleven meters, is remarkable for the stuccoes and frescoes of its presbytery and choir. The colors are garnet, dark blue, yellow ocher, sky blue, violet, and imitation marble. The presbytery had a half-vault painted with daisies on a blue ground; below were panels, blue on ocher; the cornices were red and blue; in the apse, lozenges in dark blue rectangles; the dado was painted in diagonal stripes, red, ocher, and blue. At the bishop's throne was a representation of twisted columns, painted light blue. The altar, stuccoed, stands against the wall. The choir presents columns in imitation marble, with acanthus capitals. In the body of the church the piers also had acanthus capitals, and a shaft decoration of blue and violet lines, with a red band. There was a swastika frieze, and a motif of rosettes in squares and rectangles. The excavator compares this with the décor of the Jewish cemetery at Gammarth.

The baptistery thirty meters to the south-southeast is church-shaped, and revetted in Simitthu marble. An inscription mentions a bishop named OVODBVLTDEVS, barbaric for "As-God-Wills." There was a chancel rail. The baptistery, four steps down, is rectangular, not cross-shaped as usual; there is a tank on either side of it for asperging candidates for baptism.

Another church, Basilica III, is Byzantine. It was large—seventy-eight by thirty-five meters—with an unusual triple apse, like the Church of the Nativity in Bethlehem, and two side aisles and a martyr's chapel. A mosaic from one of the apses portrays a cock, pheasant, partridge, hawk, and hare; in front of the central apse is a mosaic with lionesses and a stag, amid palms. The apse shows the footings of the bishop's throne; the altar table was marble. An arcade connected the columns of the nave; at the entrance end was another apse, roofed with a half-dome; the arrangement implies a liturgical procession. Between the second apse and the vestibule were several burials.

Yet another basilica, three hundred meters northeast of Macomades' Byzantine citadel, is double-apsed, and measures fifty-five by thirty-two meters. It has four aisles and two narthexes. One of these, opposite the counter-apse, portrays in mosaic a hemicycle out of which flow the four rivers of paradise.

Despite the evidence of vitality in the building of churches, it is also clear that thinking men of the fifth century felt a sense of *mal de siècle*. Augustine's *City of God*, begun in 413, may be interpreted as a consolation for the decline of the empire. Augustine himself died in his see of Hippo—now Annaba, Algeria—in 430, when the Vandals were hammering at the gates. But a law of Honorius, promulgated in 422, shows cultivated land in Tunisia not much reduced from what it had been in the high empire. Literature, however, shows signs of decadence. Luxorius, Latin poet of the Vandal court at Carthage, has left ninety-one poems of the utmost triviality, composed in the style of the Silver Latin epigrammatist Martial. He writes about Vandal princes' pets, herb gardens, or decease; a poem on a dwarf, and another on a female dwarf in pantomime, recall the dwarfs from the Mahdia wreck (fig. 2.6). Two only of the poems show any social conscience, one on an informer, the other on a rapacious official. Luxorius is impressed by oddities, often obscene: a catamite lawyer, a eunuch, a magician-beggar, an elderly virgin bride, a physician-pimp, a gouty hunter, an impotent girl-fancier, an alleged blue-blood hunchback, a monkey riding a dog, the philosopher Diogenes with a harlot, a cat having a stroke over a mouse. Perhaps symbolic of failed creativeness is a wedding song for a friend that is a sixty-eight-line patchwork of lines from Vergil, like inscriptions of the high empire in reuse in a fifth-century basilica.

We end this chapter with a description of the flourishing though watchful state of Ammaedara (Haïdra) in Byzantine times. The arch of Septimius Severus (195) was then transformed into a bastion. The bridgehead citadel itself, a massive affair, measuring 200 by 110 meters, with imposing square towers—the round ones are modern—has never been excavated. There is a parallel at Limisa (Ksar Lemsa) fifty-seven kilometers south of Thuburbo Maius—a particularly handsome, picturesque, and nearly complete Byzantine fortress splendid in its isolation. It is roughly thirty meters square, and has battlemented towers with slits for firing. It must be nearly contemporary with Ammaedara's. Others, more or less well preserved, are at Thelepte, Feriana, Lares, Vaga, Agbia, Sufes, and, as we have seen, Mactar and Sufetula.

Fifty meters north of the Ammaedara citadel, on a high podium at the back of a spacious precinct (eighty by forty-seven meters) cut in two by the modern road, was a tetrastyle temple, perhaps the capitolium. Its setting is strikingly like that of the Temple of Mars in Augustus' Forum in Rome (*MSS*, fig. 6.1), but without the exedras. As far as I know it has not been dated. Its walls are in *opus Africanum*—fist-sized stones set in mortar between cut stone uprights. Two hundred meters to the east is a low-arched building, seventeen by twenty-two meters, with troughs, one of many in North Africa; others have been found at Sicca, Mactar, Bulla Regia, Thugga, Thuburbo Maius, Gigthis, and Sufetula in Tunisia; and at Madauros, Theveste, and Timgad in Algeria. These buildings have been variously interpreted, as stables, bakeries, warehouses. Perhaps the least unsatisfactory explanation is that they were distribution points for a dole, either civil or religious.

The best excavated and reported buildings of Ammaedara are the five basilicas, ranging in date from the fourth to the seventh centuries. Basilica I, of Bishop Malleus (fig. 4.16), is dated firmly in 568–69. In it were found a reliquary of Saint Cyprian, with his name spelled out ingeniously in a sort of rebus on the cover, and 148 tomb inscriptions, found packed into nave and aisles. They are mostly of clerics: a Vandal bishop, priests, deacons, subdeacons, readers, nuns. The church itself is noteworthy for flying buttresses and for the use of polychrome Simitthu marble; services were held here down into the seventh century. Basilica II, of Candidus, is a martyr's memorial, thirty-seven by sixteen meters in dimension, begun in the fourth century, rebuilt in the sixth. Basilica III is the citadel chapel, of A.D. 533. It measured twenty-three and a half by thirteen meters, and had gray marble Corinthian columns. Basilica IV was a Vandal chapel, dated by inscriptions of 510 and 526. It measured nine by twenty-one meters, and was of crude workmanship. Basilica V was built over a spring just outside the southwest corner of the citadel. It has so far yielded no inscriptions, probably because burials would have polluted the water. It had Corinthian columns and a raised apse.

FIGURE 4.16 *Ammaedara, Basilica of Malleus,* A.D. *568/69*

The Byzantines under Justinian's eunuch general Solomon had needed only five thousand men to beat the Vandals in 533. Their presence in Carthage is signalized by a funeral chapel and subterranean baptistery containing an inscription with the name Asterius. It lay between the lycée and the Fountain of the Thousand Amphoras, and is dated to 582 by coins of the emperor Mauricius. It had mosaics, some geometric, others representing fish and birds, such as peacocks, in medallions. But the end of Greco-Roman rule in North Africa was near. The Arabs threatened; they defeated the patrician Gregory near Sufetula in 647, built their famous mosque at Kairouan in 670, and in 698 Carthage fell. The culture of Tunisia ever since has been Islamic, in recent times with a thin veneer of French.

PART 2: LIBYA

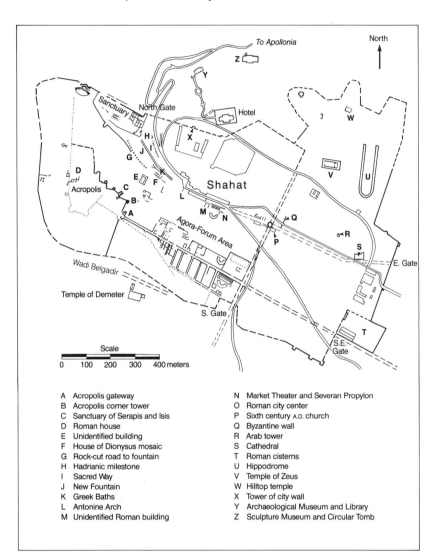

FIGURE 5.1 *Cyrene, plan*

5. CYRENAICA

Cyrene, modern Shahat, is unique among North African sites: it remains delightfully green the year round. Its average annual rainfall of over six hundred millimeters makes it extremely fertile; Djebel Akhdar, its Arabic name, means "Green Mountain." The Dorian Greeks, who founded it from the Aegean island of Thera in 632 B.C., had a fine eye for a site—on a plateau a safe twenty kilometers back from the pirate-infested sea— though they modestly gave the credit to the Delphic oracle. According to Herodotus, who visited Cyrene after 440, the place reaped three successive harvests, one at sea level, one on the slopes, one on the high plateau. Cyrene had had some commercial contact with the Aegean long before Herodotus; the evidence is Cretan sherds of Late Minoan III A 2 (fourteenth century B.C.).

Cyrene's early history is an inextricable tangle of myth and history, out of which emerges a fact: from its founding to about 440 the city was ruled by eight kings called alternately Battus and Arcesilas. Battus I was allegedly cured of a stammer by an encounter with a lion, which elicited from him a loud, clear yell. The nymph Cyrene, a well-known lion slayer, captivated Apollo with her prowess, and gave the city its name: a relief of Roman date showing her strangling the king of beasts is now in the British Museum.

A minor benevolent daimon, Opheles, was venerated at a cenotaph in the agora (see plan, fig. 5.1), over which the east stoa was later built. Battus I was worshiped at a circular monument just southeast of the agora's west stoa. It contains an altar base, a semicircular bench, and drains for carrying off the blood of sacrifice. (But this monument is held by some to be a sanctuary of Demeter.)

Arcesilas II, surnamed the Cruel, is immortalized on a Laconian cup, now in the Cabinet des Médailles, Paris (fig. 5.2), which shows him supervising the loading of silphium, a product, perhaps asafoetida, whose export made Cyrene prosper. The greed of goats and of humans wiped out the herb in the age of Augustus, but it appears on Cyrene's coins, and Pliny the Elder says it was worth its weight in silver. The ancients regarded it as a panacea—it could be used as forage, vegetable, pickle, sauce, apéritif, purgative, astringent, antiseptic, or aphrodisiac. The scene on the cup has usually been taken to represent a ship, but it may portray Cyrene's agora, with a storeroom below. The king is supervising the weighing of the plant, which is shown on the scales, packed in wicker for the circulation of air. Slaves, labeled on the vase, like the king himself, do the carrying and stowing and preside over the scales. The king is attended by exotic fauna: a tame leopard, gecko, monkey, crane, and kites.

The precinct of Apollo Archegeta, in the agora's southwest corner, formerly called the Temple of Demeter, is dated between 620 and 600. Near it were found the famous Edicts of Augustus, dated in the years 7/6 and 4 B.C., now in the site museum. They show that Cyrene under Roman rule still functioned under Greek law: capital cases involving a Greek and a Roman were to be tried before a mixed tribunal; disputes between Greek and Greek by Greek juries; new Roman citizens were liable for compulsory public service; procedures in extortion cases were to be speeded up; the accused was liable to a claim for recovery but not a capital charge.

Outside Cyrene's Ptolemaic circuit wall, across the wadi, two hundred meters south of the agora, lay a sanctuary of Demeter, currently in process of excavation by an American team. It was laid out on the hillside in five terraces covering forty-two hundred square meters. Finds show that it was in use from about 600 B.C.—only a generation after the colony's founding—till a great earthquake destroyed it in A.D. 262. One precious find was a fragment of an archaic *kore* (maiden), dated 575–550, which made a join with a piece in the museum whose provenience had hitherto been unknown. Pottery, also archaic, from both Corinth and Athens—and some, but less, from Rhodes, Chios, and Samos—show the early trade connections. In a number of shrines, their footings cut in the bedrock, pig bones were found; pigs were a favorite sacrifice

FIGURE 5.2 *Cyrene, Arcesilas vase, ca. 550 B.C., in Cabinet de Médailles, Paris*

to Demeter. The torso of a Vestal Virgin, of Roman date, has a sixty-three-inch waist, which the excavator—perhaps with Victoria in mind—describes as "queenly." A fine head of an adolescent girl, from the end of the fourth century B.C., represents an initiate; she is sister to the young devotees of Artemis, called "bears," at the sanctuary of Artemis at Brauron, in Attica (*GSS*, 256–60). An Antonine marble head of a Libyan, with a short Afro haircut, curly beard, and mustache, can serve as a Libyan type, along with the bronze, of about 350 B.C., also from Cyrene, in the British Museum (fig. 5.3). But most of the finds were votive offerings, ritually buried in *favissae* (pits) when the tables of offerings became overcrowded. These included ritual vessels, gifts (among them miniature clay vases, cheaper than the real thing, the goddess being apparently expected to accept the will for the deed), and jewelry, some perhaps

FIGURE 5.3 *Cyrene, bronze head of a Libyan, ca. 350 B.C., in the British Museum, London*

intended to hang on statues or statuettes of the goddess. Of the 110 pieces of sculpture thus far reported from the sanctuary, not one has escaped defacement; this looks like deliberate iconoclasm, by Libyan Arian Christians.

Returning to the agora, we find under the north stoa remains of buildings dated 550–450, and a temple-like building, remodeled from a fountain house, now thought to have been an Augusteum, for the Roman imperial cult.

In 525 the Persians invaded, and destroyed the temple of Apollo, who as lover of the nymph Cyrene was patron of her city. He was also lord of the oracle at Delphi, which had directed its founding. The temple had been the focal point of a sacred precinct, some 530 meters northwest of the agora and accessible from it by a Sacred Way leading down the valley. Phase I of Apollo's temple, which the Persians destroyed, was a simple rectangular hall, like a Mycenaean megaron (*GSS*, 63), with no columnar surround, for marble was scarce near Cyrene. It dated from about 550. Just north of Apollo's temple his sister Artemis was honored. The Artemision had two cellae, with separate entrances; perhaps Apollo was worshiped here before his own shrine was built—the latest dating for the Artemision is about 600. Its favissa (foundation deposit) yielded offerings in amber and precious metals, as well as iron, shell, and ivory.

A third important cult center in Cyrene's vast expanse is the temple of Zeus, outside the circuit wall, on a height 660 meters northeast of the agora. It is tentatively dated just after the Persian invasion, but its earlier phases are hard to restore because of the thorough destruction wrought by the Jews in their revolt of A.D. 115. The Jews brought down the columns by undermining their plinths and inserting wooden props that they then set afire. Seventy years later, in Commodus' reign, the temple stood larger than either the Parthenon or the temple of Zeus at Olympia: seventy by thirty-two meters. The blocks of the bottom courses of the cella measure two by four meters each, and in the cella sat, on a wooden throne and clothed in gilt stucco, a colossal statue of the Father of Gods and Men, eight times life-size, as we can tell from the size of the fingers and toes preserved in the site museum. An Italian team is doing an impressive job of reerecting the columns (fig. 5.4). The head of Zeus in the museum, put together from over a hundred fragments, belonged to the temple's prevolt phase.

Cyrene, which had at its peak a population of three hundred thousand, needed a place to bury its dead. Its necropoleis, spreading to the cardinal points of the compass, are the most extensive known in any Greek city. Archaeologists have catalogued 1,360 tombs, and many more were rifled in antiquity or remain unexplored. They cover twenty square kilometers, and are arranged along regular streets of the dead. (In 1940 the Italian

FIGURE 5.4 *Cyrene, temple of Zeus, Commodan phase, in process of reconstruction*

commander in Cyrenaica, Marshal Rodolfo Graziani, appropriated a section of the necropolis as his personal air-raid shelter, modifying, extending, paving, electrically lighting it, and embellishing it with statues from the environs.) Some tombs are rock-cut; in others sarcophagi were placed about a flowered court. Many of the sarcophagi have a horizontal setting left in the pitched roof to hold a curious kind of faceless statue (fig. 5.5) carved from the waist up, as though issuing from the earth. One series of tombs, of Hellenistic date—about 300 B.C.—is rectangular, with the sides cut board-and-batten fashion, elegant ornately carved doors, and shelves within for as many as twelve bodies. One handsome round carved tomb for two (fig. 5.6) lies by the site museum. It is 8 meters wide, 1.72 high, and stands on a square base with four steps. The elegant moldings find a match in Cyrene's treasury at Delphi. Vases date it to the fourth century B.C. Chamber tombs cut in the cliffs are dated from the sixth to the second century; individual sarcophagi were the fashion in the fourth and third. When a multiple tomb was full, it was so marked: PLERES in Greek. In 1971 was published an account of the discovery of fragments of a coffin, made of cypress and ash, and dated by a Panathenaic amphora to 425 B.C. With it were found an alabaster perfume bottle, a glass bowl, a silver-gilt wreath representing olive leaves and olives, a strigil—for scraping the body after exercise—and the skeleton.

Death, the Emperor Augustus thought, ended life's drama. Cyrenaicans in life had no lack of buildings for drama: no fewer than four theaters. The

FIGURE 5.5 *Cyrene, faceless statue*

FIGURE 5.6 *Cyrene, round tomb, fourth century* B.C.

oldest, perhaps dating in its earliest phase from a little after 500 B.C., lies two hundred meters west of the Apollonion, from which it was separated in Severan times by the Wall of Nicodamos, as a kind of *cordon sanitaire*. The Romans, who preferred a good beast-fight to a tragedy of Aeschylus, transformed the Greek theater into an amphitheater (fig. 5.7). It was rock-cut, with cages not under the arena as usual, but built more cheaply around the edge, from which the beasts could be released through a choice of ten doors. Also Severan is the theater south of the Roman forum, where perhaps the local assembly met. In the late empire the soldiers, who had turned the forum into a fort, tore down the upper courses of the theater walls and its architectural-backdrop stage to afford an unobstructed field of fire. A third theater building, the odeon, west of the Roman forum, is Trajanic; it was perhaps used for meetings of the whole Pentapolis—the group of five Cyrenaican cities of which Cyrene was at one time the head. The fourth, or market theater, two hundred meters northwest, is the latest; it dates from after the earthquake of A.D. 365.

Though Cyrene in Roman times had its own circus, for chariot races, the last of the Battiad kings, Arcesilas IV, preferred to compete in the international races at Delphi. He won in 462 B.C., with a four-horse chariot, and commissioned the great Theban lyric poet Pindar to celebrate his

FIGURE 5.7 *Cyrene, theater-amphitheater*

victory. This Pindar did in the longest and most splendid of his odes, the fourth Pythian, probably coming to Cyrene to deliver it in person.

Shortly after this, a so-called democratic revolution unseated the dynasty. Its constitution survives (and is published in *Supplementum Epigraphicum Graecum*, 9.1). It reserves the franchise to ten thousand property-owners, and vests the government in a senate of 101, a popular assembly of 500, renewed in rotation, and a council of generals. Cyrenaicans were living under this government when Herodotus, who hated absolute monarchs, visited them. In this period the precinct of Apollo was monumentalized by the addition, at the expense of a priest of the god, of the Greek propylaea (the gate to the sacred enclosure), tetrastyle, with architrave, reerected by the Italians between 1932 and 1934. South of it, in 308, rose the strategeion, the generals' headquarters, built with the spoils of victory over native tribes. Restored, it is now an adjunct to the sculpture museum. The Artemision was also remodeled in the fourth century and given a new marble doorway in fine masonry.

Cyrene's "democratic" period ended in 322 B.C., when an aristocratic revolt prompted the intervention of Ptolemy I of Egypt, a Macedonian who had been chief of Alexander the Great's general staff. Cyrenaica remained under Ptolemaic rule until its last king, Ptolemy Apion, bequeathed it to Rome in 96 B.C. This was the period of Cyrene's intellectual prime: three of her native sons made names for themselves elsewhere, Callimachus the poet (305–240) and Eratosthenes the scientist (275–194) in Alexandria, and Carneades the philosopher (214–129) in Athens. Ptolemy III (reigned 246–221) and his beautiful and redoubtable wife, Berenice II, looked after Cyrene's material needs particularly well. The Cyrenaicans expressed their gratitude to the queen, who was born in their city, with a particularly striking portrait statue, the head of which, with formally waved hair and pierced ears, was found in 1915 and is now in the site museum (fig. 5.8). A similar head, much battered, was found in 1976 in the extramural sanctuary of Demeter. Closely connected also is the so-called Cleopatra in the British Museum. To Cyrene's Ptolemaic period probably belongs the gymnasium, measuring 240 by 300 Attic feet, which underlies the Roman forum. Connecting the gymnasium with the agora was built, at an uncertain date, a 130-meter colonnade, the Stoa of the Herms (of Hermes and Heracles, no two heads alike), whose north side has recently been reerected by the Italians (fig. 5.9). A row of

FIGURE 5.8 *Cyrene, head, possibly of Queen Berenice II, reigned 246–221 B.C.*

FIGURE 5.9 *Cyrene, Stoa of Hermes and Hercules*

columns ran down the center, as in the Stoa of Attalus in Athens (*GSS*, fig. 7.10); onto the street opened windows flanked by the herms.

Cyrene's early Roman period (96 B.C.–A.D. 115) is marked by the creation of the province of Cyrenaica—in 74, not until twenty-two years after Ptolemy's bequest—and the combining of this province with Crete (67 B.C.): Cyrene is closer by half to Crete than it is to Alexandria. The Victory on a ship's prow now reerected on the east side of the agora (fig. 5.10), and strongly reminiscent of the Victory of Samothrace in the Louvre, may commemorate the victory over pirates in 67 of the Roman general Pompey "the Great," though some scholars think it celebrates Octavian's victory over Antony and Cleopatra's combined fleets at Actium in 31. The battle of Actium was important enough in Cyrene for an era to be dated from it. Certainly in the reign of Augustus, perhaps between A.D. 4 and 14, according to a recent redating of an inscription on its propylaea, was built the spacious forum (model, fig. 5.11) which rose over the Ptolemaic gymnasium, and which the Italians have handsomely restored. Its ample dimensions made it an ideal strolling place,

FIGURE 5.10 *Cyrene, agora, Victory, perhaps 67 B.C.*

FIGURE 5.11 *Cyrene, Roman forum, model*

aptly compared to the Piazza San Marco in Venice, and, by an early traveler, to the Palais Royal in Paris.

The basilica beside the forum to the north is now thought to be Flavian in date, not much later than A.D. 79, while the temple in the midst of the forum's open space is said by some to be not a Caesareum, but a Hadrianeum. The juxtaposition of forum and basilica anticipates the arrangement of the even more grandiose Severan forum area at Lepcis Magna (see chapter 6). From the Julio-Claudian era we should pause to remember a humble citizen of Cyrene, Simon, who was made to carry the cross for Christ. From Trajan's reign dates the previously mentioned odeon, just west of the forum. Also Trajanic are probably the propylaea and certainly the first phase of the baths that encroach upon the precinct of Apollo below (fig. 5.12). Destroyed in the Jewish revolt, they were restored under Hadrian, and again destroyed by the earthquake of 365; their final phase is Byzantine. They were richly adorned with statues. The most famous, the Venus (fig. 5.13), from a Praxitelean original, now in the Terme Museum in Rome, was laid bare by a cloudburst in 1913, and provided the incentive for all future Italian excavation at Cyrene.

From the time of the Jewish revolt of 115 to the earthquake of 262 the latest report lists eighty-seven monuments. The most important of these

FIGURE 5.12 *Cyrene, Hadrianic Baths from above*

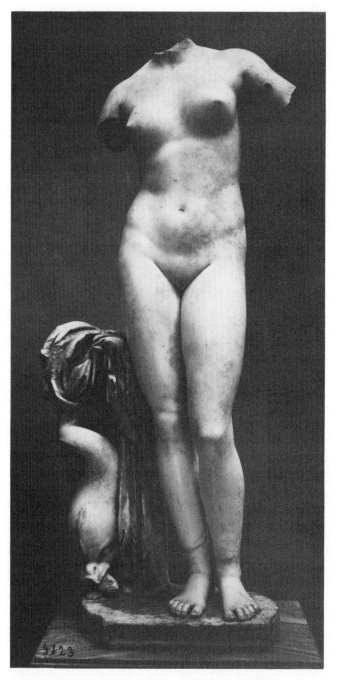

FIGURE 5.13 *Rome, Venus of Cyrene, from fourth century original*

have already been mentioned: the colossal temple of Zeus, and the conversion of the theater into an amphitheater. Also worthy of note is the arch of Marcus Aurelius (164–166), part of which has been reerected at the top of the Valley Road (fig. 5.14). To Commodus' reign (180–192) is usually dated the palatial House of Jason Magnus south of the Stoa of Herms. The rich owner was eponymous priest of Apollo—that is, he gave his name to the year—and probably also gymnasiarch, in charge of public works. The complex covers two blocks, the western half with a mosaic-paved "Rhodian" (two-story) peristyle and a banqueting hall with statues of the nine Muses; also a reception room with a mosaic of the Attic hero Theseus killing tbe Minotaur—half bull, half human—in the middle of the Cretan labyrinth. The peristyle capitals are carved to include tragic masks. The eastern half begins on the north with a double temple, perhaps to Hermes and Heracles, the gods of the gymnasium, whose herms adorn the street outside. The rooms to the south, once assigned to the House of Jason Magnus, are now thought to be two separate houses, called by the Italians "of the Hippocamp" and "of the Stellar Mosaic." The former has a mosaic of the sea nymph Amphitrite astride a sea horse; in its corners are shown the four Seasons.

Fronting on the eastern extension of the Valley Road is the propylon of Septimius Severus, from which are preserved, and exhibited in situ, reliefs depicting his battles against the Parthians, and an inscription describing him as "benefactor of the whole world."

Further still to the east was the civic center, which the late Richard Goodchild was in process of excavating at his untimely death in 1968. It contained five temples, one to Heracles, Commodus' patron; a public fountain, a private house (of Domina Spata), and a small church, thought by Goodchild's Italian successor to be the cathedral. It contains a mosaic in which a lion cub is cruelly used as a decoy; there is a similar motif in the large hunt mosaic at Piazza Armerina (*MSS*, ch. 13). Here the master on horseback issues from a fortified farm to hunt.

Bulldozing for the new town of Shahat brought to light a deposit of archaic Greek sculpture compared by Goodchild to the "Perserschutt" on the Athenian acropolis. It included a *kouros* of 540, a *kore* of 560/50 (compare *GSS*, fig. 4.15), a sphinx, a relief of wrestlers, and a Gorgon's head. Goodchild thought the deposit was motivated by an invasion from Egypt under King Amasis in 514.

FIGURE 5.14 *Cyrene, arch of Marcus Aurelius*

To this period, though not to this place, belongs a Greek papyrus of 190/91 in the Vatican, from the Marmarica, the area between the Egyptian border and Cyrene. It shows how the Romans assessed taxes: the district is divided into six major circumscriptions, called *paratomai*; four villages are listed, along with the properties, the proprietors by name (eight long columns), and the quality of the land.

The century between the earthquakes (262–365) at Cyrene presents a lugubrious record: the earthquake of 262 destroyed the extramural sanctuary of Demeter; that of 365 the Apollonion; in 303 Diocletian transferred the capital of Cyrenaica to Ptolemais (see map, fig. 5.15). The only constructive things to report are the arches at either end of the forum-agora street, one of which dates from Claudius II Gothicus (268–270), and the building of the market theater after the 365 earthquake.

After that cataclysm Cyrene had 277 years of declining civic life before the Arabs destroyed it in 642. As is often true of the late empire, the only bright spots, personal and architectural, are provided by Christianity. Cyrene was the birthplace of an unwilling bishop, Synesius (370–413), whose see was in the new capital, Ptolemais. He was a squire-bishop, persuaded to serve because he was a prominent citizen, an orator, a diplomat, a defender of the plebs, and a match for the imperial bureaucracy and soldiery. He was more of a rhetorician than a philosopher (his rhetorical *Praise of Baldness* survives), but more of a philosopher than a theologian. He was a friend to the redoubtable bluestocking Hypatia (about whom Charles Kingsley wrote a novel, once much read), who held a chair of philosophy at Alexandria. His letters reveal him as a foursquare personality, a man of culture placed over uncultured Christians. He had doubts about the primacy of soul over body, the Last Judgment, and the Resurrection. He wrote that as bishop he would miss the hunt (he liked to hunt ostriches), his wife, and the contemplative life—in that order. He took the bishopric only on condition that he could continue to neoplatonize at home, professing the Christian myth only in public. Thus he became the first baptized Neoplatonist.

Among Synesius' correspondents was one Hesychius, whose house has been excavated north of the forum-agora street. Built on top of another house, which had been destroyed in the earthquake of 365, it contains a

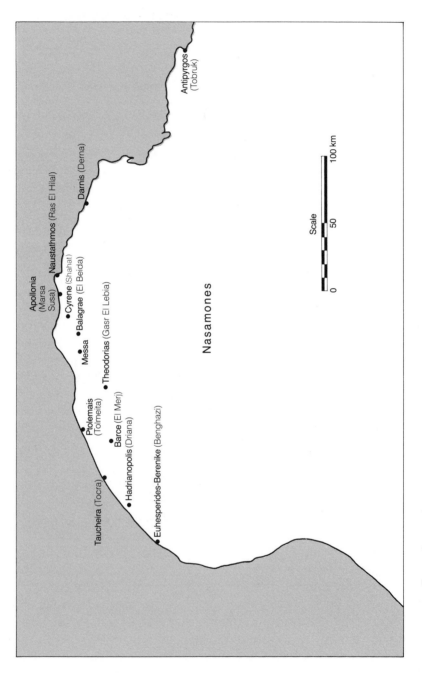

FIGURE 5.15 *Cyrenaica, map*

number of mosaics recording the owner's name, rank (Libyarch—he presided over the provincial council), and religion (Christian).

Four hundred meters east of the civic center was built in the fifth century the eastern basilica, which Goodchild called the cathedral. A traveler in 1821 described it as "indefinable heaps of church." Excavated and cleared of native houses, it proved to have had two phases. In the first, its apse was on the east and it measured forty by thirty meters, with arches defining an unusually broad nave. In the second, Byzantine phase, the apse was transferred to the west end, a throne for the bishop was added, a defensive wall was built round the church, which was extra-mural, and the nave, sacristy, and vestibule received mosaics: birds, animals, a limp gazelle suspended from a pole, rabbits, a milking scene, and a Nile scene—like Tunisian El Alia—with fishermen hauling in a teeming net, a crocodile dragging a cow into the river, and another trying to make off with a steer, while the owner holds on to its tail. The scene may seem inappropriately pagan, but the Nile was a river of paradise, and the crocodile symbolized Satan. The baptistery, up a flight of steps in the northeast corner, consists of a sarcophagus in reuse—nearly all the elements in the church are second-hand—under a six-columned canopy. Pagan motifs have been chiseled away and steps hacked in with crosses to mark the neophyte's point of entrance and exit.

The fortified church was no proof against Berber nomads and the invading Arabs, who allowed Cyrenaica to exist as a Berber kingdom under their suzerainty. Arabs lived in the fortified east church of Cyrene's port, Apollonia. Nomads, goats, and camels ruined ancient Cyrene; terrace walls were not kept in repair. Cyrenaica fell to Turkey and then to Italy. (In World War II the Cyrene museum was successively headquarters for Marshal Graziani and for RAF bombing operations against Italy.)

Apollonia (Marsa Susa), Cyrene's port, was the second of the five cities of the Pentapolis—which became Hexapolis with the addition of Hadrianopolis in the reign of Antoninus Pius. Its most remarkable remains are dated respectively very early and very late in its history. The early remains are the harbor works, which in their earliest phase must date from not long after Cyrene's founding. They had to be studied by scuba divers: the water level has risen two meters since antiquity. The divers found that the city wall (Hellenistic, 1.2 kilometers long, with nineteen towers, one every sixty meters) extended north and east to a reef (plan, fig. 5.16). A mole at the east end of the town ran out to a lighthouse island and formed an oval inner harbor with a narrow (eight-meter), tower-flanked entrance. The harbor had warehouses, quays, and slipways for berthing ships; the northernmost is a set of ten, each measuring six by forty meters. (While on a nautical subject, we may note that the *Rudens* of Plautus, the saltiest of his plays, is set on the seacoast near Cyrene, and that a temple a kilometer to the west may figure in the play.) Apollonia's theater, like its defensive wall, is Hellenistic, but later than the wall, which cuts short the western end of its twenty-eight rows of seats, partly rock-cut. An inscription of A.D. 92–96 in which the name of the hated Emperor Domitian is, as often, erased, shows that it was rebuilt at that date. It was stone-robbed in the late empire to build the east church.

This, the largest Christian edifice in the city, was built over a Hellenistic or Roman building. Two phases, fifth and sixth-century, are recognized. To the latter phase belongs a mosaic from the south transept, showing Noah releasing the dove from the ark. There was an elegant clover-leaf baptistery, marble-revetted and perhaps cupolaed; there is provision for heating the baptismal water—Cyrenaicans were notorious for their luxury. The central church, of Justinian's reign, contrasts marble fittings of fine quality with shoddy masonry. Goodchild's inference was that the locals got a shipment of church fittings and improvised a building to receive them. The west church has its apse fitted into a tower of the city wall. It also had heated water in its baptistery.

Finally, Apollonia boasts a sumptuous governor's palace, of about A.D. 500, in which lived the beautiful and talented Theodora—unjustly vilified by Gibbon (following Procopius)—who was the governor's favorite before she married Justinian. The city wall forms its south side, and some of its rooms project into a bastion. A vestibule with benches, in the northeast corner of the west wing (fig. 5.17) gives access to an apsidal audience chamber, with built-in shelves for law books. The building centers on a trapezoidal court, its columns connected by low Byzantine arches. It opens on the west into a high apsidal council chamber. In the apse a dais—rather like a High Table at Oxford or Cambridge—made this the governor's throne room on emergent occasions. Off the south side of the court opens a small chapel which yielded a marble reliquary, now lodged, along with the mosaic of Noah and the dove, in the site museum in the southwest corner of the city wall.

At Balagrae (El Beida, fifteen kilometers southwest of Cyrene) there was from Hellenistic times a sanctuary of Asklepios (Roman Aesculapius) in a porticoed precinct adjacent to a theater, as at Pergamum (*GSS*, 354–55). A hoard of 259 bronze coins, ending with Valentinian I (364–375), testifies to the havoc wrought by the earthquake of 365: the burier of the hoard did not survive to retrieve it. The fourth-century Roman historian Ammianus Marcellinus describes the earthquake—the lightning, tides receding, then engulfing whole cities; ships driven two miles inland.

The third city of the Pentapolis was Ptolemais (Tolmeita), named after Ptolemy I of Egypt. It was the successor of a nameless port founded about 525 B.C. In its building history it exhibits all the amenities of a prosperous Greco-Roman city: amphitheater, a theater for the upper and another for the lower city, an odeon, made over in the late empire for water ballet; monumental arches; baths, as late as the time of Honorius (393–423 A.D.), and set among formal garden hedges; rostra, and a number of palatial private houses. One of the most impressive finds (1935) is an early relief of maenads dancing, from a statue-pedestal or an exedra: it is on a curved base. The Dionysiac subject suits a date in the reign of Ptolemy IV (222–203 B.C.), who called himself the New Dionysus. There are seven scenes. In the first, the leader, wearing an ivy crown, a snake bracelet, lotus necklace, and disc earrings. Next, a maenad in ecstasy, head thrown back, hair streaming. Third, a maenad, knife in hand, sacrifices a goat. The fourth maenad matches the second, except that she carries the thyrsos (pinecone-tipped rod) of a bacchante. The Italian discoverer called the fifth maenad (fig. 5.18) "La Stanca," that is, "the Weary One": her head droops, she is caught in the moment before drunken prostration. Of the sixth, only the thyrsos-staff survives. The seventh plays the tambourine. The reliefs, returned from Naples in 1961, are now in the Ptolemais site museum.

The city's most impressive monument is the Palace of Columns, an aristocratic residence that may have been the governor's quarters. It was

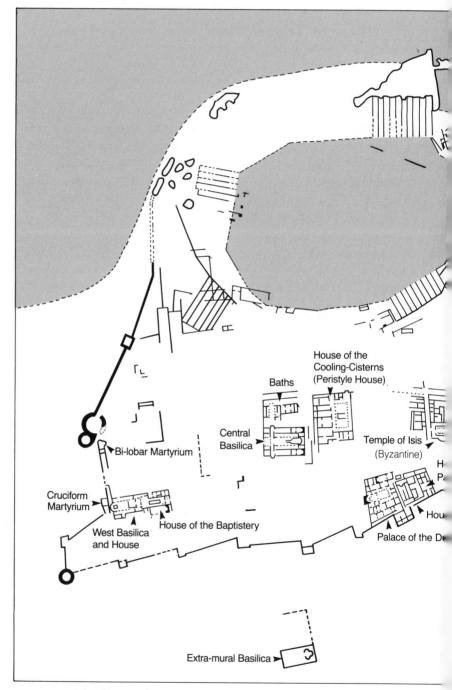

FIGURE 5.16 *Apollonia, plan*

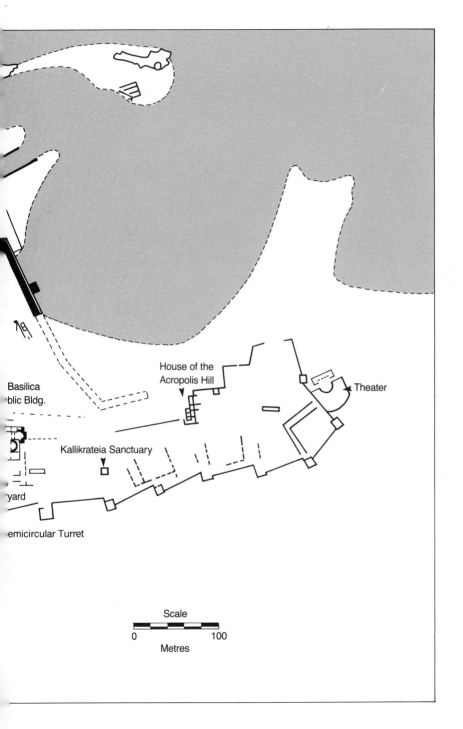

Basilica
blic Bldg.

House of the
Acropolis Hill

Theater

Kallikrateia Sanctuary

yard

emicircular Turret

Scale

0   100

Metres

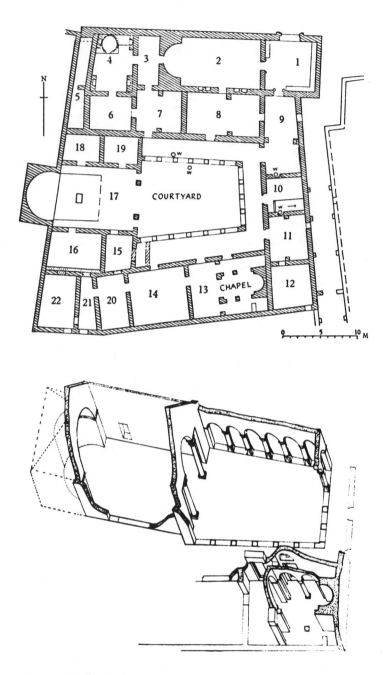

FIGURE 5.17 *Apollonia, the*
Governor's Palace, ca. A.D. *500, plan*
and axonometric projection

FIGURE 5.18 *Ptolemais, relief of a maenad, "La Stanca," 222–203 B.C.*

in use from Hellenistic times to late Roman, and must have begun as the dwelling of Ptolemy III's representative in the city. It measures 164 by 37 meters; its level descends from south to north. It is built of local reddish sandstone, in two faces with rubble fill. Its walls are sometimes plaster, painted and figured (swan, griffin, woman, Gorgon, sphinx); sometimes of marble veneer, black, violet, white, or violet-grained white, called *pavonazzetto*, "peacock-stone." Since no tile was found, the excavators assumed the house was roofed with brush supported on poles. The Great Peristyle of the palace (see reconstruction drawing, fig. 5.19), measured twenty-four by twenty-nine meters, was two-storied, and had eighteen Ionic columns on the ground level, Corinthian above, stuccoed, and with

FIGURE 5.19 *Ptolemais, Palace of Columns, Hellenistic-Roman, reconstruction drawing*

put-holes for a balustrade. There was a fishpond in the open court, marble-revetted, and with a low rail. The discovery of jewelry left behind in it shows that the final destruction of the house was sudden. The north side rose higher than the rest, with three aediculae above, the central one having a half-dome and palmette acroteria, giving a baroque effect like that of the Severan arch at Lepcis Magna; the south side had an aedicula in the center, and two wings. There were theatrical masks in the cornice of the lower architrave. The portico was marble-revetted. Its north side had apsidal ends. Off the portico opened two rooms with columned entrances; the column capitals bore likenesses of gods—Dionysus, Sarapis, Apollo, Ares, Artemis—and mythological figures—Actaeon being torn to pieces by hounds, a Pegasus, perhaps an Ariadne. One of the rooms had a Medusa, of Antonine date, in the mosaic floor. Opening off the portico to the north was a fine lofty columned hall, measuring 17.6 by 13 meters, and with clerestory windows. It was paved with *opus sectile* (cut marble) and alabaster. The bottom drums of the columns were carved into acanthus shapes, an East Greek trait. Opening off it to the west was an atrium with an impluvium, a pool that collected rainwater from inward-sloping roofs. Perhaps the rooms surrounding this were women's quarters. The palace of course had its own private baths, sumptuously decorated in polychrome marble and roofed with barrel vaults; latrines adjoined. North of the baths were shops—a wineshop, a fuller's—with back rooms but no connection with the residential part of the house.

The suite east of the columned hall was built round a narrow court where one column is ingeniously hollowed to take runoff water. Beneath the court is a *cryptoporticus* (underground gallery). One room, once a cistern, was made over into a prison; the excavators found skeletons in it. North of this block was a set of rooms grouped around a fourteen-columned peristyle. The columns are Doric, the architrave Ionic.

Among the finds statuettes and jewelry show strong Egyptian influence, but with an admixture of Greek: gods, goddesses, Apollo killing a lizard, Heracles resting, Venus coyly covering her private parts, Eros (Cupid) with torch reversed, the drunken Silenus, Dionysus, Meleager the boar-slayer, Asklepios. The palace is grander than anything in Pompeii. It must have been the colorful scene of councils, trials, receptions, and festivals during its long life.

From a church at Gasr-Elbia, thirty-five kilometers inland, southeast of Ptolemais, comes a remarkable fifty-panel mosaic of Byzantine date (fig. 5.20). Its theme is the creation, either of the church—perhaps shown in the third panel, sixth row—or of the city, or of the universe. The birds and animals that God made according to their kind are figured, usually in pairs (in the first, second, fourth and fifth vertical rows): stag, fish, lion, bear, cattle, sheep, horse, ostrich, shellfish, jellyfish, goat, whale. The

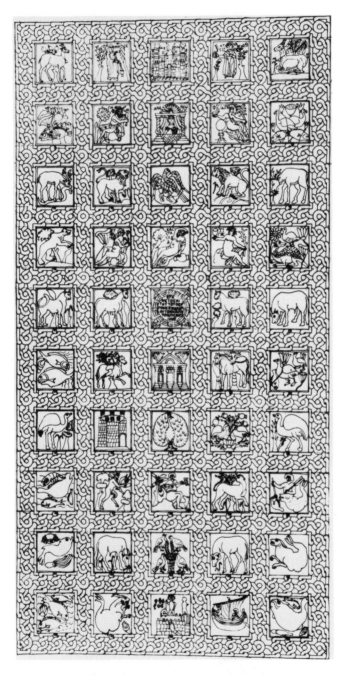

FIGURE 5.20 *Gasr Elbia, Byzantine mosaic, drawing*

second and fourth panels in the second and fourth rows represent the four rivers of paradise: between the first pair a panel shows the Eucharist, symbolized as a woman in an aedicula, with a basket of bread. The panel separating the second pair shows the spring Castalia at Delphi, center of the pagan universe. The central vertical series is the most significant: below Castalia is the inscription of Bishop Makarios, below that the (possible) church itself, then the peacock, symbol of immortality, then Orpheus, pagan analogue of Christ the Good Shepherd (on a mosaic in Ptolemais he wears a halo); then birds pecking at the Tree of Life, finally the lighthouse (at Alexandria?), which is also the Light of the World.

At the earlier end of the chronological scale may be mentioned the tomb of Menecrates, at Barca, twenty-odd kilometers south and west of Ptolemais. It is rock-cut, in two stories, with columns, and is dated 550–490 B.C.

The fourth city of the Pentapolis is Teuchira (Tocra), on the coast forty kilometers southwest of Ptolemais. It had, at various stages of its history, its gymnasium, baths, agora, temples, and private houses. Votive offerings from a sanctuary of Demeter and Persephone date from 625 B.C. onwards. The excavator describes the pottery as being "in supermarket quantity." Laconian ware predominates, but there is some Attic and Chian. The walls, 650 meters on a side, date only from Justinian. Within, an orthogonal street grid, and two basilicas; two more are extramural. Quarries contained Roman tombs, which yielded jewelry.

Hadrianopolis, a later foundation, outside the Pentapolis, can be little discussed, as even its site is uncertain. But traces of its aqueduct have been found, running for seventeen kilometers at a point forty kilometers east of Benghazi, sixty kilometers west of Ptolemais. It would have supplied enough water for a population of 17,700.

The last city of the Pentapolis was Berenice (Benghazi). Before Berenice was renamed in honor of Ptolemy III's queen, the site was called Euesperides. Since modern Libya's second largest city is built over the Ptolemaic settlement, little can be said about it. But Euesperides was *behind* the modern city, centered on an acropolis only nine meters high, surrounded by a salt marsh. It was in the fourth century B.C. extended southward; its streets, probably of Roman date (late first or early second century), may have been laid out as a rectangular grid, and extended north and south of its agora. There were private houses with polychrome mosaics, including one of the nymph Cyrene at her lion-slaying. In the Sidi Krebish quarter, blocks of houses of Hellenistic, Roman, and Byzantine date have been distinguished.

Finally, a word about the Altars of the Philaeni, in ancient as in modern times regarded as the boundary between Cyrenaica and Tripolitania. Two low tumuli were mythologized into the graves of Carthaginian brothers who out of love for their country had submitted to being buried alive. Diocletian marked the spot with four marble columns bearing statues, two tall ones for the Augusti, a shorter pair for the Caesars. In recent times, the Italians erected a grandiose monument there, now dismantled; British soldiers in World War II called it Marble Arch.

6. TRIPOLITANIA AND ITS HINTERLAND

Tripolitania is a convenient way to refer to the three coastal cities of western Libya: Lepcis Magna, Oea (now Tripoli), and Sabratha, and their hinterland. They owed their foundation to the Phoenicians, and fell successively under the sway of Carthage and the Numidian kings. Augustus placed them under the governor of Africa Proconsularis; Caligula assigned their southern marches to his new legate of Numidia. It was not until Diocletian that the province of Tripolitana was created, with Lepcis as its capital.

Archaeologists have found traces of Phoenician Lepcis under the stage of the Roman theater, and under the Old Forum (see plan, fig. 6.1). The graves under the theater date from about 500 B.C. The Old Forum area is more complicated: four levels have been distinguished. The oldest spans 150 years, beginning in about 650 B.C., and includes evidence for impressive building. The next level above dates from between 500 B.C. and 241, the end of the First Punic War. Among the finds was pottery from Athens and Corinth, now on display in the site museum. Level II (241–118 B.C.) covers the period down to near the end of Numidian domination; it yielded many coins, including Numidian ones, which provide the terminal date. The topmost Phoenician level lasts until the late first century B.C., when the Romans took over: its most noteworthy find is a lithostroton floor, of pounded clay with bits of marble inset at random, to which parallels were found at Punic Kerkouane (see chapter 1). Traces of a Phoenician "factory" (trading station) were found on the islets facing Lepcis harbor. It is difficult to distinguish between Phoenician and Carthaginian pottery, but it is plausible to connect these finds with the economic expansion of Carthage after her victory over Greek competition off Alalia, Corsica, about 540 B.C. By about 515 Carthage was strong

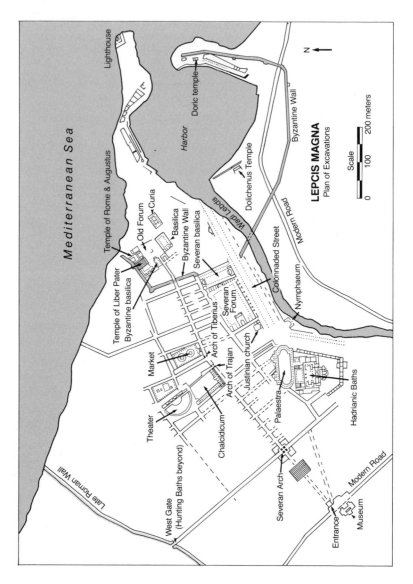

FIGURE 6.1 *Lepcis Magna, plan*

enough to drive off a Greek attempt, under the Spartan Dorieus, to settle at the mouth of the river Cinyps, now the Wadi Caam. Carthaginian influence remained strong in the Three Cities; the vitality of the Punic language, religion, and political institutions is striking, as we shall see.

Lepcis chose the losing side in the war between Pompey and Caesar. The Pompeian Cato the Younger spent the winter of 47/46 there. Caesar, after his victory, fined Lepcis heavily for her bad judgment: she had to furnish three million pounds of olive oil annually to Rome as tribute. That she was able to meet the demand, even if it was with the help of her sister cities, is eloquent evidence of the fertility of her territory.

This fertility tempted the nomad tribes of the Fezzan, the Garamantes. Against them Augustus' proconsul L. Cornelius Balbus Minor mounted a successful expedition into the Fezzan, for which he received the honor of a triumph, a particular distinction for one born in the Phoenician Gades (Cadiz). Lentulus Cossus' defeat of the Gaetulians (A.D. 6) consolidated Balbus' gains. By early in Tiberius' reign (A.D. 15–16) the frontier was for the moment secure, and Lepcis became the terminus of a military road that was also the commercial artery of the olive oil trade.

The security of the hinterland and the prosperity of export trade made possible the beginning, in 8 B.C., at Lepcis, of an Augustan wave of urban development. The first building in the series is, appropriately enough, a market, consisting of a rectangular portico—later altered to a trapezoid to conform to a change in the street plan—enclosing two pavilions, each consisting of a drum with arched windows, surrounded by an octagonal portico (fig. 6.2). An inscription in Latin and neo-Punic records that the market was the gift of a local worthy, Annobal Tapapius Rufus. His name reveals Punic blood and Roman influence. The original entrance to the enclosure was through an archway, displaying on its keystone the caduceus of Mercury, god of trade. The enclosure wall was stuccoed inside and out and embellished inside with painted Cupids and garlands. The connection of Cupid with market business is obscure; he is conventional bourgeois décor, like wallpaper. Of the pavilions, one is in limestone, the other in sandstone and marble—in a Severan restoration that also monumentalized the market entrance. The marble of the col-

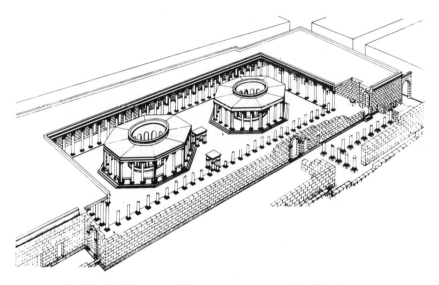

FIGURE 6.2 *Lepcis Magna, market, 8 B.C., reconstruction drawing*

umn shafts is green *cipollino* ("onion stone"); the capitals, displaying lotus and acanthus motifs, are white, making a combination of colors appropriate to a maritime city.

The colonnade was rebuilt in the Severan age with granite columns. Lining it on its inner side was a series of market tables with supports in the shape of dolphins or griffins. Six busts of Lepcitanian men of distinction were found in the market. One was named Boncarth son of Muthurbal; the bust was a dedication to Liber Pater (Punic Shadrach), god of wine—a Punic votary to a Punic god. Adjoining the pavilions are several miniature four-way arches, embellished with representations of ships in crude relief. One of the dedicants was honored for giving his city four live elephants—Lepcis was the shipping point for ivory from the back country. A miniature and highly pattable elephant, a quarter life-size, and with an enchanting crisscross of lines indicating pachydermy, from in or near the market, is on display in the site museum; fig. 6.3 is of a cast in the Castle Museum, Tripoli. The space between the pavilion columns is also occupied by market tables: most interesting is a stone block marked with three standards of linear measure, the Punic cubit (51.5 centimeters), a Greco-Roman foot (29.6 centimeters), and the Ptolemaic cubit (52.5 centimeters); this excellently symbolizes the heterogeneous nature of Lepcitanian trade. Spanning the street at the southeast corner of the market is the simple limestone arch of Tiberius, built in 35/36.

FIGURE 6.3 *Lepcis Magna, elephant, cast*

An inscription in bronze letters set into the pavement dates the Old Forum to the proconsulship of Cn. Calpurnius Piso, 5 B.C.–A.D. 2. Roughly fifty-five meters square, the forum was raised above street level, so that like the market it was free of wheeled traffic. Civic buildings and temples surrounded it. Clockwise from the north, the first temple was dedicated to Liber Pater. The high podium is in part composed of box-like compartments, like the caissons of the concrete sanctuary of Fortune at Praeneste (*MSS*, 129), except that these intercommunicate and were used as shops. Adjoining the temple of Liber Pater on the east, and connected with it by a bridge, somewhat like the arrangement of the capitolia at Sufetula (see chapter 3), rose the two-celled temple of Rome and Augustus. Attached to the front of its high podium was a speakers' rostrum. An inscription in neo-Punic from over the cella door records that the temple was completed while Balyathon and Bodmelqart were suffetes (note the Punic names and the Punic term for the highest munici-pal office), and that it held statues of Roma, Augustus, Tiberius, Livia, and other Julio-Claudians. These statues, in whole or in part, were found near the temple, and a very impressive array they make in the Tripoli Museum. The head of Augustus was pieced together from over twenty fragments; it is ninety-two centimeters high. Like the others, this was an acrolith; that is, only the hands, head, and feet were carved; the rest, left unworked, could be draped with cloth. The head of Roma is seventy-three centimeters high; it was originally helmeted, like the goddess on the Altar of Peace in Rome (*MSS*, 162–70), and on the Carthage altar (chapter 2). Germanicus, the Emperor Tiberius' nephew and adoptive son, is represented with sideburns; Drusus the Younger, Tiberius' second son, with a very Roman nose. A rather pained-looking Claudius, on a colossal scale—rendered as Jupiter, as Horatio Greenough rendered George Washington—and a number of unidentified heads, male and female, complete the set, the richest and best preserved of its kind in existence, and an important document for ruler cult as an instrument of Romanization in North Africa very early in the empire.

The temple of Rome and Augustus was joined by another bridge to a smaller temple farther east, which may have been dedicated to Hercules. Off the southeast corner of the Old Forum was sited a temple-like building in whose cella were ranged, on three sides, broad, low steps on which town councilors' seats could be placed: this was the curia. It dates from the second Christian century, perhaps from the time when Trajan made Lepcis a colony. On the Old Forum's south side was the civil basilica, which did double duty as law-court and covered market. There was a quadriportico within, and at the east end three open exedrae for the judges. A second phase of the building, dated A.D. 53, was reconstructed under Constantine: this is what the visitor sees today. This is also the date of the repaving of the forum and the addition of a portico, at the expense of one Gaius, a Roman citizen, son of Hanno, a Carthaginian name. The small temple at the southwest corner was dedicated in 71/72, early in Vespasian's reign, to Cybele, the Anatolian earth-mother, by one Idibal—another evidence of Punic survival and prosperity in this superficially Romanized town. Centered on the forum's west side was in Trajan's reign a temple which was metamorphosed in Byzantine times or slightly earlier into a church, to which belongs the baptistery in the middle of the forum. The church had a Christian cemetery attached that is even more pathetic than usual, because it contained the graves of three children of the same father, aged eight, three, and one, who all died within three days of each other, probably in an epidemic. Infant mortality was high: another brother lived only a week; a daughter died at the age of one. The northwest corner of the Old Forum contains a three-sided portico of Antoninus Pius' reign (138–161). It is paved in marble and has at the back a shrine to that emperor. An Italian team, excavating between the Old Forum and the Wadi Lebda, has uncovered temples to Vespasian and Titus, later combined for the worship of Domitian. In Byzantine times the fortified area of Lepcis was much contracted: the Byzantine defensive wall runs north and west of the Old Forum, then curves eastward to embrace the harbor works.

Any provincial city that aspired to be thought Roman had to have a theater, though not necessarily for the performance of classical plays;

pantomime, as we shall see, became more and more the popular taste as the empire wore on. The theater at Lepcis is dated by a bilingual inscription to A.D. 1/2; it was a gift to the city by the same philanthropic Annobal Rufus who donated the market. As Marcel Leglay has epigrammatically remarked, "Generosity plus vanity equals embellishment." The splendid limestone drum of the *cavea*, ninety-five meters in diameter, rests in its lower third on a natural slope, in the middle on fill, at the top on massive stone-faced concrete vaults. The theater was constantly remodeled; the little temple of Augusta-Ceres at the top of the cavea was dedicated by one Suphunibal in 35/36, six or seven years after the death of the dowager empress Livia; the cult statue represented her both as Ceres, with garland, grain-ears, poppy, and fillet, and as the Fortuna or Tyche of the city, with the conventional attribute: a turreted crown. The cipollino colonnade dates from Antoninus Pius' reign. The orchestra originally had a painted stucco floor, which was renewed thirteen times before it was replaced by a pavement of greenish-white marble. The first six rows of the cavea were reserved for town councilors, as is indicated by their inscribed names. A part of the forest of statues that decorated the theater—the published catalogue contains over a hundred—consisted of portraits of these worthies. Inscriptions from the theater also give the names of eleven of the *curiae* (electoral divisions) into which Lepcis was divided. Most are associated with Trajan, who gave the city colonial status: Ulpia, Nervia, Traiana, Germanica, Dacica, Augusta, Iulia, Matidia (after Trajan's grandmother), Plotina (after his wife), Marciana (after his mother), and the lone exception, Severa, after Lepcis' imperial native son, who did so much to monumentalize his city. The stage (fig. 6.4) is fifty meters long by nine deep; it is flanked by statues of the Dioscuri—Castor and Pollux, protectors of sailors—and by herms of Dionysus and Hercules, the patron deities of Lepcis; details from their myths appear on the elaborate pilasters of the Severan basilica. The architectural backdrop of the stage, three stories high and with three apses, is Antonine (156/57). The curtain ran down into a slot in the stage floor, as we have seen to be usual in Roman theaters (*RF*, 67). Opening out behind the stage is a trapezoidal colonnade enclosing a temple to the Di Augusti, and four four-way arches. The resulting thicket of columns has been compared by an irreverent Italian archaeologist to an asparagus bed; this would have been even more appropriate to their green cipollino phase, which preceded the granite Antonine one. An inscription in the colonnade tells us the kind of actor who was popular in Caracalla's reign; he was a pantomime artist, the toast of Verona, Vicenza, and Milan, of

FIGURE 6.4 *Lepcis Magna, theater, from* A.D. *1–2, stage*

which he was an honorary citizen. He was entitled to free admission to every theater in Italy, and he was the emperor's freedman.

The sculpture from the theater, gathered in its storeroom on the site, reminded its excavator, with its fragments of heads, arms, feet, fingers, and torsos, of an orthopedic ward, or a battlefield. Besides the statues already mentioned, there is in situ at the top of the cavea, near the Ceres temple, a statue of Hadrian's empress, Sabina, seated in a *sella curulis* (chair of state), not a throne, but a folding camp-stool, appurtenance of office of Roman consuls. She has the attributes of Ceres, and of Venus as well, for a Cupid stands beside her. Considering the shabby treatment she got from Hadrian, she had need of all the aid the goddess of love could give her. Another fine piece has a head that was at first believed to represent Septimius Severus portrayed as Hercules; it may perhaps represent the god, but not the emperor. All the sculpture, which is a cut above the usual run of official provincial art, may best be seen as a blend of local tradition with influence from Rome and from the Greek East, especially Aphrodisias in Caria.

Adjoining the theater on the south is a colonnaded portico, referred to in its dedicatory inscription of 11/12 A.D. as a *chalcidicum*: perhaps it was a cloth market. The portrait of its donor, Iddibal Caphada Aemilius, found in it, is a masterpiece of Lepcitanian sculpture. The chalcidicum's east side forms an impressive colonnaded stepped façade, giving onto the decumanus. It centers on the small temple of Venus Chalcidice, flanked on each side by five shops. Off the chalcidicum's southeast corner stands the four-way cross-vaulted arch of Trajan, of 109–110, another commemoration of his grant of colonial status to the city.

In 56, at Nero's urging, advantage was taken of a seaside quarry east of the city to build in it an amphitheater, its podium painted in a "fried-egg" imitation of Greek island marble. The arena measured fifty-seven by forty-seven meters; its partial excavation required the removal of sixty thousand cubic meters of sand. The seating capacity was thirteen thousand. The seats were rock-cut, then faced with limestone. Occupants of the best seats were protected from the wild beasts by a fence. A tunnel gave access to the amphitheater from the city. A vaulted, stuccoed room on the west side could have been the gladiators' greenroom, to judge by the graffiti. On the east, the side away from the city, was an impressive entrance arch. On the arena level were six numbered stalls for the animals, with portcullises on the arena side and access from above for feeding them.

Scholars of repute think that a historical event that took place in this amphitheater is represented on the famous mosaic of gladiators, now in the Tripoli Museum, which originally framed four sides of a floor in a villa near Zliten, thirty-five kilometers east of Lepcis (see map, fig. 6.5). The event was the games marking the victory of Valerius Festus over the Garamantes in A.D. 70; the mosaic, it is alleged, shows native chiefs pitted, unfairly, against wild beasts in the Lepcis arena. The prisoners do indeed have burnt yellow skins, like Sahara tribesmen today, and armor and hairstyles are those of the 70s or a little later. In fig. 6.6, which does not show the entire mosaic, the scenes begin with the herm at the upper left. It is death-to-music: brass and organ. In the background is a bed for a victim. To the right, a supine gladiator raises his arm in a plea for mercy. The second register shows a group of five gladiators, one pair dueling; at the right, a trainer suspends a match—a gladiator is bleeding copiously. These two sides represent the first two days of the games, devoted to gladiatorial combat; the other two sides show *venationes* (beast fights). In the third register, a leopard grips and claws the chest of a victim bound to a stake in a miniature cart like a chariot; in the next scene an attendant with a whip pushes a dark-skinned victim toward a rampant leopard. Above, a dog pursues an antelope; below, a spearman and a dog harass a stag; a dwarf, right, is grotesquely and unevenly matched with a boar. The lowest register shows a wounded wild horse bleeding from the nose; beside him, a bear and a bull are chained to-gether, and a naked victim, with a hook, must loose them. On the right, an attendant has a victim by the hair, and is pushing him toward a lion. The mosaic, whatever its date or occasion, is a gruesome masterpiece, showing the callous side of the Roman nature that survives in Spanish bullfights.

To the Roman or Romanized African, the companionable joys of the public baths rivaled the pleasures of seeing the early Christian get the fattest lion. The water for Lepcis' Hadrianic Baths of 126/27 was sup-plied from reservoirs—one dated by an inscription to 119/20—by an

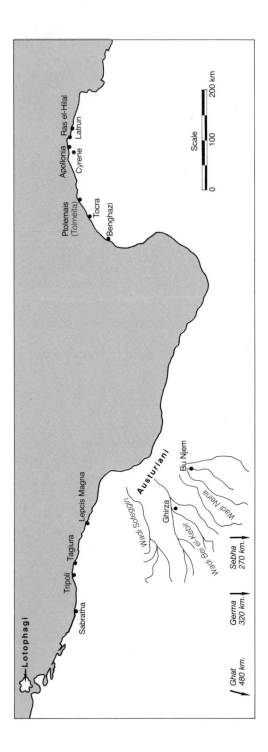

FIGURE 6.5 *Tripolitania, map*

FIGURE 6.6 *Zliten, gladiator mosaic, perhaps Flavian*

underground aqueduct. Lepcis' river, the Wadi Caam, was disciplined by walling; the course of the Wadi Megenin, behind Oea, was controlled by massive dams, the largest 210 meters long. The Hadrianic Baths were among the largest in the Roman world, covering about half the area of Rome's Baths of Caracalla, and, like the Antonine Baths at Carthage, they were axially symmetrical, perhaps for the same reason: aesthetics, and bathing for both sexes. The component parts we saw there were already present here: open-air pool; cold plunge, with statue of Mars still in situ (this central area, roofed with three lofty cross-vaults, measures thirty-three by seventeen meters); *tepidarium* (warm bath); *caldarium* (hot bath); *laconicum* (steam room). Lateral chambers and unroofed spaces would have served, as appropriate, as *apodyteria* (dressing rooms), gymnasia, and library. The two latrines are tastefully equipped with statue-niches as well as with marble *chaises percées*. Adjoining the baths to the north, and set at an angle to catch the sea breeze, is the spacious *palaestra*, or exercise ground, with curved ends; its peristyle had columns with cipollino shafts and Corinthian capitals. The baths were crammed with statues; among the survivors are one of Hadrian's favorite Antinous, as Apollo; a charming rendition of an ephebe (adolescent); a young magistrate; Hermes with the tortoise out of which he will make the world's first lyre, which a youthful Apollo Musagetes carries in another statue. There were also a satyr, a Meleager (lover of Atalanta, and slayer of the Calydonian Boar), a draped Aphrodite, and two of old women, one of whom, sour-faced, the Italians call "The Mother-in-Law."

During the second century, Lepcis continued to prosper. Part of the evidence is the circus, dated by an inscription to 161/62. It adjoins the amphitheater, with which it is connected by a bridge and two tunnels. Two-thirds of the south side, half the *spina* (axial rib), and most of the *carceres* (starting gates) have been excavated. Four hundred fifty meters long, seventy wide, it is not so large as Carthage's, nor the Circus of Maxentius in Rome. It had eleven rows of seats: on the north, they rested on an artificial mound; on the south, on the natural rock. Of the starting gates enough remains to permit conjecture about how they worked. Thirteen piers survive, each originally with a herm in front. The gates swung on pivots set into the foundation courses of the piers; other cuttings suggest that some form of wooden post ran across the top of the gates, and when raised from above, released them. A lead tablet, found in front of

one of the gates, laid a curse upon four named horses and their charioteer. The spina, 231 meters long and 6.2 wide, had fountains in the *metae*
(turning posts) at each end, and five basins along its length; in these were
found the footings of a small temple, and fragments of a statue and of the
ova ("eggs"), which, set up on posts, represented the laps of the race and
were taken down one by one as it proceeded. The Lepcitanians expressed
their gratitude to Marcus Aurelius for prosperity with a four-way arch,
the city's west gate.

The landowners enriched by Tripolitania's fertility in Antonine times
lived in luxury villas like Zliten, which survived beyond the Flavian era;
Tagiura, to be discussed later; and two discovered more recently near
Silin, fifty-five kilometers east of Lepcis. They are part of a group of six
in a seven-kilometer stretch, associated with warehouses where luxury
goods were stored that came by caravan from the desert and oasis hinterland, and with olive and wine presses, housing for the hands, and irrigation works. One of the villas, that of the Maritime Odeon, is named
from a rock-cut stepped semicircle fourteen meters wide on the seafront.
Centered behind this stretches the villa, with a portico eighty Ptolemaic
cubits long, and at either end, projecting octagonal wings with floors
paved in geometric and floral mosaic. Behind the portico ran a cryptoporticus, and behind that a range of twelve rooms. Baths were housed in
separate quarters at the back. The other villa, that of the Small Circus,
had a terraced seafront that stretched for three hundred meters, with
winter quarters behind. The summer block has both a belvedere tower
and a central bay with a sea view. There are baths, adjoining the small
circus for which the villa is named; the circus served for "constitutional"
walks. Some rooms were richly revetted in red porphyry, with *opus
sectile* floors; there were geometric mosaics, and fragments of stucco in
ocher and turquoise show how richly decorated were the walls.

Chronology now requires that we leave Lepcis briefly to describe another
monument to Antonine prosperity and provincial gratitude at Oea
(Tripoli): the four-way arch of Marcus Aurelius (fig. 6.7). Since Tripoli is
the capital of modern Libya, and much built over, the arch is the only
survival from antiquity for which a survey of this kind can find space. It

FIGURE 6.7 *Tripoli, Antonine arch*

stood near the port, at the crossing of the cardo and the town's north-ernmost decumanus. The northeast side, which faces the harbor, and the southwest were treated alike, with projecting composite columns, and statue-niches in the piers. One of the statues, of the emperor's col-league Lucius Verus, was mutilated by the Arabs as being an idol. His victory over the Armenians in 163 may have occasioned the arch. In the spandrels—triangular spaces between the curve of the arch and its rect-angular surround—were Victories; below them, attributes of Apollo and Minerva, Oea's tutelary deities: tripod, raven, laurel, owl. The northwest and southeast faces also make a pair; the piers bear barbarian families grouped around trophies. Barbarian males wear trousers, and one, clearly a king, is dressed in a cloak trimmed with ermine tails. To his right is a young woman, seated and veiled, holding the hand of a small boy, who cries into her lap; in the spandrels, Apollo and Minerva. Identical inscrip-tions dated 163 ran across each face of the monument above the arches. A cupola roofed the arch. Diagonal blocks with floral motifs carved on the underside reduce the square—14.5 meters a side—to an octagon for the cupola to rest on. The cupola is made up of three concentric rings to a keystone: the decoration is rosettes, lozenges, acanthus, shields; the keystone is a sunflower with a leaf surround.

We return to Lepcis at its apogee, the era of the Severan dynasty, whose founder, as we saw, was a native son. His sister, we are told, had a strong Punic accent of which her imperial brother was ashamed. The chief surviving Severan monuments are another four-way arch and the forum-basilica complex. The arch is being painstakingly restored in situ by Italian experts. The sculptural scheme involved four major panels in the attic—the upper story above the cornice—and twenty-four smaller panels arranged vertically in threes on the inner faces of the four piers. Two of the four major panels show triumphal processions; the third propagandizes Severan piety in a scene of sacrifice; the fourth symbolizes family Concord (fictional) by showing Septimius and his son Caracalla clasping hands; between them is the other son, Geta, whom Caracalla murdered. The major triumph-scene, commemorating the emperor's visit in 203 to his native city, shows him (fig. 6.8) frontally in a four-horse chariot, flanked by his sons, whose faces were deliberately mutilated in antiquity. Reliefs on the body of the chariot portray the Fortuna or Tyche of the city, with the patron deities Liber Pater and Hercules on either side. On another panel is a winged Victory, out of perspective, with palm. The spokes of the chariot wheels are made of six Herculean clubs. Behind the horses is a grave, bearded group of spectators in togas—the town councilors. Leading the horses is an adolescent wearing a large round *bulla* (amulet) with the emperor's portrait; he is either a groom or a symbolic likeness either of the Luck of the Army (Genius Militaris, Lar Militaris) or of the Septimian clan. To his right the swagger-stick identifies a centurion, with a barbarian prince on his left; the building in the upper right corner is the lighthouse of the Severan harbor, to be discussed below. In the sacrificial scene, the central figure is the emperor; to his right, working outwards, the goddess Roma, Geta, and the empress, the Syrian bluestocking Julia Domna. To Septimius' left, the consul, and with the sacrificial ox about to be despatched by the *popa* with upraised mallet; a *victimarius* forces the beast to his knees. In the foreground, behind the ox are soldiers and a centurion; in the background, bearded spectators, perhaps including the emperor's favorite, the praetorian prefect Plautianus, whose daughter married Caracalla. The Concord panel, called the Dextrarum Iunctio, centers on the royal father and sons (Geta's head, deliberately sawn off, was found buried beside the arch); behind them stands Fortuna with a cornucopia, and tutelary Hercules with his club. To Fortuna's left, Liber Pater, a field officer, and a centurion. To Hercules' right, Minerva, Julia Domna, and Virtue personified. The twenty-four minor panels are wretchedly preserved. One shows the siege of a Parthian

FIGURE 6.8 *Lepcis Magna, arch of Septimius Severus, triumph-scene*

city, the captives marshalled by Hercules; it has its parallel on the contemporary arch in the Forum at Rome. Another shows Africa personified,
beside her an elephant's trunk; Julia Domna as Juno, imperial eagle at
her feet; Septimius Severus as Jupiter, and Minerva with her owl. In
another, Hercules, in his lion-skin headdress, stands behind Septimius
and Caracalla; the panel below shows a sacrifice at a burning altar engraved with a patera, a ewer, and a small chest with half-open lid;
flanking the altar are a bull and ram, ribbon-bedecked for sacrifice.

The baroque grandiosity of the arch is continued in the vast Severan forum and basilica, inspired by the imperial fora in Rome, and executed by imperial army engineers. The Lepcis forum is a rectangular colonnaded area measuring a hundred by sixty meters, about six-sevenths the size of Trajan's Forum in Rome. Centered against the southwest wall towered a temple of Italic type (fig. 6.9)—that is, on a high podium, approached by a three-sided flight of twenty-seven steps. The plinths on which the red Egyptian granite columns rest are carved, after a Near

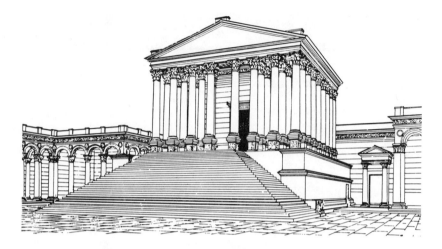

FIGURE 6.9 *Lepcis Magna, forum and temple of the Severan* gens, *reconstruction drawing*

Eastern fashion first seen at Ephesus (*GSS*, 315), with reliefs of the battle of gods and giants, symbol of Severus' "civilized" victory over the "barbarians" of Parthia. The cipollino columns of the forum portico carried a limestone arcade, with medallions between them carved with Medusa heads—as charms against the evil eye—alternating with Nereids. On the south and east, wedge-shaped blocks containing shops compensate for a different alignment between forum and colonnaded street on one side, and forum and basilica on the other. The central segment of the east side is a semicircular exedra, with a central door giving access to the basilica. This (fig. 6.10) is a double-apsed, two-storied building with a nave and two side aisles, about half as long and three-fifths as wide as the Basilica Ulpia in Rome. Its floor was marble, its walls marble-revetted, its Corinthian columns of the same red Egyptian granite as the forum's. An inscription over the lower columns showed that the basilica, begun by Severus, was finished by Caracalla in 216. Intricately carved marble pilasters frame each apse: that to the left of the north apse portrays Dionysus (Liber Pater) with his crew of Sileni, satyrs, and maenads; Theseus' castoff Ariadne, who became the god's consort, is there, and two scenes illustrate Euripides' *Bacchae*: the skeptical Pentheus, king of Thebes, killed by maenads; and his crazed mother Agave gloating with macabre cheeriness over his severed head, which she believes to be a lion's. On the pilaster on the right of the apse are carved the Labors of Hercules. The décor links the basilica to the forum; the sculptured illustration, with its emphasis on the tutelary deities, links it to the arch.

FIGURE 6.10 *Lepcis Magna, Severan basilica*

Central at the back of the apses, pairs of higher columns bore exotic entablatures involving winged griffins. The room to the left of the north apse became in the fifth century a synagogue, in Byzantine times a chapel; Justinian converted the whole basilica into a church.

The monumental street that abutted on the forum and basilica on the south led to the Severan harbor. A sharp bend in the street southwest of the forum, making a hinge between the Hadrianic and the Severan quarters of the city, was masked by a striking three-story nymphaeum (artificial fountain-grotto), enlivened by statues in the intercolumniations. It is related to the Septizonia at the southeast corner of the Palatine Hill in Rome and at Cincari in Tunisia (see chapter 3).

Severus simply monumentalized the harbor of Lepcis. It was he who made the city truly Magna, though the title is older than his reign; the port had been established at the mouth of the wadi since Augustus. Severus's engineers linked reefs together by moles on north and east, thus creating a basin, now entirely silted up, of about four hundred meters each way—three-fifths the area of Carthage's harbors, one-third the size of the port at Ostia. They left an entrance eighty meters wide that could be closed by a chain. If the line of the colonnaded street were extended, it would hit the lighthouse on the tip of the north mole. It rested on a platform twenty-one meters square, and rose in stories diminishing in size to a height of between thirty and thirty-five meters, as tall as a ten-story building. Also on the north mole were warehouses, fronted with porticos. The east mole has pierced mooring-blocks; ships were offloaded into a portico fronting an eighty-five-meter string of warehouses with twenty doors, ending in a room strongly reminiscent of the basilica in Trajan's Market (*MSS*, 269), which was designed by a Syrian, and looks like a Near Eastern souk. There was a semaphore tower on the end of the mole; between it and the warehouses, a small Doric temple. The main feature of the harbor's south side is a temple to the Syrian deity Jupiter Dolichenus, whom the empress Julia Domna delighted to worship.

The last Severan public building at Lepcis to be mentioned is the Hunting Baths, west of the excavated site. As accurately restored by the Italians, it presents a remarkably modern-looking medley of domes and barrel-vaults, which nevertheless is a characteristic Roman concrete building, designed to enclose interior space in a way that produces a strikingly unclassical exterior effect. The décor is as interesting as the architecture. It includes frescoes, the most impressive monumental painting in Roman Tripolitania. These include a fragmentary lion-hunt, with named hunters, and a better-preserved leopard-hunt, with named leopards, and an arena in the background. The east apse of the frigidarium contained, in mosaic, a Nile scene with hippopotamus and villa. A rectangular room to the northeast, outside the main bath block, had painted panels in which animal-skin trophies alternated with huntsmen, whose guild perhaps met here, and from which the baths take their modern name.

Under the military anarchy, Lepcis' harbor began to silt up, and the

Roman army could no longer protect the city from marauding nomads. An evidence of the resulting decline is the unfinished "Imperial Baths" on the seacoast 250 meters north of the theater. They were in fact part of a palace, dating from the reign of Gallienus (253–268), their extension interrupted a century later by a raid of the Austuriani (363), against whom the Roman general Romanus refused to defend Lepcis unless the city met his impossible demand for four thousand camels and copious stores. The unfinished palace-block includes a hexagonal domed hall (the caldarium), a frigidarium, a peristyle hall, and a square hall with a niche for the governor's seat of honor. North of the hexagon, and facing the sea, was a monumental building with a peristyle on three sides and three rooms on the inland end, from the central of which justice might have been dispensed; it was perhaps a civil basilica. A Lepcis milestone of 290–292 proves that the Limes Tripolitanus was not then abandoned, as some scholars had believed.

The only evidence of the Vandal occupation of Lepcis is a hoard of coins found in the market. In the end, the restricted area—the Old Forum and the mouth of the wadi—of the Byzantine walls shows how far Lepcis had to retrench, even before the Arab invasion of 643.

Sabratha, the third major city of ancient Tripolitania, began life, like Lepcis, as a Phoenician trading station, perhaps as early as the eighth century B.C.; there is solid archaeological evidence for the sixth or early fifth century; it fell under Carthaginian influence in the fourth. A restored Punic mausoleum in the southwest outskirts of Sabratha, triangular in section, and twenty-three meters high, dated in the late third or early second century B.C., shows both Egyptian and Greek influences. Egyptian are the false door, and over it the uraeus (asp's head), and, in a metope, the comic god Bes taming lions. Greek are the engaged columns, the lions supporting consoles for *kouroi* (statues of youths) three meters high, and the metope of Hercules slaying the Nemean lion. Both traditions combine in the column capitals, which show both the Ionic, Aeolic (an ancestor of Ionic), and composite varieties of Greek style and the traditional lotus-motif of the Egyptians.

Sabratha reacted to Roman influence more slowly than Lepcis. The Romans built the submerged concrete breakwaters that protected the harbor. A hoard of 22,500 coins, divided between the local and the Tripoli museums, but belonging together, was found by sponge divers.

They came from a wreck, this being a notoriously inhospitable lee shore, and date from the reign of Constantine's rebellious colleague Maxentius (295–310).

The core of the Roman city established itself in the early empire round the forum (visible in the air photograph, fig. 6.11, along with the Oceanus Baths and the temple of Isis), where, however, some buildings show by their different orientation that they are earlier—for example, in the north-west corner, the temple of Serapis, an Egyptian deity aptly described as the only ancient god ever created by a committee (in Ptolemaic Alexandria, to please both Greeks and Egyptians). The benign, bearded head of his cult statue, found in the Sabratha temple, resembles Olympian Zeus; like Egyptian Osiris, he was a god of the underworld. His temple at Sabratha stands on a high podium, centered in a rectangular portico raised above street level. Columns and pilasters were of sandstone overlaid with stucco, a characteristic building method at Sabratha, which was not so rich as Lepcis, and in its early phases, at least before the Antonines, felt the need for economy.

Some of Sabratha's oldest phases underlie the temple of Liber Pater, on the east side of the forum of the high empire. A sturdy wall under the later temple's north portico belonged to the Punic town, and an earlier temple, dating from early in the first Christian century, lies under the

FIGURE 6.11 *Sabratha, air view*

podium of the later. At this time the forum stretched farther eastward than now, and was surrounded with shops. They were replaced by a U-shaped double portico, with unfluted columns of stuccoed sandstone, the inner Ionic, the outer Tuscan (unfluted Doric). The columns of the temple itself, five of which have been impressively reerected, were fluted Corinthian, also stuccoed, and gaudily painted, as were the podium blocks. This is not necessarily Punic taste; classical Greek temples were not plain white or weathered gold, as now, but were brightly hued. Oscar Wilde might have reacted as he did to sunsets: "Ugh! Primary colors."

Central on the forum's west side, adjoining the Serapeum, was the capitolium, whose earliest phase dates from the first half of the first Christian century. The temple was Italic, with no columns in back; the front of the high podium was extended to form a rostrum for orators; a flight of steps at each corner gave access to it. Rooms under the triple cella, used in antiquity for religious gear, now house *disiecta membra*: fragments of inscriptions, a remarkable number of hands and fingers, and busts of Jupiter and Concordia, dumped in the podium after the Austuriani sacked the city in the late fourth century A.D.

A civil basilica of the mid–first century occupied the forum's south side. The judges' tribunal was also used as a chapel for the imperial cult; a number of statues of early emperors (including Vespasian, whose consort had been the mistress of a Roman knight from Sabratha) was found in it. The tribunal was placed at the center of the long side, opposite the entrance. Here, about A.D. 157, the rhetorician and novelist Apuleius of Madauros, whom we have met before in our discussion of Carthage, brilliantly, in a surviving speech, the *Apologia*, defended himself against a charge of witchcraft, brought by the relatives of a widow of a certain age (so wealthy that she owned four hundred slaves), whom he had persuaded to marry him. Apuleius, with all the resources of unbridled invective, tells us that the prosecutor was hideously bald, a stage dancer, and married to a prostitute.

After the sack by the Austuriani the basilica was rebuilt with a double apse like the Severan building at Lepcis, but only a little more than half the size.

A cruciform annex off the northwest corner of the basilica, built between A.D. 150 and 200, was made over into a meeting room, with tiers of seats facing one another as in the British House of Commons. This may have served as the curia, until a separate structure was built in the fourth century on the forum's north side, with similar seating arrangements. It was paved with inscriptions, laid with the inscribed face down; access to it was through a peristyle court.

To return to the basilica: about 450 it was reduced in size and re-modeled into a church; the northwest room became a baptistery, with cruciform font, and bishop's throne under a canopy, in the recess where the president of the town council had once sat.

South of the basilica the South Forum Temple, dedicatee unknown, was built in Antonine or Severan times, in the new fashion: marble or marble veneer where it would show, stuccoed sandstone still where it would not. It stood against the back wall of a U-shaped portico, with apses at each end of the temple.

Facing the basilica to the east was the Antonine Temple, dated by its façade inscription to A.D. 166–169, just after Sabratha achieved colonial status. On the same plan and of roughly the same size as the South Forum Temple, it is distinguished for the number of inscriptions and statues it has yielded. Some of these are stored in the vaulted crypts under the podium; others are on display in the site museum. They include bronze busts of the "Bedouin sheik," Philip the Arab (244–249), under whom Rome celebrated her millennium, and Trajan Decius, his successor (249–251), notorious persecutor of Christians. One of the inscriptions, like one from the Lepcis theater, names some of Sabratha's wards, only three of which—Augusta, Faustina (respectively aunt and wife of Marcus Aurelius), and Hadriana—bore the names of members of the imperial house. Four others were named for deities: Jupiter, Caelestis, Mercury, Neptune.

The Antonine and Severan ages were Sabratha's apogee; mosaic floors of the time of Commodus in the Piazzale delle Corporazioni at Ostia (*MSS*, 260–62) show that Sabrathan businessmen, presumably prosperous, had offices there. Thanks to discreet and skilful Italian restoration, Sabratha's theater, Antonine or Severan, is Sabratha's glory, and perhaps the most striking monument in all Roman North Africa (fig. 6.12). The ninety-six columns of the three-storied stage building—total height 22.75 meters—were restored in all their variety of size, color, and form. The originals decreased in height from the bottom story to the top; they were of pavonazzetto (bottom story), Greek white marble (middle), and black granite (top), and also of black marble and cipollino; some were fluted, vertically or spirally, some unfluted. The restorer, Giacomo Guidi, had a

FIGURE 6.12 *Sabratha, theater, Antonine or Severan*

keen eye for joins, of ashlar or of reliefs, veining, patina—sometimes rendered, with surprising success, in colored cement. Sandstone for reconstructing the cavea came from the original quarries; the blocks were cut so that two modern filled the space of one ancient, in order to distinguish restoration from original; for the same reason the faces of the new blocks were cut slightly sloping, and bear modern masons' marks different from the ancient. Friezes were restored sheer, since modern local craftsmen could not match ancient workmanship. The stage floor was newly laid down in wood and made liftable to allow scholars to examine the slots below, for curtain and for scenery. Restored also were the stairs to the second level of the stage building. (The stairs were necessary when plots called for rapid aerial takeoffs, as in Euripides' *Medea*.)

Access to the auditorium, which measures 92.5 meters across and is one of the largest in North Africa, seating five thousand, was by twenty-six arches, leading either directly to the orchestra, or to one of two superposed semicircular corridors with stairs to upper seats, or to vaulted rooms used as refreshment bars or for storage. The orchestra measures fifteen meters across; the seating tiers had carved dolphins at either end. The stage is 42.7 meters long, 9 meters deep, and 1.38 high. Alternating rectangular and half-round niches, decorating its front, were embellished with twenty-one reliefs, of which all but three (Reliefs 6, 10, and 12) survive. Taken together, they mirror the total function of a Roman theater.

Reliefs of dancers occupy either end. Perhaps the second relief—a pair of philosophers disputing—and the penultimate one—a mock duel in pantomime between the Theban brothers Eteocles and Polynices—are scenes from a school for actors or rhetoricians. (The rhetorician Apuleius would have pleaded his case in this theater if it had been built at the time.) Relief 3 shows a sundial, scrolls, and a writing tablet, all school equipment. Relief 4 represents Fortune with her wheel. Reliefs 5 and 17 are related: the one shows three Muses, the other the three Graces, a satyr, and the Judgment of Paris, wherein Venus does a striptease to assure her being judged the fairest. Relief 7 portrays, mysteriously, a basket and part of a couch. Relief 8 is a scene from mime: an English scholar says it is a slave caught stealing; an Italian says it is an adulterer caught in the act, the basket in Relief 7 being for him to hide in, like Falstaff. Relief 9 is a tripod table. Relief 11 (fig. 6.13) is of central importance: Rome and Sabratha—personified, with turreted crown—clasp hands in a scene of sacrifice, with ox, acolyte, and figures that have been identified as Septimius Severus, Caracalla, and the legate Plautianus. Relief 12 is Mercury with the infant Dionysus. Relief 14 is a scene from tragedy, perhaps Sophocles' *Trachiniae* (about Hercules), flanked by comic and tragic masks; Relief 16 is Hercules himself. The emphasis on him puts the series in the ambiance of the Antonine emperor Commodus, who fancied himself in that role. Relief 18 is a Victory.

The stage building has three apses as at Lepcis, with a door in each. The profusion of columns upon it has been described above. Some capitals on the second level bear masks: a female, Silenus, a Gorgon, a bacchante, the forepart of a lion. Behind the stage was a pair of greenrooms, the western one paved and paneled with *opus sectile—rosso antico* (Simitthu red), coral-colored *breccia, portasanta* (brown-veined pink), and *verde antico*, in lozenges, rectangles, lunettes. The walls are compartmented as if for bookcases. The theater also yielded paintings now in the site museum: from the stage, Thalia, Muse of comedy, and a still life; from the greenroom, a comic poet, perhaps Menander, and the daughters of Niobe, one with an arrow in her thigh. Behind the theater a U-shaped portico gave shelter from rain and sun, and made a gathering place for holiday makers, citizens, natives in from the country on market days, naturalized veterans, and their descendants, full citizens.

The theater is oriented to the grid of a new eastern quarter. The peristyle house near it is earlier; it has an underground room with a mosaic floor, as in Bulla Regia. In the new quarter, four blocks north and two

FIGURE 6.13 *Sabratha, theater, relief of Rome and Sabratha*

blocks west of the theater, was a temple of Hercules, dated by an inscription in 186—Commodus again.

In the next block east is one of Sabratha's three sets of baths, called the Theater Baths, from which come two mosaic medallions, now in the site museum. They extol the virtues of cleanliness: "bene lava" (Wash well); "salvom lavare" (Washing is good for you). A second set, the Oceanus Baths, also has a fine mosaic; Ocean is portrayed as a handsome old man with a flowing beard, and the whole scene is done in tiny cubes of rose, yellow, gold, brick red, gray-green, blue, black, and ivory. The third and largest set, the Seaward Baths, lies northeast of the temple of Liber Pater. It has an elegant hexagonal latrine, and mosaics both black-and-white and polychrome. Halfway between the Theater Baths and the Oceanus Baths are two Christian basilicas, late fourth century, with Byzantine alterations. The larger has a reliquary recess in an aedicula with colonnettes, as in the shrine under Saint Peter's in Rome (*MSS*, fig. 13.10).

East of the Oceanus Baths, on the sea cliff, is the temple of Isis, of Flavian date (77/78) in stuccoed sandstone, with a monumental entrance on the east, a peristyle of fourteen by twenty columns surrounding the temple proper, and eight small shrines on the west, of deities connected with Isis—Serapis, Aesculapius, Anubis, Astarte, Hecate, Osiris. Under the steps and within the podium a cistern, three corridors, and two barrel-vaulted rooms had something to do with the mysteries of Isis, much favored among sailors. Coins of King Micipsa of Numidia suggest that the temple had a pre-Flavian phase; it continued in use down to the reign of Julian the Apostate (361–363). Eight hundred meters east of the temple of Isis and 250 from the sea lies the amphitheater (late second century A.D.), two-thirds the size of Rome's Colosseum.

The most impressive building of Byzantine Sabratha is the Basilica of Justinian, between the forum and the sea. Its great glory is its remarkable polychrome mosaic floor, relaid in the museum. It represents a vine covered with grapes, inhabited by a phoenix, another phoenix caged, peacocks, and other birds.

Sabratha's domestic quarter contained a number of villas, enriched with mosaics of Nile scenes, Orpheus charming birds and animals, and others. But the most impressive villa, second in richness only to Zliten, is at Tagiura, twenty kilometers east of Oea. Like those at Silin, it is on the sea, and terraced. It had forty-five rooms, including baths, and 350 square meters of mosaics. Stamped tiles from Marcus Aurelius' mother's brick kilns date it to shortly after 157–161. In the mosaics maritime motifs predominate; the sea nymph Amphitrite often recurs, once accompanied by the four winds, looking as though they were smoking cigars. She appears again in a medallion, with a sea dragon collar, and dolphins and lobster claws in her hair. Nereids race, riding sea monsters: a sea horse, sea dragon, sea panther, sea bull. A coin of Gratian (367–383) shows that the villa lasted down into the fourth century.

We can touch here only the high spots of recent exploration of the Libyan hinterland. Human habitation there goes back a very long way. At Djebel Bu Ghneba in the Fezzan (see map, fig. 6.14) it dates from the fifth millennium B.C., when cave drawings show that the desert was more hospitable

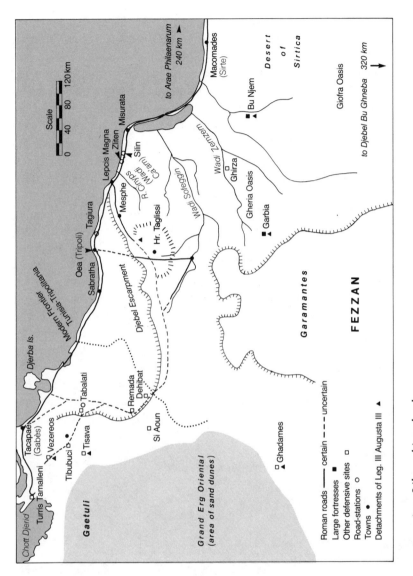

FIGURE 6.14 *Libyan hinterland, map*

than now; fauna included elephant, rhinoceros, giraffe, ostrich, antelope, cattle, and sheep. Milestones show the height of Roman exploitation of the back country in the third century, between the reigns of Caracalla and Diocletian (elsewhere the crisis-time of military anarchy), but the best of the Ghirza mausolea date from the fourth century, and a church of Donatist schismatics (identified by their slogan "laudes Deo") of the same date has been identified at Henchir Taglissi.

A sample of the development should include two caravan forts, Bu Njem and Gheria el-Garbia, and a Romanized Berber settlement, Ghirza. Bu Njem, a French excavation, is a camp of conventional playing-card shape, in an oasis 240 kilometers southeast of Lepcis Magna. It measures 135 by 90 meters, and is dated by an inscription to 201; it lasted till 273. Adjoining the camp were baths and *canabae*—a walled native settlement—ten hectares in area, which outlasted it; it had a grid of streets, and a niched building that was probably a commercial center; civilian epitaphs were found in the camp necropolis. The camp proper held ten barracks-blocks and a *praetorium* (headquarters building); at the back of a 17.85 by 22.6 meter court was a *vexillarium* (shrine of the imperial cult), measuring 6.6 by 4.6 meters. An inscription refers to Philip the Arab's empress, Marcia Otacilia Severa, as *mater exercitus*, "mother of the army."

Gheria el-Garbia, 200 kilometers west of Bu Njem, is of late Severan date (230–235), another oasis fort on a caravan route. At 183 by 132 meters, it is the largest in Tripolitania, built to protect the cultivated areas

FIGURE 6.15 *Ghirza, reaper frieze, ca.* A.D. *350*

of the wadis Solfeggin and Zemzem. When the Legio III Augusta was disgraced and disbanded in 238, *limitanei* (local militia) took over garrison duties. The fort had four gates; pentagonal towers flanked the main one. Natives hunting for stone for their mosque found a necropolis to the south-southwest, which yielded, among others, three inscriptions in bad Latin showing that a detachment of the cashiered legion returned here after its rehabilitation in 253.

At Ghirza, some 250 kilometers south of Tripoli, the settlement contained over forty sizable buildings, including six fortified farmhouses three stories high, facing inward onto courts. Here lived limitanei. There was a native temple, along with altars bearing inscriptions in Libyan. The most interesting aspect of the site is provided by the mausolea, of temple or obelisk type, in the two necropoleis. The temple tombs, of the mid–fourth century A.D., are embellished with friezes, primitive in style, fascinating in content. They show scenes from native life: plowing with camel power, a camel suckling its calf, a plowed field, the furrows rendered vertically; also an ostrich, and an antelope. An exceptionally flat and primitive piece (fig. 6.15) shows two reapers at work, beside them a man carrying on his shoulder a loaded basket.

PART 3: ALGERIA

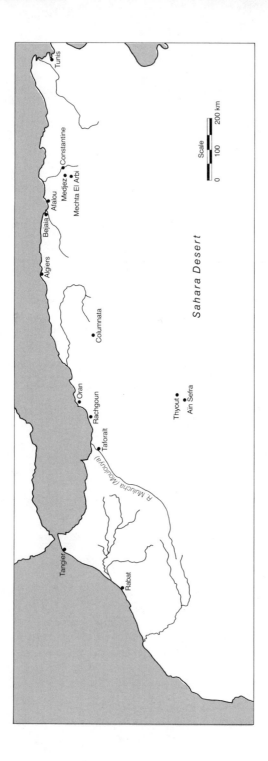

FIGURE 7.1 *Algeria, prehistoric sites, map*

7. FROM PREHISTORIC TIMES
THROUGH THE JUGURTHINE WAR

In historic times the inhabitants of Algeria have lived along the Mediterranean shore like frogs beside a pond, the settled area seldom reaching more than two hundred kilometers inland. In the prehistoric era, on the other hand, the Sahara was much wetter than now; bone harpoons have been found on sites between 17° and 20° north, nowadays deep in the desert. This permitted settlement ten times farther from the sea. Since our concern is not with paleontology, we need not go back further than the Iberomaurusian period—after 12,500 B.C.—represented by Mechta el-Arbi man, a brutal-looking Cro-Magnon type with a prognathous jaw, receding forehead, flat nose, and deliberately pulled incisors. The type site (see map, fig. 7.1) lies about fifty-five kilometers southwest of Constantine; the findspots stretch westward for nearly nine hundred kilometers to Columnata and Taforalt. This was never desert country; it is the High Tell of the Atlas Mountains, in Iberomaurusian times a forested country of pine, cedar, ash, oak, cypress, olive, poplar, and elm, the haunt of zebra, antelope, panther, lion, hyena, jackal, bear, and stag. Mechta el-Arbi man lived in sandy clearings in this forest area; his settlements were small but enduring—up to a millennium—though his life span was only just over twenty years, and his mortality rate high: 46 per 1,000, like India's in 1900. He was peaceful and endogamous. He hunted big game: rhinoceros, bison, aurochs, elephant. In addition he ate jackal, fox, mongoose, civet cat, wildcat, hare, hedgehog, monkey, lizard, tortoise, and shellfish (also used as jewelry). His burial rite was inhumation, the body stretched out on its back on a bed of pebbles. In a burial at Afalou, fifty kilometers east of Bejaia, the corpse has been thoughtfully supplied with a pot of rouge, to beautify it in the hereafter. At Columnata, the excavators found actual tombstones, which marked graves bearing corpses with the flesh stripped from the bones, the skull painted ocher, and the skeleton disarticulated. The deliberate tooth-pulling involved the upper incisors, and was probably a "rite of passage" at puberty.

A superior civilization called Capsian, after the type site in southern Tunisia, began about 7000 B.C. Capsian man was long-headed, his nose less flat, his jaw less jutting. He it was who lived on the shell heaps called *escargotières*, mentioned in chapter 1. His diet, besides the menu mentioned above, included beef, horsemeat, and mutton, though the animals from which this meat came had not yet been domesticated. Besides being a hunter he was a gatherer—of wild spelt, millet, sorghum, barley, beans, peas, fennel, asparagus, wild olive. He painted the skeletons of his dead with red ocher, and made human bones into ritual objects or weapons: a humerus is shaped into a phallus, a skull becomes a trophy, a tibia a dagger. Like his descendants, the modern Tuareg, he probably tattooed his body. He made ostrich eggs into hanging baskets, with an incised décor of chevrons or ladders. An important type site is Medjez II (El Eulma), near Sétif. As with artistic influences later, the source of his contacts is ambiguous: Mediterranean, African, or Near Eastern.

Neolithic Algeria—from about 6430 B.C.—has become famous through the discovery and publication of cave drawings and paintings from the Hoggar and Tassili N'Ajjer (map, fig. 7.2), the former area 2,072 kilometers south of Algiers, the latter 700 kilometers northeast of the airport at Tamanrasset, in the Hoggar. This is the area where the Algerians have struck oil, which creates a striking juxtaposition of ancient and modern. In this cliff and cave art the experts distinguish four periods. The oldest, from before 4500 B.C., portrays little round-headed figures, who look as though they were wearing deep-sea divers' helmets, or came from Mars. They are negroid types, tattooed, and with facial scars; perhaps they came from the Sudan. Their helmets are sometimes horned or plumed; they are armed with bows or lances. At Séfar, the canyon is cut by gorges so as to create the impression of the streets and squares of a city. Among the motifs: women praying to a god eight meters high; an ox three meters long; a painting nine meters long in which female archers hunt the mouflon; negro masks; elephant, antelope, giraffe, wart hog.

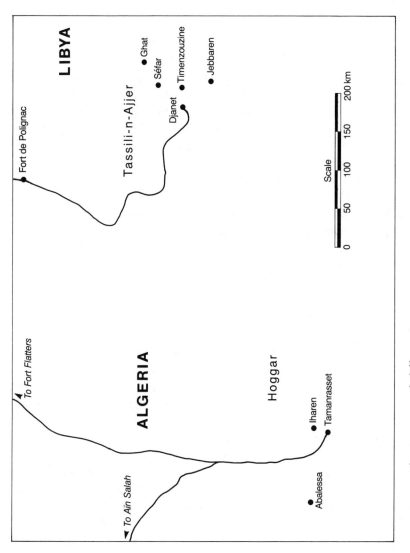

FIGURE 7.2 *Algeria, cave and cliff art, site map*

The second period, called the Bovidian, was at its height between 3550 and 3070 ± 300 years B.C., but the style persists until as late as 1500. The cattle after whom the style is named have lyre-shaped horns; the women—paler than the men—have beehive coiffures. Men in a trial scene, "the justices of the peace," also wear pretentious hairdos. Cattle are shown in their corrals, or harnessed and ridden by women carrying skins of water. Some scenes are anecdotal, having to do with fertility, and not without humor, as in a picture from Timenzouzine, in which a woman beats time for a couple having intercourse, while a male, interpreted by a Frenchman as the cuckolded husband, approaches, bow in hand. At Iheren is a masterpiece of the Neolithic naturalist school, including elegantly coiffured women on oxen, oxen drinking, 116 giraffes, a lion hunt, flocks, and herds. Very similar motifs and styles have been catalogued from the Constantine area and the Grande Kabylie, the mountain range between Bejaia and Dellys. On the oasis of Thyout, in the Algerian far west, near Aïn Sefra, on the Moroccan border, can be seen drawings of men with bow and spear, hunting ostrich; an elephant (fig. 7.3); other scenes of sexual intercourse; and an enormous cow.

Charming legends of elephant sagacity survive from this remote past. If a member of the herd falls into a pit-trap his mates fill it in with stones and logs to rescue him; elephants fleeing from hunters put the beasts with broken tusks at the front. They will wave branches as flags of truce. They worship sun and moon, and, unlike Indian elephants, resist domestication.

Bovidian also are many of the five thousand figures at Jabbaren, twenty-five hard kilometers south and west of Séfar. The paintings show herds of cattle, giraffes, elephants, antelope, wild asses, goats. The principal scene, covering twenty square meters, includes 135 figures: a gazelle and antelope-hunt, a wounded rhinoceros about to charge, archers about to attack a herd of cattle, a mythological scene with a bull in the coils of a serpent, seven animal heads symbolizing the sons of the first man (in a myth that survives in the modern Peul tribe), a gigantic figure nicknamed "the Abominable Sandman" (reproduced, with many others, in the Musée de l'Homme, Paris), a female figure in red ocher with white spots. A Bovidian drawing shows a cow being milked, with her calf; modern Algerian cows, it is said, will not let themselves be milked without their calves.

From about 1200 B.C. chariots begin to appear in the art: two or four-horse, the horses at a flying gallop, the charioteers armed with spears, daggers, and shields, but no longer the bow; their tunics are drawn as

FIGURE 7.3 *Thyout, elephant, fourth millennium* B.C.

two triangles point to point, closely resembling figures on Mycenaean vases of the same period. The chariots are light, prestige vehicles, for a warrior class. The alleged "chariot routes" following the northern edge of the Sahara from Egypt to the Atlantic are imaginary; they link points in fact inaccessible to light vehicles. Egyptian influence is, however, visible in this period: bird-headed women, ritual boats. By this time the Sahara was beginning to dry up: representations of hippopotamus, rhinoceros, and elephant disappear.

Finally, at about 50 B.C. or a little later, the camel, "the ship of tbe desert," appears in art; also drawings of climbers harvesting dates; the cave paintings of this period are on the main caravan routes.

The late cave drawings of camels, dating from 50 B.C. or after, show that the culture that produced them did not die out with the coming of Punic entrepreneurs or Roman conquerors.

But (if we glance back at earlier history) there is a gap in the archaeological evidence between the chariot phase of Berber art and the earliest datable Punic artifacts—seventh century B.C.—from the ports of call along the thirteen hundred kilometers of Algerian coast (see map, fig. 7.4). It has been argued that these are staging-points on a shuttle service between Carthage and the West, and indeed some of the sites are a

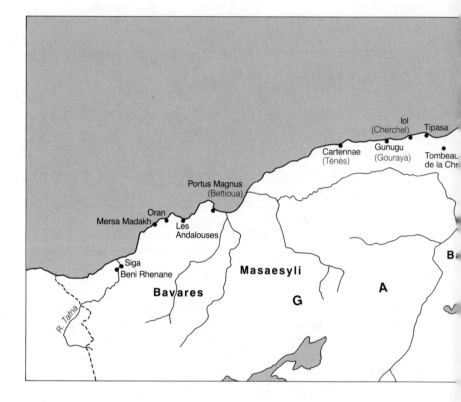

FIGURE 7.4 *Algeria, Punic ports of call and hinterland, map*

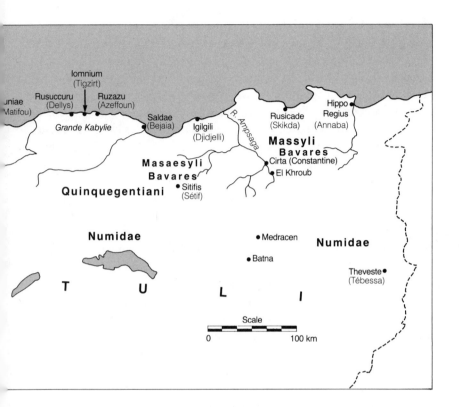

day's slow sail apart: for instance, Ruzazu (Azeffoun)-Iomnium (Tigzirt)-Rusuccuru (Dellys); Tipasa-Iol (Cherchel, where Punic artifacts of the fifth century B.C. have been found on Joinville Island)-Gunugu (Gouraya)-Cartennae (Ténès); and the stations west of Oran—Les Andalouses-Mersa Madakh-Rachgoun-Siga. Also, many of the names are Punic (*rus-*, *ras-* means "cape"; *i-* means "island"). The typical Punic site is a promontory or offshore island where boats may be easily beached; the first stage of Punic (or Carthaginian) settlement perhaps began when some crew members agreed to stay behind until the vessel's next trip. And some of the archaeological evidence is Punic: rock-cut tombs near Igilgili (Djidjelli) are dated between the sixth and the fourth centuries B.C. There is Punic evidence from Saldae (Bejaia), Ruzazu, Icosium (Algiers), Tipasa, Iol, Gunugu, and Cartennae, and it has been studied with special care at the sites west of Oran. But these must have been communities largely of Punicized Berbers, natives assimilated by intermarriage, though this hypothesis does not exclude the possible arrival of later drafts of settlers from Carthage or even the Near East.

Icosium (Algiers), nowadays a capital city with 1.5 million inhabitants, naturally resists excavation, but its name (Isle of Thorns, Owls, or Seagulls—scholars disagree) is Punic, and it is plausible to suppose that it offered an alternative anchorage to Rusguniae (Cap Matifou), depending on wind direction. Most of the ancient remains come from the Casbah and the adjacent port area, in the northern part of the modern city: here was found during road-building in 1940 a hoard of Punic coins, mostly in lead, of the late second to early first century B.C., bearing the likeness of the god Melqart (assimilated to Hercules) and the Punic legend IKOSIM. A false etymology derived the name Icosium from Hercules and the Twenty, the Greek for "twenty" being *eikosi*. But most of the scanty archaeological evidence—walls, towers, pavements, architectural members, inscriptions, mosaics—is Roman.

At Tipasa, sixty-nine kilometers west of Algiers, to which we shall return to discuss its Roman phases in chapters 8 and 9, there are Punic graves whose contents go back to the sixth century B.C. These are chambers closed by slabs, deep enough to require access by stairs; they lie by the tiny harbor and eastward to the promontory of Ste. Salsa, the burials much disturbed by Roman construction. Later excavation, of the necropolis west of the harbor, records "Punic" ware going back to the seventh century B.C., Apulian fish-plates, from South Italy, of 350–300 B.C., and a Kertch vase, all the way from the Crimea, of 370–360. But some graves contain shells filled with rouge, a Berber burial practice.

There are amphoras from Punic Spain, dated from the fifth to the third century B.C., and decorated ostrich eggs, for which Spanish (Andalusian) parallels from the sixth and fifth centuries B.C. can be adduced. Egyptian scarabs were found, dating from the fifth to the third century B.C. The excavator warns against thinking of all this as evidence for the site as a Carthaginian "factory" or trading post; it is much more likely to have been an outlet for federated Libyo-Berber tribes.

At Gunugu the excavator reports a Punic funeral mask of the seventh or sixth century B.C., and thinks that until about 200 B.C. the place was a small Punic factory of mixed population, influenced from Greece (Attic pottery) and the Near East. Another report mentions the ubiquitous painted ostrich eggs again.

The most careful excavation of Punic sites has been done by Gustave Veuillemot in the area west of Oran. At Les Andalouses, about thirty kilometers west, he excavated a cliff house whose lowest level is of the sixth century B.C.; nearby are five tumuli of the fifth century. The cliff-edge town covered three hectares; the houses were rectangular in plan, of adobe brick, with flat roofs, beaten earth floors, and a curtain for a door. Despite the proximity of the sea, there is little evidence of fishing; on the other hand, the inhabitants ate dogs. The local language was Punic, but there were Berbers there as well. At Mersa Madakh, about fifty kilometers west of Les Andalouses, Veuillemot found houses datable to the sixth century B.C. Rachgoun Island was the port for Siga, where he found fifth-century pottery. Siga was later the capital of the Numidian kingdom of the Masaesyli, a tribe of whom more will be said in the sequel. On the island, near the lighthouse, there is a necropolis of 120 cremation graves, dated by vases to the seventh or sixth century B.C. Rachgoun town, at the island's south end, covers three hectares; it flourished between 650 and 450 B.C. The inhabitants raised sheep, cows, goats, and swine; they domesticated the donkey and the horse, and ate dog, partridge, and pigeon. As in the Phoenician homeland, they made the expensive and profitable purple dye from the murex, a shellfish. The evidence points to massive Punic colonization in the sixth century B.C.

After the prehistoric cave-painters and the Punic trader-settlers, we now turn to the native Numidian kings and their monuments. Their major achievement was to turn at least some of their people from nomads into farmers, or at least into semi-nomads, who fold their tents into a corner of their huts for the winter. The kings knew that the nomad is fiscally dead, whereas the sedentary farmer is the ideal taxpayer. But it is wrong to suppose that the Numidian Berbers had to wait for the Carthaginians to teach them agriculture: long before Mago, they cultivated wheat and barley, the date, the olive, the almond, and the vine; the best Algerian wine, as developed in modern times by the French, is still a good deal better than metropolitan French propaganda will allow. The inhabitants of Neolithic Columnata already used weighted digging sticks, handmills, and sickles made of bone, with flint teeth inserted. Iron Age Berbers used a plow and knew how to graft the olive and the fig; there are Berber words for these activities without Punic, Latin, or Greek roots. The Berber farmer is a conservative by nature; out of context, one cannot tell a modern Berber handmade pot from an ancient one. The ancient Berber's clothes were fringed leather, or the highly practical burnoose, still worn, and already pictured in the cave drawings. The chief offerings to the dead were containers for steamed grain, or couscous, still the staple of the local diet throughout the Maghreb. The sizable Berber tombs, of which more hereafter, show a highly organized social structure, able to mobilize large gangs of workmen, voluntary or captive.

Berber tribes are almost bewilderingly numerous: we have heard or shall hear of the Austuriani, Baquates, Bavares, Gaetuli, Garamantes, Libyes, Mauri, Nasamones, Lotophagi (lotus eaters, from the Tunisian island of Djerba), Quinquegentiani, Troglodytes (whose descendants still live in underground houses at Tunisian Matmata), Numidae, Masaesyli, and Massyli. The Massylian kingdom had its capital at Cirta (Constantine), a city with a population of perhaps two hundred thousand. The axis of its territory ran from Hippo Regius (Annaba) to Theveste (Tébessa).

Its greatest king, Masinissa (ca. 240–148 B.C.) is the strongest personality that native North Africa produced in ancient times. His name perhaps means "Master of them all." He passes in the sources as conqueror, agronomist, economist, linguist (the Libyan alphabet was invented at his court), religious reformer, and philosopher (in Cicero's *Dream of Scipio*). He was also virile to extreme old age: he had 44 children, one of whom he fathered at the age of 86. His estates, forerunners of Roman latifundia, were vast enough to enable him to leave to each of his children 875 hectares of land. To his Berber heritage—his mother was a prophetess—he added a Punic education and an openness to Greek culture (and commerce as well); between 168 and 163 B.C. one of his sons won a chariot race at the Panathenaic games in Athens.

In 203 he beat the Masaesylian king, Syphax, took over his kingdom (capital Siga), and as we saw, sent poison to Syphax' widow Sophonisba to save her from captivity in Rome. Between 200 and 170 B.C. he supplied vast and increasing amounts of grain to the Roman army in Macedonia, while at his palace at Cirta he played at being a Hellenistic monarch, with gold and silver plate at his banquets, Greek tutors, and Greek court musicians. But his attitude to Greeks was a good deal this side idolatry: when they wanted to buy monkeys he inquired, "In your country don't the women bear children?" And his treasure house was less Greek than Anatolian, like Croesus' in Herodotus. He grew rich, too, from taxes paid in kind—grain, cattle, horses. Beginning in 174, he made a series of carefully timed seizures of Carthaginian land: over seventy places, as we saw, between 174 and 172, and fifty more between 153 and 150, allegedly retaliating against Carthaginian military preparations. He goaded the Carthaginians into breaking their treaty with Rome by attacking him; in retaliation, the Romans destroyed Carthage in 146, an event Masinissa did not live to see, since he died in 148. He had demanded of Carthage an indemnity of five thousand talents spread over fifty years, but after the Roman destruction all his heirs got, as we saw, was its library, including Mago's agricultural treatise. But the territory he seized was enormously fertile; the geographer Strabo (flourished 7 B.C.) says all the farmer had to do after reaping was scratch the soil with twigs, and the dropped grain gave a new harvest.

The historian Polybius knew and admired the old patriarch—Masinissa ruled for nearly sixty years—speaking of his endurance (day and night on horseback) and calling him "the most accomplished and happy prince of our time." The lasting peace of his long reign did much for agricultural prosperity, but under his feudal sway the subordinate Numidian chiefs were restive and unruly.

It is highly probable that his mausoleum is known—El Khroub, fourteen kilometers from Masinissa's capital of Cirta, and visible from it. Its present state (fig. 7.5) is due to an unfortunate reconstruction of 1915–16, which at least revealed the funeral chamber with its contents, of mid-second-century date. The structure rested upon a base 8.4 meters square. The reconstruction was carried up to the level of four cubic blocks, embellished on their outer faces with round shields in relief. Architectural fragments show that above this level was a loggia with either eight or twelve unfluted Doric columns, enclosing a bronze statue

FIGURE 7.5 *El Khroub, mausoleum, ca. 150 B.C.*

and supporting a coffered ceiling. Above this in turn was a sculptured group or an *acroterion* (ornament at the peak or corners of a pediment). The funeral chamber was approximately a double cube, in dimension two meters by one meter by ninety centimeters. When opened it proved to contain a silver vessel for the ashes and calcined bones of the deceased; the vessel was so badly oxidized that it decomposed on exposure. Around it were placed a helmet, coat of mail, sword, spears (some thrust between the ceiling slabs), the silver mouthpiece of a trumpet, a silver cup, medallions, seven amphoras, one with a datable Rhodian stamp, some containing the bones of sacrificial victims, some having originally held oil or wine.

Two other royal tombs in Algerian soil deserve mention here, the Medracen and the "Tomb of the Christian Woman." The Medracen rises (fig. 7.6) a twenty-three-stepped cone 18.5 meters high and 59.2 meters in diameter, just off the age-old route southward to the Sahara, and thirty kilometers northeast of Batna. It had already been robbed when the Zouaves (themselves Berbers) excavated it in 1873, and the masonry

FIGURE 7.6 *The Medracen, late third century* B.C.

was vandalized to get at the lead clamps that held it together. A platform 11.4 meters wide at the top of the cone might have held statuary or have been the scene of funerary rites. On the west was an antechamber, now in ruins, which probably also served funerary purposes. On the east was a rectangular *prothyron* (vestibule) 25 meters wide and 14 deep, leading to a false door—a Punic and Egyptian usage—and the building has under-cut Egyptian moldings. But the cone rests on a cylinder embellished with sixty Doric half-columns, a Greek architectural feature. The real entrance was hidden by a stone portcullis, sliding in grooves, at the cone's third step. It opened on an eleven-step stairway down to a tunnel leading to the tomb chamber, measuring only 3.3 by 1.5 meters, and intended for an ash urn, probably in precious metal; all that survived the tomb-robbing were a few scales of ancient copper. The tunnel was supported by cedar props and beams; the burial chamber had cedar double doors, practicable versions of the false doors at the end of the prothyron. It proved possible to take carbon 14 readings on these, of 2170 years before present (B.P.), ± 155 years, and 2270 B.P., ± 110 years; that is, 300–200 B.C. This makes the Medracen older than El Khroub, older than Masinissa; the latest conjecture is that it was built for his father Gaïa, who died before 205 B.C. The Medracen stands in the midst of a walled necropolis containing a variety of burials, some in princely tumuli, some bodies buried face-down, like criminals. In sum, we have in the Medracen a monument with Egyptian, Punic, and Greek features, built to honor a Berber king.

The other major monument of the Medracen type—in fact, an enlarged imitation of it—is the Tomb of the "Christian Woman." It stands 10 kilometers east of Tipasa, 360 kilometers west and north of the Medracen as the crow flies. Sited on a hill 271 meters above sea level, it is a stepped cylinder (fig. 7.7), 32.4 meters high, and 65 meters in diameter, a total mass of 80,000 cubic meters. It is built of sandstone, with sixty Ionic half-columns, and has trapezoidal false doors at the cardinal points of the compass. The panels of the doors, which form a cross, account for the misnaming of the monument. A curious local legend was invented to account for the name. The "Christian Woman" is said to be one Count Julian's daughter, seduced by the king of the Visigoths. In vengeance, the Count delivered Spain up to the Arabs. A shepherd followed a cow—by the tail—into the woman's tomb, and emerged with his pockets full of gold. Greedy and destructive attempts to demolish the monument failed; the workmen were routed by bird-sized mosquitoes. Coins of the fourth and fifth Christian centuries show that tomb-robbing dates from that time. Another legend would make it the monument of Cleopatra Selene, daughter of *the* Cleopatra by Mark Antony, and wife of Juba II, puppet king of Mauretania. But the architectural style is older than Juba II, who reigned 25 B.C.–A.D. 23; the latest informed guess is that it may be the tomb of Bocchus II, king of Mauretania, son of the man who betrayed his son-in-law Jugurtha to the Romans.

The entrance to the monument is only 1.10 meters high, under the east false door, and sealed by two blocks disguised to look like the rest of the structure. As in the Medracen, it worked like a portcullis, and gave access to a corridor so low as to require stooping. The corridor leads to a cradle-vaulted vestibule 5.73 meters long, 2.52 meters wide, and 3.2 high. Over the door of another corridor are carved a lion and lioness. This corridor leads to a flight of seven steps, giving access to a gallery circular in plan, 141 meters long, 2 meters wide, and 2.4 meters high, with fifty-one lamp-niches, one every three meters. The floor of the gallery is the square platform that supports the tomb cylinder. At the level of the south false door the tunnel bends sharply inward to a door at the center of the monument, closed by another portcullis, which leads to another vestibule (4.04 meters long, 1.58 wide, 2.73 high), with yet another portcullis at the far end. This gives on a vaulted cavity, 4.04 by 3.06 by 3.45 meters, oriented north and south, with niches for ash urns on the north, south, and west walls.

Another monument of a Berber prince, not of the same importance as the Medracen or the Tomb of the Christian Woman, is the mausoleum of

FIGURE 7.7 *The Tomb of the Christian Woman, first century B.C.*

Beni Rhenane, on the right bank of the River Tafna four kilometers from its mouth, and opposite Siga, the capital, as we saw, of the Masaesylian king Syphax. The monument is triangular, like the ones at Sabratha and Lepcis Magna; it measures seventeen to eighteen meters on a side. It had three doors, all closed by portcullises, and also Ionic capitals, as in the Tomb of the Christian Woman. The cradle-vaulted underground rooms were hermetically sealed; there was a hiss of air when the door was opened. An Arab lamp found in the corridor was the mark of a tomb-robber; the sepulture was deliberately violated, the tomb furniture deliberately broken; the amphoras, however, could be dated, to the second century B.C., the ointment vases to the third or second. Veuillemot thinks the tomb might have been of Vermina, Syphax' son, who ruled over a reduced puppet-kingdom, 201–191 B.C.

Siga town, Syphax' capital, across the river from Beni Rhenane, lay on two hills, of which the eastern was the arx or acropolis, above the mosquito line, a natural marketplace where the smugglers' route crossed into Morocco. Coins and a milestone show that it flourished twice: once in Syphax' reign and again under the Severi. Syphax' coins, of before 160 B.C., have as their device a horseman with two javelins. Another coin, its obverse a diademed head, the reverse a trotting horse, is of the reign of

Masinissa's son Micipsa (148–118); his funerary inscription has been identified in the dedication of a statue at Iol (Roman Caesarea, modern Cherchel).

Cirta (Constantine), Masinissa's capital and scene of Sophonisba's tragic end, is modern Algeria's third largest city, after Algiers and Oran, and does not take kindly to excavation. Its early Roman phase will be discussed in the next chapter. Here it is appropriate to describe a Punic sanctuary of the second century B.C., excavated in 1950 at El Hofra in the southern quarter of the city, on a small plateau adjoining the Hôtel Transatlantique, with a vertiginous drop to the River Ampsagas (Rhummel) a hundred meters below. There is a hillside temple overlooking ravine and river, a typically Punic site, built on the module of the Punic cubit (53 centimeters), and measuring 26.5 by 32 meters; 140 meters west of it lies the richest part of the excavation, a series of fourteen furrows in which were footed the five hundred stelae now in the municipal museum—formerly the Musée Gustave Mercier, where also are housed the finds from El Khroub. Many of the stelae bear Punic inscriptions in Greek letters; they record sacrifices, to Ba'al and Tanit, dates (163/62, 148/47, 128/27), high priests, names of professions and trades (physician, scribe, carpenter, bowyer), places, and people, including Masinissa and his sons Micipsa, Gulussa, Mastanabal. Hermes is there, Greek adjutant to a Semitic god; a rosette symbolizes Astarte, syncretized with Venus; the ram symbolizes Ba'al; the warhorse, the bellicose Hadad (Roman Mars). The arms shown on the stelae are Punic, and much resemble those found in the tomb chamber at El Khroub—oval shield, pointed helmet, short sword. The presence of so much that is Punic in a Numidian capital reminds us that Masinissa was educated in Carthage and that modern Algeria has also a Semitic (Islamic) culture on a Berber base.

The wide distribution of the various mausolea symbolizes Masinissa's unification of Numidia; their very existence, the prosperity brought by his long, peaceful reign.

Under Masinissa's son Micipsa, Numidia had another thirty years' surcease. But at his death dissension broke out among his heirs, two legitimate, and one, Jugurtha, illegitimate but adopted. He was worth adopting, for at the siege of Numantia (for which see *ISS*, p. 111) he had acquired the friendship of influential Romans. Jugurtha's high-handed behavior to his brothers (he had the one murdered, and attacked and eventually murdered the other) provoked Roman intervention and war, for which our principal source is the historian Sallust (ca. 86–35; his *Jugurthine War* was published in 41). Since Sallust had served in Africa, in both military and civil capacities (Caesar appointed him the first governor of Africa Nova), and had extensive estates near Cirta, one might have expected some valuable topographical and archaeological data to emerge from his treatment of the war, but the expectation is dashed; Sallust's interest is political rather than strategic. His aim is rhetorical: to show the criminal incompetence of the aristocratic generals to whom Rome entrusted the conduct of the war before the emergence and final victory of the plebeian Marius. Sallust in fact mentions only three rivers—Muthul, Tanais (still unidentified), Mulucha (Moulouya, in Algeria's far west)—and seven places, of which only one is in Algeria—Cirta. The others are Vaga (Béja), Sicca (Le Kef), Zama, Thala, Capsa (Gafsa), and Lares (Lorbeus).

An immediate cause of the war was Jugurtha's execution of a number of Italians who had been doing business in Cirta, the Numidian capital. Syme and Leschi argue that Sallust never saw the city, since he describes siege-works that could not possibly have been effective on that ravine-girt site. But Sallust does evoke the sempiternal picture of African warfare: guerilla tactics, scorched earth, poisoned wells, cattle-rustling, ambushes, raids, in the midst of "the desert, the scrub, the broken country, the elusive enemies, thirst and intrigue, treachery and murder" (Syme). He does give a picture, however perfunctory, of Numidian geography and peoples, the desert heat, the inaccessibility, the rough, harborless sea, the fertile land, the aridity, the native Numidians—healthy, fleet-footed, all-enduring—and the Gaetulian and Libyan nomads—a restless, roving people, pitching their tents wherever night compelled a halt (*Jugurthine War* 18). He notes with true Italian scorn—Italians prefer pasta—the primitive Numidian diet—the flesh of wild beasts. He evokes, picturesquely, the native huts (*mapalia*), "oblong, having roofs with curved sides, like the hulls of ships." An emendation (*Jugurthine War* 66.2) would have him refer to the cult of the Cereres (Demeter and Kore, ultimately Greek), as a day of holiday and entertainment, celebrated all over Africa.

At the war's outbreak (112 B.C.), the Romans governed, through magistrates, nearly all the Punic cities, plus the Carthaginian territorium. Jugurtha ruled Numidia as far as the Mulucha; the king of Mauretania was Bocchus, an unknown quantity who at first supported Jugurtha and then, as we saw, betrayed him to the Romans. Jugurtha was under no illusions about the Romans; their own rhetorical history describes them as sinking into decadence after the destruction of Carthage, and Sallust has Jugurtha describe Rome as "a city up for sale, if only she can find a buyer." But Sallust's rhetoric leads him to portray Jugurtha, at the news of Marius' imminent arrival at the head of the consular army, as behaving with barbarian lack of self-control, weeping, babbling, "showing little fortitude in bearing mortification." He might well weep: in the far west, Marius took the seemingly impregnable fortress on the River Mulucha that held the king's treasure. At this very point in his narrative Sallust introduces Marius' lieutenant Sulla, who persuaded Bocchus to betray Jugurtha. The captive prince walked in Marius' triumph and was then taken to Rome's dank prison, the Tullianum, and strangled. "Hercules!" he said as they dropped him in, "your bath is cold!" Thus ended another of the resistance heroes called forth by the challenge of Roman expansion, an equivocal hero this time, devious, treacherous, yet proving himself a match for all but Rome's best generals. And the war against him brought to the fore a soldier's general, preparing the way for the use of the army in politics and for further Roman expansion in North Africa after the campaigns of Marius' nephew, Julius Caesar. But for the moment the Roman Senate was content to leave the area of Numidia and Mauretania in the hands of native rulers. The chief Roman gain from the war was economic, not political; Roman businessmen could now resume their African trade with impunity. Western Algeria was not organized as a province until Claudius' reign, and Numidia itself was not called by that name as a Roman province until late in the reign of Septimius Severus.

8. FROM JUGURTHA TO TRAJAN, 105 B.C.–A.D. 98

Algerian history from the close of the Jugurthine War to Caesar's settlement of 46 B.C. is pretty much a blank. Roman senators, by and large a conservative lot, were not interested either in annexation or in colonization: the profits of the one would be cancelled by the cost of occupation; colonies would either be wiped out or soon demand independence. The solution was to entrust Numidian territory to satellite kings. The choice of Juba I, great-great-great-grandson of Masinissa, proved an unhappy one; chafing at being a puppet king, he aimed to annex Roman Africa, joined Pompey against Caesar, and survived the battle of Thapsus; but universally hated and rejected, he committed suicide in 46 B.C.

Caesar's reaction was threefold. He annexed Juba's kingdom to the proconsular province as Africa Nova; he gave the Numidian capital, Cirta (see map, fig. 8.1), and its territory for at least forty-eight kilometers south to a partisan, the adventurer P. Sittius of Nuceria in Campania; and he founded new colonies. A perhaps overingenious interpretation of Vergil's reference (*Eclogues* 1.64) to Italian farmers going reluctantly overseas to the *sitientes Afros* ("thirsty Africans"), would make it a pun on Sittius' name.

Cirta's setting, which has been aptly compared to Toledo's in Spain, is stupendous (fig. 8.2)—on a bluff, averaging over six hundred meters above sea level, its sides dropping sheer to the River Rhummel coiled like a snake a hundred meters below, spanned at dizzying heights by bridges, one of which still bears on a pier the relief of two elephants carved there in Roman times. Defensible, well-watered, at the crossing of roads west-

FIGURE 8.1 *Roman Algeria, map*

FIGURE 8.2 *Cirta, gorge*

ward to Carthage and southward to the Sahara, it had a busy market, which one can imagine humming with activity as the caravans were unloaded of their rich cargoes from the oases and beyond: ostrich plumes, elephant tusks, gold dust. It had its intellectual side as well; Marcus Aurelius' tutor, the rhetorician Fronto, came from here. Now a city of over three hundred thousand, it is, as we saw, an unlikely subject for excavation, but with its stepped streets, blind alleys, dark shops, and tiny squares, it cannot look very different now from the way it did when a polyglot crowd of speakers of Punic, Greek, Libyan (Berber), and Latin thronged its thoroughfares.

Sittius lasted only two years; he was assassinated by a native chief. His fief, by then grandiosely named Colonia Julia Juvenalis Honoris et Virtutis Cirta, became the chief town of a unique confederation of four colonies; the other three were Colonia Sarnia (the Sarno is a river near Campanian Pompeii), Milevitana (Milev), Chullu (Collo), and Rusicade (Skikda, formerly Philippeville). These three had no magistrates, territory, or treasury of their own; they were run by *praefecti* from Cirta, a set of municipal pro-magistrates. Rusicade had a theater, amphitheater, Mithraeum, baths, and cisterns. Of the 4,187 inscriptions from the area published in *Inscriptions latines d'Algérie*, over a third, mostly late, come from Cirta; these name 226 Julii and Sittii, naturalized citizens who took the name of their sponsors. There are 378 from Rusicade and 608 from Tiddis, a dependency of the confederation. The number of inscriptions makes possible the compilation of statistics on longevity: for example, that 25.9 percent of known dwellers in the confederation throughout antiquity lived to be over seventy; the average life span was 46 years, compared with 33.3 at Carthage. But, as Hopkins has shown, the very old exaggerate; the average age at death here is implausibly high. Of 1,309 Cirtans on surviving inscriptions, 1,162 were Roman citizens.

Though ancient Cirta cannot be uncovered, its dependency Tiddis, fifteen airline miles north-northwest, which has been thoroughly excavated, can give us, on a small scale, some idea of what Cirta was like. Tiddis clings to its mountainside, a rose-red town of stairs and sanctuaries, of grottoes, towering rocks, terraces, hairpin turns, ramps, and steps, all planned to reduce to order the steep slope on which it is built (fig. 8.3). Its prime function was military; there is a sword carved on the keystone of the rebuilt north gate. The pavement of the cardo is grooved to prevent

FIGURE 8.3 *Tiddis, forum from above*

slipping; the decumanus has thirty-eight steps and five landings. Mithras, Persian god of light, the soldiers' favorite, has his rock-cut sanctuary, whose entrance bears on each jamb a phallus, winged, and with spurred feet, like a cock. The forum, at a crossroad marked by two arches perpendicular to each other, is minute, the smallest in Roman Africa—only thirty by ten meters—and the curia that opens upon it is correspondingly minuscule. The town has no natural water, and is therefore honeycombed with cisterns. One set of three, dated A.D. 251, which fed the baths, was lined with waterproof cement and would hold 350 cubic meters of water. A hoard of 9,748 coins shows by its variety how the Roman Empire brought the world to this remote Algerian eyrie; it includes silver of Numidian Cirta—an unbroken run from Masinissa to Juba I, with devices like a galloping horse, or Ammon with his ram's horns (obverse) and elephant (reverse)—Athenian tetradrachms, Carthaginian shekels, Roman denarii. (Roman money was still legal tender in Tébessa [ancient Theveste] when the French came in the 1830s.) Other coins came from Rusicade, Utica, Hippo, Iol-Caesarea, Egypt, Spain. The latest are of Arcadius, whose rule ended in 406; apparently the town ceased to exist as an economic entity before the Vandal invasion. In this latest phase kilns for crude pottery occupy the middle of the streets and the caldarium of the baths; the counterweights of oil presses are reused in rude hovels. But in its prime the townsfolk throve in the healthful mountain air: the average life-span, if recorded ages are to be believed, was 52.8. Inscriptions, perhaps exaggerating, record thirty-one Tidditanians who lived to be over a hundred, and a beautifully cut inscription to Fortuna Augusta from the center of the town was made by one Sittius (a common name in the confederation; there are seventy-six examples from here), who lived to be ninety-two.

Besides observing the imperial cult, the people of Tiddis worshiped Semitic Ba'al—Roman Saturn—in the Semitic fashion, on a High Place. At the topmost point of the town, 575 meters above sea level, with a magnificent view down on the Rhummel gorge, they placed Saturn's sanctuary, with four rock-cut terraces, a man-made cave, and fifty Saturn stelae. Saturn would have been worshiped by the town's petty bourgeoisie, like the potters whose quarter, north of the decumanus stair, was thick with kilns, twenty in fifty meters. Potters' tools from Tiddis, 250 objects, fill seven cases in the Constantine Museum; there are metal spatulas and styluses for applying or incising decoration, stone blades, scrapers, sharpeners, smoothers, stirrers, cups for glaze, terra-cotta molds, and rings to rest unfired pots on. Pottery objects, besides vases (including imported South Gaulish, Arretine, and Campanian ware), were very various, including lamps, kitchenware, figurines, votive animals, perfume holders, toys, tiles, water pipe, plaques, and storage amphoras.

A number of middle-class houses (with rock-cut mangers) were identified, and one large villa, with mosaic floors and its own baths. In such a villa might have lived a nabob like Q. Lollius Urbicus, Tiddis' most famous son, who among other duties served Hadrian as legate in the Jewish War of 132–135. Urbicus was not much of a stay-at-home—inscriptions attest his presence in Rome, Lower Germany, Noricum, and Britain—but he came home to die: his sumptuous circular mausoleum is still visible four kilometers to the north. Nearer town, just east of the north gate, a necropolis contains other mausolea, a *columbarium* ("dovecote") with nests or niches for ash urns, Berber funerary circles called bazinas, and *cupulae*, sarcophagi with rounded tops, common in Africa and with parallels in Spain. The inscriptions epitomize the cultural makeup of the place: they are in Libyan, neo-Punic, and Latin. Unassuming Tiddis, aspiring to the sky, inspired in one romantic French archaeologist the familiar thought that civilizations are mortal; ruins are like amputated limbs and suppliant hands.

Thibilis (Announa), eighteen kilometers southwest of Calama (Guelma), was another dependency of the Cirtan confederation, and may conveniently be described here. It was first recorded in modern times by the indefatigable traveler Sir Grenville Temple, whose archaeological survey coincided with the French siege of Constantine in 1837. This meant that the natives were hostile, and he was forced to draw the antiquities of Announa without getting off his horse. Thibilis' chief remains date from the middle and late empire; it did not become a municipium till Diocletian's reign (305), and retained its Punic and Berber culture until the end, with Punic names, Saturn stelae, and gods with names like Bacax, Juno as Caelestis, Venus as Astarte. In 411 its bishop was Donatist—a peculiarly Numidian schism. It has (fig. 8.4) three monumental arches (one late fourth-century), a porticoed forum, which could be closed off by a grillwork gate, and a basilica and a Hadrianic curia. The market was surrounded by shops and had an altar to Mercury in its midst, and a table of linear measures on three systems, like the one at Lepcis Magna. The sumptuous house of the chief local family, the Antistii, has been excavated. They supplied consuls in the reigns of Marcus Aurelius and Commodus. Their elegant, marble-paved house bears their name in stucco relief and has an altar to the family Genius (tutelary spirit). Another altar

FIGURE 8.4 *Thibilis, air view*

is dedicated to Fortuna Redux (Lady Luck Who Giveth Safe Return), for the Antistii were great travelers. Their house had a formal garden with a statue of a small boy fishing (the finds are in the Guelma Museum). There are two Byzantine churches, a chapel, a baptistery, and some rooms that might be monastic cells. A Byzantine coin hoard, now, alas, largely dispersed, is interesting because it contains some native counterfeits, common under the Vandals but now proved to have outlasted their regime.

The Cirtan confederation, of which Thibilis was a dependency, was Caesarian. But Augustus was Rome's first successful overseas colonizer. He sent out colonists—mostly veterans—as reward and as riddance. Their labor would increase Rome's grain supply, their military experience would provide a buffer against Berbers, and the policy would make Octavian-Augustus popular. From the modern Marxist viewpoint, this policy combined security with profit, thus satisfying a central imperialist aim. A string of Augustan colonies lined the coast from Igilgili westward: Saldae, Tubusuctu (Tiklat), Rusazu,[1] Rusguniae (Cap Matifou; this a colony of Augustus' obscure and cruel colleague Lepidus), Icosium, Aquae Calidae (Hammam Righa) and Zucchabar (Miliana; these two inland), Gunugu, and Cartennae.

These were all in the kingdom of Mauretania, which Augustus assigned in 25 B.C. to a client king, Juba II, "the student prince," who was to reign for forty-eight years. He was Numidian born, Punic in culture, Greek by education, Roman in experience; having walked as a small boy in Caesar's triumph, he was brought up in the Julio-Claudian circle and married to the fifteen-year-old Cleopatra Selene, daughter, as we saw, of Cleopatra by Mark Antony. This piece of canny Augustan matchmaking turned the children of two enemies into devoted vassals.

---

1. A sarcophagus from here, Severan in date, now in the Algiers Museum, bears a rare treatment of the Bellerophon myth. We see the hero giving to the Lycian king the letter asking for his own execution; in another panel, he is about to lasso Pegasus; then we see Pegasus drinking, the Chimaera dead; then Bellerophon refusing Queen Stheneboea's advances.

Juba's capital at Iol, which he renamed Caesarea (nowadays Cherchel) after Caesar Augustus, he made into a cultural center. The city has been described as a corner of Greece transplanted to Algeria; the very mosque is a replica of a Greek temple. Juba surrounded himself with Greek architects, artists, actors, and physicians, and accepted honors from Athens. He also ruled the back country, from Zaraï (Zéraïa) to Thabudeos (Thouda). He was a prolific compiler, writing, in Greek, works including a short history of Rome and a long (fifteen books) comparative study of Greek and Roman antiquities; by his works, now mostly lost, proving himself, however derivative, a historian, geographer, naturalist, grammarian, art critic, and more or less a poet. He was also a connoisseur of fine furniture. (The grammatical tradition crops up again in the voluminous Priscian, born here, though his *Institutiones Grammaticae*, in eighteen books, were written in Constantinople, in the early sixth century A.D.) It was natural, then, that Juba should people his capital with statues and adorn it with buildings.

The mean annual rainfall (633 millimeters) made Caesarea fertile and prosperous (though the average life span was only 28.2 years), so that eventually it became the capital of a Roman province. Ptolemy, Juba's son and successor, was murdered by Caligula in 40. What is possibly his portrait bust as an adolescent, in Greek marble, was published in 1955. He is shown wearing a diadem, his hair in a fringe. He has a heavy chin, a short, swollen upper lip, long, narrow eyes, and a low forehead.

Claudius in 42 divided the Mauretanian kingdom into two, Tingitana in the west and Caesariensis in the east, with a Roman procurator of the equestrian or middle class stationed at Caesarea, like Pilate in Jerusalem. The procurator was at once army commander, customs officer, tax collector, head of the department of public works, administrator of citizen and native affairs, including distribution of the dole, and judge in both civil and criminal cases; later, he was chief persecutor of Christians. His term of office was not limited to a single year. The walls of his capital, built about A.D. 150, enclosed 370 hectares, with a perimeter of seven kilometers; Augustan Rome was eleven kilometers around. Only about 150 hectares were occupied, allowing for a population of about seventeen thousand, roughly the same as today. The rest of the walled area was given over to gardens and fields, and could serve as a place of refuge in emergencies. The wall had thirty-nine towers and three fortlets; its maximum width was 4.7 meters. The gate at the south end of the cardo was the most impressive, being set back thirty meters from two octagonal towers flush with the wall. The wall was destroyed in

Firmus' revolt (371), and its remains dismantled by the Vandals (ca. 439). Caesarea's peak came in the Severan era; Macrinus, a pretender to Caracalla's throne, came from here.

Within the wall were all the appurtenances of a Roman city—baths, temples, theater, circus, amphitheater, private houses, rich with fresco and mosaic; purveyors of luxury goods, and of bad poetry for inscriptions. The town was hospitable to all the gods; inscriptions mention the Di Mauri, Saturn (a temple and seventeen stelae), the Olympic pantheon, Mithras, Cybele, Serapis, and Isis (also on coins, a tribute to Juba's Egyptian queen), and, as time wore on, deified emperors. There was a synagogue, and in Christian times Augustine preached in Caesarea against the Donatists.

The theater, originally of 19 B.C., with twenty-seven rows of seats built into the hillside, was later (in the fourth century) remodeled into an amphitheater, the arena measuring thirty-four by twenty meters. The stage was three stories high, as at Sabratha; its back wall formed one side of a portico—as in Pompey's theater in Rome—which enclosed the forum. The West Baths, called locally "the Sultan's Palace," are as big as a football field. They contained the usual amenities, symmetrically arranged, as at Carthage. They were especially rich in statues, now thought to be Hadrianic, and mostly in the local museum: a Mercury, Ceres, Jupiter with eagle, Neptune with dolphin, Bacchus, Pan, Aesculapius, a satyr extracting a thorn from Pan's foot, a famous Venus, this last taken to Algiers. The central room, a frigidarium, was expensively paved in yellow-brown, white-veined onyx from Oran. The baths were fed by an aqueduct of the mid–second century whose course followed the contours from a source forty-five kilometers away in the foothills of the Atlas Mountains. The aqueduct's course includes several splendid, perhaps overdaring pieces of engineering, among them a three-level bridge of ten arches and a great bridge (fig. 8.5) 228 meters long and 26 high, with twenty-five arches on the first level and twenty-nine on the second. In other places there is alleged evidence of four unsuccessful tries at bridging a ravine, of an elbow-bend bridge subject to landslides, of shoddy and overfragile construction, of too-steep gradients, insufficient allowance for sharp changes of temperature or high winds. While some will use the example of Saldae (discussed in chapter 9) to generalize about botched work, others may prefer to view the engineering of Roman aqueducts as Gibbon did: "The boldness of the enterprise, the solidity of the execution and the uses to which they were subservient, rank the aqueducts among the noblest monuments to Roman genius and power."

FIGURE 8.5 *Caesarea, aqueduct, ca.* A.D. *150*

Gibbon goes on to say that Roman aqueducts make insignificant towns look like "the residence of some potent monarch," and writes of flourishing cities amid the solitudes of Asia and Africa, "whose populousness and even whose existence, was derived from such artificial supplies of a perennial stream of fresh water."

The port at Caesarea, the next most important in North Africa after Carthage, was, like Carthage's, double, naval and commercial. The naval harbor is still in use, now for commercial purposes; sunken Roman war galleys were found in it. It was protected by Joinville Island, on which was a lighthouse in *opus reticulatum*—brick, set lozenge-fashion—dating from Claudius' or Nero's reign; the commercial harbor lay farther east. The area of the Eastern Baths and adjoining amphitheater has been transformed into an outdoor museum, to relieve the overcrowding of the indoor one. It contains some fine mosaics, including one of the triumph of a marine Venus in which the goddess sits, flanked by Tritons, in her scallop shell, trying on a necklace; before her on either side are Nereids mounted on sea monsters. The amphitheater, rectangular with apsidal ends, measured 120 by 70 meters. Its seats rose on ramping vaults; underground rooms with portcullises served as beast cages. This was the scene of the martyrdom of Saint Marciana, a virgin from Rusuccuru who was repeatedly protected by a magic wall from the lascivious advances of gladiators and was even rejected by a pious lion before a bull and a leopard finally finished her.

It remains to speak of the Cherchel Museum, referred to by some as "the Chamber of Horrors," by others as the best in Africa for statuary. Juba II had a gallery of copies, many of which are on display here. One female figure with an elephant-head coiffure may be Cleopatra or her daughter; there are a priestess of Isis, with rattle, and a colossal Hercules, to whom Juba II was devoted, as well as a gladiator-owner, identified by the staff he holds, throwing in the towel, a gesture acknowledging defeat for his man. There are also a young Bacchus (school of Praxiteles), an Aesculapius, a mounted Achilles with a mortally wounded Penthesilea, an Augustus in armor, with Mars the Avenger instead of a Gorgon on his breastplate, a Venus Genetrix (patroness of Julius Caesar), and Caesar himself, deified and crowned by a Victory. But the prize exhibits are the mosaics: Achilles hiding among the women on Skyros, to keep from being sent to the Trojan War; the Muses, a leopard and a stag, the Three Graces; and two very fine depictions of farm labor, aptly called "the *Works and Days* of African agriculture." In one, dated about A.D. 250, we see scenes of plowing with oxen, sowing, vine-dressing, and weeding with a hoe; grain and olives grow in the vineyard. The other, dated in the fourth century, is a bird's-eye view of a trellis in fact inhabited by a lively population of birds—swallow, partridge, blackbirds. Workmen are shown engaged in autumn pursuits: grapes are plucked, put in baskets, and carried on shoulders to an oxcart that hauls them to be pressed; a pig is hung up and butchered, while a dog devours the entrails; one workman with a pruning hook has taken time off for hunting, for he holds a hare by the hind legs. An air photograph (fig. 8.6) shows the villa from which this mosaic comes, and the large peripteral temple adjoining it. Of about the same date is a mosaic of the wedding of Peleus and Thetis, of which Achilles was the offshoot. Peleus has a groomsman, perhaps his erstwhile companion Acastus, or Telamon; Mercury, the gods' messenger, is also present. Thetis, a sea nymph, enthroned and diademed, has Nereids for attendants. Eros (Cupid) aims his arrow at Peleus. It is a horsy scene; Chiron the centaur, who is to be Achilles' tutor, is in attendance, and above are Achilles' immortal and loquacious chariot-horses, gift of Neptune.

FIGURE 8.6 *Caesarea, air view*

Hippo Regius, three kilometers south of Annaba (formerly Bône, now Algeria's fourth largest city—170,000 inhabitants), was allegedly a Punic foundation, older than Carthage, but nothing older than 200 B.C. has been found there. Its epithet "Regius" (Royal) shows it to have been a residence of Numidian kings. It is of course chiefly famous as the see of Saint Augustine, who was bishop here from 395 till the Vandal invasion in 430, having great trouble with the Donatist schism that was strongly favored in this part of Numidia. Under the hideous nineteenth-century basilica dedicated to him (which enshrines his right elbow), on the hill overlooking the ruins, lies a three-cella sanctuary to Ba'al-Saturn, from which come seventy-three stelae now at the site museum. Punic was still spoken in Hippo in Saint Augustine's time. Near the temple was a large cistern (fifty by forty-five meters), divided in two, with a compartment like an underground hypostyle hall, with ten piers on one side and seven rectangular compartments at right angles to it on the other. It has been put into use again to supply the needs of modern Annaba.

Also outside the site proper, and divided from it by the modern highway, is the theater, on an extension of the decumanus. Partly of brick, partly of ashlar, and marble-revetted, it is built into the hillside. The cavea is fifty-five meters wide, with a loge in front, perhaps once reserved for the Vandal king, though the theater as a whole dates from Augustan times or a little later. The orchestra was sixteen meters wide, the stage forty meters long, fourteen deep, and a meter high. The stage building had three half-round statue-niches. A fragmentary inscription referring to a discontented husband may conceal the title of a comedy. Built into the masonry were *dolia* (jars) placed mouth-outward, to help with the acoustics.

Hippo was a municipium under Augustus, achieving colonial status under the Antonines. The biographer C. Suetonius Tranquillus probably came from here, and was a *flamen* (priest; the word is related to "Brahmin") of the local imperial cult. Since Hippo was important as a shipping point for grain to Rome, an imperial procurator was stationed here. The Vandal king Genseric made it his capital until 439. It was a city of no great size, covering about sixty hectares. Its forum (seventy-six by forty-three meters; fig. 8.7) is the largest and oldest datable one in the Maghreb; in monumental bronze letters in its pavement can still be read the name of C. Paccius Africanus, patron of the town and proconsul in 77/78. A head of Vespasian, found in the forum and now in the museum, confirms the date. But there are earlier levels—for example, under the curia off the forum's northwest corner; from here came a huge bronze trophy two and a half meters high, erected to celebrate Caesar's victory at Thapsus (46 B.C.). A huge Gorgon's head, a meter high, its gaping mouth thirty centimeters across (fig. 8.8), decorated a fountain off the porticoed decumanus.

The market, 120 meters east of the forum, is the most important in the Maghreb. Its colonnade, five meters wide, encloses a rectangle measuring 37 by 105 meters, with swastikas in the mosaic pavement. There is a round building, nearly ten meters in diameter, in the middle of the open space, much as at Lepcis. From a late fourth-century house in the metal-workers' quarter on the south side of the market comes a mosaic showing a child victor in a chariot race where the motive power is a duck; there is a parallel at Carthage (see chapter 4) and in the Sicilian Piazza Armerina villa (*MSS*, 339).

Adjoining the market (see air photograph, fig. 8.7), is the Christian quarter, where Augustine must have sat on the bishop's throne in the apse of the Great Basilica (twenty by forty-two meters). An apsidal chapel runs at right angles to it, and forty meters southwest is a clover-leaf

FIGURE 8.7 *Hippo Regius, forum, Flavian and after, from the air*

FIGURE 8.8 *Hippo, Gorgon*

building, perhaps a baptistery. One of the rich houses nearby may have belonged to the patrician Julianus, who made Augustine his heir. A number of mosaics, from houses perhaps predating the basilica, were found in this area, including one of the Muses, another of Cupids fishing, and a third representing in medallions the animals that Noah took into the ark. In the Christian era the rooms of the rich pagan houses perhaps became monastic cells.

Next to the Christian quarter on the northeast is the "seafront" villa quarter, now a good distance from the sea. A complicated series of walls, dated by pottery to Hippo's Numidian phase (90/80 B.C.), is interpreted as breakwaters. The seafront villa itself went through six phases, dated by mosaics from the first to the fifth century. To Phase II (150–250) belongs a mosaic of Amphitrite, a fishing scene (dated 210–260), and an unusual one (fig. 8.9) showing ancient Hippo viewed from the sea. At the left edge of the photograph can be seen the left edge of the wooden bridge across the local river, the Boudjemâa, and the edge of a tetrastyle temple

FIGURE 8.9 *Hippo, sea-front mosaic, A.D. 150–250*

surmounted by a four-horse chariot; to the right appear the seafront buildings, porticoed, arcaded, pedimented, barrel-vaulted, with a loggia having an *à jour* (pierced) stone balustrade. From Phase III (280–330) comes a spirited though cruel rendition of hunting wild animals for the circus. The hunters, behind large oval shields, use burning torches to frighten the wretched beasts—lions, leopards, ostriches, gazelles—and drive them into the oval of a net; one hunter has been downed by his intended quarry. At the bottom left, a cart with a cage on it awaits the delivery of a catch. At the right center, outside the net, tethered domestic animals serve as decoys for the beasts and as food for the hunters; in the corner a mounted hunter with a lasso pursues a wild horse. At the bottom right, in front of a tent, the cook prepares a meal; some of the hunters are already eating. From Phase IV comes a mosaic that features the Triumph of Amphitrite. An earlier (second century) example, from a house on the decumanus, near the market, shows two panels, Autumn and Winter, from a mosaic of the Seasons.

The great North Baths, fed by an aqueduct from the picturesque Seraïdi hills to the west, were dedicated to Septimius Severus, and are curiously asymmetrical. The frigidarium had four apses and was marble-paved and revetted, white on gray for the floor, saffron yellow for the walls; the vaulted ceiling had mosaics. As usual, the baths were heavily populated with statues: Minerva, a Venus like the Venus de Milo, a colossal, muscle-bound Hercules, 2.6 meters tall, resembling the brutal Farnese type to be seen in the Naples Museum, and a Dionysus in Parian marble, in the style of the Parian sculptor Scopas (fourth century B.C.). The caldarium, as often, had hypocaust (radiant) heat in floor and walls; the tepidarium had frescoes. A smaller and older set of baths lies four hundred meters south: it yielded a gaming board inscribed SECVRVS LVDE—"Play it safe". Seventy-five meters southwest of them is a villa with a mosaic whose central panel shows a rather sheepish Minotaur—bull's head, human shoulders and torso—immured in his labyrinth.

Most of the finds from the site are collected in and around the museum, which is partly in the open air. It has been in its time a fort, a military prison, an agricultural station, and an army post. Outdoors, in picturesque profusion, are column capitals, stelae, millstones, sarcophagi, boundary markers, milestones, altars; in the courtyard, inscriptions to Ba'al-Saturn, Jupiter, Mercury, the Cereres, Pluto; also a Genius with a torch; and the Noah's Ark mosaic. Within are coins, terra-cotta plaques (one depicting the sacrifice of Isaac, another Eve and the serpent tempting Adam), Christian and Jewish lamps, and necklaces, hairpins, rouge boxes, locks, keys, door knockers, bells, bronze outlets for fountains, a bronze jug and spoons, a bronze statuette of Apollo (fished from the sea), weights, measures, molds, fishing gear, a marble *crater* (punchbowl) with a Dionysiac scene, and also a mosaic of a Nereid, from a villa with upper stories, of Severan date, on the southern part of the site (some ninety meters south of the South Baths), in which perhaps the Roman procurator lived—until the Vandals came.

The discussion of Hippo, an Augustan municipium, has taken us 430 years down into the Christian era. Returning now to the Augustan age, we may note again a series of military triumphs celebrated under Octavian-Augustus, in 34, 33, 28, 21, and 19 B.C., emphasized by Marxist commentators as evidence of native resistance provoked by the spread of Roman settlements, which interfered with the age-old nomad practice of transhumance; that is, taking the flocks from winter to summer pasture and back again. The triumph of 19 B.C. was celebrated by the proconsul L. Cornelius Balbus over the Garamantes. Thenceforward the African frontiers were kept secure for the settlers, Roman and native, by the Legio III Augusta and by a network of military roads, such as the previously mentioned south Tunisian one from Tacapae via Capsa to Ammaedara, opened in A.D. 14, the first year of Tiberius' reign. The French learned from the Romans how to pacify native nomads by the use of a few crack troops—hence the Foreign Legion, which has for British and Americans of a certain age a romantic aura derived from the novels of P. C. Wren and films featuring Ronald Colman; in the mind's eye dance visions of white horseshoe arches, minarets against a dusty-blue sky, an olive-green horizon, storks on the tiles, camels at the tether. But the Foreign Legion was in fact a mercenary army comparable more to Rome's auxiliary units from Pannonia, Chalcidice, Commagene, Spain, Portugal, Mauretania, Thrace, and Palmyra than to the Legio III Augusta itself. (However, the legionnaires got citizenship after five years, the Roman auxilia after twenty-five. In the later empire, citizenship was actually offered as an inducement to non-Roman recruits.) Both forces, ancient and modern, had experts—draftsmen, masons, carpenters—in their ranks; both made fortified camps for each night's bivouac; the permanent camps of both became civilian towns; both fed on pasta, not meat, and became inured to desert sandstorms and to desert extremes of temperature, which can fluctuate more than eighty degrees Fahrenheit in a day; both manned but never entirely pacified a desert frontier, and both were a tiny minority—perhaps only 12,000 Roman, and 3,500 (growing in 130 years to 80,000) French Foreign Legionnaires—compared with the population they were assigned to police.

Resentment at urbanization and land-grabbing, coupled perhaps with a deserter's rancor and a thirst for liberty, produced the revolt of Tacfarinas, who is revered by modern Algerians as a "freedom fighter," fierce, full of bravura, indomitable, impetuous in attack, agile in retreat, an able guerilla warrior. He had in fact been an officer in the auxiliaries, like Vercingetorix in Gaul and Arminius in Germany. (In ancient as in modern times, insurgent chiefs had often been trained in the armies of colonial powers.) For seven years—A.D. 17–24—he held Roman consular armies at bay, delivering ultimata to Tiberius and besieging Romanized settlements like Thubursicu Numidarum, perhaps abetted by Roman traders inconvenienced by long warfare. Tiberius retaliated by offering land to deserters from the rebel camp; the Roman army itself took up guerilla tactics. The campaigns had their ups and downs; Roman generals celebrated triumphs, including Q. Junius Blaesus, uncle of Tiberius' ill-fated advisor Sejanus, who was the last general not a member of the imperial house to be allowed full military honors (acclamation by his troops as *Imperator*). In a tumultuous battle at Auzia (A.D. 24), marked by Roman war cries and the slaughter of Numidians like sheep, Tacfarinas' son was taken. The distraught father rushed into the melee to rescue him, and died; with him, for some twenty years, died the spirit of revolt.

Evidence for the involvement of Thubursicu Numidarum (Khamissa) in Tacfarinas' revolt rests upon an almost certain emendation (Thubursicum for Thibuscum) in Tacitus (*Annals* 4.24). The place, thirty-two kilometers southwest of Thagaste (Souk-Ahras, Augustine's birthplace), on the military road from Hippo to Theveste, was the seat of the Musulamii, Tacfarinas' own tribe, and of another, the Numidae, from whom the whole area took its name. Trajan in 113 made it a municipium; it became a titular colony before 270. Its area, sixty-five hectares, was too hilly for a rectangular street-grid. In spite of two Ba'al-Saturn temples and 173 stelae, and of a preponderance of indigenous names among the over 750 inscriptions, the place was thoroughly Romanized, with two fora, baths, a monumental arch, a nymphaeum like Zaghouan's at the spring that was the source of the Bagradas River, and one of the most beautiful and best-preserved theaters in North Africa (probably Severan; fig. 8.10). Romanization went so far that Khamissa in the early fourth century produced a Latin lexicographer, Nonius Marcellus, whose dictionary treats exhaustively of grammar and of the names of ships, clothing, containers, colors, food and drink, weapons, and human relationships. The site was healthy; the average life-span was 48.8 years, and an inscription from nearby Tipasa Numidarum (Tifech) records a teetotaler who lived to be 123, though as usual, allowance must be made for pardonable exaggeration.

The Old Forum, cut into a hillside and surrounded by a portico, was free of vehicular traffic, the only approach being by a stair on the northwest. Off the south side was a chapel dedicated to the Genius of the Numidian *gens*, with the *aerarium* (town treasury) underneath it. As at Lepcis Magna and elsewhere there was a table of standard measures, this time dry and liquid. Off the southwest corner was a temple, possibly oriented to sunrise; it stood on a podium; its columns had Ionic capitals. Perhaps a splendid Jupiter of Trajanic date—now in the Guelma

FIGURE 8.10 *Thubursicu Numidarum, theater, Severan (?)*

Museum—came from here. The same museum also has a statue from here of Geta, his face deliberately mutilated after his brother Caracalla murdered him. A basilica nearly as large (thirty-nine by twenty-nine meters) as the forum occupied the east side; it had superposed orders of architecture and was revetted in Simitthu marble. Storerooms, shops, or offices as at Ostia's Piazzale delle Corporazioni filled the forum's north side. A public lavatory adjoined. Two hundred fifty meters to the north was the theater, probably Severan, perhaps left unfinished at the end of the dynasty. It was seventy meters wide, smaller than Thugga's or Caesarea's. There were eighteen rows of seats built on vaults, and a stage, forty-four by nine meters, and one meter high. One story of the architectural backdrop is preserved, with a stair to the roof. A mask inscribed EVNVCV refers to a pantomime actor, not to Terence's play. Audiences, as we have seen, preferred mime, rope dancers, or magicians to classical drama; the Church frowned impartially upon them all. Adjoining the theater was the nymphaeum monumentalizing the spring Aïn el-Youdi, also visible in fig. 8.10. It had a horseshoe basin and a rectangular one, with an ingenious lock-like arrangement for filling and for raising and lowering levels. Next to it is visible a palaestra with a marble-revetted portico on three sides, and a little square marble-paved sanctuary opening upon it.

In A.D. 39 Caligula, fearing the conjunction in North Africa of civil and military power, took the latter away from the governor of Africa and placed it under his own personal legate. Claudius, as we saw, created the two Mauretanias as provinces, giving limited (Latin) rights to Tipasa, of which more anon; the future emperor Galba, as proconsul, put down a revolt of the Musulamii in 45. To reduce disaffection, the new provinces were soon provided with a cult of the emperor, presided over by the *flamen provinciae*; Vespasian, as the founder of an upstart dynasty, was especially keen on this. In fact, in administration, defense, colonizing, and Romanization, Vespasian's Flavian dynasty made North Africa definitively Roman. Among minor Flavian foundations were Tigisis (Aïn el-Bordj), east of Sigus, in Cirta's territorium, where there survive a Severan arch and a Byzantine fortress; Mascula (Khenchela), station of the Legio III Augusta en route from Ammaedara to Theveste and Lambaesis, and findspot of a villa particularly rich in mosaics; and also nearby Aquae Flavianae (Aïn el-Hammam) whose warm swimming pools are still in use. Under the Flavians a military road was built connecting Lamasba (Henchir Merouana; later, in Alexander Severus' reign, the site of an elaborate irrigation project) with Zaraï and Auzia. Of major Flavian sites Theveste (Tébessa) may best be postponed to chapter 10, which will treat its late flowering. Tipasa, the lovely seaside town so lyrically praised by Albert Camus, and Lambaesis, headquarters for five generations of the Legio III Augusta, will be treated here.

Tipasa deserves Camus's panegyric: an intrinsically lovely seaside town has had its beauty enhanced by making the ruins into a tasteful archaeological park, and the basilica and cemetery of Saint Salsa to the east is a gem among Christian monuments of the western world. The description of this last, and of the corresponding Christian basilicas and necropolis outside the walls to the west, is best postponed to chapter 10. The town was made a municipium in Claudius' reign, and a colony in Hadrian's, or more likely, in that of Antoninus Pius. An inscription found at the east gate of the circuit wall now establishes that it was built, the whole 2.3 kilometer perimeter at one go, in 146/47, against the danger of a Moorish attack; a family of captives, manacled, appears in a mosaic from the civil basilica, now in the local museum. Slits in the footings of the wall, too narrow to allow the smallest enemy to pass, allow the local stream to flow under. The wall had twenty-five towers, eleven round, fourteen square, and a bowshot apart; they projected one story above the wall, which itself was monolithic, in concrete, averaging 1.5 to 1.6 meters thick, wide enough for a wall-walk. The west and south gates are monumental, as at Caesarea; the east or Algiers gate simply had flanking towers; nearer the sea on the east side there is a postern. For the expected assault upon the town in 145/46 a detachment was brought in by sea from Pannonia; they landed at the port, outside the wall to the east, discovered by modern diving investigations to have been formed artificially by moles projecting shoreward from two islets.

On the peninsula about 900 meters west of the port were the forum and civil basilica (Severan), with capitolium and curia. By the sea, 130 meters west of the basilica, is the sumptuous, partly two-storied House of the Frescoes (fig. 8.11), with mosaic floors as well as painted walls, built over a cemetery dating from pre-Roman at least to Flavian times. It went through three phases (Antonine to the Vandal and Byzantine eras). In its second (Severan) phase its eastward run of rooms was—proudly—made

FIGURE 8.11 *Tipasa, House of the Frescoes, Antonine and after*

over into private baths; a summer dining room, with sea view, was installed, and on the practical side a loading and unloading dock was added on the southeast corner. In the final phase (mid–fourth to sixth century) its north rooms were transformed into a factory for manufacturing *garum* (fish sauce); large storage jars were found in what had formerly been a private apartment. They were stoppered in the adjoining one, and before pickling, the fish were kept alive in what had been the fountains of the central peristyle. Accurate dating was possible because of careful attention to pottery, but also because of the discovery of three hoards of coins, one of them of 1,560 pieces, ranging in date from Claudius Gothicus (268–270) to the reign of Justinian (527–565). The coins included a number of unofficial strikings, not exactly counterfeited, but minted to make up for shortages. A few graffiti date from a time when the house was occupied by transients, tramps, and slum families.

From the sea just west of the villa the colonnaded cardo led inland. At its crossing with the decumanus rises the "New Temple," to an unknown god; across the street is another. The decumanus runs southwest, leaving on the left an amphitheater eighty meters long, and passing, two hundred meters further along its course, an elaborate semicircular nymphaeum of the early fourth century, rendered in polychrome marble, with monolithic Corinthian columns. It is built on a module in multiples of four, its length twice its depth. Parallels to this theater of water-play are to be seen at Zaghouan, Lambaesis, and in the Piazza d'Oro of Hadrian's villa at Tivoli, near Rome. The nymphaeum masks the terminus of an aqueduct, which discharges into it at three levels. The Tipasa aqueduct served the Great Baths, which rise in gaunt brick ruin amid the houses of the modern town. Just north of the point where the decumanus reaches the west gate was the theater, built on radiating vaults; only four rows of seats are preserved.

The traveling Legio III Augusta finally, in 81, in the reign of the Flavian emperor Titus, came to rest at a strategic crossroads: Lambaesis (Tazoult), 11 kilometers southeast of Batna, 170 due east of its last "permanent" camp at Theveste. Three camps are known at Lambaesis, the last and largest Hadrianic. The adjoining canabae became under Severus a municipium, and capital of his newly created province of Numidia, until Constantine transferred the seat of administration to Cirta, renamed Constantina in his honor. Of the earliest (east) camp, 1,750 meters southeast of the conspicuous praetorium (taken by the Scots traveler Bruce—in 1765—for an elephant stable), the remains recently excavated measure 148 by 120 meters. It contained a basilica, with a *vexillarium* (shrine for the legionary standards) in an apse midway in one long side. The west camp, 2.4 kilometers from the praetorium and 200 meters square, was built in 128 especially for a visit by Hadrian; his congratulatory address to the troops, inscribed on stone, was found in the camp and is now in the Algiers Bardo Museum. The Great Camp (see air photograph, fig. 8.12), dating from 129, was much larger (500 by 420 meters). Its central building, the praetorium, essentially a four-way arch, is the most impressive in North Africa after the Severan basilica of Lepcis Magna. The north façade, whose entrances could be closed for immigration and customs control, is a triumphal arch; since it was made of sandstone, it needed frequent repair. The architrave bears inscriptions of Diocletian (of 286–293) and Gallienus (of 267/68), and symbolic reliefs in the keystones—Victory, hand with wreath, bull's head, eagle, Genius. The whole was tile-roofed, and originally stuccoed bright yellow, with the joins in the stonework picked out in red. Proportions were carefully observed: the structure was 100 Roman feet long, 75 wide, and 50 high. The Gallienus inscription is to be connected with the rehabilitating of the Legio III Augusta in 263, after it had been in disgrace for fifteen years.

The central building gave access to a paved courtyard (sixty-five by

FIGURE 8.12 *Lambaesis, praetorium,* A.D. *129, air view*

thirty-eight meters) surrounded on three sides by porticoes with rooms opening off them; some rooms were arsenals, in which were found several thousand terra-cotta and stone missiles. Other rooms were workshops, for the camp and town were between them quite self-sufficient, like an antebellum Virginia plantation: there were smiths, carpenters, potters, masons, tailors, dyers, fullers, tanners, saddlers, cobblers, tentmakers, ropemakers, brickmakers. On the fourth (south) side was a three-aisled, open-sided basilica (fifty-two by thirty meters), approached by a flight of steps and embellished by statues, some of them colossal. At the back was a series of rooms, to which the Gallienic reconstruction added apses; the central one was the vexillarium, and flanking it were shrines of Mars, Fortuna Augusti, the Genius of the Camp, and Minerva, and also *scholae* (clubrooms) for the noncommissioned officers. The statutes of their guilds have been found: their dues provided bonuses at promotion, demotion, transfer, discharge, and death, and also paid for sacrifices to emperors. The whole camp plan is strikingly like that of the restored Saalburg, on the German limes (*RoR*, 104–7). Cutting into the basilica is the kitchen garden of the penitentiary built in 1851 for opponents of the Second Empire; the prisoners did some of the first excavating. The prison buildings have obliterated most of the camp's southwest quadrant; however, in the southeast are baths—a luxury unthinkable in the pre-Hadrianic Roman army—and barracks. North of the praetorium were more barracks, for infantry and cavalry officers and men, and perhaps a hospital. There was parking space for wagons in the northeast corner.

The civilian town grew up east of the main camp. Its monuments include the arch of Commodus, an amphitheater of A.D. 169 (104 by 95 meters, heavily stone-robbed), a meat market, of the end of the third century, about 150 meters southeast of the camp, and a necropolis. Canabae grew up round the east camp, 1,200 meters southeast of the praetorium; veterans, engaged in viticulture, were among the inhabitants. There were a cardo (the Via Septimiana), a Severan arch, the "Legate's Baths," and a complex including a capitolium, a Septizonium, a sanctuary of Aesculapius, a Mithraeum, and the Chasseurs' Baths, so-called because excavated by that regiment. The capitolium, of the Corinthian order, built in 246, restored 364/367, stood on a podium twenty steps high— allowing for vaulted rooms underneath—at the back of a porticoed precinct. It had two cellae instead of the usual three.

The Aesculapeum complex, ranging in date from 162 to 210, is small in size but extraordinary in plan (fig. 8.13). It stands at the back of a

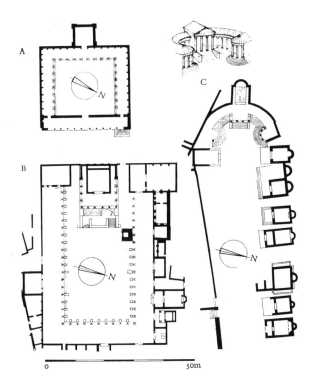

FIGURE 8.13 *Lambaesis, Aesculapeum,* A.D. *162–210, plan*

hemicycle, approached by three adjoining flights of steps, the end ones convex in plan, the central one concave, interrupted by a rectangular tetrastyle portico in veined white marble. The cella is paved in red stone and revetted in reddish marble. One approached the shrine along the façades of a series of chapels; eight on the north (which broke into the southeast wall of the east camp), and one on the south are preserved. Inscriptions, of which the whole site has yielded some fourteen hundred, many on display in an epigraphic garden near the main camp, reveal that the pair of chapels nearest the Aesculapeum was dedicated to Jupiter Valens and Silvanus. One inscription pithily summarizes the hoped-for effect of all attendance at religious services: BONVS INTRA, MELIOR EXI— "Go in good, come out better." Another stone mentions a temple of Saturn, which has not been identified, though 198 Saturn stelae have. Other chapels were dedicated to Diana, Jupiter Depulsor (Jupiter Who Puts to Flight), Apollo, Mercury. Therapeutic baths, part of the health regime prescribed by Aesculapius, adjoined.

Opposite the Aesculapeum, at the other end of the Sacred Way, were the frescoed Mithraeum and the Chasseurs' Baths. The Septizonium, at the junction of the Via Septimiana and the Via Sacra, is in plan a hemicycle flanked by rectangular wings; it masked aqueduct outlets, like the nymphaeum at Tipasa, but here there were not one but four. One of them came from a source thirty-nine kilometers away; it was built in eight months, in 225/26. Six hundred meters along its course, southward, is the spring Aïn Drinn (*aïn* is Arabic for "spring"); close by it, the sanctuary of Neptune, god of fresh water as well as salt. Under the houses of Tazoult village were Roman villas from which have come the mosaics in the rich but crowded local museum. Statues there, provenience not always known, include Mercury, Bacchus, Venus, Minerva, Neptune, Fortuna, Commodus, and Septimius Severus. One treasure from Lambaesis, the bronze Child with Eaglet, is in the Algiers Museum. Seven hundred meters east of Tazoult a Byzantine fort testifies to Lambaesis' longevity. In the surrounding necropoleis the most interesting monument is the mausoleum, three kilometers north, of one Flavius Maximus, prefect of the Legio III Augusta in Alexander Severus' reign. In a theatrical, imperialist, but somehow moving gesture in 1849, the commandant of a French detachment, Flavius' modern opposite number, marched his troops past the tomb with an "Eyes right," a salute, and a round of musket fire.

Lambaesis was originally a Flavian camp. To Nerva (A.D. 96–98), successor to the Flavians, Algeria owes two foundations: Sitifis (Sétif), and Cuicul (Djemila, "the Beautiful" in Arabic). Since excavations at the former have so far revealed chiefly monuments of late antiquity, discussion of it will be postponed to chapter 10, but we may well conclude this chapter with a description of Cuicul. It has an austere beauty very different from the romantic attraction of Tipasa, but as striking in its own way. It was built for veterans, eighty kilometers west of Cirta, on a ridge between wadis, nine hundred meters above sea level, in stark but not infertile mountain country (1,250 to 1,450 meters above sea level); wheat will grow on these high plains. Little but the south gate of its original circuit wall survives (it was demolished in 211, under Caracalla, when Cuicul was enlarged), but it originally enclosed an area of four hundred by two hundred meters. The city first developed in its northern sector, reached by the colonnaded cardo maximus (in the center of the air photo-

FIGURE 8.14 *Cuicul, air view*

graph, fig. 8.14), leading through an arch to the porticoed forum, measuring forty-four by forty-eight meters, bounded, clockwise from the west, by the civil basilica (A.D. 169; thirty-eight by fourteen meters) and by Cosinius' market, measuring twenty-eight by twenty-two meters, surrounded by eighteen shops (it cost him—a Carthaginian merchant, not a veteran—18,000 sesterces). An inscription of 160 or 162 mentions a *pollicitatio*, a procedure of financial self-estimating, gone through by more or less willing benefactors in order to avoid outbidding by greedier candidates. The market has a hexagonal building in the middle, a table of official measures in the portico, and in the south wall put-holes for suspending the official scales. Next comes the capitolium, on a high podium, reached by a monumental stair, with arches under; the Corinthian columns are fourteen meters high, a meter and a half thick, and fluted in stucco. In the northeast corner is the curia, with the Terentius Baths behind it, and, across the street from the baths, to the south, the House of Amphitrite, whose mosaic will be discussed below. The temple in the southwest corner, in its own precinct, has been called "of Venus Genetrix," but an inscription makes Cybele, the Anatolian earth-mother, another possibility. In the middle of the forum an altar of the mid–third century A.D. has on one face an unusual sacrificial scene (fig. 8.15): a *victimarius* raises his mallet over the hapless head of a calf-sized bull;

beside him flames an altar; beyond, a large (out-of-scale) *urceus* (pitcher); above, *patera* and cleaver; below, cock and ram.

The north quarter has four major houses, the west quarter—across the cardo—three,[2] and the Severan square, one. Altogether they have produced thirty-six mosaics and thirty-two fragments, mostly, but not quite all, of the fourth and fifth Christian centuries, evincing the taste of Cuicul's late élite. Four houses monopolize the best figured mosaics. The oldest, Severan, comes from the House of Europa, near the north end of the cardo maximus, and shows Cupids vintaging. Next in time (third century) comes the Marriage of Neptune and Amphitrite, much ruined, from the House of Amphitrite, mentioned earlier. The bridal pair is gone, but attendants remain: a Nereid with a curly brunette bob, wearing gold bracelets and necklace and carrying a fan; a Triton with a Napoleon III beard, holding the bridle of a four-horse chariot; a wingless Cupid, whipping dolphins; Hymen, god of marriage, with his torch. The House of the Ass, in the cardo south of the "Temple of Venus Genetrix," has two major mosaics. One, the largest figured mosaic from the site, depicts the Toilet of Venus; the central motif dates from about 350, the border from the early fifth century. Below a central drain—the mosaic was intended to be viewed under water, which brightens the colors—sits Venus in her conch shell, upheld by a pair of sea monsters. The shell is comfortably lined with cloth. Naked to the waist, she wears a diadem and two gold necklaces. Her son Cupid, a garland of roses in his left hand, with the other helps her to uphold a mirror, which reflects her face, though it faces outward, toward the spectator. Nereids, seminude and bejeweled, adorn the four corners; their mounts are a sea horse (whose Nereid gives him a drink), a sea ram, sea griffin, and sea leopard. In the center of the upper register stands a statue of Neptune, bronzed, bearded, naked except for a sea-green mantle. He leans on a gold trident, carries a dolphin, head down, and is flanked by sea horses. The (later) border's right side is almost all lost, except for a man who bears on his shoulder an amphora, which he is preparing to load onto a ship against a background of a port with arcades. Across the bottom border boats are featured; one is loaded with musicians, plus a man dancing and a woman clacking castanets. Beside the music boat, a Cupid with a whip threatens an aggressive sea horse. In the corner, a minute Hero leans out a tower window with a

2. The west quarter also has a basilica (forty-four by twenty-two meters), of poor materials and late date (367–400) containing in the choir a saint's burial surrounded by graves of children, one a baby girl buried with her little glass beads with their rock-crystal cabochon.

FIGURE 8.15 *Cuicul, altar from forum, with sacrificial implements;
after* A.D. 250

torch to light the way of a giant Leander, as tall as the tower. Central in
the left border, a boat with five convivial passengers ties up to an islet
with arcaded, vaulted, windowed and towered buildings. One passenger
plays a huge Pan-pipe, another dances, a woman embraces a man from
behind. In the bow, a man in a dalmatic holds a silver wine-cup and
pitcher. In the corner, a Nereid, Orpheus or Palaemon, and cattle. The
top border has fishing scenes, a teeming net between two boats; in the
corner, a much-ruined Perseus and Andromeda—she is bigger than he is,
but the dragon bleeds at his feet.

The other major mosaic in the House of the Ass is elaborate, with
eighty panels, one of which bears the legend ASINVS NICA, "The Ass
conquers," half Latin, half Greek, perhaps a pun on a proprietor named
Asinius. (A panel in another room portrays an actual ass.) The panels, in
five rows of sixteen, portray birds and animals (often paired between
Rows 1 and 5, and 2 and 4): ostrich, stork, parrot, crane, bustard,
hen, duck, crow, pigeon, peacock, heron, goose, partridge, boar, gazelle,
hound, hare, horse, elephant, griffin, stag, bull, antelope, with seven
panels of winged Genii (Geniuses) for good measure. The central set
appears to convey a message: Asinius celebrates his victory (perhaps in a
beast fight—there is a bull in one panel) with a banquet; slaves carry
buckets, braziers, and linen, and there are punchbowls at either end; the
master himself appears in robe and stola.

In the mosaic that gives the House of Europa its name, also fifth-
century, the lady rides happily on her kidnapper's taurine back and feeds

him roses from a basket. There is a pair of Cupids; one pulls the bull, the other pushes. There is a very close parallel, somewhat earlier in date, in a Roman villa at Lullingstone, Kent. Finally under this head, the House of Castorius—first right off the cardo—is the most imposing in area (fifteen hundred square meters), but poor in mosaics.

In the southern quarter, the House of Bacchus, next to the Commodan Great Baths, consists of two peristyle houses thrown together. The mosaic for which the house was named, dated 340–400, shows the murder of the god's nurse Ambrosia by the Thracian king Lycurgus; she was metamorphosed into a vine that strangled the murderer. The border shows scenes from the god's life—for example, the Athenian Icarius sacrificing to him in gratitude for the gift of the vine; a votary revealing a phallus in a basket to a horrified initiand (compare the Villa of the Mysteries fresco from Pompeii, *MSS*, fig. 8.15). From a seven-apsed hall, perhaps for dining, north of this mosaic, comes an ingeniously ordered one of an animal hunt in an arena, where huntsmen, mounted, kneeling, or standing, pursue the stag or face the charge of curiously human-faced lions, leopards, or boars, whose jaws break the hunting spear in two. At one side a huntsman with a net over his left shoulder carries a hare by the hind legs in his right hand. In the upper left corner, a hunting dog with collar; running across the top, an arcaded portico fronting a row of houses with pitched tile roofs.

Cuicul, like many North African towns, has two fora (frontispiece). The spacious (thirty-two hundred square meters) second, or Severan forum marks the transition between the north and south quarters; its features are an arch of Caracalla (216), spanning the road westward to Sitifis,[3] an apsidal cloth market and a conical fountain, a civil basilica of 364–367, built over a temple of Saturn, and the grandiose temple of the Severi (220), tetrastyle, approached by a double flight of steps. A street curving eastward from its northeast corner led under the arch of Crescens (169) to the theater, whose twenty-four tiers of seats held three thousand, with magnificent views across the town from the top rows (fig. 8.16). It has proved necessary to provide cement footings to keep the seats from washing out. The stage measures about thirty-nine by six meters; the stage building is well preserved.

Finally, in the eastern part of the southern quarter there grew up in the fifth century a Christian area, with three basilicas, a circular baptistery (restored) with annexes for ritual ablutions, and the bishop's house. The

---

3. Near this arch were found a number of milestones, indicating road upkeep right through the third-century anarchy and beyond; the latest is dated 402–408.

FIGURE 8.16 *Cuicul, theater,* A.D. *161*

northern basilica was perhaps used for eucharistic meals; it had a mosaic with medallions of animals, and the names of donors. The southern, with double side-aisles, was dedicated to martyrs, and perhaps Donatist; a mosaic inscription mentions a Bishop Cresconius, of whom there were two—one died in 411, the other in 553. If the later is the one meant, then the Christian quarter was flourishing in Byzantine times.

The language of architecture, in this remote Algerian mountain fastness, is universal, in temples, fora, mosaiced houses, theaters, basilicas, baths; from end to end of the Roman Empire, official architecture was one, as it is in our day from Chandigarh to Brasilia. But here at Cuicul the adaptation to the terrain and the craftsmanship are local. However, the unity was more artistic than political or religious: this was the area of mountaineers' revolt and Donatist schism, as we shall see in ensuing chapters.

9. THE HIGH EMPIRE IN ALGERIA, A.D. 98–238

Most Mediterranean countries have their "Pompeii," a site that evokes with special vividness the life of the past. In Greece it is Delos; in France, Vaison-la-Romaine; in Spain, Mérida; in Libya, Lepcis Magna; in Morocco, Volubilis. In Algeria it is, by common consent, Timgad, though it must be admitted that the place does not move the spirit, as do Tipasa and Cuicul. Rather, it evokes the essential orderliness of the Roman mind. Its ancient name was Thamugadi. It lies thirty-eight kilometers east of Lambaesis. Trajan planned it (A.D. 100), on a regular grid twelve hundred Roman feet on a side (see air photograph, fig. 9.1), to be a colony for veterans. Over the years it expanded from twelve to fifty hectares, the additions not conforming to the grid. Its population, estimated at fifteen thousand, had the use of most of the Roman amenities, including no less than thirteen public baths. It will be most convenient to describe the site topographically. Having passed the excellent local museum, one enters at the north gate, of A.D. 149, which gives onto the cardo maximus, paved with blue limestone slabs, set on the bias to minimize slipping and ruts. Five blocks south on the left is the library, the gift—it cost him 400,000 sesterces—of a wealthy citizen (third or fourth century), to be compared with that of Celsus (Trajanic) at Ephesus (*GSS*, 422). A U-shaped portico precedes an apse, twelve meters across, with shelves, on ground floor and gallery, to hold twenty-three thousand books, and a central niche for Minerva, goddess of wisdom. The pavement was green and white marble; graffiti, some obscene, show that the young used—and abused—the building.

Halfway through the town, at the junction of the porticoed decumanus maximus, the cardo comes to a dead end at the forum, whose porticoed central space (forty-three by fifty-meters), paved in blue limestone, was

FIGURE 9.1 *Timgad, air view*

surrounded by public buildings. The central entrance from the decumanus was flanked by shops and an elegant latrine, its twenty-six seats separated by stone dolphins. A complex at the forum's southwest corner has been plausibly identified as the police station, or it might be an *atrium publicum*, a building for municipal offices, as at Cosa in Etruria. Next to it an elegant polychrome marble-revetted building, approached by steps and with a columnar screen, its uprights grooved for grilles, is the curia. It had a dais at the far end, where the magistrates sat. Many statues in the museum came from here, including one of Trajan. From here also came a municipal *album* (list of officials) of late date—362 or 364—posted, if of the former date, as a notice of evaders of town duties; if of the latter, as an assurance to the upper bourgeoisie of their privileges. It includes bureaucrats of the imperial civil service, priests of the imperial cult, and Christian clergy, as well as town officers. Next to the curia a small temple—the only one within the original gridded area—was probably dedicated to Trajan. Vaulted rooms beneath housed the town treasury; a projection from the front into the forum was the speakers' rostrum. A square building in the northwest corner remains unidentified. On the opposite corner the small but elegant House of the Jardinières may have been the quarters of the legate of Legio III Augusta when he visited Timgad on his official rounds. Round the sides of its peristyle were the large flowerpots from which it takes its name; they were decorated with theater masks. A basilica occupied the southeast corner; coins date it as Hadrianic. It is thirty-eight meters long, fifteen wide, and fourteen high, with two superposed ranges of columns, one Ionic, one Corinthian; there are windows on the forum side, a row of offices or shops on the other, a raised tribunal at the south end, and three statue-niches at the north, the central one apsidal; there was room also round the walls for standing statues of emperors. A row of shallow rooms across the forum's south side may have housed the offices of the town's various curiae (wards). These building ingredients, disposed very much as at Gigthis, were standard for fora all over the empire: here was the center of civic life, the scene of oratory, at elections and funerals, of swearings-in, religious sacrifice on holidays, official approval of public works, distribution of the dole, consecration of statues, conduct of business and of lawsuits, posting of notices, and, above all, idling and gossip:

> VENARI LAVARI
>
> LVDERE RIDERE
>
> OCC EST VIVERE

says a forum graffito (which also, with its thirty-six letters, must have been a game with counters)—"Hunting, bathing, gambling, laughing— *that's* living!" Certainly it is a hearty invitation to the brainless life—but there was always the library, a block away.

Down the decumanus to the east lay the East Market, late in date, like the library, but like it, interesting in plan. A portico faced the street. Behind it, on either side of a hemicycle vestibule, was a range of shops; behind that, a pair of partly intersecting apsidal courtyards, each lined with shops. Beside the east or Mascula gate, of 146, rose the East Baths, dating from the colony's beginnings but enlarged in 167. They held, though not in symmetry, the usual amenities: changing rooms, cold, warm, and steam baths, latrines, reservoirs, radiant heating, a mosaic in the frigidarium. Another gate, of 171, two hundred meters south-east of the Mascula gate, shows how far the town had burst its original boundaries in two generations.

Returning to the forum and turning south, the visitor reaches the theater (of A.D. 160). Its seats, set into a gentle slope but also resting on vaults, would hold thirty-five hundred, and were more than the towns-folk needed, but spectators would come from miles around on market days. The attraction was usually pantomime; an acrostic inscription of the second or third century, found in reuse in the Byzantine fort, re-

FIGURE 9.2 *Timgad, theater (A.D. 160), and forum, Trajanic*

cords in unintentionally limping iambics the virtues of a pantomime
actor named Vincentius, as good as he was talented, who died at twenty-
three. The air view (fig. 9.2) shows the relation of the theater to the
forum.

Timgad's southwest quadrant was its aristocratic quarter. It included
the House of the Piscina, the small but elegant Central Baths (which
yielded a mosaic of the Seasons), and outside the original grid, the House
of the Hermaphrodite—named from a mosaic—and the House of Sertius
(dated A.D. 200–250 and built over the original town circuit wall),
residence of the nabob who gave Timgad its main market building, described below. Into a pentagonal space immediately south of the House
of the Hermaphrodite were cunningly fitted the South Baths, oblique to
the grid, with apses and exedrae filling in the angles. One exedra was,
says Gsell, for conversation; another housed a sumptuous twenty-eight-
seat latrine. From without, the vaulted rooms must have been as striking
in appearance as the Hunting Baths at Lepcis Magna.

Four hundred meters south of the South Baths looms the great bulk of the Byzantine fort of 539, measuring 112 by 67 meters, the best and best-preserved example of Byzantine architecture in North Africa. Its walls were 15 meters high and 2.5 meters thick; seven of its eight square towers doubled as storehouses (oil and grain jars were found in them), and within the walls were symmetrical barracks along arcaded streets, the commandant's baths, and a chapel. Beneath the Byzantine level was found a Severan sanctuary, with embellishments, dated by an inscription in 213. In it three temples shared a podium; there were two porticoes, and a marble-lined pool (27 by 7 meters, and 1.7 deep), with, originally, a bronze balustrade and a colonnaded garden. Colossal statues of Serapis and Saturn were found here; also dedications to Diana Augusta and to the Dea Africa, the latter with an elephant-mask headdress, a military standard, a cornucopia, and a lion. The inscription calls the sanctuary Aqua Septimiana Felix, obviously a sacred (and therapeutic) spring, whose waters Septimius Severus himself may have taken. Three hundred meters further southwest was a vast Christian necropolis containing ten thousand tombs and two chapels, one built about 645, on the eve of the Arab conquest, by the Byzantine patrician Gregory.

The western suburbs included artisans' quarters (with vats and kilns) and luxury houses. Off the southwest corner of the original grid, and facing obliquely toward the forum, rose the capitolium (fifty-three by twenty-three meters), on a podium thirty-eight steps high; its Corinthian columns were fourteen meters tall. Its precinct measured ninety by sixty-two meters. One hundred thirty meters behind the capitolium to the west (visible in the air photographs) was a unique complex, the Donatist quarter, the seat in the late fourth century of that "mitred bandit," the schismatic bishop Optatus, *bête noire* of Saint Augustine. Optatus and his movement will be discussed in the next chapter. Here we limit ourselves to describing his headquarters, which may be not unfairly called a great monastery. It contained Optatus' cathedral, preceded by an atrium, and identified by a mosaic inscription naming the bishop and ending QVANTA LAVS NOMINI EIVS, "how great the praise to his name." In the nave was buried a much-revered saint: could it have been Optatus himself? At right angles to the cathedral was a chapel; adjoining it, rooms opened onto a peristyle. The complex includes apsidal rooms, a dining room, and the bishop's own house, identified as such by the inscription, and a baptistery with a hexagonal font embellished with delicate floral mosaics in the carpet-like pattern characteristic of Timgad. The area yielded some engraving on glass, now in the Algiers Museum, that showed Christ curing the man born blind, and Isaac saved from sacrifice.

A walk northward along the avenue that passes in front of the capitolium brings the visitor to Sertius' market, a Severan building whose seven shops arranged in a semicircle face a rectangular portico and a set of six more conventional stalls, these with fixed counters so that the clerk had to crawl under them to serve his customers. The Sertii, man and wife, did not suffer from false modesty—and perhaps not from true, either: statues of each adorned the building their philanthropic vanity provided. Off the market's northwest corner was a cloth market, a smaller building from the reigns of Valentinian and Valens (364–367). Across the porticoed Lambaesis road from Sertius' market is the little temple to the Genius of the Colony, dedicated in 169 at a cost of 64,500 sesterces by a patron who was a great builder (he also sponsored the East Baths and the theater). The emperor Commodus had him murdered and his name chiseled out of inscriptions—the practice known as *damnatio memoriae.*

The Lambaesis road passed under an arch of 167, a twin to the Mascula gate on the east. Two hundred meters beyond the arch is a pagan necropolis of the second century, with cremation burials. The road emerged from the city proper through Timgad's most famous monument, the Arch "of Trajan" (fig. 9.3), actually built between 166 and 169. Flanking its central vehicular bay are two lower pedestrian passageways; above each are statue-niches framed by colonnettes. Pairs of tall Corinthian columns, with eagles and thunderbolts in the capitals, frame each side-arch and niche. The columns supported bowed rather than gabled pediments. The whole structure, now heavily but accurately restored, was twelve meters high.

Outside the gridded area, off its northwest corner—matching in size the capitolium precinct to the southwest—was another elaborate Christian complex, this time presumably orthodox: a church (thirty-nine by seventeen meters), baptistery, and courtyard (thirty-three by eighteen meters), all in a poor technique of late date. Within the gridded area in the northwest quadrant the House of Julius Januarius, elegant enough to have its own private baths, was in Byzantine times made over into a religious complex, with burials in the atrium, a small (twelve by ten meters) chapel with nave and aisles, and a baptistery in the next block.

Outside the grid to the north were two bath complexes. The smaller, the Philadelphus Baths, is so called from the name at the top of a mosaic of 220–230, now in the museum, where a panel within an elaborate floral frame shows Jupiter, disguised as a satyr, with a glint in his eye, making advances to the almost naked nymph Antiope, who waves coyly

FIGURE 9.3 *Timgad, arch,* A.D. 166–169

at him and carries—apparently ready for anything—a tambourine. The third-century North Baths, the city's largest, measure eighty by sixty-five meters, and are conventionally symmetrical, like those of Caracalla in Rome from which they derive. This is Timgad's only brick-revetted building.

Finally, there are the treasures now collected in the museum, a little gem, especially noteworthy for its mosaics. From a house in the block between the forum and the library comes a Triumph of Venus, Hadrianic or Severan, with a very elaborate floral surround. From one of the baths, appropriately, comes a mosaic of the hunter Actaeon surprising Diana, goddess of the hunt, as she bathes; in punishment (not shown) he was turned into a stag, and torn to pieces by his own hounds. The mosaics, here as elsewhere, range in date over five hundred years, representing an even wider range of taste, a Frenchwoman remarks, than Garnier's Opéra with a ceiling by Chagall. In front of the museum a large group of Ba'al-Saturn stelae gives evidence of native beliefs, as does a temple to Ba'al-Saturn, of Severan date, which lies one hundred meters off the main road to Batna, beyond the hotel. It measures forty-eight by twenty-two meters, and stands, triple-celled, at the back of a large porticoed court containing a monumental altar. It serves to remind us how thin, even in Timgad, was the veneer of Romanization; a deep pulse of native inspiration beat beneath the banality that it is so easy to think of as at the heart of Roman provincial life.

Civilian centers at Timgad and northward flourished because they were guarded by the Limes, or Fossatum Africae, farther south—a zone of protection in depth, taking advantage of natural obstacles, or in default of these, a man-made ditch, with a fortified road network running behind—a system well known in other parts of the empire, from Britain (Hadrian's Wall) to Syria (a desert limes very like the one we are concerned with here; see also *RoR*, figs. 3.5, 4.1, and 4.15, and *DSS*, fig. 5.1). Recent, usually Marxist commentators have argued that imperialist interests used the Limes to intervene in local life, impose a stringent New Order, increase restraints, raise the tax base, restrict freedom of movement, and set up concentration camps for dissenters. On this analysis, granting of municipal status means occupation of land, which invariably leads to native uprisings. To Jean Baradez, a French army officer who used air photography to study 750 kilometers of the Algerian Limes, its functions seemed less restrictive. He points out how it served the needs of the military, the civil administration, colonizing, and irrigating; how it provided a buffer between Roman and barbarian, a static obstacle, with no gaps in the watch and alarm system, which protected a dense population. Those who lived peacefully inside it—the *limitanei*—had a vested interest in defending it. It created oases of culture—and prosperity—in the desert, and made possible the peaceful existence of splendid cities without walls behind its protective line.

The Limes and the road network went closely together. We have seen that the road from Tacapae to Capsa in Tunisia dates from as early as A.D. 14. The Flavians established a line that made it possible for colonies (for example, Cuicul, Sitifis) to be founded under Nerva. Trajan fortified this line, Hadrian consolidated it, and successive emperors, including especially Septimius Severus, called in his own propaganda PROPAGATOR IMPERII,[1] and Diocletian, added to and strengthened it. Baradez's air survey covers it from Capsa westward to Auzia (see map, fig. 9.4). The line ran nearly straight west through Ad Maiores (Négrine) and Thabudeos (Thouda), then southwest to Gemellae (M'Lili), with a Severan extension another 175 kilometers further south to Castellum Dimmidi (Messaad). Under Hadrian, however, the line was made to run northward from Gemellae to Thubunae (Tobna) and Zaraï (Zéraïa), then west again to Auzia (formerly Aumale), Rapidum, and Thanaramusa (Berrouaghia); thence (fig. 9.5) southwest by stages to Columnata (Sidi Hosni, formerly Waldeck-Rousseau), Tiaret, Cohors Breucorum (Takhemaret), Ala Miliaria (Beniane), Altava (Ouled Mimoun, formerly Lamoricière), Pomaria (Tlemcen), and Numerus Syrorum (Marnia). The question whether the Limes continued onward into Mauretania Tingitana is controversial; it would seem to have been a military necessity, but archaeological evidence is thus far lacking. The best-informed authority, Pierre Salama, points out that between Marnia and the Taza pass in Morocco it is possible to travel on the plain without a road.

Along the eastern Limes, almost nothing is visible on the ground except in a raking light. Baradez notes that in two days sand can cover a meter-high truckload of rails under a six-meter dune. However, the stretch for forty kilometers east of Thubunae is typically rich in Roman remains:

1. The historian Herodian, Severus' contemporary, describes him as enterprising, experienced, violent, hard-working, keen in planning and execution. A French historian (Gautier) pictures him "munching dates on the Imperial throne." Marxist historians have criticized his stamping out pockets of resistance, extending the area of Roman domination, and building forts.

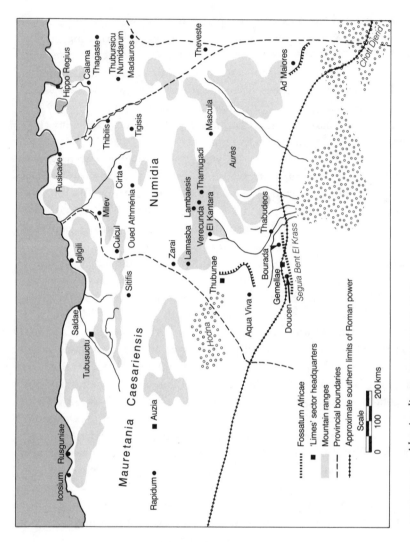

FIGURE 9.4 *Algerian limes, eastern part, map*

two *fossata* (defensive ditches with earthworks), a *castrum* (camp), thirty blockhouses, a hundred kilometers of road, irrigation works, retaining walls, farms, olive oil presses, villages. The blockhouses, sited below the skyline to conceal them from possible enemies, needed outposts for observation; one two-kilometer stretch has two blockhouses and twenty-one watchtowers. South of Gemellae the fossatum, there called the Seguia bent el-Krass, runs for fifty kilometers east and west; the natives believe it continues eastward all the way to Mecca. Bourada, about thirty kilometers east, is Constantinian (after 334). At Doucen, thirty-two kilometers west of Gemellae, there are *castella* that protected estates of the time of Gordian III (238–244), attested by inscriptions.

An inscription dates Gemellae as Hadrianic (126/27). As a military architect, Hadrian was, as Baradez remarks, a veritable Vauban. The camp, surrounded by wall and ditch, measures 150 by 190 meters; it would hold some thirteen hundred men. Its wall was three meters thick, presenting a sheer vertical face on its Sahara side; its towers projected inward, two at each rounded corner, others every thirty meters. Its headquarters building measured thirty-six by forty-five meters; like that of Lambaesis, it had its armory, shrine for the standards, inner court, and offices. On the walls were three layers of stucco, which once bore frescoes portraying palm trees, flower baskets, columns with vine leaves and grapes, a horse and rider. There are statue bases—of Hadrian, Pertinax (who ruled for three months in A.D. 193), Severus, and Gordian III. On an inscription the name of the Legio III Augusta is chiseled out, a token of its disgrace for having supported Gordian's enemies. But an altar dedicated to Military Discipline commemorates its return fifteen years later. Canabae in a two-kilometer circuit surround the town; they are walled, with towers and gates, an amphitheater (whose arena measures fifty-two by seventy-two meters), baths, and temples.

Ad Maiores, 5 kilometers south of Négrine oasis, 180 kilometers east of Gemellae, well on the way to Capsa, is a Trajanic desert fortress of A.D. 105, measuring 170 by 110 meters, with a capacity of about eight hundred men. It had four gates and four square corner towers (fig. 9.6). Traces of the canabae are visible outside the camp walls; a kilometer north of the oasis, in a palm grove, are the remains of a villa with an apsidal room, hexagonal pool, and a mosaic (now destroyed), with the word FLAVIORVM repeated in a ninety-square checkerboard.

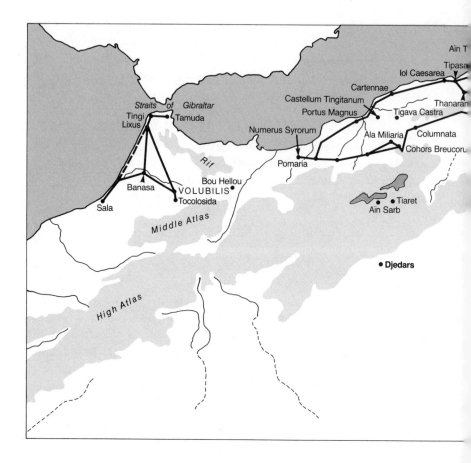

FIGURE 9.5 *Algerian limes, western part, map*

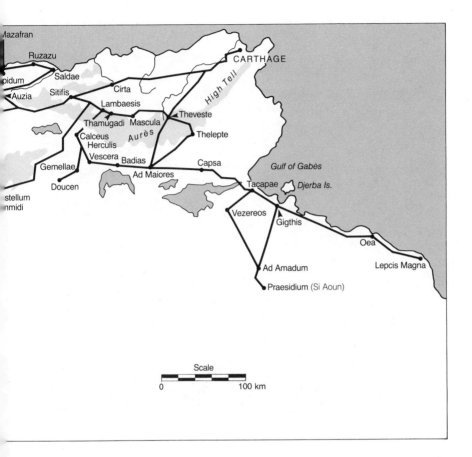

Mazafran
Ruzazu
pidum
Saldae
Auzia
Sitifis
Cirta
CARTHAGE
High Tell
Lambaesis
Theveste
Thamugadi Mascula
Aurès
Calceus
Herculis
Thelepte
Vescera
Gemellae
Badias
Capsa
Gulf of Gabès
Doucen
Ad Maiores
Tacapae
Djerba Is.
stellum
midi
Vezereos
Gigthis
Oea
Ad Amadum
Lepcis Magna
Praesidium (Si Aoun)

Scale

0   100 km

FIGURE 9.6 *Ad Maiores, desert camp,* A.D. *105, air view*

Aqua Viva, thirty-five kilometers southwest of Thubunae, is a Dio-cletianic fortress dated 303 by an inscription that calls it a *centenarium*, though being eighty-five meters square, it would have held 330 men. Tombs show that it survived into the fourth or fifth century, and burials of women and children suggest that it was defended by limitanei, who lived with their families on fortified farms.

A military road from Aqua Viva led some two hundred kilometers southwest to Castellum Dimmidi (Messaad), Rome's deepest outpost in the Algerian Sahara. It is four hundred kilometers south of Algiers, but Algeria's southern border is a journey of a further seventeen hundred kilometers. The half-hectare fort was designed for five hundred cavalry. Its headquarters building dates from 198, and the Legio III Augusta occupied it until its disgrace in 238; a roster of A.D. 225 held a hundred names, including a bookkeeper, stonemason, orderly, and veterinarian. The detachment defended itself with ballista balls the size of oranges. In the unrest of 235–238 the camp was set on fire and evacuated. The detachment of Palmyrenes, skilled in desert warfare, that succeeded the legion set up its own chapel with bronze libation vessels like half-pint beer mugs, and frescoes strongly resembling those from Dura-Europos on the Euphrates (*GSS*, fig. 8.24). They worshiped Malagbel, equated with Mercury. The most interesting fresco shows two figures, one with a brick-red face, short red beard, purple-striped white overgarment, gray-blue tunic, and a wide red leather belt; the other wears a long purple silk garment and white shoes with a purple binding, a pitcher in his left hand. Both are putting pinches of incense into a burner set between them. The one is a centurion, the other a Palmyrene high priest—it is a scene from home. The Palmyrene detachment did not long survive the troubles of 238; its withdrawal marks the first recoil before the barbarian in this part of the empire, rationalized as "shortening the front."

Once the established Limes had controlled or kept out the nomads, hydraulic works could be undertaken, necessary because the mean annual rainfall was only 250 millimeters. Installations took three forms: terrace walls, against erosion; reservoirs and dams, for retention; canals, for channeling to centuriated farms. The result was oases, in one case, near El Kantara, twenty times the present size. Thanks to an inscription from Lamasba, thirty-five kilometers northwest of Lambaesis, dating from Elagabalus' reign (218–225), we know something about how water supply was controlled and distributed there and then. The inscription gives a list of fields, owners (the majority with naturalized African names like Rogatianus, Africanus, Rogatus, Felix, Exspectatus, Saturninus, Victor, Fortunatus), and the length of time each is entitled to water. It is distributed from a dam to proprietors above and below its water level; those below get, in the winter months, sixty-five to seventy units an hour; those above, forty-one to forty-two. What it amounts to is rationing, imposed and regulated by local magistrates and voluntarily accepted by the farmers. Since it was organized locally and was not exclusive—the water went to eighty-nine recipients—the rationing probably did not generate social and political tensions.

An inscription of A.D. 150, found at Lambaesis but now in Bejaia (formerly Bougie, ancient Saldae) on the coast 135 kilometers northwest of Lamasba, shows the kind of engineering work performed under such security as the Limes provided—and also how the Romans rectified mistakes. It has to do with a tunnel, part of an aqueduct twenty-one kilometers long that fed Saldae from the west. The tunnel's course—nearly five hundred meters—had gone awry, because it had been begun from both ends, and instead of meeting, the two galleries diverged. The expert surveyor called in to mend matters fell among brigands who wounded and stripped him. He escaped, and found the army engineers "bewailing" the tunnel. Entrusting the work, referred to in another inscription as an "incredibilis labor," to the rivalry between some sailors and some Alpine troops, he finished it satisfactorily, and was mentioned in despatches as "indispensable, zealous, and dependable." The inscription bears, above the text, the heads in relief of three allegorical females, labeled PATIENTIA, VIRTVS, SPES.[2] This tunnel is only one of the "projects fit for omnipotence," as Ramsay MacMullen calls them, executed by the army; after all, its accomplishments included whole colonies—Timgad, its neighbor Verecunda (Marcouna), just east of Lambaesis, Theveste (Tébessa, to be discussed in chapter 10)—and innumerable bridges, harbors, roads, fora, porticoes, and works of slum clearance.

The inscription now at Saldae may be interpreted to suggest that nomad "brigands" sometimes slipped through the Limes net. This was not difficult, since 150-meter gaps were left at intervals as customs posts for the passage of caravans. One of the points of passage was Zaraï (Zéraïa, thirty kilometers northwest of Lamasba), where in 1858 an illuminating list of tariff rates (Severan, dated at 202)[3] turned up, engraved on stone. A selection of the facts should prove illuminating. The table on p. 249 reproduces the list in a somewhat modernized form, giving the original rates in sesterces (s) and denarii (d). To try to give modern equivalents amid inflation is risky, but a rough approximation is one denarius to twenty cents or one gold franc uninflated. The sesterce is worth a quarter as much. The price of wine works out at thirty cents a liter. (In Rome in 1950 a liter of Frascati cost twenty-two cents.) Clearly the tariff was not protective in intent: the rate never exceeds 3.75 percent. The parity in value among slaves, horses and mules is interesting; also the comparatively low rate on such luxury items as a purple cloak. Since Zaraï is in

2. An inscription from Saldae, dated 253 or 289, mentions a paramilitary corps (*iuvenes*, like those at Mactar) loyal to Jupiter and the *gens Maura*, that is, having a foot in each world, Roman and indigenous.
3. At this date the two Mauretanias were united under one procurator—a sign of emergency.

Severan Tariff Rates from Zaraï

Item	Tariff	Total Value
Per head		
Slave	1.5d*	500d
Horse, mare	1.5d	500d
Mule, she mule	1.5d	500d
Ass, cow, or bull	.5d	133.3d
Pig	1.0s*	66.6d
Suckling pig	.5s	33.3d
Sheep, goat	1.0s	66.6d
Kid, lamb	.5s	33.3d
Imported clothing		
Dinner mantle	1.5d	75d
Tunic	1.5d	75d
Blanket or counterpane	.5d	25d
Purple cloak	.5d	50d
Hides		
Hide, dressed	.5d	25d
Hide, with hair	.5s	25d
Sheepskin or goatskin	.5s	25d
Coarse hides, per cwt.	.5d	25d
Glue (birdlime?) per 10 lb.	.5s	25d
Sponges, per 10 lb.	.5s	25d
Miscellaneous		
Wine or garum, per amphora	1.0s	40s
Dates, per cwt.	.5d	80s
Figs, per cwt.	[text lost]	
Peas, per 10 modii (pecks)	[text lost]	
Nuts, per 10 modii	[text lost]	
Resin, pitch, or alum, per cwt.	[text lost]	
Iron, [text lost—other metals]	[text lost]	

* d = denarii
  s = sesterces

pastureland, on the transhumance route, cattle and their products are significant items. Alum was used in tanning. The dates would have come from Chott Djerid, in south Tunisia, the purple from Djerba Island, the lotus eaters' land, off the Tunisian coast. In general the exchange is between the undeveloped and the developed parts of Africa. The tariff documents relations between Berbers and Romans; the former found it worthwhile on the whole to keep on good terms with the Romans, for the sake of access to luxury goods. The inscription was set up at the departure of a cohort. It was not that it actually collected the money; that would have been done by the procurator's revenue men. The point probably was that the soldiers were exempt from tariff, and their departure made the previous schedule obsolete.

The western part of the Limes developed comparatively early: the camp at Rapidum (Sour Djouab, thirty kilometers west of Auzia,[4] sixty-five kilometers south of Algiers), is Hadrianic, of playing-card shape, with a praetorium like (and earlier than) Lambaesis'. West and south of the camp there grew up canabae, fifteen hectares in extent, divided by walls into three sections, which may suggest segregation of natives from Roman soldiers. The exterior walls, built in 167 by soldiers and natives in collaboration, were destroyed in the mid–third century (a coin hoard stops with Gallienus, 253–268), but restored soon after, under Diocletian (284–305). Within the camp were baths (two sets thrown into one, for civilian use), a granary with damp-proof floor, and an unusual ironclad north gate. The town had a grid of streets, courtyard houses, a capitolium, and a temple of Ceres; a Severan relief from here portrays Africa with elephant-trunk-and-tusks headdress, a lion to symbolize land and a Triton for water, and also a horn of plenty and wheat-ears. Comparison with Tellus/Italia on Augustus' Altar of Peace in Rome (MSS, fig. 6.14) is inevitable. Outside to the northeast lies a temple to Saturn-Caelestis (Punic Ba'al-Tanit). To the west and north were necropoleis. Milestones of emperors from Severus Alexander through Aurelian (270–275) show that roads were kept up through the troubled times of the third century.

One hundred and sixty kilometers farther west, Tigava Castra (north

4. An inscription from Auzia records a revolt of the Baquates, "desperatissima turba et factio," in 227 (reign of Severus Alexander).

of El Attaf, formerly Wattignies), a Limes camp of 167/68, the same year
as the circuit wall of Rapidum's canabae, measures 111 by 147 meters,
which would comfortably house a detachment of five hundred; it has
semicircular corner towers, off which ballista balls would ricochet, and a
main gate with a dual carriageway. There is the usual praetorium, also
an aqueduct and extramural baths. At Tigava municipium, fifteen kilometers east, a black basalt head of a boy has been identified as Juba II.
An inscription, in execrable Latin, shows, though dated A.D. 354, by a
reminiscence of the *Aeneid*, that a pious son who here commemorates his
mother had some contact with Vergil at school.

Much farther west, only seventy-five miles from the Moroccan border,
the Severan camp (of 201) of Altava (Ouled Mimoun, formerly Lamoricière) lies in a handsome setting in a well-watered plain, with a view of
distant saw-toothed mountains. It controlled a crossroads that invading
nomads might threaten. In Arabic it is called Hadjar Roum, "the Roman
stones," but these, though rich, are inscriptions, not part of buildings, for
the buildings were destroyed by road-building, the modern village, and
the railway, whose line bisects the Roman camp—the station overlies the
praetorium. The vast camp (370 by 317 meters) would have housed a
legion. Within the walls little can be discerned but the cardo, a mosaic
floor, and some oil presses. But Diocletian did not abandon the province
of Caesariensis, for an Altava inscription mentions a wall of 349/50,
built by the local authority under promise of tax remission. As late as
509 one Masuna, describing himself as "king of the Mauretanian tribes
and of the Romans," ordered a castrum built. Inscriptions, now mostly
in the Oran museum, are Altava's richest harvest, especially a series of
epitaphs, valuable because precisely dated, ranging from 302 to 599.
They make it clear, from the names (Berber, like Sammac, Mazio; or
Romanized, like Donatus, Felix, Fortunatus, Victor), that Romanization
was very superficial here, on this defense highway, in the zone under
surveillance, where troops had to be constantly on the *qui vive*—in the
fifth century, more against Berbers than against Vandals. An epitaph of
329 shows that Altava was then run on modified Roman lines. Its subject, one Donatus, was a princeps, head of the *decemprimi*, an in-group
of ten men who outranked the town councilors and ran the town; this
man's family was long prominent, from 250 to 494. Though Altava had
commercial advantages, life was not idyllic: one epitaph is of a man who
died "gladio percussus a barbaris"—run through by a barbarian sword.
The inhabitants worshiped both Roman and native gods: Disciplina Mili-

taris, but also the Di Mauri. From the early fourth century onwards, there were Christians, with a basilica, as yet unexcavated, that contained a martyr's memorial.

The Limes would have been impracticable without the road network. The roads served political and commercial as well as military needs, and were a boon to religious pilgrims; they also contributed to the security in which peaceful sedentary life might flourish. The roads helped to make the Romans masters everywhere, without which mastery the settled provincials could be secure nowhere. The roads isolated and encircled the fastnesses of mountain tribes and facilitated patrol against the camel-mounted nomads. The network was a great tactical apparatus which, as we saw, was kept up, and its dependent settlements extended, right through the third-century crisis. The network contributed largely to the peaceful growth of the several hundred colonies and municipalities known in Africa by the end of that century. Antiimperialists stress how extension of the Limes and the road network sparked revolt; apologists, how it fostered settled urban and agricultural life. The Limes and the roads follow the line of 400 millimeter rainfall, which with the aid of irrigation made cultivation possible over a wider area than in Algeria today. The roads connected water holes; they also, of course, had their military importance: the straight Roman road that ran along the thousand-meter contour from Sitifis to Auzia was used by the French for a visual (semaphore) telegraph in 1850–51. For an arterial road to run straight through a town might involve delay for the traveler and dangerous traffic for the town; thus, like a modern motorway, the main road bypassed Thibilis and Calama.

The structure of highways shows the Roman genius as road engineers. The main Carthage-Theveste artery was six to seven meters wide; the minimum width of a Roman road in Africa was four meters, to allow the passage abreast of two wagons of 1.45 meter gauge. Our roads are elastic; Roman roads were thick, the main ones up to five layers (eighty centimeters), on a bed of sand, slabs, and mortar, then fine gravel, then crushed stone, finally the cemented stone pavement on which traffic rolled. In the Aurès Mountains the practical-minded Romans placed by the roadsides snow markers up to fifty centimeters high. But this seemingly sophisticated technology had its failings. Apuleius of Madauros records (*Florida* 21) the inconvenience of travel by wagon: the nuisance of baggage, the clumsy vehicle, the balky axles, the jolting over ruts, boulders, and jutting roots; the washouts, the steep grades. Indeed, ordinary African roads were so casually made that we know more about them from milestones than from roadbeds. In the Cirta confederation, abutters were allowed, under Antoninus Pius, to levy tolls for road upkeep. Besides, there was the expense of building bridges, draining swamps, reinforcing embankments. At oases, crossroads, and watchtowers, there were inns—every thirty or forty kilometers a *mansio*, with stable, forge, and granary; every ten or twelve, a *mutatio* (post-house, for changing horses). Some picturesque inn-names survive: the sign of the Cock, the Ostrich, the Dragon, the Wheel, the Birds, the Partridge. The frequenters of these inns included businessmen, journeymen, sculptors, wandering scholars, hypochondriacs (on their way to spas), tourists (attracted by theaters), beggars, pilgrims. Monastery hospitality sprang up because the Church did not approve of secular inns. Thus the road network, solid evidence of the logical, skilful, rigorous, ambitious Roman mind, unified and consolidated empire; the amount of injustice this involved to those who resisted Romanization we shall try to assess in the final chapter.

We conclude this section by describing in chronological order seven sites selected for their unusual significance. First, Madauros (M'daourouch), on a main Roman highway ninety kilometers south of Hippo. Though a Flavian foundation, Madauros is chiefly famous as the birthplace, ca. 123, of the rhetorician and novelist Lucius Apuleius, whom we have met just above, and elsewhere. Though he has been accurately—and pitilessly—described (by Gsell) as "superficial, colorful, excessive, disordered, intemperate, and redundant," his fellow citizens were proud of him, describing him, though with little justification, in a surviving inscription, as a "Platonic philosopher" as well as an ornament to the community. Apuleius' father was rich; he left an estate of 2 million sesterces. Another nabob gave 375,000 to build the theater (seen incorporated into the Byzantine fortress in the air photograph, fig. 9.7), memorializing in the process himself, his father, mother, grandfather, and three cousins. The theater, Severan in date, though small, was costly because the cavea, being on a downslope, had to be supported on expensive vaults. It was only thirty-three meters wide, the stage only twenty, the seating capacity twelve hundred. The squarish forum (thirty-two by twenty-seven meters) adjoined the theater on the southeast, and served as

FIGURE 9.7 *Madauros (Flavian foundation), air view*

its portico. It was built on fill, and required retaining walls. Its limestone pavement was patched in the third century with inscriptions in reuse; the site yielded eight hundred, mostly epitaphs, in bad Latin and limping verse. They mention more buildings than have been found, including four monumental arches. They boast, perhaps exaggeratedly, of unusual longevity; the average life span was 52.2 years, and one bishop lived to be 86.

North of the forum and west of the theater was a small (twenty by eight meters) civil basilica; on the forum's west side, the little curia (16.5 by 6.5 meters) with U-shaped seating arrangement. An adjoining temple, perhaps of Mars, is dated in the late empire. An impressive Byzantine fortress, dominant in the air photograph, consumed at a single bite a quarter of the forum. It is an admirable ruin. Its reused stones (many inscriptions upside down) have acquired a golden patina. Its wall rises in places ten meters high. An inscription, in Latin and Greek, of A.D. 534–536, over the entrance arch, mentions Justinian, his empress Theodora, and his viceroy (*magister militum*, praetorian prefect) for North Africa, Solomon. One hundred fifty meters northeast of the fortress are two baths, small (thirty by thirty-four meters) for winter, large (thirty-nine by forty-one meters) for summer; the latter's latrines, in the east apse, were open to the sky and unusable in inclement weather. The small baths had four large windows on their south side, to catch the winter sunshine, as at Ostia (*MSS,* 257–258). Carefully built, the baths are probably Severan. They were repaired between 361 and 364, in and just after Julian the Apostate's reign, and again in 407/408; thereafter they were allowed to deteriorate into a slum, its hovels patched with inscriptions in reuse. One stone has Julian's name chiseled out—his attempted revival of paganism did not sit well with Christian bureaucrats.

Excavation has revealed two churches, one in the southeast corner of the site, dated about 450; the other, two hundred meters northwest of the Byzantine fort, yielded the epitaph of the long-lived bishop mentioned above, who was a Catholic delegate, from Donatist country, to the Council of Carthage in 411. Madauros had, however, its quota of mid–fourth-century Donatist martyrs, with names like Namphano, Miggin, Saname. The accusations against them, though vague—*nefanda facinora,* "unmentionable behavior"—suggest that they belonged to the hated schism; perhaps even to its terrorist fringe, the Circumcellions, to be discussed further in the next chapter. Christian Madauros was enough of an intellectual center to attract the young Augustine to school here, before 370, and before he went to Carthage. But it had been a notoriously pagan community. Its capitolium, referred to in an inscription, has not been found, but there are many Saturn stelae and references to many non-Roman gods with Roman disguises: Caelestis, the Cereres, Liber Pater, Mercury, Hercules (Melqart), Aesculapius (Eshmoun), Venus. The art is banal, the surviving statues of an honest mediocrity, typically "official," this too an aspect of half-hearted Romanization.

Calama (Guelma), seventy-four kilometers south-southwest of Hippo, is, like Madauros, chiefly important for its association with a famous man, this time M. Cornelius Fronto (100–160), who, though born in and patron of Cirta, was also patron of Calama, before 143. Educated, like Apuleius and Augustine, in Carthage and resident most of his life in Rome, where Antoninus Pius made him tutor to the young Marcus Aurelius, he could nevertheless express nostalgia for the *laetissimum caelum,* the sunny skies, of his homeland. His letters, discovered in 1815, show him without false front, among students, friends, and family; ill with gout, generally hypochondriac, self-centered; in style highly mannered and archaistic. His correspondents are people in or on their way to power from all over the Roman world—Italy, Paphlagonia, Baalbek, Ephesus, Cirta, Arles. Rhetoric is the open sesame to advancement. The

letters to his imperial charge, dated 139–165, show that they did not really get on; the young prince found the schoolmaster too finicky. Fronto may be taken as typical of the growing number of Africans in the Roman Senate—under Hadrian, 16.2 percent; under Pius, 26.8; under Marcus, 30.5; under Commodus 31.4, then decline under the Severans, to an average of 26.2 percent. African equestrians in the imperial service increased from 15.5 percent under Trajan to 38.8 percent under the last two Severi, with slight declines from A.D. 161 to 217. It was an African knight, from Thaenae in Proconsularis, who murdered Commodus and put Pertinax on the throne.

The town of which Fronto was patron had been a municipium since Trajan. Though it had baths, and a Byzantine fort (278 by 219 meters, with thirteen towers), its most conspicuous surviving monument is its theater, which cost 400,000 sesterces. Larger than Madauros', it is fifty-eight meters wide, with twenty-two rows of seats. Between 1902 and 1918 it was so heavily reconstructed as to be virtually rebuilt; fig. 9.8 shows the new stage building as a curiosity. The statue to the right is of Neptune, and comes from Thubursicu Numidarum. Others from there, and from Calama, Thibilis, and Madauros are kept in the small museum made out of the theater's greenroom. One, of a schoolboy, is called, with more sentiment than scholarship, "The Young Saint Augustine"; there

FIGURE 9.8 *Calama, theater, early third century* A.D., *restoration*

are the ubiquitous Saturn stelae and (again from Thubursicu) a mosaic of Amphitrite in cortège. A spectacular postwar find, of 1953, was a hoard of 7,499 Roman coins; they stop in 257 and are, as usual, a sign of local unrest.

Our next site, Oued-Athménia, a rich working villa forty kilometers west of Cirta, will serve as a symbol of the prosperity the Limes allowed to Numidia. It is chiefly noteworthy for its fifteen rooms of mosaics, eight hundred square meters of them, which at the Paris Exposition Universelle of 1855 won a gold medal. The villa has built-in baths; from their apsidal caldarium comes a mosaic showing six named horses in a stable, with saddle blankets. The owner was a lover of horseflesh, and his stables, seventy meters square, with forty-three troughs on one side, are among the largest known from the classical world. One horse, Actus, is apostrophized in verse: "unus es, ut mons exultas" (You're one of a kind, you loom up like a mountain). Of another, Polydoxus, is written, "Vincas non vincas, te amamus" (Win or lose, we love you). Others are named Pullentianus, Delicatus, Scholasticus, Titas. A charioteer, the Moor Crescens, in 115 had won 47 firsts, 130 seconds, and 111 thirds, earning over 1.5 million sesterces. In an adjoining room we see the lady of the manor in her pleasure garden (labeled "Philosophical Area"), with armchair and fan; a slave has her pet dog on a leash, and shades her mistress with a parasol. An inscription from nearby Kharba records the conventional qualities expected of a matron: FIDEM SERVAVIT, EXIBVIT PVDICITIAM, COLVIT MARITVM, TOLERAVIT PAVPERTATEM, FILIOS MONVIT BENE—"She kept her plighted troth, was a model of chastity, cherished her husband, bore up under poverty, gave her children good advice." In a labeled "Hunting Area" a brace of hounds chase three gazelles in a park. Another area is the corral (PECVARI LOCVS). The middle room of the central suite of the baths, the frigidarium, has a mosaic showing the proprietor, Pompeianus, mounted, hunting gazelles, with two dogs, Fidelis and Castus; his beaters are Liber and Diaz. Also represented was (the mosaic is now destroyed) the house, with one to three-story outbuildings and a tower. In rooms flanking the frigidarium, Nereids, seminude, with colored cloaks, pearl necklaces, bracelets, and anklets—and one with a parasol—recline on couches. These in the late 1920s were in the storerooms of the Trocadéro in Paris. Coins of Commodus and Caracalla date the complex as Antonine-Severan. In the early fourth century the house was sacked, and squatters built fires on the mosaic floors.

Our fourth site, Sitifis (Sétif) belongs in this chapter because, though founded as a colony under Nerva, it flourished in the high empire. It lies at 1,116 meters above sea level, 110 kilometers west of Cirta and 35 southeast of its sister Nervan colony, Cuicul. Excavations begun in 1959 have continued despite the breach in relations between Algeria and France. Important evidence emerges for Sitifis in the second and third centuries, including a temple, a gridded town plan, and a necropolis east of the old French military quarter, now transformed into an archaeological park; the burials, east of the late Roman city wall, were found in digging a new swimming pool. Most of the bodies were inhumed, not cremated; cremation in Africa became much rarer in the third century, and almost disappeared in the fourth. They were buried in a flexed position, which is not Roman. Names like Felix, Fortunatus, and Saturninus betray African origins. Motifs from Saturn worship include the ladder, the fat-tailed sacrificial ram, the seven planets, the moon and the sun. In 1967, 360 new tombs were discovered; 3,500 finds are on display in the site museum. Many of the inscriptions bear a precise date. Individual longevity, if the stones are to be believed, is remarkable—one man died at 110—but the average is only 38.6 years.

In the territorium of Sitifis, a revolt in Alexander Severus' reign prompted the rebuilding of a number of castella. When Diocletian reorganized the empire, Sitifis became the capital of Mauretania Sitifensis, carved out of the eastern part of Caesariensis. There was a Jewish colony, date uncertain. Evidence for Christianity begins about 350; Augustine in a sermon takes note of an earthquake there. But the city recovered, and built a new quarter, with circus (five hundred by eighty meters), restored amphitheater, baths that yielded a mosaic of the Toilet of Venus, and in 1971, a Triumph of Bacchus; also a temple of Magna Mater, the settling basin of an aqueduct, and two Christian basilicas at right angles to one another, dated 375–400—the smaller has a martyr's burial, and may be Donatist. The late fourth century was important for African cities; that phase at Sitifis is more important than that of the high empire. And a gold solidus of the Byzantine emperor Zeno (474–91) is tenuous evidence of survival through the Vandal occupation. There is a Byzantine citadel, probably built over the Roman forum.

Mascula (Khenchela), halfway between Theveste and Lambaesis, is important for the evidence it gives for Berber continuity and Roman provincial luxury. It was in the territory of the Musulamii, a hardy lot— an inscription records in verse a man of 83 who went haring with the hounds. Their holy place, the Medracen, is only seventy-five kilometers west-northwest. Its inscriptions show indigenous names; it yielded Numidian coins; there are Saturn stelae, one of an infant consecrated to the god. There are Christian catacombs. In Christian times it was Donatist; Donatism has been argued to be an aspect of Berber continuity. But the Romans recognized the strategic importance of the place: seven roads radiate from here, and Aquae Flavianae was settled before Mascula became a municipium, in Severan times or earlier; its "tribe" (traditional Roman voting district) was the Papiria, the same as Trajan's. There is evidence of a shrine of Mithras, a favorite god of the soldiers, as we have seen. A recent discovery (1960) is a villa as sumptuous as the one at Oued Athménia, with fifteen mosaic floors, including the familiar Triumph of the Marine Venus, and a charioteer riding in triumph amid a shower of roses.

Portus Magnus (Bettioua, formerly St.-Leu) flourished in Severan times; it is our farthest west Algerian coastal site. It lies forty kilometers east of Oran, and was the Oran of antiquity. Like the upper city of Oran, it lies high above the sea, which is 600 to 800 meters away from the cliff on which it perches. It was a Punic port of call, and its pottery shows close connections with Spain. In order to conserve it, its first excavator, Mme. Vincent, bought the forty-hectare site outright. Its forum (fifty by forty meters) has economical stuccoed columns, as at Sabratha, and a sea view, a cryptoporticus, and huge cisterns; on its west side lies a small curia (twenty by eight meters), and 120 meters farther west a capitolium approached by a monumental stair, where an inscription mentions a temple to Juno Regina (perhaps Tanit). Hollow tile walls that could be heated show that there were public baths; a terraced, split-level peristyle villa on the decumanus had private ones, and also an elaborate late third-century mosaic, now in the Oran Museum. Its four registers show refreshingly original scenes: Hercules pinning the centaur Chiron in a wrestling match; Latona, mother-to-be of Apollo and Diana, being borne by Aquilo, the North Wind, to the island of Delos for the holy birth; Apollo and Marsyas, whom he had flayed for daring to compete with him in music; and the myth of the Cabiri, a mysterious non-Greek quartet of deities worshiped on Samothrace, especially by sailors. Pagan Portus Magnus seems to have declined after our period; there are no pagan inscriptions later than Gordian III, but a fifth-century tomb-mosaic shows a Christian praying, with a candelabra and a bird, perhaps the dove of peace.

Our last high empire site is Rusguniae (Tametfoust) at Cap Matifou, on the east side of the Bay of Algiers. Though it was an Augustan colony, as we have seen, its milestones suggest that it flourished under Elagabalus or Severus Alexander, between 218 and 235. A find, on the beach, of 273 silver sesterces ranges in date from Vespasian to Trebonian (251–253), with peaks in the reigns of Hadrian, the Antonines, the late Severans, and Gordian III. The urn containing the hoard was turned up in World War II by an American bulldozer moving gravel for the Algiers airport runway. The coins must have been buried in a panic, as is usual with hoards, though connoisseurs of revolts have not dated any at this period. The town baths yielded a mosaic of a labyrinth dated to the mid–fourth century by a coin of Constantius II (324–361). A basilica, perhaps of the Vandal period, with eleven bays and originally three naves, had these enlarged to five in Byzantine times. It was double-apsed, and yielded a mosaic of Christ the Good Shepherd. It is well to close the chapter on this note, since Christianity dominated Algeria in the last phase of the empire.

10. ALGERIA FROM THE GORDIANS
TO THE ARAB INVASION

The central fact of North African history in the late empire is the rise and fall of the Donatist schism and of its terrorist fringe, the Circumcellions. The split arose out of the persecutions (303–305) under Diocletian. Donatus and his followers held, puritanically, that those who had "lapsed" and handed over the Scriptures to imperial officials had forfeited the right to call themselves Christians. Refusing to recognize the new Catholic bishop of Carthage, they elected Donatus as his rival (313). Their precedent was the refusal of Bishop Cyprian, in the mid–third century, to reinstate apostates. Their puritanism was combined with a strong, even morbid attachment to martyrdom: "the blood of the martyrs is the seed of the Church." Their watchword was *Deo laudes*—"Praise be to God." Their adherents centered in Numidia; the question how far theirs was a social, economic, and political (nationalist) movement is controversial, though we may accept that "in some obscure corner of men's minds there was something that said 'no' to the Empire" (Markus). When the emperor Constantine's conversion, perhaps as early as 312, made the Catholic church the established state religion, the Donatists were driven still further into opposition.

The archaeological evidence for Donatism is slim, since it is rarely possible to detect from the physical remains of churches which sect they belonged to. But that Timgad had a Donatist quarter is, as we have seen, not in doubt, and the cult of martyrs at a site creates a plausible presumption that it was Donatist. Inscriptions are also informative, though not always unequivocally, and the minutes of church councils sometimes tell us which bishops were Donatist. At the Council of Carthage in 411, in which was involved the great Augustine, who never understood the depths of Donatist fanaticism, there were either 279 or 286 Catholic bishops to 284 Donatist. Despite the council's pronouncement against the schism, it survived into the seventh century; the evidence is a record, inscribed on lead, of the deposit of relics, dated 637. To the end, Donatism opposed the ideal of the establishment as expressed by the senatorial historian Dio Cassius, described by P. R. Brown as that of a "stable, centralized, sharply-graded society avoiding at all costs disorder and change." Catholicism was an ecclesiastical vested interest; Donatism was a reaction against it, but it was primarily doctrinal, not political: in the fourth century, doctrine would be more divisive than nationalism or socialism today.

Donatism has been accurately described as a chapter in the extinction of classical culture; another way of looking at it is to say it accompanies "a revival of Berber art." It is significant that the pro-pagan Julian, "the Apostate," called in an inscription from Thibilis RESTITVTOR SACRORVM, tried to restore Donatism, presumably to divide the Christian ranks. It is also significant that Donatism flourished in non-Latin-speaking areas where the Saturn cult had been strong. It also took root in Africa Proconsularis, but not so firmly as in Numidia, because Proconsularis was more prosperous, and Donatism appealed to the poor. Yet Donatists as such never advocated communal property, manumission of slaves, or remission of debt.

Political activism was left to the storm troopers, the Circumcellions, from whom the Donatists were careful to dissociate themselves. These men of violence first appear about 340, seven years before Donatus, who might have restrained them, was exiled. Augustine, as Catholic bishop of Hippo and indignant spokesman for the establishment, justifies the use of force against the *rusticana audacia* ("clodhopping effrontery") of these *dementissimi greges* ("herds of lunatics"). They insult good Catholics (at Lemellef, fifteen kilometers east of Equizetum, in 362, they climbed to the church roof and pelted the congregation with tiles, and a holy-water vessel there shows the mark of their heretical pickax); they poison the minds of runaway slaves against their masters; their weapons are clubs and the torch of the arsonist; they destroy records of debt; they yoke *generoso cultu educati*, "men of liberal education," to the grain-mill and whip them round and round; they eject masters from their carriages and let slaves ride instead—it is the world turned upside down.

The Circumcellions had their place in society; a schedule of fines, of

412, shows them lower than the plebs but above coloni and slaves. They were apparently journeyman agricultural workers—the very clubs that horrified Augustine doubled as rods for knocking olives from the trees at the harvest. Not all landowners were Catholic, and some *latifondisti* no doubt protected the Circumcellions because they needed their manpower on their estates. The cellae that they haunted were apparently grain stores attached to chapels, in monasteries like the one at Aïn Tamda, fifteen kilometers west of Rapidum, with the cells ranged round a fifty-eight by twenty-nine-meter court. Also at Mechta Azrou and Bir Djedid, in the high plain east of Chott el-Beida (see map, fig. 10.1), were shrines with space for grain storage, and others are now known at Sitifis and Old Theveste (Tébessa Khalia). All these were also places hallowed by martyrs' graves. The Circumcellions were keen on martyrdom: like Buddhist monks in Vietnam, they would set themselves alight; near Aïn M'lila, forty-three kilometers by road south of Cirta, a set of roughly hewn boulders lying at the foot of a precipice, each marked with a name, a month, and the word *redditum* ("account paid"?) is thought to mark the site of Circumcellions' ritual suicide.

The Donatist involvement with the revolt of Firmus (372–375), though attested by Ammianus Marcellinus (the greatest neglected historian of antiquity), by Augustine, and by the great pagan proconsul Symmachus, must be marked not proven. An earlier revolt of Bavares under Faraxen, put down in 260, occurred before the Donatists became a factor to reckon with. Firmus, a high Roman officer, son of a petty Mauretanian king, proclaimed himself, allegedly aggravated by overtaxation, to be Augustus, and occupied Caesarea, Icosium, and Cartennae. It took all the military skill of Count Theodosius, father of the emperor Theodosius, called "the Great," operating out of Sitifis, to put him down; his end was suicide.

Local magnates who could and did hold the imperial organization at their mercy facilitated revolts like this. Firmus' brother Gildo, also a high Roman officer, also revolted (397–398); this time the involvement of at least one Donatist in the affair is not in doubt. This was Optatus, schismatic bishop of Timgad, whom we have met before. He is systematically vilified by ancient and modern sources. His Catholic enemies told how he oppressed widows, overturned trustees, betrayed patrimonies, broke up marriages, sold the property of innocent men, and divided the spoils with

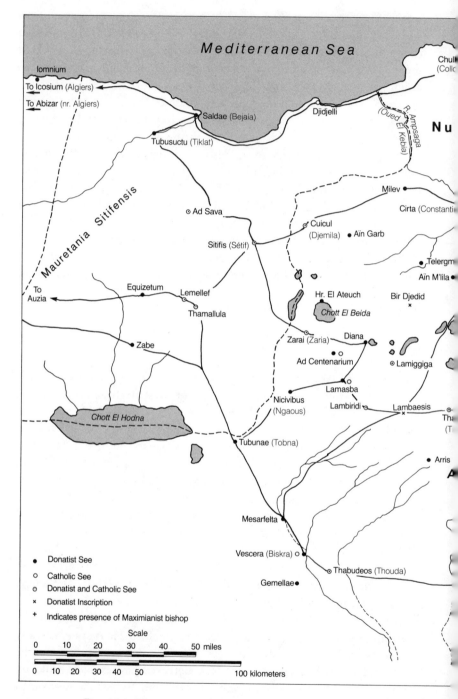

FIGURE 10.1 *Donatist sites, map*

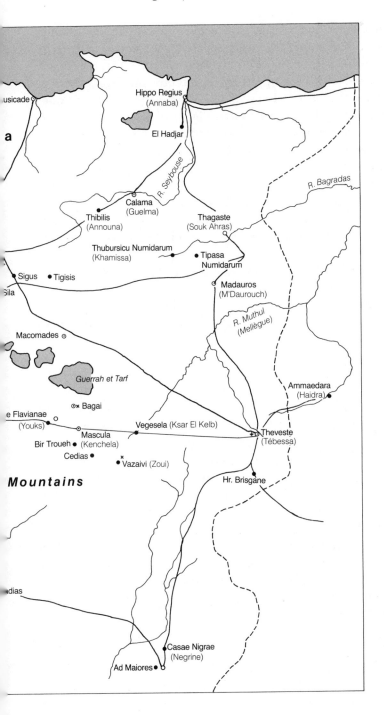

the local landowners; a modern critic, Peter Brown, calls his relation with Gildo "sinister toadyism." They were apparently a precious pair: Gildo himself had amassed immense wealth through control of the grain supply to Rome, and indeed his attempt to cut this off brought about his downfall. His brother Semmac, whom Gildo had murdered, had a fortified estate "the size of a city" (landed estates in fourth-century Africa were often more impressive than the towns). Stilicho, the power behind the throne in Italy, declared Gildo a public enemy, and sent Gildo's own brother Mascezel against him. The fraternal armies faced one another near Theveste. The Catholic Mascezel had more potent medicine than his Donatist-supported brother: Ambrose, the great bishop of Milan, appeared to him in a dream, and spurred on his forces, though outnumbered, to victory. Gildo fled, but was imprisoned at Thabraca, and like Jugurtha five hundred years before, strangled. Marxist critics say he was defeated because abandoned by the "freedom-thirsty" natives, whom he had betrayed. At any rate his downfall shows that the Roman Empire in 398 was not so far gone as is commonly supposed. An imperial tribune besieged a successor of Optatus, Bishop Gaudentius, in his cathedral, in 420.

Though as we saw, Donatism, attenuated, survived, its heyday ended with its condemnation as a heresy by the Council of Carthage in 411. The very full minutes of this council, which survive, list the bishops present and their affiliation. Many major cities, and some minor ones, had prelates of both persuasions. These cities included Augustine's own see, Hippo; Calama, birthplace of Augustine's biographer Possidius; and Cirta and its satellites, Rusicade, Collo, and Milev. Milev was the see of one of Donatism's greatest enemies: confusingly enough, another Optatus. Cirta's bishop, about 390, was Petilian, one of the sect's best apologists. Other ambivalent sees were Sitifis and Theveste; Bagai, where a council was held in 384, and in 404, the basilica burned and the bishop left for dead; Mascula, Macomades, forty-five kilometers north of Mascula, and of course Timgad. Lesser known are Lambiridi,[1] twenty

---

1. Lambiridi is the findspot of a mysterious mosaic, now in the Algiers Museum, dated 295. It probably has nothing to do with Donatism. It shows, above, a shrouded corpse labeled VRBANILLA; below, the cynical and frequent cliché, "I was not; I was; I am not; I care not," written in Greek. The main motif is a medical consultation: a physician feels the pulse of an emaciated patient, who has

kilometers west of Lambaesis, and Lamasba, Lamigiggi (*lam*- in Berber means "people"), Zaraï, Thabudeos, Tubunae, Mesarfelta, Gemellae, Thamallula, Lemellef, Ad Sava, and Equizetum.

One in this category that deserves slightly more notice is Vegesela (Ksar el-Kelb), between Mascula and Theveste, where the Donatist church building survives, identified as such by the inscription DEO LAVDES in a keystone, and by the memorial of a martyr, one Marculus, a lawyer, a pagan turned bishop, who in 347 was flogged in a persecution and pitched over a cliff. A site almost twin to this, with two churches, catacombs, and farm buildings nearby where Circumcellions might have been fed is Henchir el-Ateuch, fifty kilometers southeast of Sitifis.

Donatist sees included Thibilis; Thubursicu Numidarum, heretical enough for Augustine to have visited it twice; Sigus; Tigisis; Sila, where there was a martyr cult in one of the basilicas; Casae Nigrae, birthplace of Donatus himself; M'Dila; Vazaïvi (Zeui); Aquae Caesaris (Youks); Badias; Vescera (Biskra); Nicivibus (N'Gaous);[2] Zabe; and Equizetum.

Inscriptions containing the catchphrase DEO LAVDES, citations from the Psalms,[3] or holier-than-thou sentiments (BONIS BENE; IVSTI PRIORES) or dedications to martyrs are likely to be Donatist; examples have been found in Tébessa Khalia, Mascula, Cedias, 20 kilometers southeast of Mascula, Novar (Beni Fouda, formerly Sillègue), Bagai, Sitifis, Castellum Tingitanum (El Asnam, formerly Orléansville, where there is also a probably Donatist basilica, dated 324), Tigava, Cirta, Timgad, Aïn Ghorab, in the Aurès between Theveste and Badias, Ala Miliaria (Beniane, in the far west, 106 kilometers southeast of Oran), Calama, and Thamallula (Ras el-Oued, formerly Toqueville). Iomnium (Tigzirt), some seventy-five kilometers west of Saldae, has an impressive late-fifth or

---

both beard and breasts. The physician is either Aesculapius or Hippocrates, whose pupil Perdiccas fell in love with him.

2. A hoard of sixty-two coins from here dates from Diocletian's reign. The mints represented are widespread: Cyzicus, Alexandria, Carthage, Rome, North Italy. They are lighter in weight after 295, and stop altogether between 300 and 305. This may have some bearing on the attempt at fiscal control in the price edict of 301. The pitiful hoard, silver-washed copper and bronze, bespeaks the poverty that went with Donatism.

3. For example, "Deus me paschet et nihil mihi deest" (the beginning of Psalm 23), from a rural church near Theveste.

FIGURE 10.2 *Iomnium, Donatist basilica, fifth–sixth century* A.D.

sixth-century basilica (fig. 10.2) attached to an earlier cloverleaf baptistery, perhaps Donatist. Its sculptural ornament, copious and crude, shows minimal signs of Romanization; it includes Daniel, a lion, and a subject which could be either Balaam on his ass or Paul on the Damascus road. The human figures are like gingerbread men; the treatment anticipates Gothic gargoyles and demons. Modern Berber woodcarving in this area—the Grande Kabylie—is a lineal descendant. What is noteworthy about all the evidence is its concentration in those parts of Numidia where Romanization was minimal, and where Saturn worship had been especially rife.

One of the Algerian sites where evidence for Donatism is not strong, though evidence for martyr cult is, is Tipasa, whose earlier pagan monuments we have already described. Now we focus our attention on the hilly promontory outside the town's east circuit wall; it contains two basilicas and a plethora of burials, set in the midst of lentiscus (mastic), artemisia, asphodel, and cyclamen, making it one of the most beautiful Christian cemeteries in the western world. The older basilica honors Saint Salsa, a determined young lady, though her epitaph calls her "sweeter than nectar," who at fourteen, in about 320, vexed local pagans by her iconoclasm: she threw the gold head of a venerated bronze dragon into the sea; a nineteenth-century stained-glass window in the local church shows her doing it. The infuriated mob threw her in after their idol. A storm rose; the waves brought her body back to shore, where one Saturninus, a Gaul, rescued it. The storm ceased. The teenage martyr was buried in a small apsidal monument just south of the present basilica (see air photograph, fig. 10.3). At some time between Firmus' revolt[4] and the Vandal invasion, that is, between 372 and 430, the basilica was built, and Salsa's relics were transferred to it; another sarcophagus, of another lady of an older generation but of the same name, was placed beside it by mistake. Salsa's sarcophagus received a masonry surround; above it, a pagan sarcophagus with scenes from the myth of the handsome Endymion, with whom the Moon fell in love, was used as a container for relics. In the seventh century, piers were introduced to hold up the nave roof; then the basilica was reduced to half its size, and confined in width to the nave. Meanwhile, around the shrine of the beloved martyr clustered an incredible number, over five hundred, of sarcophagi of the faithful desiring burial as close to the saint as possible. The sarcophagi are usually quite primitive: the mosaics inset into one show the healing of the man born blind; Christians praying, hands upraised; Noah in the ark, with a crow and a dove (the ark has feet, through confusion with *arca*, "a coffer," the Ark of the Covenant); Daniel and the lions; and the three Hebrew children in the fiery furnace— each child has a kiln to itself. Some of these motifs are Donatist. At all events the shrine was a place of pilgrimage for the faithful from all over the empire.

The other basilica in this eastern area, that of Saints Peter and Paul, is set directly against the circuit wall. Coins date it to the mid–fourth

4. That the revolt spared Tipasa was due in part to its strong defenses, not least in its territorium, which embraced 60,000 to 70,000 hectares and stretched an average of thirty kilometers southwest, west, and eastward as far as Mazafran, where Icosium's territory began, and a late fourth-century castellum has been found. This large territory explains the large size of Tipasa's Great Basilica and theater.

FIGURE 10.3 *Tipasa, Saint Salsa basilica,* A.D. 372–430

century. In Byzantine times a hole was knocked through the circuit wall to give access to it, now enlarged from 11 by 12 to 11 by 16.5 meters, and with three reliquaries in its ambo. A sarcophagus in the right aisle proved to contain a headless skeleton, almost certainly of a martyr. The nave may have been open to the sky; certainly the piers, footed in earth, would not have supported a substantial roof. Outside the church to the south an enclosure contains two rows of six sarcophagi, very late, all different, and with more than one body or head in each, including a four-year-old child. Clustered about are 450 burials, some three deep.

From the House of the Frescoes a sandy path leads westward to the Great Basilica, just inside the circuit wall. At fifty-eight by forty-two meters, it is the largest Christian building yet excavated on Algerian soil. It dates from the end of the fourth century. Its nave is thirteen meters wide; it has three pairs of aisles (fig. 10.4), separated by columns supporting arches, four of which are still standing. Its apse is buttressed to keep it from falling into the sea. To the north of it were baths for ritual ablution before baptism, a baptistery, and possibly a bishop's house.

On a promontory outside the circuit wall is the vast west necropolis, containing, besides the crowded sarcophagi (fig. 10.5), a circular martyrium twenty meters wide: within are fourteen arched niches that contained tombs; the basilica, identified in a mosaic, of Bishop Alexander; and a martyrs' enclosure. The basilica is funerary, devoted to a cult that

FIGURE 10.4 *Tipasa, Great Basilica, late fourth century* A.D.

FIGURE 10.5 *Tipasa, basilica of Bishop Alexander, sarcophagi, early fifth century* A.D.

brought the living and the dead together in an *agapē*, or ritual meal. The bishop's sarcophagus, with two others, is in the west aisle; it dates from a little after 400. The area in front of the apse is decorated with seven registers of sea creatures, fish, and shellfish. At the opposite end are aligned nine tombs of persons called in another mosaic IVSTI PRIORES, possibly Tipasa's earliest bishops, perhaps taken thither from the crypt, which has rock cuttings for eleven burials. North of the church a stair leads to the martyrs' enclosure. There a pious mosaic inscription reads RESVRRECTIONEM CARNIS FVTVRAM ESSE QVI CREDIT ANGELIS IN CAELIS SIMILIS ERIT: "Whoso believes in the resurrection of the body, at the Resurrection will be like the angels in Heaven." Still further to the north are catacombs. Appropriately, among the ancient tombs rises a stele to the memory of Albert Camus, Algerian born, and a lover of Tipasa's beauty.

A discussion of Theveste (Tébessa) belongs here, because of its impressive late basilica and Byzantine fortifications, though the Roman impress on the place began, as we noted in passing, much earlier, with Vespasian's camp for the Legio III Augusta. This became a civilian municipium in 75, when the legion moved on to Lambaesis. No less than seven hundred inscriptions reveal the bureaucratic importance of the place, full as it was of imperial freedmen, slaves, and Augustales (freedman priests of the imperial cult). Also recorded are benefactors like the prefect of a legion who in 214 gave 250,000 sesterces for bath oil, and a like sum for the arch of Caracalla, in the passageway of which his generosity is recorded, together with a precise list of the sixty-four days on which it will be dispensed. Another philanthropist, A. Titinius, and his son gave, somewhere between A.D. 163 and 165, sums of 35,000, 15,000, and 13,000 sesterces to supply a cella with a gilt coffered ceiling, and a statue of Saturn, a banquet, and *ludi scaenici* (stage shows) for the Augustales and curiales (minor religious functionaries). The same family is known from Uchi Maius in Africa Proconsularis, where it provided civil and religious officials for five generations. The Titinii married into the equestrian and then into the senatorial order, down to the Severi. An epigraphic curiosity from Theveste is a lead curse-tablet, in Greek, dated by its first editor to the first century, by a stern critic (Louis Robert) much later. A jealous husband invokes the curse upon his wife Saturnina; he wishes her "bitter and terrible things until death; let her be cut in pieces, let her go mad, now, now, now, quickly, quickly, quickly." This breathless violence is unique in the literature of cursing.

A monument Flavian in origin, but with a history running down into the fifth century, is the amphitheater, a hundred meters west of the southeast corner of the Byzantine fort. It measures 60 by 40 meters within, 86.5 by 80.5 without. It has two monumental gates, and thirteen rows of seats survive, plus loges. Over four lintels are inscribed the names of the four circus factions; on the balustrades, the names of Thevestan first families. In its latest period, squatters' houses occupied the site, as at Arles (*RF*, 62–63).

Just inside and halfway along the north stretch of the Byzantine wall is the so-called Temple of Minerva, almost perfectly preserved (fig. 10.6). It stands on a podium four meters high, and was originally surrounded by a portico. It has monolithic Corinthian columns of blue-veined white marble. Its frieze motifs include crossed cornucopias, rosettes and swags, trophies, warriors, Bacchus and Hercules (the latter adopted as patron by Commodus; both, as we saw at Lepcis Magna, by Septimius Severus), Castor and Pollux, and Medusa. In the metopes are wingspread eagles holding serpents, enlacing vine shoots, and bucrania (bulls' skulls). The architrave's underside is carved with flowers and baskets of fruit. The temple, having served since the early nineteenth century as engineers' office, officers' quarters, canteen, fodder store, and prison, is now a museum. It contains mosaics: Venus, Neptune, Muses, and Daphne's metamorphosis into a laurel tree. The temple as a whole closely resembles that of Mars at Augusta Emerita (Mérida) in Spain (*ISS*, 135).

Thirty meters east of the temple is the four-way arch of Caracalla, built in 214, incorporated into the Byzantine wall in 539 (fig. 10.7). Its provincial rococo architectural ornament has caused it to be described, somewhat condescendingly, as "a rude Numidian tenant-farmer overdressed for a holiday," and more accurately as epitomizing "the very soul and taste of Romanized Africa." It is an eleven-meter cube from which projected on each side two pairs of monolithic unfluted Corinthian columns. Like the arch of Marcus Aurelius at Oea, it had a cupola resting on stone corner crossbeams within; an aedicula with monolithic colonnettes in polychrome marble rises above. Over the keystones on the three visible sides are medallions containing busts in high relief: a lion, a Minerva-Medusa (as in the Severan Forum at Lepcis), and the Fortune of Theveste, wearing her turreted crown. Each of the visible friezes bears an inscrip-

FIGURE 10.6 *Theveste, temple of Minerva, Antonine or Severan*

tion to a Severan: Septimius, his wife Julia Domna, and Caracalla, who has suffered *damnatio memoriae.*

The jewel of Theveste, the Christian basilica complex, lies six hundred meters north of the arch. It dates from the early sixth century, but before the Byzantine reconquest—an extraordinary testimony to prosperity here under the Vandals. Entrance was by a monumental arch on the east, which gave on to a broad east-west avenue (see fig. 10.8) leading, between the basilica itself and a formal garden, to a building of which the lower floor, which has what look like mangers and hitching holes, may have been a stable, and the floor above an inn, for Theveste became a place of pilgrimage, perhaps because of its association with the aristocrat Crispina, martyred under Diocletian in 304. Her shrine may be the trefoil building, older than the basilica, with access from it by fifteen steps down. The martyrium contains eleven mosaic inscriptions, of about A.D.

FIGURE 10.7 *Theveste, arch of Caracalla,* A.D. 214

351, to which correspond eleven sarcophagi, one buried below each. The names match fairly closely those of Crispina's recorded companions. One, Bishop Palladius, had his brown hair still intact when his wooden coffin was excavated in 1868. The basilica proper is on a podium fifteen steps high, leaving room beneath for the catacomb, really a crypt, of one Gaudentia and several other martyrs. Off the atrium opens the baptistery, a circular building with twelve niches, one for each of the apostles. The basilica measures eighty-one by twenty-two meters, counting narthex, atrium, apse, and the rooms behind it. It was two stories high, its upper gallery accessible by stairs. From hooks in the narthex columns could be suspended the hangings used on holy days. The nave, 8.3 meters wide, and the aisles, each 4.5 meters wide, were paved with geometric mosaics. Against the basilica walls, accessible from the walled precinct, was a series of twenty-four cell-like rooms for visitors and dignitaries; against the precinct walls, sixty-five more, for monks; in the space between, library, refectory, and kitchens. Berbers—not Vandals—destroyed the complex about 536; the Byzantine Solomon rebuilt it, and turned it into a concentration camp; the cells now locked from the outside, and were overlooked by towers projecting inward, to control prisoners, not to ward off exterior attacks. The warders were housed in the inn; they worshiped in the small (ten by eleven meters) chapel of Gabinilla north

FIGURE 10.8 *Theveste, Christian basilica, early sixth century* A.D.

of the clover-leaf martyrium. Each morning the prisoners were marched off to work on the city wall, which took eight hundred men two years to build.

The Byzantine wall is a formidable affair, measuring 320 by 280 meters, with fourteen towers, accessible by a walkway along the wall, and three gates. It was originally seventeen to eighteen meters high.

Three kilometers southwest is Tébessa Khalia, (Old Tébessa), *inter odoratos nemorum recessus*, "in the perfumed seclusion of the glades," as an inscription poetically puts it. It is the site of a complicated group of third to fourth-century buildings, perhaps part of an imperial estate. There are four Christian basilicas, one with a clover-leaf apse that has geometric mosaics, another with a double apse and more mosaics; there are baths, with a round plunge-pool, a round temple, perhaps of Aesculapius, and a huge (110 by 117 meters) rectangular enclosure containing, *inter alia*, an oil press and a pond.

FIGURE 10.9 *Theveste territorium, oil works*

The mention of oil presses is a reminder that the Limes runs fifty kilometers south of Theveste, and that the intervening area was in antiquity a fertile oil-producing country. At Henchir Brisgane, twenty-seven kilometers south of Theveste, is a particularly impressive oil works measuring 150 meters on a side, and dated by an inscription to the reign of Caracalla. Fig. 10.9 shows the equally impressive one at Bir Sgaoun, also in Theveste's territorium. The area also yielded a funerary inscription pathetically showing loyalty to the Gordians: the deceased's epitaph states that he died *pro amore Romano*.

For over a century (429–534) the Vandals dominated Roman Africa. Boniface, the Roman "count" of Africa, is alleged to have invited the land-hungry Germanic tribe over from Spain to help him against rival intriguers. A probable souvenir of their passage is a hoard of objects in silver and gold, buried at Cartennae by a panicky nabob, and never discovered until 1936. Under their able king, Gaiseric, they swept victoriously across the Maghreb, taking Hippo in 431 and Carthage, which they made their capital, in 439. In the siege of Hippo, Augustine died, aged seventy-six. Some years before, in his *City of God*, written between 413 and 426, and aptly described as a landmark in the abandonment of classical ideals, he had compared the Roman Empire unfavorably with the Kingdom of Heaven and given expression to that otherworldliness which was to be the refuge of pessimists high and low throughout the Middle Ages. Nevertheless, not everyone in his circle was poor in worldly goods (critics of the empire would say that that was precisely the trouble). His friend and protegée Melania of Thagaste was so rich that the area of her estate exceeded that of the town.

Gaiseric handed over all his conquered territory west of the Hippo-Theveste road to Berber satellite kings, of tribes like the Bavares (see chapter 11), Quinquegentanei, and Baquates. A cenotaph inscription from Arris in the Aurès, twenty-five airline miles south-southwest of Timgad (and in 1954 the original center of the Algerian revolt from France) refers to one Masties, a Berber who calls himself, from 449, "dux et imperator," and boasts, in barbarous Latin: "numquam periuravi neque fide fregi neque de Romanos neque de Mauros" (I was never forsworn, nor broke faith either with the Romans or with the Moors). He died in 516. Another such inscription is that of the Berber king Masuna from Altava, already mentioned. The Berber kings were buried in great rectangular stepped monuments, dating from the sixth and seventh centuries, called Djedars, of which a number crown the hilltops in the Djebel Lakhdar and near Ternaten, some eighty kilometers south of Tiaret. Fig. 10.10 shows Djedar A of Djebel Lakhdar, with its excellent masonry, and stepped construction above. Within were corridors and a funerary chamber, with a cunningly wrought door-frame, placing the whole in the tradition of the Medracen and the Tomb of the Christian Woman. Djedar A has Christian symbols in reuse on its façade. The largest of the Djedars, in the Ternaten necropolis, is forty-eight meters on a side and must originally have been forty meters high. The Djedars were only the most prominent monuments in large necropoleis, in which camel-nomads may also have been buried. Perhaps contemporary with Djebel Lakhdar Djedar A, though the precise date is uncertain, is a relief inscribed in Libyan from Abizar, about ten kilometers south of Iomnium (Tigzirt) in the Grande Kabylie (fig. 10.11). On it a horseman with a pointed beard carries a buckler and three lances; he holds an unidentifiable round offering between thumb and finger; in front of him is an ostrich. He is either a member or a god of a warrior-hunter caste.

Another piece of evidence for Berber prosperity, from as early as the third Christian century, is a Romano-Berber villa at Aïn Sarb, about

FIGURE 10.10 *Djebel Lakhdar, Djedar A, sixth–seventh century* A.D.

twenty kilometers west of Tiaret, where the peristyle has Aeolic capitals, and the pool is lined with waterproof cement. One room had painted wall or ceiling plaster, molded or carved with classical details like dentils, egg-and-dart, and rosettes; the colors included red, green, yellow, brown, gray, and blue. There is also a Christian chi-rho emblem. On the working side of the villa were many amphora sherds, and a marble weight (a hundred Roman pounds). Classical details in a Berber working villa symbolize both how the two cultures existed side by side and how forces of resistance could assimilate without yielding. So far as there was assimilation, a French colonial (Mercier of Constantine) in 1896 called it "the formation of a Creole race."

Berber riches of the reign of Constantine are illustrated by the tomb of Tin Hinan, found near Abalessa, in the Hoggar (see map, fig. 7.2), the area of the much earlier cliff paintings and drawings. She was, according to legend, the first queen of the Sahara. Her skeleton, now in the Algiers Museum with the rich furniture from the tomb, was found in a large tumulus, with jewelry in gold, silver, and colored stones. She lay on an elaborately carved bier upholstered in red leather. Her skeleton shows her to have been "tall, slim, and aristocratic."

The Vandals knew and capitalized on the propaganda value of the

FIGURE 10.11 *Abizar stele, Algiers Museum*

imperial cult; its *flamines* are attested in Vandal times at Cuicul, near Theveste, at Ammaedara, and elsewhere. Though they themselves followed the Arian creed, which subordinated the Son to the Father, rather than the Athanasian creed of the Catholic church, Vandals, as we saw, did not vandalize Catholics overmuch; an epitaph of 505 from Pomaria (Tlemcen) suggests that Vandal tolerance extended to that region. Jews and Berbers united in resistance to Romanization, and medieval Arab sources report a large Jewish population in the Aurès.

Not only the modest and numerous churches, with their mosaics, but also what we know of individuals in the Vandal period attest to the continuing attractiveness of the Catholic church, not least to the Roman aristocracy. A case in point is the senator Volusianus, proconsul of Africa in 411/12. His wife was Catholic; his cousin was the first man to sit in the Roman Senate dressed as a monk (this was in 360 or thereabouts). His niece was Augustine's rich friend Melania, who finally converted him, and had him baptized by the Archbishop Proclus, in 437, in Constantinople, where he had gone to arrange Valentinian III's marriage to the princess Eudoxia. He and his circle knew everyone of mark and influence. His brother was urban prefect in Rome, and figures as a guest, along with the distinguished pagan Symmachus, at the symposium in the *Saturnalia* of Macrobius, himself a proconsul of Africa (410), and probably of African origin. The Gallic urban prefect (414) and poet, Rutilius Namatianus, was his friend. During his proconsulship in Carthage Augustine worked at converting him. A proselytizing poem to him appears in the works of Paulinus, bishop of Nola. Yet his uncle was a priest of Vesta, an uncle by marriage was a votary of Mithras, and his grandmother had been a priestess of Isis. The pagan survival is as significant as the Christian conversion. From El Hadjar (formerly Duzerville), now the site of a major ironworks, only eleven kilometers south of Augustine's see of Hippo, are reported nineteen pagan tombs, dated by coins as late as Valentinian III (425–455).

Though life went on in Vandal Africa less bleakly than is commonly portrayed, the alliance of Berber mountaineers and Sahara nomads that the Vandals permitted was destined in the end to doom Roman civilization in North Africa. To hasten the process, inflation was a continuing problem: according to Szilagy's calculations, between the Julio-Claudians and Diocletian the price of grain had risen 150 percent; of wine, 240 percent; of clothing, 550 percent; of oil, 25 percent; all for an average of 230 percent. Purchasing power decreased by 46 percent, the standard of living by 80 percent. For the third century A.D. Duncan-Jones calculates the rate of inflation at 4 to 4.9 percent per annum.

The most interesting economic documents from Vandal Africa are the Albertini Tablets—named from their first editor—a set of thirty-four, written in ink on grooved cedarwood. They include the record of a dowry, the sale of a slave, accounts, and land transfers. They were found by natives in a sealed jar, at a place near the Algerian-Tunisian border, a hundred kilometers south of Theveste, and sixty-five west of Capsa. They are dated 493–496, in the reign of the Vandal king Gunthamund. They are written in bad Latin, in a cursive hand, with many complicated ligatures, on diptychs or triptychs, linked and sealed; the hands of nine different public scribes have been distinguished. They recorded date, place, name of seller, object sold, buyer, price, legal provisions, obligations and guarantees, especially against eviction (a fine of twice the selling price), and signature. Thirty-one signatories were illiterate, signing with an X. No woman could write, but widows owned property. The vendors were Romanized Berbers. The lots sold were widely dispersed, with twenty-six different owners. The provisions of the *leges Marciana* and *Hadriana*, of over four hundred years before (see chapter 3) were still in force. The area involved has deteriorated since antiquity. Nowadays it is a steppe, thinly populated with nomads; in antiquity there was an olive press at least every fifty square kilometers, but the land clearly *was* almost desert: one of the tablets mentions camels. Roads, canals, reservoirs, boundary stones, and place names defined the parcels of land; rights of access, and water rights, were sold with the land. Crops were olives, figs, a few almonds and pistachios; grain is not mentioned. The dowry tablet equates 12,000 *folles* with 750 olive trees, and 9 olive trees with a pair of shoes. The bride's trousseau included clothes—more Berber than Roman—jewelry, and a loom. She dressed well: a cloak at 2,000 folles was worth nearly three times as much as a six-year-old well-behaved white slave. The overall picture given by the tablets is of smallholders selling off little parcels of land, or olive presses, one after another, annihilating their capital. One theory is that the buyers were émigrés, ruined by the Vandal invasion, who had returned and were buying up the family that had dispossessed them a generation before. This return to the land, if it ever happened, is a forerunner of the Byzantine reconquest that began in 533.

Some *ostraka* (potsherds) from Bir Troueh, south of Mascula, also from Gunthamund's reign, but earlier (between 485/86 and 492/93) than the Albertini Tablets, register the delivery of measures of grain or oil, with names of teams of workmen, proprietors, and property. The area was centuriated, as was, with three different orientations, a wide region from north of Ras el-Oued (formerly Toqueville) to east of Cirta; the centuriation has been published but not dated.

The rather remarkable Byzantine reconquest of North Africa under the eunuch Solomon, *domesticus, magister militum,* and praetorian prefect of Justinian's famous general Belisarius, has left its impressive mark on the archaeological record in the shape of fortresses of 534/35 in Tunisia and Algeria, like those we have described at Limisa, Mactar, Sufetula, Ammaedara, Timgad, Theveste, Madauros, Sitifis, and Thibilis. Here we might add an irregular one at Numidian Tipasa (Tifech). It lay fourteen kilometers east of Thubursicu, on the main Carthage-Cirta military road. Its impressive maximum dimensions are 246 by 130 meters; the northern apex was separately walled off as a citadel. Of its original ten square towers only one has survived local stone-robbing. Other Byzantine citadels worth a passing mention are at Diana, Tigisis, Tubunae, and Bagai, whose locations show that the Limes was being kept up. Byzantine Bagai had walls 2.2 meters thick, with a rubble fill; in 1894 a forty-meter stretch survived, with three square bastions.

Besides the basilicas like Theveste's that survived into Byzantine times, there are other, though scanty, pieces of evidence for the state of Christianity in seventh-century Algeria. The lead plaque mentioned at the beginning of the chapter comes from Telergma, thirty-five airline kilometers southwest of Cirta; it records the deposit, as late as the twenty-sixth year of the reign of Heraclius, of relics of Saints Stephen of Jerusalem, Phocas of Sinope, Theodore, possibly of Alexandria, and Victor, a Syrian. Peter the Patrician, exarch (governor) of Carthage, is recorded as in charge of the province. Finally, from Basilica III at Sila, some thirty kilometers south of Cirta, comes a limestone pyxis, reliquary of one Georgius, lector (a minor functionary) of the basilica, who may, for a reason unknown, have suffered persecution, a late survival of man's inhumanity to man.

PART 4: MOROCCO

11. MAURETANIA TINGITANA

Morocco's history, like Cyrenaica's, is different from that of the rest of the Maghreb. For one thing, its connections with Spain, from remote antiquity, including a raid thither by Moorish pirate-bandits in 178, have always been close if not friendly; for another, it was added late to the roll of Roman provinces, dating its provincial era only from A.D. 40. Finally, Roman penetration, both geographically and culturally, was remarkably thin, confined to an isosceles triangle 270 kilometers on the sides, 150 across the base. It never extended south of Rabat (see map, fig. 11.1), and was perhaps restricted still further after Diocletian's reign.

Moroccan prehistory may be briefly dismissed. It goes back to the Günz-Mindel period (500,000 B.C.). A Neanderthal jaw has been found at Rabat; there is little evidence for a Bronze Age; there are dolmens in the northwest, where, as we shall see, Berber tumuli from the seventh Christian century are also known; and there are cave drawings and paintings in the pre-Sahara and High Atlas, many of them in increasing danger of destruction by tourists, mining interests, road extension, or commercial expansion. Their motifs and phases are those we have met elsewhere: roundheads, Bovidians, chariots; fauna include ostriches, gazelles, elephants (one standing on its head), antelope, giraffes, large felines, and in the late period, camels.

Lixus, the oldest dated historic site in Morocco, lies on the Loukkos River four kilometers from the Atlantic, just to the south of white cliffs like Dover's, and 82.5 kilometers by road from Tangier. As at Utica, its legendary foundation date, 1100 B.C., is not borne out by archaeology; the oldest finds are of the seventh or sixth century. It is rich in mythology: the Gardens of the Hesperides were here (the loops of the river would be

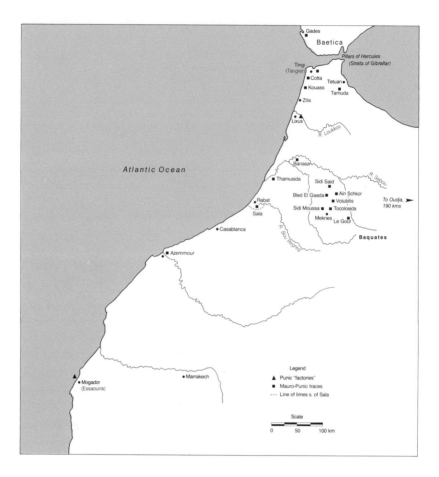

Legend

▲ Punic "factories"
■ Mauro-Punic traces
---- Line of limes s. of Sala

Scale

0   50   100 km

FIGURE 11.1 *Roman Morocco, map*

FIGURE 11.2 *Lixus, air view*

the coils of the guardian dragon); here Hercules, sent to get the golden apples, wrestled with the giant Antaeus; knowing that his adversary gained strength from his mother Earth every time he touched the ground, he won by holding him over his head until he cried for mercy. (Hercules, Punic Melqart, was popular in Tingitana; there is evidence for him in Tingi, Banasa, Volubilis, and Thamusida, and the Ras el-Hadid south of Sala is Cape Hercules.) Lixus was a Punic port of call on the way to Mogador, 700 kilometers southwest, and to Guinea gold, perhaps the true source of the myth of the golden apples. The rampart that runs across the bottom of the air photograph (fig. 11.2) is variously dated, between the fourth century B.C. and the first century A.D.; the masonry resembles Hippo's. The wall perpendicular to it cuts off the acropolis, 80 meters above the river marshes. It contains no less than eight temples, one to Hercules-Melqart, and must in its oldest levels go back to Punic times. One temple (called F), not excavated when the air photograph was taken, stands in a precinct 1,500 meters square: one of its apses is just visible in the unexcavated area of the arx in the picture. Four hundred meters east of the acropolis stood the theater-amphitheater, westernmost in Africa, and with one of the largest orchestras—at 32.5 meters in diameter, wider than either Athens' or Epidaurus'. When, like Cyrene's, it was made over into an amphitheater, the arena level, for safety against the wild beasts, was 4.2 meters below the lowest seats. Baths adjoin, of

Severan date; a mosaic of the god Oceanus paved their tepidarium. This is not without its Punic reminiscence, since Oceanus has traits in common with Syrian Hadad.

South of the acropolis, in the workers' quarter of the lower city, a complex 170 meters long, made up of twelve buildings, was a factory, with fifty vats (fig. 11.3) for making *garum*, the fish sauce prized by Roman gourmets as ours prize caviar; the tuna from which it was made appears on Lixus' coins. The factory was in use from the reign of Juba II until the fourth century.[1]

Lixus became a colony under Claudius. From the Roman period date rich houses, one named from its mosaic of Helios (Punic Shamesh; he too appears on coins), another from its mosaic of Mars and Rhea; both are visible on the left of the air photograph. The mosaic from the latter house, dated in the third to fourth century, is in the Tetuan Museum, along with others of the Three Graces and Venus and Adonis, and bronze statuettes of Hercules and Antaeus and Theseus and the Minotaur. Yet another mosaic, showing a pair of Cupids, winner and loser in a cock-fight, is dated about 250. (Cocks were fed onions for valor, and equipped with bronze spurs.)

A series of Punic ports of call[2] leads finally to Mogador (Essaouira), where an offshore island contains a factory for making purple dye, the most expensive of Roman luxuries. (The extraction of the dye from the murex shellfish was a simple process. The shells were boiled with sand, which catalyzed production in a matter of four or five days; the resulting liquid was filtered through cloth, and the product was quite stable.) Mogador dates from Juba II's reign, and lasted, on the evidence of coins, to Julian's. Pottery, Punic, Attic, and Ionian, shows that it had been a port of call since the seventh century B.C. It was at places like this that the Phoenicians would have carried on the system of silent trading that Herodotus describes: the traders signaled their arrival by lighting

1. Another impressive garum factory is at Cotta (Jibila), fifteen kilometers south-west of Tangier. Covering 2,240 square meters, and with vats two meters deep, it is the largest architectural complex thus far discovered in the region. It dates back to the third or second century B.C.

2. Including Azemmour, eighty kilometers below Casablanca, the terminus of a caravan route, where three thousand rock-cut graves suggest that the settlement was something more than a mere "factory."

FIGURE 11.3 *Lixus, garum vats, first–fourth century* A.D.

a smoky fire, the natives laid out goods, and the traders gold, in turn, till both sides were satisfied—all this without a word being exchanged. Mogador would also have been one of Hanno's ports of call on his famous voyage. In this connection it is worth noting that his exploit was repeated in 116 B.C. by Eudoxus of Cyzicus, subsidized by Ptolemy Euergetes of Egypt. He sailed from Gades (Cadiz), with flute-girls, physicians, and carpenters aboard. Though obviously equipped for almost any emergency, he ran aground south of Morocco, returned, and mounted another expedition, from which he never came back.

In pre-Roman times a villa, which grew to have twenty rooms, with baths and a mosaic of peacocks, was built on the island; it lasted to the fifth Christian century. From it came an Arretine bowl with a beautiful likeness of Apollo the lyre-player, perhaps occasioned by the battle of Actium, which was fought in waters below a headland bearing a temple of the god. In the nineteenth century, the island housed a prison. The picturesque mainland town is now the center of a fascinating craft of inlaying wood, the very same cypress wood (thuya, arbor vitae) from which tables were made that were the delight of Roman connoisseurs— the philosopher Seneca was said to own five hundred.

Tingi (Tangier) must from Punic times, as now, have had close connections, via the Pillars of Hercules (Gibraltar), with southern Spain. The modern city so overlies the ancient that we know more of its history than of its archaeology, but there were Roman baths under the Casbah, the square called the Petit Socco was probably the forum, and the street leading westward out of it the decumanus maximus; there is a Roman temple under the Great Mosque; a Christian basilica is reported in the rue de Belgique. The Voyage of Venus mosaic from Volubilis, to be described below, has been brought to the Casbah Museum, where there are also replicas of other Volubilis treasures (originals in Rabat). In the hinterland more than a hundred sites have been reported, including villae rusticae (working farmsteads), and necropoleis to the northwest, west, and south. Two major roads led southward from it, one coastal, to Sala (Chellah, suburb of Rabat), the other inland, to Volubilis.

In 81 B.C. the Roman renegade Sertorius invaded Tingi from Spain; in 38 Octavian made it a colony, as a reward for its having chosen the right side in his war against Antony; it is the westernmost of the string of coastal colonies listed in chapter 8. It was probably administered from the southern Spanish province of Baetica. Under Diocletian it was a base against the Moors, and a place of persecution, with its own martyrs.

Kouass, a port twenty-five kilometers southwest of Tangier, is chiefly noteworthy for its forty surviving aqueduct arches; its name means "arches" in Arabic. There is also a Roman blockhouse, forty-eight and a half meters square. It was probably one of the Carthaginian Hanno's ports of call on his voyage to West Africa. It yielded hundreds of amphoras. The town it served in Roman times was probably Zilis (Arzila), thirteen kilometers northeast, which has a circuit wall, temple, houses, baths, cisterns, and possibly a theater. Augustus "displaced" its inhabitants to Spain for having supported Antony, and replaced them with Iberians.

Another settlement originally Punic, with Roman overlay, is Tamuda, five kilometers southwest of Tetuan. The pre-Roman community, covering four hectares, had regular streets, in accordance with the canons of Hellenistic city planning at the beginning of the second century B.C., but the houses were poor, built of mud or adobe, with no peristyles or atria. First destroyed in about 38 B.C., in an internecine struggle between Mauretanian rulers, the pro-Octavian Bocchus II and his brother Bogud, who sided with Antony, and had a Greek wife, Eunoe, who was said to have had an affair with Julius Caesar, it was rebuilt, but destroyed again in the troubles of A.D. 40, involving the murder of Juba II's son and successor Ptolemy II, the revolt of the Moorish freedman "vizier," Aedemon, and the emperor Claudius' making Mauretania Tingitana into a province. (Tingitana and Caesariensis were combined for civil and military administration in emergencies eleven times between Claudius and Diocletian.) Late in the first or early in the second century A.D. the Romans built in Tamuda a camp eighty meters square (see air photograph, fig. 11.4), with twenty semicircular towers and four gates. Excavation has revealed only the remains of houses, with no public buildings, religious or secular. The Roman necropolis, to the west (top of photograph) overlies the Punic one. The coins are an interesting sequence: Numidian, Mauretanian (with wheat-ears and meander as devices), Iberian, and Roman from the Republic to Arcadius (reigned in the eastern empire, 383–405).

FIGURE 11.4 *Tamuda, air view*

Banasa (Sidi Ali bou-Jenoun) is a Punic-Roman site of particular importance for its wealth of inscriptions. It lies on the River Sebou, 30 kilometers from the Atlantic, 178 kilometers south of Tangier and 100 northeast of Rabat. In antiquity it was directly on the military road from Tingi to Sala, and an important station on the Limes: nowadays a detour of 8.5 kilometers is required to reach it. Its Punic remains, dating from the fourth century B.C. or earlier, are in part buried under thick layers of silt. Between 33 and 25 B.C. Octavian-Augustus made it the Colonia Augusta Valentia Banasa; it developed, by the end of the first Christian century, into a grid-planned town (see air photograph, fig. 11.5) with a decumanus maximus 4.5 meters wide, insulae 260 Roman feet long, a forum measuring 37 by 34 meters; fig. 11.6 shows an arched exit from the forum northward onto one of the minor decumani. Fig. 11.7 shows the plan of a sacred building with five or six cellae (somewhat like the vexillarium of a military camp such as Lambaesis), in which some have seen a capitolium. Parallels are known from Ulpia Traiana in Dacia (see *DSS*, 109). There were temples to Isis and the mother of the gods, at least five sets of public baths, a *macellum* (meat market), private houses, and shops. One of the houses has a mosaic of Venus; it has been ingeni-

FIGURE 11.5 *Banasa, air view*

ously if implausibly suggested that the prevalence of Venus mosaics in Mauretania is a delicate reference by Cleopatra Selene, consort of Juba II, to the Venus-like appearance of her mother to Mark Antony, in her barge at Tarsus, which we know from the descriptions by Plutarch and Shakespeare. In one of the shops was found part of a branding iron: this was cattle country. The shops included a remarkable number of bakeries. In the oven of one of these was discovered a hoard of 457 coins, and the House of Fonteius yielded another 51; they range in date from Caracalla to Gallienus. The latest issues are of 257–259, shortly after which Banasa was presumably destroyed. Their legends propagandize virtues rather desired than realized by the establishment: Loyalty of the Army, Victory, Concord, Security, Happiness, Chastity, Equity, a New Age (this minted by Philip the Arab, the "Bedouin sheik," under whom, as we saw, Rome celebrated her millennium), Peace, Abundance, Lushness (*Ubertas*), Fecundity, Hope, Liberty. A rampart with a circuit of 1,100 meters, 1.6 meters thick, and equipped with towers, was built in Severan times, but proved ineffectual. To the west, on the Limes, was a camp measuring 105 by 86 meters.

Inscriptions at Banasa include a *tabula patronatus* in which the colony names the prefect of Legio III Augusta as its patron, and he accepts the colonists as his *clientela*. More important is a series of no fewer than thirteen *diplomata* (certificates of military discharge), dated from 88 to 157. The dates include 109, 121/122, 124, 129–132, and 156/57—but Marxist critics have suggested that the first two may represent times of revolt. Also, the presence under Trajan of only three cavalry units and five auxiliary cohorts shows Moorish loyalty: no larger force was needed. A third epigraphic document of importance is the Tabula Banasitana of 177, which lists twelve members of the imperial privy council and grants citizenship to a Berber chief and his family—the wife was native, the children had Roman names. The privy council included three ex-proconsuls of Africa: it was an ad hoc blue-ribbon committee. Grants of citizenship were a part of deliberate policy; Romanizing native persons of importance was calculated to retard, deflect, or prevent Berber incursions. Finally, an inscription of Caracalla (215/16) remits back taxes; in gratitude the community makes a gift of "celestial animals" (lions or elephants) to the praetorian prefect. Pliny the Elder reports that the area was infested with elephants; one of the finds from the site was an elephant head in blue schist with white marble tusks.

Sala (a southern suburb of Rabat) is another Punic foundation, of the seventh or sixth century B.C., Romanized from the time of Juba II.

FIGURE 11.6 *Banasa, forum arch, late first century* A.D. *(?)*

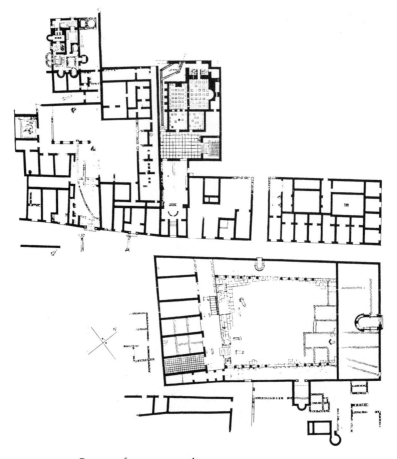

FIGURE 11.7 *Banasa, forum area, plan*

It lies on the Oued bou-Regreg, four kilometers from the sea. Its coins bear neo-Punic inscriptions; the devices, wheat-ear and grapes, symbolize the fertility of the region. From Juba II's reign dates the agora, where the five-celled Temple A recalls Banasa's. The agora also yielded a diademed statue of the monarch, its head inclined like Lysippus' Alexander, or the Prima Porta Augustus. There is also a rendition of Juba's son and successor, Ptolemy II, after the manner of Polyclitus' Doryphorus. Other temples of the period were discovered under the Roman decumanus maximus. The soft stone of the region is stuccoed over, as at Sabratha.

Sometime not long before A.D. 50 Sala's Mauretanian agora gave way to the Roman forum, measuring 750 square meters, with shops, and, in time, to the Curia Ulpia (Trajanic), a basilica, and a three-bay arch of

Antoninus Pius' reign. There was a capitolium in a portico on two terraces, which gave room for nine large rooms underneath. On a secondary
decumanus were baths, and shops dating back to Sala's Mauretanian
period. In 142/43 Sala got a circuit wall, perhaps prompted not so much
by military danger as by prosperity (*oppidum*, the Roman word for a
town like Sala, implies a place walled to protect its *opes*, wealth). We
know about this wall because it is mentioned on Sala's most famous
monument, a statue base inscribed to honor M. Sulpicius Felix, prefect of
a "Syrian" cavalry squadron of Roman citizens, thanked and made an
honorary magistrate for having saved them from "the usual lawlessness,
and cattle-rustling" (*solitis iniuriis, pecorumque iactura*). He seems to
have done this by bribing native brigands. The statue was erected not by
the community as a whole but by thirty-eight "friends" (*amici*), whose
names are listed, as Sulpicius was leaving his command. The inscription
mentions sending a delegation to Rome. Some scholars think that this
suggests that Sulpicius was leaving under a cloud. If so, was it because he
had been too lenient to raiders? Or too kind to the rich? The "friends"
were probably wealthy: they represent only thirteen *gentes* (clans); eight
are Fabii, eleven Valerii. In 144 the two Mauretanias were under a single
governor, and twenty-two different units from Pannonia, Moesia, Upper
and Lower Germany, and Spain were in service, two facts that suggest
that now there *was* an emergency; the enemies were the Baquates, of
whom more when we discuss Volubilis. That the "friends," at least, were
thoroughly Romanized is shown by the inscription's fulsome style; Felix
is called "moderate, modest, gentle, moral, a lover of the people, devoted
to his duty."

Not all Roman officers bribed rebels: it was in pursuit of them that the
praetorian C. Suetonius Paulinus had been the first Roman to cross the
Atlas Mountains (A.D. 41). Here may also be mentioned a Moorish chief
who fought for Rome: Lusius Quietus, whose kinky-haired cavalry appear on Trajan's Column (*DSS*, 192), fighting in the Dacian campaign of
105/106. Trajan had him made a senator; he was consul *in absentia*,
in 117, probably as a reward for his savagery against the Jews in Cyrene.
His fall was as sudden as his rise had been meteoric: this powerful,
wealthy, bold, sinister man was suspected of conspiring to seize the
throne, and Hadrian had him executed.

Though there was probably no Mauretanian Limes at the time Sala's
wall was built, air photography has now revealed a V-shaped ditch,
running below the crests of the hills for sixteen kilometers, from the sea
ten kilometers south of Sala to an inland reach of the Oued bou-Regreg.

The accompanying wall had towers at intervals, and air photography has also revealed a very considerable Roman camp, five hundred meters on a side, in a bend of the river eleven and a half kilometers from the sea. Thus protected, Sala was not abandoned by Diocletian; inscriptions run down to the reign of Constantine. Two necropoleis are known, running along the Islamic east wall of Rabat; burials are concentrated between the first century B.C. and the second A.D., with a scattering down into the fourth.

The description of Sala would not be complete without mention of the rich Rabat Museum, which houses the Sala finds, as well as the Tabula Banasitana and the wealth of bronze sculpture from Volubilis, the most impressive and richly documented site in Morocco.

Volubilis (Ksar Pharaoun) lies twenty kilometers north of Meknes, on a fertile plateau 390 meters above sea level, with a view of the Djebel Zarhoun, from which some of its building-stone came. On the plateau grow figs, olives, vines, the dwarf palm, carob, bay tree, thyme, lavender, live oak, wheat, barley, maize, sorghum, and with irrigation, vegetables. It also supports sheep and cattle.

Excavation at Volubilis was opened in 1915 by Hubert Lyautey, governor-general of the French protectorate of Morocco; it was carried on in 1916–17 with German prisoners of war as workmen. Though it has continued sporadically ever since, the west and south quarters are only partially uncovered. What has been revealed, *inter alia*, is that Volubilis had a vigorous life as a Libyo-Punic settlement in the third and second centuries B.C., governed by suffetes and worshiping its native chiefs, to which a sizable tumulus in the center of the excavations bears witness. A total of 598 funeral stelae of Punic or Carthaginian type have been found, and under the Roman levels are temples to native gods; one, miscalled a temple of Saturn (see plan, fig. 11.8) is of impressive dimensions: fifty-four by thirty-six meters. The plan also shows traces of the town's wall, of the Hellenistic period (third–second century B.C.), which enclosed fifteen hectares. The site grew to forty hectares, with a polyglot population of 10,000 to 12,000—Spaniards, Syrians, Jews, and Libyo-Punic speakers. This phase flourished under the long reign of Juba II, a descendant of Masinissa who had, as we saw, a Greco-Roman education and a Macedonian wife, Cleopatra Selene. Volubilis may have been his western capital, though there is no firm archaeological evidence for this.

In the face of Aedemon's revolt in A.D. 40 the inhabitants of Volubilis

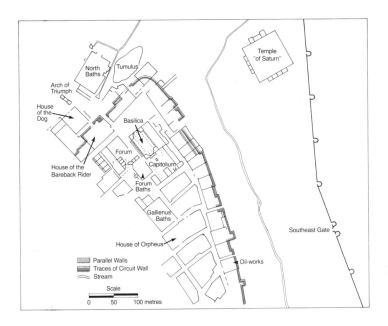

FIGURE 11.8 *Volubilis, Hellenistic phase, plan*

took the side of Rome. Their leader, M. Valerius Severus, had a native father, Bostar, as we learn from an inscription; the sculptured head of a youth in the local museum may represent the son. The Volubilitanian reward was citizenship rights, and ten years' exemption from taxes, under Claudius, with enrollment in the emperor's "tribe," the Quirina. An early phase of the forum dates from Nero, but what the visitor sees today is Severan (fig. 11.9), with double-apsed basilica (reerected arches visible), capitolium, on a high podium at the back of its precinct (upper left), small Forum Baths, to the right of the capitolium, and porticoed area (bottom center) with four cellae to the right. About a hundred meters north of the Severan Forum rises the arch of Caracalla (fig. 11.10) dated by its inscription to 216/17. In its present state it is 19.28 meters wide and 9.23 high, bearing reliefs with military standards and trophies, and two inscriptions; it was surmounted by a statue of the emperor in a six-horse chariot. It had two pairs of projecting Corinthian columns on each face, as at Theveste and Ammaedara. Between each pair are statue-niches, and above them medallions, each representing a Season. A Caracallan inscription on bronze, not from the arch, remits all outstanding debts to the imperial fisc, and very broadly hints that the emperor expects a draft of soldiers and elephants in return. Facing the arch on the east are

FIGURE 11.9 *Volubilis, arch of Caracalla*, A.D. 216–217

FIGURE 11.10 *Volubilis, forum, air view*

the North Baths, Trajanic or Hadrianic; at fifteen hundred square meters they are Volubilis' largest public ones; the other set in this quarter, those of Gallienus, measure only nine hundred square meters, but had a rich polychrome marble décor.

Surrounding the arch on the other three sides are houses: to the north, that of the Ephebe, of the Columns, and of the Horseman; west and south, the House of the Compass, the Dog, and the Desultor (bareback rider). These are named from their décor or finds. The Ephebe is a bronze statue of an ivy-crowned youth, now in the Rabat Museum. The House of the Columns (early 200s) has spiral fluting. In the House of the Horseman (third century) was a mosaic showing Bacchus, guided by Cupid as seeing-eye dog, discovering the sleeping Ariadne. The House of the Dog is named from a splendid bronze statue of a native saluki (greyhound); it too is in Rabat. The House of the Desultor is named from a mosaic showing a figure, perhaps Silenus (compare Conimbriga, *ISS*, 214), riding backwards. One other house, the richest in this quarter, deserves mention, that of the Orpheus, south of the Gallienus Baths, with cypresses in its garden. It has central heating, its own set of baths, and several mosaics, of which the one that gives the house its name is the most interesting (fig. 11.11). It professes to show the familiar scene of the bard charming animals and birds with his lyre-music, but the animals—

FIGURE 11.11 *Volubilis, Orpheus mosaic*

elephant, horse, monkeys, oryx, antelope, bull, deer, griffin, leopard, bear, etc.—are of different sizes, and face in different directions, paying Orpheus no attention whatever; they come from various pattern books, and the mosaicist has not bothered to integrate them into a total design. This is one of the ten houses in Volubilis that incorporate a room for pressing oil—that is how these Berber-Roman tycoons made their money. Also, as we shall see, they were not ashamed of having shops in the front or rear of their houses; a total of 121 shops have been identified, many of them bakeries.

Under the Antonines, Volubilis expanded, and with it the new northeast quarter (see the city plan, fig. 11.12) surrounded by a wall 2.35 kilometers in circumference, with eight gates and thirty-four towers, one every fifty meters. The wall is dated 168/69 by a coin, deliberately embedded in antiquity in the northeast (Tangier) gate. The northeast quarter, enclosed by this wall, is split in two by a noble decumanus maximus, with sidewalks, porticoes, and arcades (fig. 11.13). On either side of it twenty-three houses have been excavated. They are listed below, and the most important starred. Beginning from the lower left (southwest corner of the street), we have the House of:

*1. the Labors of Hercules (Commodan?)
2. Flavius Germanus
3. Dionysus and the Four Seasons
*4. the Baths of the Nymphs (Antonine?)
5. the Wild Beasts (Antonine/Severan)
6. the Pompeii (west of the palace; after A.D. 238)
7. South Cardo I
8. the Gold Coin (Severan)
9. the Marble Bacchus ⎫
10. the Sundial   ⎬ after A.D. 238
11. the Two Olive Presses ⎭
12. the Nereids ⎫
13. the Half-columns ⎬ Severan
14. the Apse (third century A.D.)
15. No Name
16. No Peristyle ⎫
17. the Cloverleaf Basin ⎬ A.D. 250–260
18. the Portico ⎭
*19. the Voyage of Venus (A.D. 250 or earlier)
20. the Bronze Bust (before A.D. 238)

21. the Gold Ring (late third century A.D.)
22. the Fat Pilasters (Severan)
23. the Crypt (ca. A.D. 250)

The first house shows, in its dining room, the Labors of Hercules, and scenes from his life, in sixteen medallions, of which twelve are legible: the infant Hercules strangling serpents, the golden apples of the Hesperides, Cerberus, the Cretan Bull, the Augean stable, the Stymphalian birds, the Erymanthian boar, Antaeus, the Lernaean hydra, the Amazons, the Nemean lion, and an enigmatic one of the hero apparently erecting pillars (work for Laomedon at Troy?). Because of Commodus' Hercules-fixation, the house has been thought to date from his reign. It has forty-one rooms, covering two thousand square meters. Another room with mosaics shows Jupiter and Ganymede in a central medallion, the four Seasons in the corners. The house has eight shops, and, as elsewhere, a porter's lodge. Some rooms have frescoed panels imitating marble, in yellow or pale blue, veined with white.

The House of the Baths of the Nymphs portrays three of them, one in a necklace, another removing her sandals, a third dancing. Also portrayed are the winged horse Pegasus drinking from the spring Hippocrene, and the hunter Actaeon. The house also has three shops, a bakery, and an oil press.

The House of the Voyage of Venus (no. 19 on the list) is the star attraction: it had mosaics in eight rooms and seven corridors. The mosaic that gives the house its name, now in the Tangier Museum, decorated the dining room (11 on plan, fig. 11.14). Venus is on the poop of a galley rowed by Graces, manned by Cupids, and convoyed by Tritons and Tritonesses with baskets of flowers. The triclinium entrance had a panel portraying a mock chariot race, as at Piazza Armerina, the chariots drawn by outsize red ducks, green peacocks, and white geese (the colors of three of the teams which competed in chariot races in the Roman circuses, but also of Seasons). Room 16 had a mosaic of the handsome Argonaut Hylas abducted by nymphs, a favorite theme of Hellenistic poetry, elaborated by both Theocritus and Callimachus. It also contained one of the prize Volubilis finds, a superb bronze bust of Cato the Younger (fig. 11.15), now in Rabat. It was sand-cast, with details inlaid in silver, and a dozen patches on the shoulder and left breast, invisible, but sensible to the touch. An expert dates it to the reign of Nero or Vespasian, a superb copy of an original contemporary with Cato's suicide. The adjoining room, Room 17, contained a mosaic of Diana and three nymphs

North Baths

House of the
Cloverleaf Basin

House of
Venus

Palace of
Gordian

House of
the Pompeii

House of the
Baths of the Nymphs

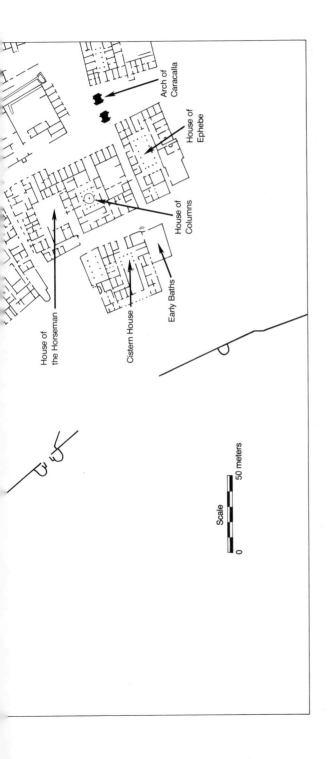

House of
the Horseman

Cistern House

Early Baths

Arch of
Caracalla

House of
Ephebe

House of
Columns

Scale

0

50 meters

FIGURE 11.12 *Volubilis, plan*

FIGURE 11.13 *Volubilis, decumanus maximus*

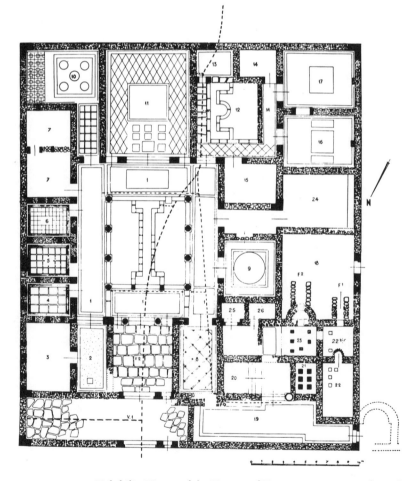

FIGURE 11.14 *Volubilis, House of the Voyage of Venus, A.D. 250 or earlier, plan*

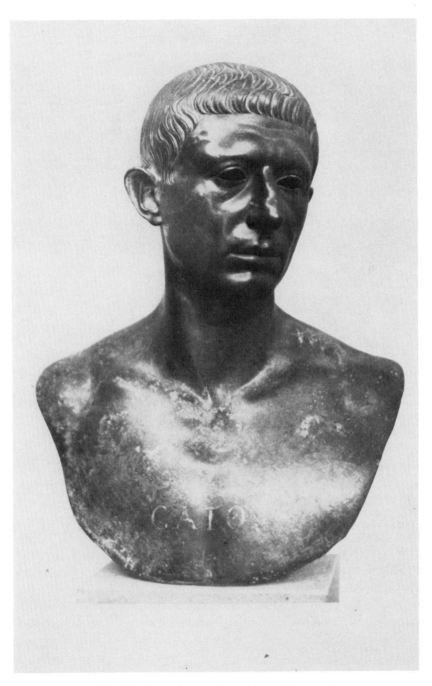

FIGURE 11.15 *Volubilis, Cato, bronze bust, reign of Nero or Vespasian, in Rabat Museum*

FIGURE 11.16 *Volubilis, Hellenistic prince, bronze bust, Rabat Museum*

bathing, with Actaeon, who is already sprouting the staghorns that will prompt Diana's hounds to rend him, as a culpable voyeur. One nymph, with bow and quiver, is oblivious of the whole affair; the second is surprised, the third frightened. An empty statue base in this room may have supported the controversial diademed bronze bust of a Hellenistic prince (fig. 11.16) actually found in a bakery across the street, and now in Rabat. It is usually identified as Juba II, but other candidates are Hiero II of Syracuse, Cleomenes III, the idealist reformer king of Sparta (reigned 235–219), who like Cato committed suicide, Juba I (another suicide), and Hannibal. Cleomenes committed suicide, samurai-fashion, in Alexandria, in the reign of an ancestor of Juba II's wife, Cleopatra Selene. The Prince is at any rate a reproduction of an official portrait; it was cast by the lost-wax process, has inlaid bronze eyelashes, inset eyes (put in place before the top of the head went on; the diadem concealed the join). Since the alloy has the same percentage of tin as in the Cato, it is reasonable to suppose that the two bronzes are of the same date. Both busts were cast in pieces for ease in transport, then assembled on the spot.

Volubilis' preeminence as a center or market for bronze work is underlined by the discovery in the excavation storeroom, reported in 1966, of a fragment of a red copper trophy from an imperial statue, probably Severan. The findspot is unknown. The technique is damascening; that is, the metal is incised, and silver leaf hammered in. As usual, the trophy is mounted on a tree trunk, and flanked by captives. The tree trunk is inlaid with silver and surmounted by a helmet with flaps and horns. The cuirass, also inlaid with silver—the motifs are acanthus leaves and sea monsters—is bronze, oxidized into red, green, violet, and orange. At the foot of the tree are shields. The captives are recognizable as a Parthian and a Briton, both in trousers, the Briton in damascened plaid.

The House of the Voyage of Venus also had its own baths, in Rooms 18–22: at twelve hundred square meters, they are larger than those of Gallienus. Two other mosaics here deserve mention. The central medallion in Room 9 portrayed Cupids throwing grain to birds; barbarians built fires upon it when they occupied the house as squatters after 270. Room 10, a bedroom, had Bacchus and the four Seasons, Spring with a flower crown, Summer a brunette with a sickle, Autumn blonde, with grapes and a basket of fruit; Winter (missing) was probably cloaked, as was conventional.

One house in the northeast quarter belongs in a separate category, the Palace of the Gordians, named after an inscription of Gordian III found in it; probably it was the governor's residence. It is prominent, as befits its lofty function, on the decumanus maximus, north of the House of the Pompeii. It consists of two houses thrown together, a total of seventy-four rooms, and though it has a colonnaded front, its own baths, and *opus sectile* (not mosaic) floors, it also has a dozen shops in a row behind the colonnade, and the northeast corner has three oil presses and an oil store. The possibility that it was ever the palace of Juba II is slight; coins found there begin with Marcus Aurelius.

An inscription found in this house in 1949 probably belongs to a significant series of "altars of peace," celebrating good relations with native tribes, in which Volubilis is uniquely rich. They generally record what are called "conversations" between the Roman procurator and the *princeps* (chief) of the Bavares or the Baquates. This amounts to recognizing officially, in law and religion, that the relations are between equals. Faced with forces beyond its control, Roman diplomacy showed itself realistic. The dates of the various colloquia are significant: 140, *169–175*, 180, 200, 203, 223–224, *239–241*, 245, 277, 280. Only those italicized belong to years of revolt. The most sensible hypothesis is that these colloquies were occasioned by a change in reign, either Roman or indigenous; in Rome's case from Hadrian to Antoninus Pius, Marcus Aurelius to Commodus, Elagabalus to Alexander Severus. The last two altars refer, with wishful thinking, to a *foederata et diuturna pax*, "a federated and lasting peace." In fact, the barbarians destroyed Volubilis between 274 and 280.

The lamps of Volubilis and other Moroccan sites give a valuable insight into what mattered in the lives of average Mauretanians in Antonine-Severan times. Their motifs include chariot races and gladiatorial shows; mythological scenes, often erotic—Leda having intercourse with a horse, a phallic Genius, a satyr, Venus and Cupid, Diana and Actaeon, Mercury, a centaur, a dove with olive branch, Vulcan, a sphinx, a cock; the animal kingdom—boar, eagle, stag, lion attacking goat, dolphin, panther, Ram, Scorpion, Crab (these last zodiacal); the vine, daisies, palm, laurel crown, Victory, the monogram of Christ, the scallop shell (of Saint James?).

Volubilis' territorium has sixty-four known sites, including villae rusticae, quarries, and castella. Sidi Said housed the Cohors IV Gallorum; the Bled el-Gaada camp measures 210 by 175 meters. Aïn Schkor housed cohorts from Spain and Belgium; its blockhouse, 90 meters square, oversaw the neighboring quarries, where one can still see abandoned squared blocks, wedge-slots, and inclined planes down which blocks were moved on rollers. Stone was extracted by cutting slots in a row, inserting wooden wedges, and wetting them. The resulting expansion of the wedges split the rock. Sidi Moussa, 95 meters square, housed a cohort of Parthians. At Tocolosida (Bled Takourart, 175 meters square; see air photograph, fig. 11.17) were stationed squadrons of Gallic and Syrian cavalry; its date is Antonine.

FIGURE 11.17 *Tocolosida, Antonine, air view*

Thamusida (Sidi Ali ben Ahmed) on the River Sebou, halfway between Sala and Banasa, and like them an army town, was inhabited by a slightly bloated bourgeoisie, many of them retired veterans. The excavations, unfinished, have revealed the largest camp of its period (Antonine), a river-front quarter with a large warehouse, a fuller's establishment, and three temples, of which one, triple-celled, may be to Ceres, Liber, and Libera; in front of it were found over a hundred kilograms of bronze, broken up for the crucible. Southwest of it were the Great Baths (three thousand square meters), with fifty-nine rooms, and men's and women's sections; and a garum works. Within a circuit wall like Tipasa's, and of the same date as Volubilis', with semicircular towers, seventeen *insulae* (blocks of houses) have been excavated and picturesquely named—the Drums, the Snails, the Lion, the Hollow Stone. The air photograph, fig. 11.18, shows a corner of the circuit wall in the east quarter, with the town's only peristyle dwelling, the House of the Stone Floor; two walls of a square temple, perhaps to Venus-Astarte, adjoining to the east; the Insula of Nigidius Albanus; and the towered circuit wall itself, which forms the southeast side of the peristyle house. This has twenty-two rooms; those facing northwest are shops, as at Volubilis. The large room backed against the circuit wall, and facing the peristyle, was the triclinium, for dining. The date is Antonine, about 150.

FIGURE 11.18 *Thamusida, Antonine, air view*

The camp is oriented differently from the town and is set somewhat apart, seventy-five meters southwest of the nearest residential block. Of the usual playing-card shape, it measures 166 by 139 meters, an area of 2.25 hectares: it would accommodate a thousand men. Some of their barracks have been identified inside the east gate. It shares its southwest side with the slightly later circuit wall, and has fourteen rectangular towers, facing inward, and four more pairs flanking the gates. It had rounded battlements, which must have given it an exotic appearance, like an Islamic ribat. Its Via Principalis, running across the front of the headquarters building, was colonnaded. A basilica, whose apse robs part of the praetorium court, is a later addition of 250–270, just before Thamusida's fall. Civilization here was composite: language and culture were Punic; architecture, amenities, and some of the cults were Roman. Still to find is the forum; still to be excavated, the rest of the camp, the industrial quarter, and the river-front installations.

The question of the Roman occupation of eastern Morocco, and of its road communications with Mauretania Caesariensis, is, as we have seen, vexed. Excavation of the region around Oujda, on the Moroccan-Algerian

FIGURE 11.19 *Oujda, Berber settlement, air view*

border, five hundred kilometers east of Thamusida, is interesting in itself, but has not settled the question. What it has revealed is 148 sites, in an area of twenty-one by fifteen kilometers, at an altitude of nearly sixteen hundred meters. These consist for the most part of low discontinuous walls, many hidden in the undergrowth or ruined by the plow. The walls are not foursquare, and are probably Berber, not Roman. A typical site is a sheer projecting isthmus, either walled or naturally defended at the base, like Djebel Matisseur (fig. 11.19), with dwellings and corrals on top, like the *citânias* of Portugal (*ISS*, figs. 4.23 and 24). The houses are irregular in plan, built, their French excavator writes, with an apparent abhorrence of linearity, regularity, order, or harmony. Though sparsely settled, this area supports cattle, sheep, and goats in tens of thousands. Since Berber conservatism is such that a given pot may be either Neolithic or contemporary, dating is difficult, but there are a few Roman coins, ranging in date from Tiberius to Maxentius (A.D. 14 to 312); some of the walls show the influence of Roman technique; and an altar is reported that dates to the third or fourth Christian century.

We end this chapter with a description of El Gour, a Berber mausoleum of the seventh century A.D. It lies twenty kilometers southeast of Meknes, and consisting as it does of a platform in which stands a masonry cylinder forty meters wide, surmounted by a truncated cone, it is distantly related to the Djedars described at the end of the last chapter, and like them it would have been the burial place of a Mauretanian prince more or less Romanized, since the dimensions suggest the Roman foot as module. An altar, now destroyed, on the side facing the sunrise, suggests a solar cult. Carbon 14 dating places the monument ninety years either side of A.D. 640. This late Romano-Berber monument illustrates some comments made by the American novelist and *grande dame* Edith Wharton, who published in 1920 a book about her travels in Morocco under the aegis of the French High Command. She writes of "the perpetual flux and the immovable stability, the barbarous customs and sensuous refinements, the absence of artistic originality, and the gift for regrouping borrowed motives, the patient and exquisite workmanship, and the immediate neglect and degradation of the thing once made." She also, perhaps unwittingly, recapitulated the experience of the Maghreb when she wrote of "the superhuman virtues of a series of rulers whose debaucheries and vices were usually cut short by assassination."

PART 5: CONCLUSION

12. THE BALANCE SHEET OF EMPIRE

"Romans," Ramsay MacMullen has written, "of course, not only built bridges, but beat their wives." This is a proper assessment of praise and blame. Modern apologists for the empire have tended to overpraise, antiimperialists to overblame. Jean Colin (to take examples of the former first), addressing French army officers in Morocco in 1925, advised them to let the indigenes know that "we Romans were here before the Arabs." In *The River War* (1899) Winston Churchill wrote, "What enterprise that an enlightened community may attempt is more noble and more profitable than the reclamation from barbarism of fertile regions and large populations? To give peace to warring tribes, to administer justice where all was violence, to strike the chains off the slave, to draw richness from the soil, to plant the earliest seeds of commerce and learning, to increase in whole peoples their capacities for pleasure, and diminish their chances of pain—what more beautiful ideal or more valuable reward can inspire human effort? The act is virtuous, the exercise invigorating, and the results often extremely profitable." Lord Rosebery (British prime minister in 1894) called the British Empire "the greatest secular agency for good the world has ever seen."

In the years since the Maghreb has gained its independence (Libya in 1951, with a coup in 1969, Morocco in 1956, Tunisia in 1957, Algeria in 1962), antiimperialist critics of the Roman Empire in Africa have become more vocal. Though French authorities state that whatever was good about their régime was due to conscious imitation of Rome by Napoleon III, the antiimperialists insist that Roman history must be "decolonized," and that underdevelopment was a necessary consequence of the ancient slave system. While even the most conservative historians admit that Roman imperial government was not uniformly virtuous, the critics select their evidence to prove too much; the balance needs redressing. The operation will require repeating, without cross-reference, of data from earlier chapters.

———————————

Agricultural productivity. Africa was Rome's granary and its agricultural output sufficed, at least till the Vandal invasion of the 430s, both to support its own population and to supply the Roman annona. Statistics on ancient African calorie-intake are not available, but in Africa Proconsularis people were generally well fed, the countryside being made fruitful by putting into practice the agricultural precepts of the Carthaginian Mago, translated into Latin for practical use in 126 B.C., by order of the Roman Senate, after the destruction of Carthage in 146 B.C. The Romans learned from the Carthaginians to preserve a monopoly by limiting the growth of vines: one does not take steps to limit that which does not grow productively. It is worth noting that the agrarian law of 111 B.C. treats land in Africa as though it were eminently worth having, affirming title to it as private property and removing the obstacles to expansion of the latifundia for which Africa became famous—or notorious. The Numidian king Masinissa had already found that latifundia made agriculture more efficient. Nero, notoriously, caused the execution of the six largest landowners in Africa: their holdings formed the nucleus of the *saltus* (imperial estates) there, about which a number of inscriptions give valuable information.

For purposes of the present argument, the most important point in the inscriptional provisions is the inducement offered to tenant farmers to take up waste or abandoned land: they would become quasi-owners of it as long as they continued to cultivate it, and they might occupy it rent-free for five to ten years, depending on the crop grown, the maximum inducement being reserved for olive-culture. Surely these provisions evince a strong imperial desire to raise production, which would not only supply more olive oil for Rome's annona, but feed and profit the local population as well. In this connection the number of oil works in the territory south of Theveste is noteworthy. This is the area where the Albertini Tablets, of the Vandal period, were found. These show that the provisions of the saltus inscriptions of four hundred years before were still in force, and perhaps imply the return to the land of a family previously dispossessed. The Bir Troueh ostraka, slightly earlier but still of the Vandal period, also show agricultural activity, with teams of workmen busy delivering grain and oil. Some have stressed the evidence the inscriptions offer for violence and corruption practiced by the imperial procurators and chief lessees, but surely the complaints would never have been carved on stone if there was not at least the will to remove the ground for them.

That Lepcis Magna was able to bear up under an annual fine, imposed by Caesar, of three million pounds of olive oil does not suggest a starving population. Even if discounted ten percent for exaggeration, average life spans of from 47.5 to 59.2 years, calculated for Sicca Veneria, Simitthu, Thuburbo Maius, Thugga, and Mactar in Tunisia; and for Thibilis, Madauros, Tiddis, Thamugadi, and Thagaste in Algeria, also do not indicate undernourishment. A significant number of buildings in Proconsularis are equipped with receptacles for grain; for example, at Sicca, Mactar, Bulla Regia, Thugga, Thuburbo Maius, Gigthis, Sufetula; and in Numidia at Madauros, Theveste, and Thamugadi; if these were distribution points for a grain dole, the poor in those centers did not go hungry. The mosaics portraying life on great African latifundia of the third and fourth Christian centuries (for example, at Uthina, Thabraca, Caesarea, and the estate of Dominus Julius, near Carthage) show an abundance in which the farmhands shared: flocks of sheep and goats, plentiful water-supply, partridges and other birds for fowling; geese, ducks; rich plow-land, olive orchards, vineyards, fruit trees, kitchen gardens. When the chatelaine receives a present of fish, we may assume that the family of the peasant donor did not go hungry.

The Boglio stele (third century) from Tunisian Siliana shows plowing, reaping of abundant sheaves, and heavily loaded wagons bringing the harvest home. Later (fourth century) and more primitive reliefs from Ghirza in the Tripolitanian hinterland show similar scenes: here one of the crops is barley, and among the draft animals are camels. Nowadays the site is desert. Mosaics and extensive stables from the working villa at Oued Athménia, not far south of Constantine, show productivity in horse-rearing. Even the steppe-like uplands of the Algerian-Moroccan border supported large flocks of cattle, sheep, and goats. The statistics for Proconsularis and Byzacena in 422—8,332 square kilometers of land taxable, 6,730 exempt—show that in the latter years of Roman rule there, cultivated land was not much reduced from what it had been in the high empire.

The fate of large areas of the Maghreb hinterland in modern times shows what happened when Rome withdrew: deforestation, springs polluted, the art of grafting, to improve the olive, no longer practiced, terrace walls not kept in repair, manuring neglected.

Public amenities. It is always a question in any culture how far apparent prosperity risks diminishing itself by sinking into conspicuous consumption. Cosinius' market at Cuicul, for example, cost 30,000 sesterces; Liberalis' fountain at Timgad cost 32,348, while an unskilled worker's daily wage was four. But the markets at Hippo, Cuicul, or Thamugadi are evidence rather for outlets for productivity than for conspicuous consumption and waste. They also show how good communications were. Harbors like those of Apollonia, Lepcis Magna, Tipasa, and Caesarea fostered communication by sea, which was exponentially cheaper than land-transport: for cargoes of similar bulk, sea freight cost 2.1 percent of its value per hundred kilometers, transport by land, 58 to 88 percent. Nevertheless, the far-flung road network, though primarily military, facilitated civil administration, commerce, and the exchange of ideas. The elaborate systems of centuriation (large-scale land partition) known from Proconsularis, Numidia, and Caesariensis would have been pointless without access from the centuriated farms to market. In Proconsularis this was provided by the major military road from Carthage to Ammaedara; in Numidia, by that from Cirta to Sitifis. Milestones in the Tripolitanian hinterland show that agriculture was at its height there precisely in the years of the military anarchy, between the Severans and Diocletian. The Tipasa cardo continues southward into the back country, to tap the exotic products of the desert and its oases—gold dust, ivory, ostrich plumes. The hoard of nearly ten thousand coins from Tiddis reveals trade contacts between this remote Numidian outpost and the wider Mediterranean world of Carthage, Athens, and Rome.

The army was responsible for public works: the Legio III Augusta built the thirty-nine kilometers of the Lambaesis aqueduct in eight months, and the legion or its temporary successor kept the roads in repair throughout the military anarchy. In some places in Numidia civilian agricultural abutters levied tolls for the upkeep of roads, their vital link to market. The engineering shows Roman genius at its practical best: large towns were bypassed, snow-markers were provided, there was an elaborate system of post houses. In Tingitana the military roads assured communications also for the villae rusticae that dotted the territorium of Tingi and Volubilis.

But it is the urban amenities, which had an economic and aesthetic value of their own, that are usually taken to be the glory of Roman North Africa: theaters, amphitheaters, baths, nymphaea, temples, Christian basilicas, seigneurial houses with their elaborate mosaics and cool underground rooms, as at Bulla Regia; the library at Timgad, the elaborate mausolea. Philanthropy not only paid for many of these buildings, but also provided child-assistance funds, like the one attested for Sicca Veneria in Marcus Aurelius' reign, where the income from 1.3 million sesterces was pledged to the support of three hundred boys from three to fifteen, and two hundred girls from three to thirteen. Even if vanity were the only motive, we ought to remember Leglay's equation: "Vanity plus generosity equals embellishment." At the very least the building and décor gave employment to many. While Apollonia's heated baptismal water, Cyrene's four theaters, and Timgad's thirteen public baths may be deemed excessive, there is no denying the usefulness of the many aqueducts, which to Frontinus and Gibbon ranked "among the noblest monuments of Roman genius and power." Water supply also helped productivity, as in the voluntary local water rationing and irrigation scheme of the 220s at Lamasba in Numidia, which did not imply, as it did in Egypt, caste, bureaucracy, or tyranny.

It is worth noting that many of the donors have indigenous names, especially at Lepcis Magna, where the names are Punic and the benefactions include market, theater, and chalcidicum. At Bulla Regia, some of the sumptuous houses with their cool underground mosaic-floored rooms may have belonged to naturalized Africans whose cognomina—Concessus, Donatus, Rogatus, Saturninus, Felix, Fortunatus, Honoratus, Victor—are Latin versions of Punic names. And the Roman-style Berber working villa at Aïn Sarb shows how the native culture could assimilate without yielding, as today in the Francophone Maghreb. The working villas remind us that the seigneurial houses were not all for show: the House of the Frescoes at Tipasa paid its way, and so did the dwellings in the northeast quarter of Volubilis, which had both rich mosaics and shops and oil presses. Nor did public building always use flagrantly expensive materials: at Gigthis, Sabratha, Portus Magnus, and Sila they made do with cheap local sandstone covered with stucco to keep up appearances.

Though Dio Cassius, historian, senator, and consul (A.D. 229), advocates adorning Rome as expensively as possible, while reducing building expenditure in the provinces, the African Lactantius, writing in 318, criticizes Diocletian's passion for building—basilicas, circuses, mint, armory, luxurious houses. In fact much of the building could be justified. Much replacement was needed after the turmoil of the previous half-century—for example, the main camp, streets, and aqueduct at Lambaesis; the rebuilding and repopulation of Rapidum. This was not extravagant but necessary, and it shows that public spirit survived: the tetrarchy was not merely a time of punitive taxes, evasion, and forced labor. Though Cyprian—martyred in 258—waxes rhetorical about exhaustion of the land, amphoras from Africa at Ostia give him the lie: they show, as do the offices (opened in the second century, but still in use in the third) of African firms in the Ostian Piazzale delle Corporazioni, that olive oil was still pouring in from Lepcis Minor and Hadrumetum at a time when he alleges the produce of Proconsularis was sadly diminished. In fact, dated mosaics from rich houses and other buildings at Thysdrus, Uthina, Cincari, Thuburbo Maius, Thugga, and Pupput (Souk el-Abiod, a shrine of Ceres and Persephone), Hippo, and Zliten (a threshing scene) show that Proconsularis was not so hard hit by the anarchical years as other parts of the empire.

Finally under this head, the number of Christian basilicas attested for the late empire certainly suggests that the many dioceses—over five hundred at the Council of Carthage in 411—were far from being churchmouse poor: the evidence is the funerary mosaics of Clupea and Thabraca, the numerous basilicas of Carthage, Sufetula, and Ammaedara, the fortified east church of Cyrene, the basilicas of Apollonia; Justinian's basilica at Sabratha, with its splendid mosaic; the Great Basilica, perhaps Augustine's, at Hippo; the other Great Basilica at Tipasa, with those of Saints Salsa, Peter and Paul, and Bishop Alexander; a whole basilical quarter at Cuicul, and another—Donatist—at Thamugadi; those of Sitifis, the firmly dated one, perhaps also Donatist, of 324 at Castellum Tingitanum, and the splendid one, testifying to prosperity even under the Vandals, at Theveste. A plethora of churches could be seen as conspicuously consumptive and wasteful, but clearly their original builders thought otherwise, and had the wherewithal to build them.

Industry. Professor Finley has told us that in antiquity the top priority went to investment in land, the only reputable source of wealth. The concept of investing for improvement in manufacturing simply did not exist. Manufacturing had a low social status, and was simply not a major source of wealth; that came from agriculture, investment in land, or mining. Because of the moral obloquy attached to "being in trade," the ancients set no great store by technological progress, economic growth, productivity, or efficiency. The only African product mass-produced for export was pottery, of which a great deal, mostly oil amphoras, has been identified at Ostia. And pottery was regarded as a legitimate extension of respectable agriculture, since potters' clay is a product of the soil. Cyrene paid for its luxury imports with an agricultural export: silphium.

But even with these caveats, there is more positive evidence for African industry. One entrepreneur who profited from tile-making was Hedulius, the dedicator of the Carthage altar which rivals the Ara Pacis in Rome as propaganda for Augustus. In this connection we may cite again the evidence of the Volubilis oil presses and 121 shops, the north rooms of the House of the Frescoes at Tipasa, metamorphosed into a garum (fish sauce) factory, and similar establishments in Tingitana, at Lixus, Cotta, and Thamusida. Also in Tingitana we have the manufacture of purple dye at Mogador island. Quarrying limestone was a noteworthy activity at Volubilis, and marble at Simitthu. And we should not forget the evidence of the cloth markets at Thamugadi and possibly Lepcis Magna (the chalcidicum). Finally under this head we should note that as the empire wore on manufacture of goods increased on the latifundia, which at the end were as self-sufficient as an eighteenth-century Virginia plantation.

The imperial bureaucracy. On the evidence of the cemetery of the *officiales* at Carthage, the album of municipal officers at Thamugadi, and the seven hundred inscriptions there, we must agree with Professor Parkinson that in ancient as in modern times, work expands to fill the time available for its completion, and subordinates multiply at a fixed rate regardless of the amount of work produced, gobbling up any surplus in the process. Of course the length of the Timgad album also reflects the government's efficiency in persuading or coercing the rich into shouldering municipal burdens. But the growth of bureaucracy made for recognition of achievement, as opposed to mere claims based on birth, and so made for social mobility and the employment of nonaristocrats in powerful posts. However cumbersome and corrupt the bureaucracy grew, especially in Byzantine times, it proved a check on the more arbitrary extortions of provincial governors, even though Dio's recommendation of education for public service remained an unrealized dream. Luxorius, idle poet of the Vandal court, can find only one rapacious governor to criticize. In the Christian bureaucracy, that not all bishops were bureaucrats is proved by the career of Synesius of Cyrene, who in the first place prejudices us in his favor by having been unwilling to serve, and then proved himself a staunch ombudsman, a defender of the plebs against the excesses of imperial bureaucracy both civil and military. Many bureaucrats were far from idle: Lollius Urbicus of Tiddis served his sovereign not only in Rome, but also from end to end of the empire— in Palestine, Noricum, Lower Germany, and Britain.

Tolerance. Under the empire, the Romans used force surprisingly little to establish political domination. On the whole, the Roman record is one of tolerance, as long as the provincials behaved and paid their taxes. Roman sources themselves deprecate annexation or colonization; against the former, they argue that occupation costs would overbalance the profit; against the latter, that colonies are either doomed to be wiped out or prone to demand independence. It was twenty-four years after the fall of Carthage before the Gracchan colony was founded. That was short-lived. A new Carthage began to rise only after a hundred years had passed since the destruction of the old, and the definitive Augustan foundation dates from 29 B.C., 117 years after Scipio Aemilianus sowed the site with salt. This hardly shows eagerness to exploit conquered territory. And outside the territorium of Carthage, Punic or Numidian political and religious institutions were allowed to survive. In Cyrene, Augustan edicts provided that Greeks should be tried under Greek law. Augustus, Rome's first successful overseas colonizer (as well as the man who curbed Roman territorial expansion overseas), sent out colonists as reward (to veterans) and as riddance (from malcontents). Once arrived, they could provide farm labor for the annona, defend the new settlements against the Berbers, and add by their gratitude to Augustus' popularity.

Most natives actively wanted Romanization, though the gloomily rhetorical Tacitus speaks of the Latin language, the wearing of the toga, and the indulgence in the luxury of baths and banquets as the instruments of servitude. The willing acceptance of Roman citizenship by members of the ruling class in African cities produced such Roman Africans as the comic poet Terence, the rhetorician Fronto of Cirta, the jurist Salvius Julianus of Hadrumetum, the novelist Apuleius of Madauros, the emperor Septimius Severus of Lepcis Magna, the Christians Tertullian and Cyprian of Carthage, and Arnobius of Sicca and his pupil Lactantius; the angelic doctor Augustine of Thagaste, the epigrammatist Luxorius of Vandal Carthage, and perhaps the biographer Suetonius (of Hippo?), and the poet Dracontius (of Carthage; late fifth century). Tacitus writes, "the addition of the strongest of the provincials was a rescue operation for an exhausted empire" (*Annals* 11.24). And Tertullian could praise the gifts of Romanization: roads, estates, flocks and herds, the culture of cities, the conquest of desert, mountain, and fen. Romanization at its best meant the rule of law: consider the shelves for law-books in the Byzantine governor's palace at Apollonia. It made a policy of granting Roman citizenship to Berber chiefs, as at Banasa in 177. This evoked loyalty, as when Valerius, son of Bostar, defended Volubilis against Aedemon's revolt in A.D. 40. A corollary of this was the recognition of Berber chiefs as equals, attested to by the series of altars of peace from Volubilis, dated between 140 and 280. The result was a composite civilization, in which language and culture might be native, while architecture, amenities, and some of the cults were Roman.

Some but not all evidence for widespread Saturn worship thinly conceals the survival of Phoenician Ba'al. Roman tolerance also allowed the cult of Caelestis (Tanit) at Thuburbo Maius and Portus Magnus, the Di Mauri at Vaga, of Liber Pater (Shadrach) at Sabratha, Malagbel at Castellum Dimmidi, Venus-Astarte at Thamusida, the Syrian Jupiter Dolichenus at Lepcis Magna. There were Jews at Carthage, Sitifis, and Pomaria. Isis worship is attested at Sabratha and Banasa.

The Romans, never ones to hide their light under a bushel, propagandized their virtues far and wide—for example, Caesar's conquests in the monument at Kbor Klib, near Mactar, and the huge bronze trophy at Hippo. Augustus' altar at Carthage connects him with the gods and the founding of Rome. Colossal heads from Lepcis Magna magnify the princes of the Julio-Claudian house and their consorts. A relief from the Sabratha theater celebrates concord between Roman and native; another from the Severan arch at Lepcis celebrates the same, as a matter of wishful thinking, between members of the ruling house. Severus calls himself "propagator of empire." Coins propagandize virtues like Loyalty, Concord, Security, Equity, Peace, Liberty—which at least conceal the existence of political subordination.

We conclude this section with a discussion of resistance movements. These are idealized by antiimperialist historians, taken by others to be nomadic incursions requiring defense. The list of African resistance leaders begins with Jugurtha, high-handed, violent, devious, treacherous, but brilliant in generalship and in political analysis (he saw Rome as venal), and enlisting the sympathy of moderns because he was betrayed at the end. From Augustus to the Vandal conquest, one could count thirty-five revolts covering 262 out of the 449 years involved, and conclude from this the failure of Roman imperialism. One could as illogically count, say, forty-four revolts in the last 450 years of British history (for example, the Gunpowder Plot, Civil War, the American Revolution, the Boer War, agitation for independence in the Indian subcontinent) and conclude therefrom the failure of the British Constitution; or one could count thirty-nine revolts in American history (for example, the Whiskey Rebellion, the Civil War, presidential assassinations, steel strikes, civil rights or antiwar demonstrations), and draw a parallel erroneous conclusion. Many of the alleged revolts were mere troublemaking by misfits, present in every society. Brigands were not necessarily Robin Hoods, nor spokesmen for class-consciousness. It is particularly hard in the present case to justify the terrorism of the Circumcellions or Gildo's deliberate policy of starving Rome by withholding the annona.

A major crux is whether the Donatist schism was a nationalist or social movement. Some distinguished Western historians argue that it was neither, but was primarily doctrinal: in the fourth century doctrine could be more divisive than nationalism or socialism. Donatists never advocated communal property, freeing the slaves, or forgiving debt. It is true that native élites stopped wanting integration into the empire, but that was not because the empire was rotten, but because they preferred local power to senatorial status. What could be seen as decadence may well have been a search for a better balance, frustrated by external and internal troubles, and perverted into militarism and totalitarianism.

Extent of social equality. Philanthropy attempted, with some success, to bridge the gap between haves and have-nots; natives often shared in the wealth, as, possibly, in the seigneurial houses of Bulla Regia. The classic example of rags to riches is the Mactar Reaper, who tells us in verse how by hard work and keeping his skirts clean he rose to prominence in his community, and full of years and honor, watched his grandchildren grow up. Punic names on many lists of benefactors show how this story of blameless social mobility could be multiplied. We have seen how incentives to tenant farmers bettered their lot. Slavery, while indefensible in absolute terms, was not an exclusively Roman institution, and indeed the total number of slaves decreased over the centuries through manumission and as the Roman peace made war captives increasingly unavailable. (A schedule of fines of A.D. 412 shows that Circumcellions, who were free journeyman agricultural laborers, were ranked above coloni and slaves and below plebeians.) Neither coloni nor slaves, under the ancient social system, had the *power* to revolutionize economics, society, or politics. Slave revolts never succeeded, and none is recorded for Africa.

Security. The provision of security was a conscious and for centuries successful Roman policy. Tacitus (*Histories* 4.74) tersely defends the empire: its aim is peace: no peace without armies, no armies without pay, no pay without taxes. Natives get military commands and civil administrative posts. Bad emperors should be treated as inevitable, like the weather, and they do not last forever. Years of good luck and training have built the empire; efforts to tear it down will involve the ruin of the would-be destroyers; obedience and security are preferable to revolt and ruin.

Thanks to the Severi, North Africa by the third century had a complete security system, partly wall-and-ditch, partly a chain of roads and forts, creating a mobile political, military, and cultural frontier, its central aim to make the nomads sedentary. Some areas were so peaceful that their cities were unwalled: Cuicul's wall was dismantled in 211 to allow for urban expansion, Sufetula had no fort till Byzantine times, and Teuchira in Cyrenaica was unwalled until the reign of Justinian. On the other hand, coin hoards or treasure from Calama, Rusguniae, Nicivibus, and Cartennae, dating respectively from shortly after 253, 267, Diocletian, and the Vandal occupation, show unrest at those dates, since the owners never returned to claim their property. The Legio III Augusta, which with its auxiliary units may be compared in size, makeup, and function with the French Foreign Legion, kept the peace for centuries on the North African frontier, with one hiatus (238–253). Castellum Dimmidi (Severan), four hundred kilometers south of Algiers, is the farthest Roman outpost in Algeria; Bu Njem, dating from 201, defended Roman interests in the Libyan desert. Fortified farms there—for example, at Ghirza—were worked by limitanei, embattled native farmers who defended their property against their compatriots from across the frontier. In Mauretania Caesariensis (not abandoned by Diocletian) the walls of Caesarea and Tipasa are Antonine; at Altava, in the mid–fourth century, the citizens got their taxes remitted for building a circuit wall; Gildo's brother Semmac had a Mauretanian fortified estate the size of a city. In Tingitana, there are Antonine fortifications around Sala, Thamusida, and Volubilis, and there is also an Antonine fort at Tocolosida; the walls of Zilis and Banasa, and the Tamuda castrum, are earlier. The dates of

Banasa military discharges show periods of peace. The visible stretch of the Carthaginian circuit wall is Theodosian (425).

The Byzantines were highly security-conscious. Cyrene had a fortified church; it and Lepcis both had Byzantine walls. Most of this defensive activity was carried out by Belisarius' lieutenant Solomon: in Tunisia his work is particularly impressive at Ammaedara, with other fortresses at Limisa, Mactar, and Sufetula. In Algeria, Byzantine Timgad and Theveste take pride of place, with other fortifications at Lambaesis, Madauros, Calama, Sitifis, Thibilis, and Tipasa Numidarum (Tifech).

Modern liberals may wish that these precautions had been unnecessary, but insecurity was a fact of ancient life, and a responsible government had to take steps to reduce it. It would be pleasant to be able to report, too, that Romanization took place without confrontation, but the fact is that the Berbers, however self-denying and enduring they were, were backward and uninnovative, with no gift for politics or urbanization. They also proved themselves, on occasion, faithless, murderous, and (in Jugurtha's case) manic-depressive. To idealize them is to do them a disservice, for to present a falsified picture of a people's past is to betray them. Historical truth, however harsh and cruel, never fails to give to those who know how to receive it—who can grasp the past with human understanding—the consistent clarity of vision that alone makes it possible to plan for a better future. The Romans were not guiltless: they sowed the site of Carthage with salt, strangled Jugurtha, martyred Cyprian. They also enriched and Romanized the African bourgeoisie, and inspired vitality in art, literature, philosophy, and Christian apologetics. The views and grievances of the "lesser breeds without the law" remain largely unrecorded. Yet the Berbers survive, like the desert palm and the desert sand, and the very impulses to independence at work in North Africa today may well be the fruit of a seed first sown by ancient Rome.

BOOKS AND ARTICLES
CONSULTED

INDEX

BOOKS AND ARTICLES CONSULTED

The following chapter bibliographies are designed to serve both as a reference list to works consulted in the preparation of the present volume, and as an annotated bibliography for those interested in further readings. Within each chapter bibliography, entries are arranged in alphabetical order, and books by the same author are then arranged chronologically. Here and there cross-references have seemed in order: when the cross-reference refers to a work within the same chapter bibliography, the name of the author and the date of the work are supplied—that is, Smith (1960); when it refers to a work in another chapter bibliography, the appropriate chapter is also supplied—that is, Smith (1960; see chapter 3). It has not been possible to take systematic account of publications after August 1978.

ABBREVIATIONS

Abbreviations for the author's own works, which appear throughout the preceding chapters, are listed in the Preface.

AA	*Archäologischer Anzeiger*
AAA	Stéphane Gsell, *Atlas archéologique d'Algérie* (Paris, 1911)
AAHung	*Acta Archaeologica Academiae Scientiae Hungaricae*
ABSA	*Annual of the British School at Athens*
AfrIt	*Africa Italiana*
AJ	*Archaeological Journal*
AJA	*American Journal of Archaeology*

AJPh	*American Journal of Philology*
AnnalesESC	*Annales: Economies, Sociétés, Civilisations*
AnnRptSocLibSt	*Annual Report of the Society for Libyan Studies*
AnnsLittsUBes	*Annales littéraires de l'Université de Besançon*
ANRW	*Aufsteig und Niedergang der antiken Welt,* ed. H. Temporini (Berlin, 1972–)
AntClass	*L'Antiquité classique*
AntsAfrs	*Antiquités africaines*
AntWelt	*Die antike Welt*
ArchClass	*Archeologia classica*
Assim et résist	*Assimilation et résistance à la culture gréco-romaine dans le monde ancien: travaux du VIe congrès international d'études classiques,* ed. Dionisi M. Pippidi (Bucharest and Paris, 1976)
BAA	*Bulletin d'archéologie algérienne*
BAM	*Bulletin d'archéologie marocaine*
BCTH	*Bulletin du comité des travaux historiques du Ministère d'instruction publique et des beaux-arts,* Paris
BEFAR	Bibliothèque des Ecoles françaises d'Athènes et de Rome
BJ	*Bonner Jahrbücher*
BSAF	*Bulletin de la Société des antiquaires de France*
CIL	*Corpus Inscriptionum Latinarum,* vol. 8 and supplements, ed. G. Wilmanns (Berlin, 1891–1942)
CahsArchs	*Cahiers archéologiques*
CahTun	*Cahiers de Tunisie*
CHistAfr	*Cambridge History of Africa,* ed. J. D. Fage and Roland Oliver (Cambridge, 1975–)
CollEFR	Collection de l'Ecole Française de Rome
CollLat	Collection Latomus (Brussels)
CorsiCultRavBiz	*Corsi di cultura ravennate e bizantina*
CP	*Classical Philology*
CRAI	*Comptes-rendus de l'Académie des inscriptions et belles-lettres*
Dessau	Hermann Dessau, *Inscriptiones Latinae Selectae*
EAAC	*Enciclopedia d'arte antica classica*
EHR	*English Historical Review*
EpigStud	*Epigraphische Studien*
EtTravArchMar	Etudes et travaux d'archéologie marocaine
FA	*Fasti archaeologici*

HAAN	Stéphane Gsell, *Histoire antique de l'Afrique du Nord*, 8 vols. (Paris, 1918–1930)
HespTam	*Hespéris-Tamuda*
HommGren	*Hommages à Albert Grenier*, Collection Latomus, 58 (Paris, 1962)
HommRen	*Hommages à Marcel Renard*, ed. Jacqueline Bibauw, Collection Latomus, 102, parts 1–3 (Brussels, 1969)
HSCP	*Harvard Studies in Classical Philology*
ILAlg	*Inscriptions latines d'Algérie*, vol. 1, ed. Stéphane Gsell (Paris, 1922); vol. 2, parts 1 and 2, ed. Hans-Georg Pflaum (Paris, 1957, 1977)
IRT	John B. Ward Perkins and Joyce M. Reynolds, *Inscriptions of Roman Tripolitania* (Rome, 1952)
JBAA	*Journal of the British Association of Architects*
JRS	*Journal of Roman Studies*
JThS	*Journal of Theological Studies*
JWG	*Jahrbuch der Wirtschaftsgeschichte*
KP	*Der kleine Pauly*
LA	*Libya Antiqua*
LinH	*Libya in History*, ed. F. Gadallah (Benghazi, 1971)
MAAR	Memoirs of the American Academy in Rome
MAL	Monografie d'archeologia libica
MEFR	*Mélanges de l'Ecole française de Rome*
MélCarc	*Mélanges d'archéologie, d'épigraphie, et d'histoire offerts à Jérôme Carcopino* (Paris, 1966)
MélPig	*Mélanges d'archéologie et d'histoire offerts à André Piganiol*, ed. Raymond Chevallier (Paris, 1966)
MemSocAntFr	*Mémoires de la Société nationale des antiquaires de France*
MiscHistEccles	*Miscellanea Historiae Ecclesiae*
MonsPiot	*Monuments et mémoires publiées par l'Académie des inscriptions et belles-lettres, Commission de la fondation Piot*
N&D	Notes et Documents, Direction des antiquités et arts, Tunis and Paris, 1908–1957; new series under the Institut national d'archéologie et arts, Tunis, 1958–
NouvArchMissSc	*Nouvelles archives des missions scientifiques*
OpuscRom	*Opuscula Romana*

PBA	*Proceedings of the British Academy*
PBSR	*Papers of the British School at Rome*
PCPS	*Proceedings of the Cambridge Philological Society*
PdP	*Parola del Passato*
PECS	*Princeton Encyclopedia of Classical Sites* ed. Richard E. Stilwell (Princeton, 1976)
ProcACA	*Proceedings of the African Classical Associations*
PSAM	*Publications du service archéologique de Maroc*
PublUTunFacLettr	*Publications de l'Université de Tunis, Faculté de lettres*
QAL	*Quaderni di archeologia libica*
RAfr	*Revue africaine*
RE	*Realencyclopädie der klassischen Altertumswissenschaft*, ed. August Pauly and Georg Wissowa
REA	*Revue des études anciennes*
RecConst	*Receuil des mémoires de la société archéologique et historique du département de Constantine*
RendLinc	*Rendiconti della classe di scienze morali, storiche, e filologiche dell'Accademia dei Lincei*
RendPontAccArch	*Rendiconti della Pontificia Accademia Romana di Archeologia*
RevArch	*Revue archéologique*
RevArchEst	*Revue archéologique de l'est et centre-est*
RevHCMaghr	*Revue de l'histoire et civilisation du Maghreb*
RevPhil	*Revue de philologie*
RevTun	*Revue tunisienne*
RIDA	*Revue internationale des droits de l'antiquité*
RivStLig	*Rivista di studi liguri*
RivStLittRel	*Rivista di studi di litteratura e religione*
RM	*Mitteilungen des deutschen archäologischen Instituts, römische Abteilung*
SEG	*Supplementum Epigraphicum Graecum*, ed. J. J. E. Hondius (Leiden, 1923–)
StudMagr	*Studi magrebini*
WdF	Wege der Forschung (Darmstadt)
YCS	*Yale Classical Studies*
ZPE	*Zeitschrift für Papyrologie und Epigraphik*

1. The Carthaginian Area in Prehistoric and Punic Times

Allibert, Jacques. "Les sacrifices d'enfants à Carthage." *Archeologia*, no. 1 (1964): 81–84.

Anziani, Dominique. "Nécropoles puniques du Sahel tunisien." *MEFR* 32 (1912): 245–303.

Astin, Arthur E. *Scipio Aemilianus*. Oxford, 1967.

Baradez, Jacques. "Nouvelles recherches sur les ports antiques de Carthage." *Karthago* 9 (1958): 47–78.

Bisi, Anna Maria. *Ceramica punica*. Naples, 1970.

Brisson, Jean-Pierre. *Rome ou Carthage?* Paris, 1973.

Camps, Gabriel. *Aux origines de la Berbérie: Massinissa ou les débuts de l'histoire*. *Libyca* 8 (1960): entire issue.

———. *Les civilisations préhistoriques de l'Afrique du Nord et du Sahara*. Paris, 1974.

Cintas, Pierre. "Le sanctuaire punique de Sousse." *RAfr* 91 (1947) 1–80.

———. *Ceramique punique*. Paris, 1950.

———. "Deux campagnes de fouilles à Utique." *Karthago* 2 (1951): 5–88.

———. "Une ville punique au Cap-Bon, en Tunisie." *CRAI* (1953): 256–60.

———. "Nouvelles recherches à Utique." *Karthago* 5 (1954): 89–154.

———. *Manuel d'archéologie punique*, vols. 1 and 2. Paris, 1970–1976. Cintas's attempt to alter the accepted view of the plan of the ports of Carthage has not found favor. The account of the Carthage necropoleis in vol. 2 is useful.

Cintas, Pierre, and Gobert, E. G. "Les Tombes de Jbel Mlezza." *RevTun* (1939): 135–98.

Deroche, Louis. "Les fouilles de Ksar Toual Zammel et la question de Zama." *MEFR* 60 (1948): 55–105. Ancient name Vicus Maracitanus, "attributed" to Zama Regia.

Dorey, Thomas A., and Dudley, Donald R. *Rome against Carthage*. London, 1971. An unpretentious, competent, lively, reliable study of the Punic Wars.

Ensslin, William. "Der Einfluss Karthagos auf Staatsverwaltung und Wirtschaft der Römer." In Joseph Vogt, ed., *Rom und Karthago*, pp. 262–96. Leipzig, 1943.

Fantar, Mhamed Hassine. "Le cavalier marin de Kerkouane." *Africa* 1 (1966): 19–39.

————. "Pavimenta punica et signe dit de Tanit dans les habitations de Kerkouane." *StudMagr* 1 (1966): 57–65.

————. "Kerkouane." *EAAC*, suppl. (1970).

————. "Récentes découvertes dans les domaines de l'archéologie et de l'épigraphie punique." *BCTH*, n.s. 7 (1971): 241–64.

————. "Un sarcophage en bois à couvercle anthropoïde découvert dans le nécropole punique de Kerkouane." *CRAI* (1972): 340–54.

Ferron, Jean. "L'inscription du mausolée de Dougga." *Africa* 3/4 (1969/70): 83–98.

Flaubert, Gustave. *Salammbô*. First published Paris, 1862; one authoritative modern edition is published by Bibliothèque de la Pléiade, Paris, 1951.

Foucher, Louis. *Hadrumetum*. Paris, 1964.
The standard work on ancient Sousse. Best on mosaics.

Gallet de Santerre, Herbert, and Slim, Latifa. "Fouille dans le nécropole punique de Kerkouane." *Africa* 3/4 (1969/70): 189–91.

Gsell, Stéphane. *Histoire antique de l'Afrique du Nord*, vols. 1 to 4. Paris, 1918–1920.
Fundamental; a classic. Complete in 8 vols. Good on Hanno's periplus, the Carthaginian constitution, military and cultural history.

Harden, Donald B. "The Pottery of the Precinct of Tanit at Salaambo." *Iraq* 41 (1932): 59–89.
The standard monograph on levels and dating.

————. "The Topography of Punic Carthage." *Greece and Rome* 9 (1939): 1–12.
Useful on circuit wall.

————. "The Phoenicians on the West Coast of Africa." *Antiquity* 22 (1948): 141–50.

————. *The Phoenicians*. 2nd ed. London, 1963.
Pages 174–76 offer a useful translation of Hanno's Periplus.

Heurgon, Jacques. "L'agronome carthaginois Magon et ses traducteurs en latin et en grecque." *CRAI* (1976): 441–56.

Hoffman, Wilhelm. "Die römische Politik des zweiten Jahrhunderts und das Ende Karthagos." *Historia* 9 (1960): 309–44.

Hurst, Henry. "Excavations at Carthage 1974: 1st Interim Report." *AJ* 55 (1975): 11–40.

————. "Excavations at Carthage: 2nd Interim Report." *AJ* 56 (1976): 177–97.
Latest results of UNESCO-sponsored excavation in the port area.

Writing in *World Archaeology* 9 (1977): 334–46, with L. A. Stager, Hurst emphasized that no archaeological evidence connects the fourth-century circular and rectangular harbors with the original Punic colony.

Kolendo, Jerzy. "Sur le colonat en Afrique préromaine." In E. C. Welskopf, ed., *Neue Beiträge zur Geschichte der alten Welt*, vol. 2, pp. 45–56. Berlin, 1965.

Kotula, Tadeusz. "Les traditions puniques dans la constitution des villes de l'Afrique romaine." In *Akten des VIten Kongresses der griechischen und lateinischen Epigraphik*, pp. 73–83. Vestigia, 17. Munich, 1972.

Lancel, Serge. "Nouvelles fouilles de la mission archéologique française à Carthage sur la colline de Byrsa, 1974–5." *CRAI* (1976): 60–75.
Records undated Punic houses with *opus signinum* floors in Sector A.

Lancel, Serge; Deneauve, Jean; and Carrié, Jean-Michel. "Fouilles françaises à Carthage, 1974–75." *AntsAfrs* 11 (1977): 11–130.
Part of a UNESCO project, on south and southwest slopes of Byrsa Hill. Clears up mistakes of earlier excavators; for example, Lapeyre's "Proconsul's Palace" and "Punic enceinte" are both proven fictitious. Punic tombs date from seventh/sixth century to 146 B.C.; second-century terraced houses resemble those of Delos or Priene. Wide (11.4 meters) porticoed Cardo Maximus dates from Julian colony; under the empire the whole hilltop was sliced off to make a monumental colonnaded esplanade with temple of Gens Augusta, a Metroon, baths, shrine of Concord, Victories with trophies.

Law, Robin C. C. "North Africa in the Period of Phoenician and Greek Colonization, c. 800–323 B.C." *CHistAfr*, vol. 2, pp. 77–137.
Useful survey; excellent maps; judicious bibliographical comment (pp. 681–87).

Leglay, Marcel. "Nouveautés puniques." *RAfr* 96 (1952): 399–415.
On a rich Thapsus burial.

McIntosh-Turfa, Jean. "Evidence for Etruscan-Punic Relations." *AJA* 81 (1977): 368–74.

Morel, Jean-Paul. "Kerkouane, ville punique du Cap Bon: rémarques archéologiques et historiques." *MEFR* 81 (1969): 473–518.

Moscati, Sergio, ed. *I Fenici e Cartagine*. Turin, 1972.

Newman, William L. *The Politics of Aristotle*, vol. 2. Oxford, 1887.

On the Carthaginian constitution, see pp. 401–8.

Pallottino, Massimo. "Scavi nel santuario etrusco di Pyrgi." *ArchClass* 16 (1964): 49–117.

Picard, Colette. "Genèse et évolution des signes de la bouteille et de Tanit à Carthage." *StudMagr* 2 (1968): 77–87.
Sacrificed infants' laughing masks.

Picard, Gilbert Charles. *Les réligions de l'Afrique antique.* Paris, 1954.
———. *Hannibal.* Paris, 1967.
Holds, against most scholars, that Volubilis bronze bust of prince is almost certainly Hannibal; otherwise good.
———. *Vie et mort de Carthage.* Paris, 1970.
Artistic verisimilitude on infant sacrifice, borrowed from Flaubert. Valuable detail on Third Punic War.
———. "Le périple d'Hannon n'est pas un faux." *Archeologia,* no. 40 (May–June 1971): 54–59.

Poidebard, Antoine. "Explorations sousmarines à Carthage." *CRAI* (1948): 379–381.
Against Cintas on ports.

Poinssot, Louis, and Lantier, Raymond. "Un sanctuaire de Tanit à Carthage." *Revue de l'histoire des réligions* 44 (1923): 32–68.
Editio princeps of Salammbô tophet.

Russell, Francis H. "The Battlefield of Zama." *Archaeology* 23 (1970): 20–29.
Well-intentioned attempt at topographical identification, by a former American ambassador to Tunisia.

Scullard, Howard H. "The Site of the Battle of Zama." In J. A. S. Evans, ed., *Polis and Imperium: Studies in Honor of Edward Togo Salmon,* pp. 225–31. Toronto, 1974.

Slim, Hedi. *Histoire de la Tunisie: L'Antiquité.* Tunis, 1969.
Good on Masinissa.

Toynbee, Arnold J. *Hannibal's Legacy,* vol. 1, pp. 28–38. Oxford, 1965.
Able summary history of Carthaginian Empire.

Walsh, Patrick G. "Masinissa." *JRS* 55 (1965): 149–60.

Warmington, Brian H. *Carthage.* 2nd ed. Harmondsworth, 1969.
Useful on Third Punic War.

Whittaker, C. Richard. "The Western Phoenicians as Colonisers." *PCPS,* no. 200 (1974): 58–79.
Against notion of mere "factories" as opposed to permanent settlement.

2. From the Conquest through Nerva, 146 B.C.–A.D. 98

Bassignano, Maria Silvia. *Il flaminato nelle province romane dell'Africa.* Exhaustive lists. Pflaum in a review, *Athenaeum* 54 (1976): 152–63, dates Sabratha as a colony to 165/66; Sufetula, to 217 as terminus ante quem; Mactar to 191/92; Picard (1954; see chapter 1) gave the date as 176–180. Uzappa was a municipium in the reign of Gallienus, Membressa in Tacitus'.

Bénabou, Marcel. "Proconsul et légat en Afrique: le témoignage de Tacite." *AntsAfrs* 6 (1972): 129–36. Tacitus *Hist.* 4.48–50, on Valerius Festus vs. Garamantes. Compare C. Daniels (1970; see chapter 6).

———. *La résistance africaine à la romanisation.* Paris, 1976. Important, controversial, written from a postcolonial point of view; shows how natives responded to incorporation in Roman Empire: diversely, with much persistence of pre-Roman religion, language, names, and social groups.

Beschaouch, Azedine. "Municipium Iulium Aurelium Mustitanum." *CahTun* 15 (1967): 85–102. Musti as Marian-Julian foundation.

———. "Clupea." *EAAC*, suppl. (1970).

Broughton, T. Robert S. *The Romanization of Africa Proconsularis.* Baltimore, 1929. Still fundamental.

Burian, Jan. "Die einheimische Bevölkerung Nordafrikas von den. punischen Kriegen bis zum Ausgang des Prinzipäts." In Franz Altheim and R. Stiehl, eds., *Die Araber in der alten Welt,* vol. 1, pp. 420–547. Berlin, 1964.

Burn, Andrew R. "Hic breve vivitur: A Study of the Expectation of Life in the Roman Empire." *Past and Present* 4 (1953): 2–31. See Hopkins (1966/67; chapter 3) for caveat.

Caillemer, A., and Chevallier, R. *Atlas des centuriations romaines de Tunisie.* Paris, 1957. Fundamental.

———. "Die römische Limitation in Tunesien." *Gymnasium* 35 (1957): 45–57.

Carcopino, Jérôme. "Sylla et les fouilles sous-marines de Mahdia." In *Mélanges offerts à M. N. Iorga par ses amis français et des pays de langue français,* pp. 167–81. Bucharest, 1933.

Chantraine, Heinrich. *Freigelassene und Sklaven im Dienst der römischen Kaiser,* vol. 1. Wiesbaden, 1967.

On Carthage cemetery of *officiales.*

Chevallier, Raymond. "Essai de chronologie des centuriations romaines de Tunisie." *MEFR* 70 (1968): 61–128.

Chevallier, Raymond, and Caillemer, A. "Les centuriations de l'Africa Vetus." *AnnalesESC* 9 (1954): 433–60.

———. "Notes sur trois centuriations romaines." *HommGren* (1962): 413–15.

Davin, Paul. "Etude sur la cadastration de la colonia Julia Carthago." *RevTun* (1930): 73–85.

Debbasch, Yvan. "Colonia Julia Karthago: vie et institutions municipales de la Carthage romaine." *Revue de l'histoire de droit français et étranger*, ser. 4, 31 (1953): 30–53.

View of collegial pagus unacceptable.

Desparmet, Hélène. "Théâtre de Cillium." *Karthago* 15 (1969/70): 13–66.

Dilke, Oswald A. W. *The Roman Land Surveyors.* Newton Abbot, 1971.

Pages 151–58 summarize work of Caillemer and Chevallier.

Etienne, Raymond, and Fabre, G. "Démographie et classe sociale: l'exemple du cimitière des officiales à Carthage." In Claude Nicolet and Christian Leroy, eds., *Recherches sur les structures sociales dans l'antiquité classique*, pp. 81–97. Caen, 1969.

Euzennat, Maurice. "Castellum Thigensium." *BCTH*, n.s. 7 (1971): 229–39.

Ferron, Jean, and Pinard, M. "Fouilles de Byrsa." *Cahiers de Byrsa* 5 (1955): 31–263; 9 (1960/61): 77–170.

Fishwick, Duncan. "The Institution of the Provincial Cult in Africa Proconsularis." *Historia* 29 (1964): 342–62.

Fishwick, Duncan, and Shaw, B. D. "The Era of the Cereres." *Historia* 27 (1978): 343–54.

The authors use Dessau 9401, from Uchi Maius, to argue that the official Roman era in Carthage was dated from 40–39 B.C.

Freis, Helmut. "Die cohortes urbanae." *EpigStud* 2 (1967): 31–89.

Fuchs, Werner. *Der Schiffsfund von Mahdia.* Deutsches archäologische Institut, Bilderheft, 2. Tübingen, 1963.

Exhaustive, completely illustrated.

Gastinel, Georges. "Carthago et l'Enéide." *RevArch* 23, part 1 (1926): 40–102.

Guey, Julien, and Pernette, A. "Lépide à Thabraca." *Karthago* 9 (1959): 79–89.

Despite Lepidus' notorious cruelty, the citizens made him a patronus.

Haywood, Richard M. "Roman Africa." In Tenney Frank, ed., *Economic Survey of Ancient Rome*, vol. 4, pp. 3–119. Baltimore, 1938.
Sources, including epigraphic, in translation.

Law, Robin C. C. "North Africa in the Hellenistic and Roman Periods, 323 B.C.–A.C. 305." *CHistAfr*, vol. 2, pp. 138–99 and bibliography.

Lézine, Alexandre. *Carthage, Utique.* Paris, 1969.

Merlin, Alfred. *Le sanctuaire de Ba'al et Tanit près de Siagu.* N&D, 4 (1910).
On Thinissut.

Merlin, Alfred, and Poinssot, L. *Cratères et candelabres de marbre trouvés en mer près de Mahdia.* N&D, 9 (1930).
The *editio princeps*; includes descriptions of all the finds.

———. "Eléments architecturaux trouvés en mer près de Mahdia." *Karthago* 7 (1956): 59–104.

Pflaum, Hans-Georg. "La romanisation de l'ancien territoire de la Carthage punique à la lumière des découvertes épigraphiques récentes." *AntsAfrs* 4 (1970): 75–117.
Record shows only limited Roman penetration from the time of Tiberius to Hadrian. It was in the Roman interest to preserve local institutions so long as their own interests were unaffected; this policy enabled them to hold the Carthaginian *territorium* without an army of occupation.

———. "La romanisation de l'Afrique." In *Akten des VIten internationalen Kongresses für griechische und lateinische Epigraphik*. Vestigia, 17. Beiträge zur alten Geschichte der Komission für alte Geschichte und Epigraphik des Deutschen Archäologischen Instituts. Munich, 1973.
Important. Ranks with Broughton, but more controversial.

Picard, Gilbert C. "Les monuments triomphaux romains en Afrique." *CRAI* (1948): 421–27.
On Kbor Klib.

———. "Néron et le blé de l'Afrique." *CahTun* 4 (1956): 163–74.

Poinssot, Louis. *L'autel de la gens Augusta à Carthage.* N&D, 10 (1929).

Poncet, Jean. "Vestiges de cadastration antique et histoire de sols en Tunisie." *CahTun* 3 (1953): 323–30.

Quoniam, Pierre. "Une inscription de Thuburnica: Marius et la romanisation de l'Afrique." *CRAI* (1950): 332–36.

Rachet, Marguerite. *Rome et les Berbères: un problème militaire d'Auguste à Dioclétien.* CollLat, 110 (1970).
Especially useful on Tacfarinas.

Romanelli, Pietro. *Storia delle province romane dell'Africa*. Rome, 1959.
Authoritative.

Salama, Pierre. "Le miliaire archaïque de Lorbeus." *Cahiers de Byrsa*
10 (1964/65): 97–115.

Salmon, Edward T. *Roman Colonization*. London, 1969.
An authoritative list of colonies in Africa Proconsularis and
Numidia appears on p. 169.

Saumagne, Charles. "Le plan de la colonie julienne de Carthage." *BCTH*
(1924); reprinted *CahTun* 10 (1962): 463–71.
Fundamental; still standard.

―――. "La centuriation rurale de l'Afrique." *CRAI* (1929); reprinted
CahTun 10 (1962): 207–12.

―――. "Les vestiges d'une centuriation romaine à l'est d'El Djem."
· *CRAI* (1929): 307–13.

―――. "Le champ de bataille de Muthul." *RevTun* (1930): 3–17.
Title conceals article on course of Fossa Regia.

Seston, William. "Les institutions politiques et sociales de Carthage,
d'après une inscription latine de Thugga." *CRAI* (1967): 218–23.

Slim, Hedi. "La vie économique à Thysdrus." *CahTun* 11 (1964):
155–58.

Slim, Latifa. "La nécropole romaine de l'actuelle place publique d'El
Jem." *Africa* 3/4 (1969/70): 243–46.

Stager, Lawrence A. "Carthage 1977: The Punic and Roman Harbors."
Archaeology 30 (1977): 198–200.

Syme, Ronald. "Pliny the Procurator." *HSCP* 73 (1969): 201–36.

Teutsch, Leo. "Gabt es Doppelgemeinden in römischen Afrika?" *RIDA*
8 (1961): 281–356.
Negative answer.

―――. *Das römische Städtewesen in Nordafrika*. Berlin, 1962.
Fundamental.

Thompson, Lloyd A. "Settler and Native in Roman Africa." In Lloyd A.
Thompson and John Ferguson, eds., *Africa in Classical Antiquity*,
pp. 132–81. Ibadan, 1969.
Statistics on Julii and on upward social mobility of Africans.

Tixeront, Jean. "Réflexions sur l'implantation romaine de l'agriculture
en Tunisie." *Karthago* 10 (1960): 3–50.

Trousset, Pol. "Nouvelles observations sur la centuriation romaine à l'est
d'El Jem." *AntsAfrs* 11 (1977): 175–207.
Area of twenty-five by fifteen kilometers, centered on Rougga,
determined by Via Hadrumetina. Actus separated by stone balks
fifteen to twenty-five centimeters high, two to three meters wide.

Dated after Thapsus; flourished into the fourth century. Perhaps a speculator intervened between surveyor and final occupant. Air photography shows dense settlement, reducing distinction between *rus* and *urbs*: baths, cisterns, wells, cemeteries, olive mills, sanctuaries, an amphitheater for nineteen hundred spectators. Two thousand olive trees per century.

Van Nerom, Claire. "Colonia Julia Concordia Carthago." *HommRen* (1969): 767–76.

3. The High Empire: Trajan through Alexander Severus, A.D. 98–235

Bénabou, M. *La résistance africaine à la romanisation* (1976; see chapter 2).

See pp. 309–30, on the Beja Di Mauri.

Berger, Philippe, and Cagnat, René. "Le sanctuaire de Saturne à Aïn Tounga." *BCTH* (1889): 7–65.

Beschaouch, Azedine. "Bulla Regia." *EAAC*, suppl. (1970).

Blanchet, P. "Les temples païens de Tunisie." *RecConst* 32 (1898): 298–311.

Review of Cagnat and Gauckler (1889). Convenient but somewhat dated list.

Boulouednine, Mongi. *FA* 13 (1960), no. 4404.

On the Bulla Regia theater.

Bruhl, Adrien. *Liber Pater*. Paris, 1953.

Cagnat, René, and Gauckler, Pierre. *Les monuments historiques de la Tunisie*, vol. 1: *Les temples païens*. Paris, 1889.

Camps, Gabriel. "L'inscription de Béja et le problème des Di Mauri." *RAfr* 98 (1934): 233–60.

Carandini, Andrea. "Metodo e critica nel problema dei mosaici de Sousse." *ArchClass* 14 (1962): 244–50.

Critique of Foucher's (1960) Severan dates: pushes all dates down into the fourth-fifth century. Foucher, *ArchClass* 15 (1963): 102–4, says this is archaeologically impossible.

Carton, Louis, "Le sanctuaire de Baal-Saturne à Dougga." *NouvArchMissSc* 7 (1899): 367–474.

Good early account, by an army doctor turned archaeologist.

————. *Le théâtre romain de Dougga*. Mémoires presentées par divers savants à l'Académie des inscriptions et belles lettres, ser. 1, 11. Paris, 1902. 2nd ed., 1922.

Castagnoli, Ferdinando. "Capitolium." *EAAC* (1959).

Convenient list with dates; plan of Sufetula's capitolium.

Chabot, Jean-Baptiste. "Inscriptions puniques de Dougga." *CRAI* (1916): 119–31.

Chtaerman, Elena M. "Afrika und Rom in der Prinzipät." In Hans-Joachim Diesner, ed., *Afrika und Rom*, pp. 53–58. Halle, 1968. In Russian; German summary. Enlightened Marxist view.

Constans, Louis A. "Gigthis," *NouvArchMissSc*, n.s. 14 (1916): 1–113.

Dunbabin, Katherine. "The Triumph of Dionysus on Mosaics in North Africa." *PBSR* 39 (1971): 52–65.

Duncan-Jones, Richard P. *The Economy of the Roman Empire: Quantitative Studies.* Cambridge, 1974. Important on philanthropy, on inflation, and on purchase of municipal office.

Duval, Noël. "Sufetula." *EAAC* (1966).

Duval, Noël, and Baratte, François. *Les ruines de Sufétula.* Tunis, 1973. Short, authoritative guidebook.

Ennabli, Abdelmajid. "Cartagine." *EAAC*, suppl. (1970).

Euzennat, Maurice. "Quatre ans de recherche sur la frontière romaine de la Tunisie méridionale." *CRAI* (1972): 7–27.

Février, James G. "Les nouvelles inscriptions monumentales puniques de Mactar." *Karthago* 12 (1963–64): 45–59. On Hathor Miskar temple lists.

Finley, Moses I. *The Ancient Economy.* Berkeley, 1973. Doubts conclusions about social mobility from Mactar Reaper stele alone (p. 192, n. 28).

Foucher, Louis. "Inventaire de mosaïques, Sousse." In *Atlas archéologique*, feuille 57. Tunis, 1960.

———. "La mosaïque d'Orphée de Thysdrus." *HommGren* (1962): 646–51.

———. "Venationes à Hadrumète." *Oudheidkundige Mededelingen* 45 (1964): 87–114. On the House of Ostriches.

———. "Les collections du musée de Sousse." *Archeologia*, no. 3 (March–April 1965): 91–96. Popular summary, with good photographs of mosaics.

———. *La maison de masques à Sousse.* N&D, n.s. 6 (1965).

———. "Les mosaïques nilotiques africaines." In *La mosaïque gréco-romaine*, vol. 1, pp. 137–45. Paris, 1965.

———. "Découvertes fortuites à Sousse." *Africa* 2 (1967/68): 183–90.

———. "A propos des cirques africains." *BCTH*, n.s. 5 (1969): 207–13.

Convenient list, with dimensions and capacities.

————. "Le char de Dionysos." In *La mosaïque gréco-romaine*, vol. 2, pp. 55–61. Paris, 1975.

Gauckler, Pierre. "La domaine des Labérii à Uthina." *MonsPiot* 3 (1896): 177–229.

————. "Fouilles de Bougrara." *NouvArchMissSc* 15 (1907): 283–330. On Gigthis.

Gauckler, Pierre; Gouvet, E.; and Hannezo, G. *Musées de Sousse*. Paris, 1902.
Out of date, but good detail on El-Alia Nile mosaic.

Golfetto, Arthur. *Dougga, Geschichte einer Stadt*. Basel, 1961.
Borrows heavily from Poinssot (1958).

Gozlar, Suzanne. "La maison de Neptune, Acholla: problèmes posés par l'architecture et la mode de conservation." *Karthago* 16 (1971/72): 43–99.

————. "Les pavements en mosaïque de la maison de Neptune à Acholla." *MonsPiot* 59 (1974): 71–135.

Hands, Arthur R. *Charities and Social Aid in Greece and Rome*. London, 1968.
Page 185, document 20, refers to Sicca Veneria *alimenta*, A.D. 169–180.

Hanoune, Roger. "Une muse et un philosophe sur une mosaïque de Bulla Regia." In *Mélanges de philosophie de littérature et d'histoire offerts à P. Boyancé*. Rome, 1974.

Heitland, William E. *Agricola*. Cambridge, 1921.
On Henchir Mettich and other *saltus*, pp. 342–58.

Hopkins, Keith. "Elite Mobility in the Roman Empire." *Past and Present* 32 (1965): 12–26.

————. "On the Probable Age Structure of the Roman People." *Population Studies* 20 (1966/67): 245–64.
Contains warning against tendency of inscriptions to exaggerate longevity.

Ifie, Jeremiah. "The Romano-African Municipal Aristocracy of the Maghreb under the Principate." Ph.D. dissertation, Ibadan, 1976.
Useful tables of number and percentage of preferment of native over settler: 181 to 110, 51 percent to 30 percent in municipia; but 103 to 89, 46 percent to 40 percent settler over native among Roman senators.

Leglay, Marcel. *Saturne africain: histoire*. BEFAR, 205. Paris, 1966.

————. *Saturne africaine: monuments*. 2 vols. Paris, 1961, 1966.

Authoritative and exhaustive collection of material.

————. "Les dieux d'Afrique." *Archeologia*, no. 39 (March–April 1971): 48–55.
Popular survey of syncretism and native survival.

Lewis, Naphtali, and Reinhold, Meyer. *Roman Civilization*, vol. 2. New York, 1955.
Pages 178–84 provide convenient translation of *saltus* inscriptions, Henchir Mettich, et al.

Lézine, Alexandre. *L'architecture romaine d'Afrique*. PublUTunFacLettr, série arch.-histoire, 9 (1964).

————. *Thuburbo Maius*. Tunis, 1968.
Authoritative guidebook.

————. "La population des villes africaines." *AntsAfrs* 3 (1969): 70–82.

————. *Les thermes d'Antonin à Carthage*. Tunis, 1969.
Authoritative guidebook.

Mahjoubi, Amar. *Cités romaines de la Tunisie*. Tunis, 1969.
Good color photographs of mosaics; rare plans of fora at Thuburbo Maius and Bulla Regia.

Merlin, Alfred. "Découvertes à Bulla Regia." *CRAI* (1906): 363–68.

————. *Le temple d'Apollon à Bulla Regia*. Paris, 1908.

————. "Une nouvelle inscription trouvée à Thuburbo Maius." *CRAI* (1916): 262–67.
Prescribed ritual purity for visitors to Aesculapius' shrine.

————. *Le forum de Thuburbo Maius*. N&D, 7 (1922).

————. "L'histoire municipale de Thuburbo Maius." In *Actes du Ve Congrès internationale d'archéologie, 1930*, pp. 205–25. Algiers, 1933.

————. "Divinités indigènes sur un bas-relief romain de la Tunisie." *CRAI* (1947): 355–71.
On Di Mauri, Béja.

Pfeiffer, Homer F. "The Ancient Roman Theater at Dougga." *MAAR* 9 (1931): frontispiece, pp. 145–56, Pls. 11–12.

Pflaum, Hans-Georg. "Une lettre de promotion de l'empereur Marc-Aurèle pour un procurateur de Gaule Narbonnaise." *BJ* (1971): 349–66.
Subject was a native of Bulla Regia. Incidental information on Bulla Regia theater.

Picard, Gilbert C. "Acholla." *CRAI* (1947): 557–62.
See also his article on Acholla in *RevArch*, ser. 6, 32 (1949): 810–21.

————. "Le monument aux Victoires de Carthage et l'expedition orien-

tale de L. Verus." *Karthago* 1 (1950): 67–93.
On Musée Lavigérie trophy.

———. "*Civitas Mactariana.*" *Karthago* 8 (1957).
Standard work on this site.

———. "Bulla Regia." *EAAC* (1959).

———. "Les mosaïques d'Acholla." In *Etudes d'archéologie classique*, vol. 2, pp. 76–95. Annales de L'Est, 22. Nancy, 1959.

———. "Le septizonium de Cincari (Hr. Tounga) et le problème des septizonia." *MonsPiot* 52 (1960): 77–93.

———. "La datation des mosaïques de la maison de Virgile à Sousse." In *Atti del 7⁰ Congresso internazionale di archeologia classica*, pp. 243–49. Rome, 1961.
Same date (A.D. 210) as Arch of Septimius Severus at Lepcis Magna.

———. "Influences étrangères et originalité dans l'art de l'Afrique romaine." *Antike Kunst* 5/6 (1962): 30–41 and plates.
Especially good on Mactar and Acholla.

———. "Les fouilles de Mactar, 1970–73." *CRAI* (1974): 9–33.
West Baths, House of Venus.

Pohlmann, Egert. "Die zwei Musen des Virgils: zur Virgilmosaik von Hadrumetum." *AA*, 1978 (pt. 1): 102–6.
Agrees with Foucher that the Muse with Vergil is not Clio but Calliope.

Poinssot, Claude. *Dougga*. Paris, 1958.
A reliable guidebook.

———. "Sondage dans le sous-sol du Capitole de Thugga." *CahTun* 15 (1967): 169–81.
On colossal head of Jupiter.

Quoniam, Pierre. "Sculptures trouvées à Oudna." *MEFR* 60 (1948): 35–54.
From baths, including a fine Severan head of Aphrodite, now in the Bardo.

———. "Fouilles récentes à Bulla Regia." *CRAI* (1952): 460–72.

———. "Uthina." *RE* 9, A1 (1961): cols. 1177–78.

Rakob, Friedrich. "Das Quellenheiligtum in Zaghouan." *MEFR* 81 (1974): 41–89.
Shorter version, in French: *Africa* 3/4 (1969–70): 133–41. See also *AA* (1969): 284–300.

Röder, Josef. "Quadermarken am Aquaedukt von Karthago." *MEFR* 81 (1974): 91–106.

Romanelli, Pietro. "Le case semisotterranee di Bulla Regia." In *Mélanges offerts à Kazimierz Michalowski*, ed. Marie-Louise Bernhard, pp. 641–47. Warsaw, 1966.

———. "Dugga." *EEAC*, suppl. (1970).

Salomonson, Jan W. "La mosaïque du 'banquet costumé' d'El Djem." *CahTun* 8 (1960): 57–62.

Sherwin-White, Adrian N. "The Roman Citizenship: A Survey of Its Development into a World Franchise." *ANRW* 1, part 2 (1972): 23–58.

Slim, Hedi. "Hadrumetum." *EAAC*, suppl. (1970).

Stager, Lawrence. "Leben in römischen Afrika im Spiegel der Schriften Tertullians." Ph.D. dissertation, Zürich, 1973.
Treats children, school, women, men, death, burial, dress, shoes, hair, cosmetics, transport, food, baths, recreation, creative arts, divisions of time, street names, seafaring, commerce, money, gods, the ruler cult, holidays, army, medicine, astrology, dreams, oracles, crime and punishment, catastrophes, climate, vegetation, water, animals.

Sznycer, Maurice. "La grande inscription dédicatoire de Mactar." *Semitica* 22 (1972): 25–43.

Thébert, Yvon. "L'utilisation de l'eau dans la Maison de la Pêche à Bulla Regia." *CahTun* 19 (1971): 11–17.

———. "Les maisons à étage souterrain de Bulla Regia." *CahTun* 20 (1972): 17–44.
Authoritative.

———. "La romanisation d'une cité indigène d'Afrique: Bulla Regia." *MEFR* 84, part 2 (1973): 247–310.

Toutain, Jacques. "Le sanctuaire de Saturnus Balcaranensis au Djebel Bou Kourneïn." *RAfr* 12 (1892): 83–124.

Trousset, Pol. *Recherches sur le Limes Tripolitanus du Chott el-Djerid.* Paris, 1974.

———. "Sur la frontière saharienne de l'Empire romaine." *Archeologia*, no. 84 (July 1975): 41–53.
Good popular summary, well illustrated.

4. From the Military Anarchy to the Arab Invasion

Andreotti, Roberto. "Problemi sul significato storico della usurpazione di L. Domizio Alessandro." In H.-J. Diesner, ed., *Afrika und Rom*, pp. 245–76. Halle, 1968.
Marxist rehabilitation of rebel.

Baratte, François. *Recherches archéologiques à Haïdra: Miscellanea I.* CollEFR, 17. Rome, 1974.
Mosaics, including Ulysses-Sirens.

Baratte, François, and Duval, Noël. *Haïdra.* Tunis, 1974.
A dependable guidebook.

Baratte, François; Duval, Noël; and Golvin, C.-Cl. "Recherches à Haïdra V: Capitole et Basilica V." *CRAI* (1973): 156–78.

Beschaouch, Azedine. "Une stèle consacrée à Saturne le 8 nov., 323." *BCTH*, n.s. 4 (1968): 353–68.
Latest dated Saturn stele.

————. "Sur la localisation d'Abitina, la cité des célèbres martyrs africains." *CRAI* (1976): 255–66.

Beschaouch, Azedine; Hanoune, Roger; and Thébert, Yvon. *Les ruines de Bulla Regia.* CollEFR, 28. Rome, 1977.
A guidebook.

Biebel, Franklin M. "The Mosaic of Hammam-Lif." *Art Bulletin* 18 (1936): 541–51.
Synagogue.

Carandini, Andrea. "Problemi dell'ultime pitture tardo-antiche nel bacino del Mediterraneo meridionale." *ArchClass* 14 (1963): 210–35.
Late dating; to be used with caution.

————. *Produzione agricola e produzione ceramica nell'Africa di età imperiale: appunti sull'economia della Zeugitana e della Bizacena.* Studi miscellanei del Seminario di Archeologia e Storia dell'Arte greca e romana dell'Università di Roma, 15. Rome, 1970.
Marxist economic history; see esp. pp. 97–119.

Cavalieri, Franchi di. "La passio dei martiri abitinesi." *Studi e testi* 65 (1936): 3–46.

Cèbe, Jean-Pierre. "Une fontaine monumentale récemment découverte à Sufétula." *MEFR* 69 (1957): 163–206.

Chastagnol, André, and Duval, N. "Survivances du culte impérial en Afrique du Nord à l'époque vandale." *BSAF* (1972): 194–98.
Flamines perpetui after 439.

Cintas, Jean, and Duval, N. "L'église du prêtre Félix (région de Kélibia)." *Karthago* 9 (1958): 157–265.

Clover, Frank M. "Carthage in the Age of Augustine." In John H. Humphrey, ed., *Excavations at Carthage*, vol. 4, pp. 1–15. Ann Arbor, 1978.
Dates Theodosian Wall 423–425. Exemplary on the fourth-century city teeming with "beggars, children, dockhands, maid-

servants, footsoldiers, housewives, thieves, deacons, shepherds, prostitutes, minor bureaucrats, priests, merchants, generals, bishops, estate-owners."

Delattre, Alfred L. *Gamart ou la nécropole juive de Carthage.* Lyon, 1898.

————. "Une grande basilique près de Ste. Monique à Carthage." *CRAI* (1916): 150–64.

Duval, Noël. "Nouvelles recherches d'archéologie et d'épigraphie chrétiennes à Sufétula." *MEFR* 68 (1956): 247–98.
On Basilica VI, of Sylvanus and Fortunatus.

————. "La chapelle funéraire souterraine dite d'Astérius à Carthage." *MEFR* 71 (1959): 339–57.

————. "Deux basiliques chrétiennes de Tunisie méridionale." *Cahs-Archs* 13 (1962): 269–87.

————. "Trois notes sur les antiquités chrétiennes d'Haïdra." *BSAF* (1963): 44–68.
Reliquary of Saint Cyprian from Basilica I.

————. "Observations sur l'urbanisme tardif de Sufétula." *CahTun* 12 (1964): 87–105.

————. "L'église de l'évêque Melleus à Haïdra." *CRAI* (1967): 221–44.

————. "Quelques tables d'autel de Tunisie." *CahTun* 15 (1967): 209–21.
Includes Junca, Douimès, Sufetula.

————. "Les églises de Sbeïtla et Haïdra." In *Atti del 7° Congresso d'antichità cristiana, 1965,* pp. 473–78. Rome, 1969.
On Bellator I, Vitalis II, Melleus, and Candidus: double apses.

————. "Haïdra 1967: rapport préliminaire." *Africa* 3/4 (1969/70): 193–225.

————. "Eglise et temple en Afrique du Nord." *BCTH,* n.s. 7 (1971): 265–317.
Sbeïtla Basilica III, Thuburbo Maius, Djebel Oust.

————. "Les églises d'Haïdra III: la citadelle." *CRAI* (1971): 136–66.

————. "Inscriptions byzantines de Sbeïtla III." *MEFR* 83 (1971): 423–43.

————. *Sbeïtla et les églises africaines à deux absides.* BEFAR, 215. Paris, 1971.

————. "Etudes d'architecture chrétienne nord-africaine." *MEFR* 84 (1972): 1071–72.
Much on Carthage, Sbeïtla, Mactar, Junca, Haïdra.

————. "L'évolution du décor figuré et ornemental en Afrique à la fin de l'antiquité." *CorsCultRavBiz* 19 (1972): 159–86.

Djebel Oust, Dermech, Bir Ftouha, Bulla Regia, Haïdra, Sbeïtla, Althiburos, Smirat, Tabarca, and Algerian sites.

————. "Plan de la leçon sur les monuments chrétiens de Carthage." *CorsCultRavBiz* 19 (1972): 95–104.

————. *Eglises africaines à deux absides II*. BEFAR 218, part 1. Paris, 1971.

Much on Carthage. See especially pp. 107–19.

————. "L'origine, la technique et l'histoire de la mosaïque funéraire chrétienne en Afrique." In *La mosaïque gréco-romaine*, vol. 2, pp. 63–101. Paris, 1975.

Richly illustrated. Includes, among much else (including Algerian sites): Haïdra, Thabraca, Thugga, Utica, Carthage, Hammam-Lif, Thuburbo Maius, Kelibia, Hadrumetum, Acholla, Sfax, Thina, Junca, La Skhira, Sbeïtla, Mactar.

Duval, Noël, and Cintas, Jean. "Etudes d'architecture chrétienne nord-africaine III: Le Martyrium de Cincari et les martyria triconques et tétraconques en Afrique." *MEFR* 88, no. 2 (1976): 853–959.

Account of a fifth-century complex now destroyed. Tébessa Khalia associated with oil works at Henchir Faraoun; troughs are later additions to original religious building.

Duval, Noël, and Duval, Yvette. "L'église dite de Candidus à Haïdra et l'inscription des martyrs." *MélPig* (1966): 1153–89.

————. "Fausses basiliques (et faux martyrs): quelques bâtiments à auges d'Afrique." *MEFR* 84 (1972): 675–719.

For example, at Haïdra. Offers the hypothesis that buildings with troughs were used for distributing the grain dole.

Duval, Noël, and Golvin, J.-C. "Haïdra à l'époque chrétienne IV: monuments à auges et les bâtiments similaires." *CRAI* (1972): 133–72.

Duval, Noël, and Hallier, G. *Recherches archéologiques à Sbeïtla I: églises à deux sanctuaires opposées*. Paris, 1971.

Duval, Noël, and Lézine, A. "Nécropole chrétienne et baptistère souterrain à Carthage." *CahsArchs* 10 (1959): 71–147.

Duval, Noël, and Prévot, Françoise. *Recherches archéologiques à Haïdra I: les inscriptions chrétiennes*. CollEFR, 18. Rome, 1975.

A total of 508 inscriptions. Statistics on African names.

Duval, Paul-Marie. "La forme des navires romains d'après la mosaïque d'Althiburus." *MEFR* 61 (1949): 119–49.

Updates Gauckler (1905).

Eadie, John W., and Humphrey, John H. "The Topography of the Southeast Quarter of Late Roman Carthage." In J. H. Humphrey, ed.,

Excavations at Carthage, vol. 3, pp. 1–19. Ann Arbor, 1977. Updates information on naval and commercial harbors, Theodosian Wall, Bir Knissia religious complex.

Ennabli, Abdelmajid. "Cartagine." *EAAC,* suppl. (1970).

———. "Althiburos" and "Macomades Minores." *PECS* (1976).

Ennabli, Liliane. *Les inscriptions funéraires chrétiennes de la basilique dite de Ste. Monique à Carthage.* CollEFR, 25. Rome, 1975.

Ennaifer, Mongi. *La civilisation tunisienne à travers la mosaïque.* Tunis, 1973.
   In Arabic, with French summary. Bad color photographs of forty-six mosaics.

———. "La mosaïque de chasse de Althiburos." *CahTun* 28 (1975): 7–16.
   Horse, dog names.

———. *La cité d'Althiburos et l'édifice des Asclepieia.* Bibliotheca Archaeologica (Tunis) 1 (1976).
   Not seen.

Fendri, Mohammed. *Les basiliques chrétiennes de La Skhira.* PublUTun-FacLettr 8 (1961).

———. "Les thermes des mois à Thina." *CahTun* 12 (1964): 59–67.

———. "Evolution chronologique et stylistique d'un ensemble de mosaïques dans une station thermale à Djebel Oust." In *La mosaïque gréco-romaine,* vol. 1, pp. 157–72. Paris, 1965.

———. "Djebel Oust." *EAAC,* suppl. (1970).
   Full-page photograph of seasons mosaic.

Feuille, Georges L. "Stucs et peintures de l'église de Iunca." *CahsArchs* 5 (1947): 131–34, 175–81.
   See also his article on Iunca in *RevTun* (1940): 21–45.

Février, Paul-Albert. "Les sources épigraphiques et archéologiques et l'histoire réligieuse des provinces orientales de l'Afrique antique." *CorsCultRavBiz* 19 (1972): 131–58.
   Good on Augustine's Carthage.

———. "L'évolution du décor figuré et ornemental en Afrique à la fin de l'antiquité." *CorsCultRavBiz* 19 (1972): 159–86.
   Well illustrated. Good on Djebel Oust, Carthage, Bulla Regia, Haïdra, Sbeïtla, Iunca, La Skhira, Althiburos, Thabraca.

Finley, Moses I. "Aristotle and Economic Analysis." *Past and Present,* no. 47 (1970): 3–25.
   No evidence for investment in improving agriculture or manufacturing; priority went to investment in land.

Frend, William H. C. "The Early Christian Church in Carthage." In

John H. Humphrey, ed., *Excavations at Carthage*, vol. 3, pp. 21–40. Ann Arbor, 1977.
Useful summary of Vandal and Byzantine buildings and activity.

Fries, Helmut. "Urbanae cohortes." *RE*, suppl. 10 (1963): cols. 1125–40.
Carthaginian detachment escorted Cyprian to execution.

Garrigue, Pierre. "Une basilique bizantine à Junca." *MEFR* 65 (1953): 173–96.

Gauckler, Paul. "Catalogue figuré de la batellerie gréco-romaine: la mosaïque d'Althiburos." *MonsPiot* 12 (1905): 113–54.

———. "Mosaïques tombales d'une chapelle de martyrs à Thabraca." *MonsPiot* 13 (1906); reprinted *CahTun* 20 (1972): 152–202.

———. *Inventaire des mosaïqués de l'Afrique du Nord*, vol. 2: *Proconsularis*. Paris, 1910. Supplement by A. Merlin, 1915.

Hanoune, Roger. "Trois pavements de la maison de la course de chars à Carthage." *MEFR* 81 (1969): 219–56.
Especially on child's chariot race. Valuable bibliography of parallels.

Hayes, John W. *Late Roman Pottery*. London, 1972.
Authoritative. Invaluable on dating.

Humphrey, John H., ed. *Excavations at Carthage*, vol. 3. Ann Arbor, 1977.
Articles by specialists, including Frend (1977). Humphrey's preliminary reports, *Excavations at Carthage*, vols. 1–4 (Tunis and Ann Arbor, 1975–78) are exemplary both as to field method and as to exposition. The Michigan sector, northwest of rectangular harbor, east of TGM railway, includes House of the Charioteer Mosaic (late fourth century) and ecclesiastical complex (mostly after A.D. 650). J. W. Hayes treats pottery; T. V. Buttrey, coins; Katherine Dunbabin, mosaic and pavements. Other information: on quarry-sites, many besides Simitthu, and closer to Carthage— for example, Hamilcar, Djebel Oust; marble for *opus sectile* came mostly from Simitthu, but also from farther afield—Chios, Scyros, Euboea, Djebel Rhouas (near Thuburbo Maius), Phrygian Synnada, Laconia. Volume 2 contains also a series of excellent photographs, taken in 1925, before Carthage was so much built over; views of Basilica of Saint Cyprian and Damous el-Karita are especially fine.

Humphrey, John H., and Pedley, J. G. "Roman Carthage." *Scientific American* 238 (1978): 111–20.

Katchatrian, Armen. *Baptistères paléochrétiens*. Paris, 1972.
Numerous plans, especially of Carthage buildings.

Kotula, Tadeusz. "L'insurrection des Gordiens et l'Afrique romaine."
   Eos 50 (1959/60): 197–211.
   Marxist. Argues economic motive for El-Djem revolt.
Lancel, Serge. "Originalité de la province ecclésiastique de Byzacène."
   CahTun 12 (1964): 139–53.
   List of Donatist and Catholic bishoprics, A.D. 411.
Lapeyre, Gabriel, and Pellegrini, A. *Carthage latine et chrétienne.* Paris,
   1950.
   Useful on history of excavation.
Lavin, Irving. "The Hunting Mosaics of Antioch and Their Sources."
   Dumbarton Oaks Papers 17 (1963): 181–286.
   Title conceals many fine photos of Tunisian mosaics.
Leynaud, Augustin F. *Les catacombes africaines—Sousse-Hadrumète.*
   3rd ed. Algiers, 1937.
   Corrections in Foucher, *Hadrumetum* (1964; see chapter 1).
Lepelley, Claude. "Déclin ou stabilité de l'agriculture africaine au Bas-
   Empire?" *AntsAfrs* 1 (1967): 134–44.
   Argues for stability.
Lézine, Alexandre. "Notes sur l'amphithéâtre de Thysdrus." *CahTun*
   8 (1960): 29–50.
Mahjoubi, Amar. "Découverte d'une nouvelle mosaïque de chasse à
   Carthage." *CRAI* (1967): 264–78.
Mahjoubi, Amar; Salomonson, Jan W.; and Ennabli, Abdelmajid. *Né-
   cropole romaine de Raqqada.* Collection N&D 8, nos. 1 and 2
   (Tunis, 1970–73).
   Rich yield of locally made vases and lamps dated from first to
   mid–fourth century, from site twelve kilometers south-southwest
   of Kairouan.
Maurin, Louis. "Thuburbo Maius et la paix vandale." *CahTun* 15
   (1967): 225–54.
Merlin, Alfred. *Forum et maisons d'Althiburos.* N&D, 6 (1913).
   Excludes ship mosaic.
Musurillo, Herbert. *The Acts of the Christian Martyrs.* Oxford, 1972.
Picard, Gilbert C. "Mosaïques africaines du troisième siècle." *RevArch*
   (1960), part 2, 17–49.
   Thugga, Hadrumetum, Themetra, Acholla, Bulla Regia, and
   Algerian sites.
———. "Un palais du IVe siècle à Carthage." *CRAI* (1964): 101–18.
———. *La Carthage de St. Augustin.* Paris, 1965.
   Excellent, especially on mosaics.
Poinssot, Claude. "Les mosaïques de la maison de Dionysos et d'Ulysse

à Thugga." In *La mosaïque gréco-romaine*, vol. 1, pp. 219–31. Paris, 1965.

Précheur-Canonge, Thérèse. *La vie rurale en Afrique du Nord d'après les mosaïques.* PublUTunFacLettr 6 (1962).
Inventory includes Uthina, Thabraca, Dominus Julius.

Rosenblum, Morris. *Luxorius: A Latin Poet among the Vandals.* New York, 1961.

Rostovtzeff, Mihail I. *Storia economica e sociale dell'impero romano.* Florence, 1946.
The best edition. Many photos and good commentary on mosaics.

Salomonson, Jan W. *La mosaïque aux chevaux de l'antiquarium de Carthage.* Archeologische Studiën van het Nederlands Historisch Instituut te Rom, 1. The Hague, 1965.

————. "Etudes sur la céramique romaine d'Afrique: sigillée claire et céramique commune de Hr. el Ouiba (Raqqada) en Tunisie centrale." *Bulletin der Vereeniging tot Bevordering der Kennis van de Antike Beshaving* 43 (1968): 80–145.
Seventy-seven tombs, down to 375; parallels at Hadjeb el Ajoun, Henchir el Aouja.

Saumagne, Charles. "Les basiliques cypriennes." *RevArch* 2 (1909): 188–202.

————. "La paix vandale." *RevTun* (1930); reprinted in *CahTun* 10 (1962): 417–25.

Saxer, Victor. *Vie liturgique et quotidienne à Carthage.* Studi di antichità cristiana, 29. Vatican City, 1969.
Based on Cyprian.

Stevens, Courtenay E. "Agricultural and Rural Life in the Late Roman Empire." In *The Cambridge Economic History of Europe from the Decline of the Roman Empire*, ed. J. H. Clapham and Eileen Power, vol. 1, pp. 89–117. Cambridge, 1942.

Tchernia, André, and Zevi, Fausto. "Amphores de Byzacène au Bas-Empire." *AntsAfrs* 3 (1969): 173–214.
New finds from Tunisia on Monte Testaccio and in Ostia.

Thirion, Jean. "Orphée magicien dans la mosaïque romaine: nouvelle mosaïque d'Orphée à Sfax." *MEFR* 67 (1955): 149–79.

————. "Un ensemble thermal avec mosaïques à Thina." *MEFR* 69 (1957): 207–54.

Toutain, Jacques. "Le théâtre de Chemtou." *MEFR* 12 (1892): 359–78.
See also *CRAI* (1893): 453–73; Cagnat and Saladin, "Chemtou," *NouvArchMissSc* 13 (1887): 385–427. A German team under Jürgen Christern has been working at Chemtou since 1970.

Townsend, Prescott W. "The Revolution of A.D. 238: The Leaders and Their Aims." *YCS* 14 (1955): 49–105.

Vaultrin, Jean. *Les basiliques de Carthage*. Algiers, 1932.
　　See especially pp. 81–100. See also his work of the same title in *RAfr* 73 (1932): 187–318, continued in 74 (1933): 118–56.

Villefosse, Heron de. Untitled note in *CRAI* (1906): 118–21.
　　Publishes late Roman or Byzantine inscription of ferry charges, Le Kram.

Yacoub, Mohamed. *Catalogue du Musée du Bardo*. Tunis, 1970.
　　Valuable, but the 139 photographs are badly reproduced.

————. "Trois chefs d'oeuvres d'art chrétien au Bardo." *CorsCult-RavBiz* 19 (1972): 351–73.
　　Especially Thabraca ECCLESIA MATER and Clupea baptistery mosaics.

————. "La mosaïque d'Achille et de Chiron au Musée du Bardo." In *La mosaïque gréco-romaine*, vol. 2, pp. 41–54. Paris, 1975.

5. Cyrenaica

Alföldi-Rosenbaum, Elizabeth. "A Nilotic Scene on Justinian Floor-Mosaics in Cyrenaican Churches." In *La mosaïque gréco-romaine*, vol. 2, pp. 149–53. Paris, 1975.

Basset, Henri. "La Libye d'Hérodote d'après le livre de M. Gsell." *RAfr* 59 (1918): 293–305.

Bates, Oric. *The Eastern Libyans*. London, 1914.
　　Excellent on natives; still not outdated.

Beechey, Frederick W., and Beechey, H. W. *Proceedings of the Expedition to Explore the North Coast of Africa from Tripoly Eastward*. London, 1828.
　　Quaint *and* valuable; good plans of Pentapolis.

Boardman, John, and Hayes, J. W. *Excavations at Tocra, 1963–5*. 2 vols. London, 1966–74.

Boardman, John. "Evidence for Dating Greek Settlements in Cyrenaica." *ABSA* 61 (1966): 149–66.

————. "Tocra." *EAAC*, suppl. (1970).

————. *The Greeks Overseas*. Harmondsworth, 1973.
　　Good on Cyrene, pp. 169–174.

Caputo, Giacomo. *Lo scultore del grande bassorelievo con la danza delle Menade in Tolemaide di Cirenaica*. MAL, 1. Rome, 1948.

Cassells, John. "The Cemeteries of Cyrene." *PBSR* 23 (1955): 1–43.

Chamoux, François. *Cyrène sous la monarchie des Battiades.* BEFAR, 177. Paris, 1953.
> Deservedly standard.
_____. "Campagne de fouilles à Apollonia de Cyrénaique, 1976." *CRAI* (1977): 6–27.
Chevallier, Raymond. "Cité et territoire." *ANRW* 2, part 1 (1974): 649–788.
> Includes plans of Apollonia, Cyrene, Ptolemais, Lepcis Magna, Volubilis, Timgad, Tunisian centuriation, and Carthage; 133 plates.
Coster, Charles H. "The Economic Position of Cyrenaica in Classical Times." In *Studies in Honor of A. C. Johnson,* pp. 3–26. Princeton, 1951.
Fitzgerald, Augustine. *The Letters of Synesius.* Oxford, 1926.
Flemming, Nicholas. Report quoted in Joan du Plat Taylor, ed., *Marine Archaeology,* pp. 168–78. London, 1965.
> Results of scuba diving exploration of Apollonia harbor. See also Flemming's expanded account in his *Cities in the Sea* (New York, 1971), pp. 95–135.
Fraser, Peter M. "Hadrian and Cyrene." *JRS* 40 (1950): 77–90.
> Reconstruction after Jewish Revolt.
Freeman, Kathleen. *Greek City States.* London, 1950.
> Reliable short popular account of history and constitution of Cyrene, pp. 181–201.
Gasperini, Lidio. "Le iscrizioni del Cesareo e della basilica di Cirene." *QAL* 6 (1971): 3–22.
> Dates the former A.D. 4–14, the latter 118 (restoration).
Goodchild, Richard G. "Chiese e basiliche bizantine della Cirenaica." *CorsCultRavBiz* 13 (1966): 205–23.
> On Gasr Elbia church and mosaic; new plan and axonometric reconstruction of Palace of Dux, Apollonia.
_____. "A Coin Hoard from Balagrae (El-Beida) and the Earthquake of A.D. 365." *LA* 3/4 (1966/67): 203–11.
_____. *Cyrene und Apollonia.* Zurich, 1971.
> Authoritative. In German.
Goodchild, Richard G.; Pedley, J. G.; and White, D. "A Recent Discovery of Archaic Sculpture at Cyrene." *LA* 3/4 (1966/67): 179–98.
Guarducci, Margherita. "La più antica catachese figurata, il grande mosaico della basilica di Gasr Elbia in Cirenaica." *MemLinc* 18 (1975): 659–86.
> Argues that fifteen of the panels were set in the wrong place;

changes do not affect analysis in text above. Mosaic presents life as an insidious, perilous sea; fortress (VII, 2) is City of God; eagle (III, 3) symbolizes resurrection; gazelles (I, 1 and 5) are the faithful.

Harrison, Richard M. "An Orpheus Mosaic at Ptolemais in Cyrenaica." *JRS* 52 (1962): 13–18.

Jones, G. D. Barri, and Little, J. H. "Coastal Settlements in Cyrenaica." *JRS* 61 (1971): 64–79.
Especially useful on Eu(h)esperides (Benghazi).

———. "Hadrianopolis." *LA* 8 (1971): 53–67.

Kraeling, Carl. *Ptolemais, City of the Libyan Pentapolis.* Oriental Institute Publications, 90. Chicago, 1962.
Exhaustive, authoritative; but see Caputo (1948) and Pesce (1956).

Kwapong, Alex. "Citizenship and Democracy in Fourth-Century Cyrene." In Lloyd A. Thompson and J. Ferguson, eds., *Africa in Classical Antiquity,* pp. 99–109. Ibadan, 1969.

Lauer, Jean-Philippe. "L'enceinte d'Apollonia à Mersa-Souza." *RevArch* (1962): 129–63.

Lloyd, J., and Lewis, P. R. "Water Supply and Urban Population in Roman Cyrenaica." *AnnRptSocLibSt* 8 (1976/77): 35–40.

Marrou, Henri-Irénée. "Synesius of Cyrene." In Arnaldo Momigliano, ed., *Conflict between Paganism and Christianity in the Fourth Century,* pp. 126–50. Oxford, 1963.

Masson, Olivier. "Grecs et Libyens en Cyrenaïque." *AntsAfrs* 10 (1976): 49–62.
Epigraphic evidence for persistence of Libyan names.

Mingazzini, Paolo. *L'insula di Giasone Magno a Cirene.* MAL, 8. Rome, 1966.
The *editio princeps.* Stucchi (1975) offers some revisions.

Norsa, Medea, and Vitelli, G. *Il Papiro Vaticano Greco,* vol. 11. Rome, 1931.
The cadaster (tax register) of Marmarica.

Oliverio, Gaspare, and Pugliese-Carratelli, G. "Supplemento epigrafico cirenaico." *Annuario della scuola italiana di Atene* 39/40 (1961/62): 219–37.
Useful, pending J. M. Reynolds' *Inscriptions of Roman Cyrenaica.* Lists 299 items (for some of which see *SEG* 9), including list of eponymous priests of Apollo, and accounts of demiurges, fourth century B.C.; dedication to Ptolemy X (181–116). For Anastasius decree, found in Apollonia, see *SEG* 9, no. 356.

Paribeni, Ettore. *Catalogo delle sculture di Cirene.* MAL, 5. Rome, 1959.
Includes the Venus (no. 246), cult statue from temple of Zeus
(no. 192) and from capitolium (no. 185).

Pesce, Gennaro. *Il palazzo delle Colonne in Tolemaide di Cirenaica.*
MAL, 2. Rome, 1956.

————. "Tolemaide." *EAAC* (1966).

Pierini, M. Grazia. "La tomba 'di Menecrate' a Barca in Cirenaica."
QAL 6 (1971): 23–34.

Reynolds, Joyce M. "Cn. Cornelius Lentulus Marcellinus in Cyrene,
67 B.C." *JRS* 52 (1962): 97–103.
Pompey's legate, in a campaign against pirates which may have
earned him a Victory monument in Agora.

————. "Inscriptiones Romanae Cyrenaicae." *LinH* (1971): 181–89.
Promises corpus of twelve hundred items. Ptolemy's will: *SEG* 9,
no. 7.

————. "Libya and Diocletian's Edict on Maximum Prices." *LA* 8
(1971): 53–57.

Reynolds, Joyce M., and Goodchild, R. G. "City Lands of Apollonia in
Cyrenaica." *LA* 2 (1965): 103–7.
Boundary dispute with Cyrene.

Reynolds, Joyce M., and Masson, Olivier. "Une inscription ephébique
de Ptolemais (Cyrénaique)." *ZPE* 20 (1976): 87–100.
Forty-five names (fourth–third century B.C.), some Cyrenaican,
some Egyptian.

Rhotert, Hans. *Libysche Felsbilder.* Darmstadt, 1952. [Not treated
in chapter 5.]
Engraved or painted rock art, fifth millennium B.C., from southeast; tattooed archers, cattle, antelope, elephant, gazelle, penis
sheaths, men with animal heads.

Romanelli, Pietro. *La Cirenaica romana.* Verbania, 1943.

Rosenbaum, Elizabeth. *Cyrenaican Portrait Sculpture.* London, 1960.
Includes the British Museum head of a Libyan; Berenice, fine
Agrippina Minor (mother of Nero).

Rowe, Alan. *The Cyrene Expedition of the University of Manchester,
1952.* Manchester, 1956.
On necropoleis. Exhaustive but disappointing; see Cassells
(1975).

Smallwood, E. Mary. "Jews in Egypt and Cyrenaica." In Lloyd A.
Thompson and John Ferguson, eds., *Africa in Classical Antiquity,*
pp. 125–31. Ibadan, 1969.
On, *inter alia,* Jewish Revolt of 115.

Stroux, Johannes, and Wenger, L. "Die Augustus-Inschrift auf dem Marktplatz von Cyrene." *Abhandlungen der bayerischen Akademie des Wissenschaften, philosophisch-historische Klasse 34,* part 2 (1928): entire issue.
Exhaustive: text, translation, commentary.
Stucchi, Sandro. "Le fasi costruttive dell'Apollonion di Cirene." *QAL* 4 (1961): 55–81.
––––––. *L'Agora di Cirene,* vol. 1. Rome, 1965.
Authoritative.
––––––. "I lavori di ristauro eseguiti dalle missioni archeologiche italiane a Cirene dal 1957 al 1965." *LA* 2 (1965): 109–22.
Especially the Stoa of Herms.
––––––. "Prime tracce tardo-minoiche a Cirene: i rapporti della Libia con il mondo egeo." *QAL* 5 (1967): 19–45.
Very full annotation.
––––––. "Apollonia." *EAAC,* suppl. (1970).
––––––. "Cirenaica—basiliche cristiane." *EAAC,* suppl. (1970).
Good on Gasr Elbia mosaic.
––––––. "Cirene." *EAAC,* suppl. (1970).
––––––. "Architettura cirenaica in età greco-romana." *LinH* (1971): 207–32.
––––––. "Per una pubblicazione scientifica del Piazzale delle Cisterne di Tolemaide di Cirenaica." *ArchClass* 25/26 (1973/74): 704–12. Gymnasium site (second/first century B.C.) of 200 by 180 Roman feet, transformed into forum after earthquake of A.D. 365, in "Honorian renaissance."
––––––. *Architettura cirenaica.* Rome, 1975.
Massive, indispensable. Some attributions and dates controversial. Good in combination with Goodchild (1971).
Vickers, Michael, and Bazane, Abdulsalem. "A Fifth Century B.C. Tomb in Cyrenaica." *LA* 8 (1971): 69–84.
Vickers, Michael, and Reynolds, J. M. "Cyrenaica 1962–72." *Archaeological Reports* 1971/72 [London]: 22–47.
Notes, with bibliography. Cyrene founder's inscription, *SEG* 9, no. 3.
Vita, Antonio di. "Libia." In F. Barreca et al., eds., *Espansione fenicia nel Mediterraneo,* pp. 77–98. Studi Semitici, 38. Rome, 1971.
On Mycenaeans in Cyrene, twelfth century B.C.
Ward Perkins, John B., and Ballance, M. "The Caesareum at Cyrene and the Basilica at Cremna (Pisidia)." *PBSR* 26 (1958): 137–94. Dates former after 12B.C., restored 115. See Gasperini (1971).

White, Donald. "Excavation of the Demeter Sanctuary at Cyrene, 1959. Preliminary Report." *LA* 8 (1971): 85–104. Third and fourth reports: *AJA* 79 (1975): 33–48; 80 (1976): 165–81.

———. "Ancient Cyrene and the Cults of Demeter and Persephone." *Expedition* 17, part 4 (1975): 2–15.

A good general survey.

———. "Seven Recently Discovered Sculptures from Cyrene." *Expedition* 18, part 2 (1976): 14–32.

A collaborative enterprise with graduate students.

6. Tripolitania and Its Hinterland

Aurigemma, Salvatore. "L'elefante di Lepcis Magna." *AfrIt* 7 (1940): 67–86.

———. "Sculture del Foro Vecchio di Lepcis Magna raffiguranti la Dea Roma e principi della casa dei Giulio-Claudii." *AfrIt* 8 (1940): 1–94.

———. *L'Italia in Africa,* vol. 1: *I mosaici;* vol. 2: *Le pitture.* Rome, 1960–62.

Zliten mosaics (Flavian date); Sabratha houses.

———. "L'ubicazione e la funzione urbanistica dell'arco quadrifronte di Marco Aurelio in Tripoli." *QAL* 5 (1967): 65–78.

———. "L'arco quadrifronte di M. Aurelio et di L. Vero in Tripoli." *LA,* suppl. 3 (1970): entire issue.

Bartoccini, Renato. "L'arco quadrifronte dei Severi a Lepcis." *AfrIt* 4 (1931): 32–152.

———. *Il Porto Romano di Lepcis Magna.* Rome, 1958.

In Italian and English.

———. "Il porto di Lepcis Magna nella sua vita economica e sociale." *HommGren* (1962): 228–43.

———. "Il tempio antoniniano di Sabratha." *LA* 1 (1964): 21–42.

Bianchi-Bandinelli, Renato; Caffarelli, Ernesto Vargara; and Caputo, G. *The Buried City: Leptis Magna.* New York, 1966. [Italian edition, 1964.]

Pictures excellent, translation opaque.

Birley, Anthony. "Apuleius: Roman Provincial Life." *History Today* 18 (1968): 629–36.

On the trial for witchcraft in Sabratha.

———. *Septimius Severus, the African Emperor.* London, 1971.

See especially pages 327–58. Out of 173 known holders of high

Severan office, 35 are African, a higher percentage than from Italy or any other province.

Boethius, Axel, and Ward Perkins, J. B. *Etruscan and Roman Architecture.* Harmondsworth, 1970.
Pages 462–94, with pictures and figures, treat the North African provinces.

Bovill, E. W. "The Camel and the Garamantes." *Antiquity* 30 (1956): 19–21.
Expeditions of Flaccus and Maternus made possible by camel; Caesar took twenty-two at Thapsus; reliefs show camel plowing, second/third centuries.

Brogan, Olwen. "The Camel in Roman Tripolitania." *PBSR* 22 (1954): 126–31.
In Cyrenaica by Augustan age, then gradually westward; needed for plowing.

Brogan, Olwen, and Reynolds, J. M. "Inscriptions from the Tripolitanian Hinterland." *LA* 1 (1964): 43–46.
This is supplement 2 to *IRT*; supplement 1 is in *PBSR* 23 (1955): 124–47.

Cagiano di Azevedo, Massimo. "La data dei mosaici di Zliten." *HommGren* (1962): 374–80.
Severan; but see Aurigemma (1960) and Foucher (1964).

Caputo, Giacomo. *Il teatro di Lepcis Magna.* MAL, 3. Rome, 1950.
──────. *Il teatro di Sabratha e l'architettura teatrale africana.* MAL, 6. Rome, 1959.
──────. "Fezzan." *EAAC* (1960).
──────. "Ritratto leptitana di Settimio Severo-Ercole." *HommGren* (1962): 581–85.

Caputo, Giacomo, and Traversari, A. *Le sculture del teatro di Lepcis Magna.* MAL, 13. Rome, 1976.

Carter, Theresa H. "West Phoenicians at Lepcis Magna." *AJA* 69 (1965): 123–32.

Crova, Bice. "Opere idrauliche romane all'uadi Caam, il Cinyps della Tripolitania romana." *QAL* 5 (1967): 99–120.

Daniels, Charles. *The Garamantes of Southern Libya.* Stoughton, Wis., 1970.
──────. "An Ancient People of the Libyan Sahara." In James and Theodora Bynon, eds., *Hamito-Semitica*, pp. 249–50. The Hague and Paris, 1975.
On Garamantes.

Degrassi, Nevio. "Il mercato romano di Lepcis Magna." *QAL* 2 (1951): 27–69.

Desanges, Jehan. "Un drame africain sous Auguste: le meurtre du proconsul L. Cornelius Lentulus par les Nasamons." *HommRen* (1969): 197–213.

Evrard, Ginette di Vita. "Les dédicaces de l'amphithéâtre et cirque de Lepcis Magna." *LA* 2 (1965): 29–37.

―――. "La dédicace du temple d'Isis à Sabratha." *LA* 3/4 (1966/67): 13–20.

Foucher, Louis. "Sur les mosaïques de Zliten." *LA* 1 (1964): 9–20.
Gladiator mosaic is Flavian; others in same villa Severan.

―――. "La villa romaine de Tagiura." *BCTH*, n.s. 4 (1968): 237–39.
Date 145–161.

Gadallah, Fawai F., ed. *Libya in History*. Benghazi, 1971.
Fifteen relevant articles, most listed here under authors. A scarce book.

Goodchild, Richard G. "Oasis Forts of Legio III Augusta on Routes to the Fezzan." *PBSR* 22 (1954): 56–68.

―――. *Tabula Imperii Romani: Cyrene; Lepcis Magna*. Both London, 1954.
Authoritative annotated maps.

―――. "The Unfinished 'Imperial Baths' of Lepcis Magna." *LA* 2 (1965): 15–28.

―――. "Roman Roads of Libya and Their Milestones." *LinH* (1971): 155–71.

Goodchild, Richard G., and Ward Perkins, J. B. "The Limes Tripolitanus in the Light of Recent Discoveries." *JRS* 39 (1949): 81–95.

Graziosi, Paolo. "Graffiti rupestri del Gebel Bu Ghnèba nel Fezzan." *AfrIt* 6 (1935): 188–97.

Guey, Julien. "Lepcitana Septimiana Altera IV." *RAfr* 96 (1952): 275–310 and 97 (1953): 273–313.
On Lepcis Magna Severan Forum and basilica.

Guidi, Giacomo. "Il teatro romano di Sabratha." *AfrIt* 3 (1930): 1–52.
Fascinating on the reconstruction.

Hammond, Norman. "The Limes Tripolitanus." *JBAA* 30 (1967): 1–18.

Haynes, Denys E. L. *The Antiquities of Tripolitania*. 2nd ed. Tripoli and London, 1959.
An absolutely model guidebook. Limpid exposition of complicated material. Maps, plans, plates.

Humphrey, John H.; Sear, F.; and Vickers, M. "Aspects of the Circus at Lepcis Magna." *AnnRptSocLibSt* 5 (1973/74): 4–12.

Ioppolo, Giovanni. "La tavola delle unità di misure nel mercato augusteo di Lepcis Magna." *QAL* 5 (1967): 89–98.

Laurenzi, A. "I grandi complessi architettonici della Tripolitania e Cirenaica." *CorsCultRavBiz* 13 (1966): 251–74.

Law, Robin C. C. "The Garamantes and Trans-Saharan Enterprise in Classical Times." *Journal of African History* 8 (1967): 181–200.
Doubts chariot routes. Sahara could be crossed to beyond Hoggar, perhaps southwest to Timbuctoo, but West African gold came to Carthage by sea.

MacDonald, William L. *The Architecture of the Roman Empire*, vol. 1. New Haven, 1965.
Good on Severan Forum and basilica at Lepcis Magna.

Magi, Felipe, and Fiandra, E. "Missione archeologica dell'Università di Perugia a Lepcis Magna." *Annali della facoltà di lettere e filosofia dell'Università di Perugia* 6 (1968/69): 245–55, 375–92.
Temples to Flavian emperors.

Matthews, Kenneth D., and Cook, A. W. *Cities in the Sand*. Philadelphia, 1963.
Good pictures, jargon-ridden text.

Pace, Biagio; Caputo, Giacomo; and Sergi, Sergio. "Scavi Sahariani." *Monumenti Antichi* 41 (1951): cols. 149–551.
Pioneer work on Tripolitanian backcountry: Germa, Garama mausolea, Zuila, Fezzan generally.

Pesce, Gennaro. *Il tempio di Iside in Sabratha*. MAL, 4. Rome, 1953.

———. "Deux ans de recherches dans le sud de Tripolitaine." *CRAI* (1969): 189–212.
Bu Njem; graffiti in Latin and Libyan. See also his remarks in *CRAI* (1972): 319–39.

———. "Recherches en Tripolitaine du Sud." *RevArch*, n.s. 2 (1971): 177–84.
On Bu Njem canabae.

———. "Trois nouvelles campagnes dans le Sud de la Tripolitaine." *CRAI* (1975): 495–505.
Ancient name of Bu-Njem was Gholia or Golas. Map of predesert and desert tracks; eleven ancient native villages near Bu Njem; in Bu Njem proper, three suburban temples, fifty more tombs, civilian and military; evidence of rapid growth but no plan. In the fort: barracks, double granary, principia, chapels, baths. Camp established (201) under elite officers, to pacify desert, at the point of furthest olive culture.

Rebuffat, René; Deneauve, J.; and Hallier, G. "Bu Njem." *LA* 3/4 (1966/67): 49–137 and 6/7 (1969): 9–168.

Reynolds, Joyce M., and Ward Perkins, J. B. *Inscriptions of Roman Tripolitania*. Rome, 1952.

Ricotti, Eugenia S. P. "Le ville marittime di Silin." *RendPontAccArch* 43 (1971): 135–63.

Romanelli, Pietro. "La vita agricola tripolitana attraverso le rappresentazioni figurate." *AfrIt* 3 (1930): 53–70.
Ghirza reliefs, Zliten mosaics of fieldwork and threshing, not mentioned in chapter 6.

———. "Lepcis." *EAAC* (1961) and suppl. (1970).

———. "Sabratha." *EAAC* (1965).

———. "Basiliche e battisteri di età paleocristiana in Tripolitania." *CorsCultRavBiz* 13 (1966): 413–24.
Good especially on Christianity in farming centers of hinterland.

———. "Tripoli." *EAAC* (1966).

———. "La Tripolitania nell'archeologia nord-africana." *LinH* (1971): 133–42.
Notes that dividing line between Greek and Roman culture passes through Libya.

Ryberg, Inez S. *Rites of the State Religion in Roman Art*. MAAR, 22 (1955).
On portraiture on Severan arch, Lepcis Magna. Profusely illustrated.

Salama, Pierre. "Déchiffrement d'un miliaire de Lepcis Magna." *LA* 2 (1965): 39–45.
Proof that Diocletian did not abandon the limes.

———. "Les trésors maxentiens de Tripolitaine." *LA* 3/4 (1966/67): 21–27.

Sartorio, Giuseppina Pisani. "Arco quadrifronte di M. Aurelio a Lepcis Magna: saggio stratigrafico." *LA* 6/7 (1969/70): 327–79.
Six phases, from first century necropolis to A.D. 173.

Squarciapino, Maria Floriani. "Problemi della Gigantomachia di Lepcis Magna." *RendPontAccArch* 28 (1955/56): 169–79.

———. *Lepcis Magna*. Basel, 1964.
Authoritative guidebook. In German.

———. "Sculture di Lepcis Magna." *LinH* (1971): 147–52.
Influence of Aphrodisias in Caria.

———. *Sculture del Foro Severiano di Lepcis Magna*. MAL, 10. Rome, 1974.

Strocke, Volker M. "Beobachtungen an der Attikareliefs des severischen

Quadrifrons in Lepcis Magna." *AntsAfrs* 6 (1972): 147–72.
Exhaustive study. Good plates.

Thompson, Lloyd A. "Roman and Native in the Tripolitanian Cities in the Early Empire." *LinH* (1971): 235–49.
Lists forty-four functionaries. Native aristocracy. Intermarriage. Septimius Severus' first wife a Paccia.

Torelli, Mario. "Le curiae di Lepcis Magna." *QAL* 6 (1971): 105–11.

Vergara-Caffarelli, Ernesto. "Ghirza." *EAAC* (1960).

Ville, Georges. "Essai de datation de la mosaïque des gladiateurs de Zliten." In *La mosaïque gréco-romaine*, vol. 1, pp. 147–54. Paris, 1965.
On evidence of costume, mosaic must be earlier than 100. Garamantes revolts not confined to the 70s.

Vita, Antonino di. "Il limes romano di Tripolitania nella sua concretezza archeologica e nella sua realtà storica." *LA* 1 (1964): 65–98.
Dates Bu Njem pre-Severan. Good map.

⸻. "Questione di metodo." *ArchClass* 16 (1964): 315–18.
On Carandini-Foucher polemic (see chapter 3). Dates Sabratha Oceanus baths A.D. 123 (tiles).

⸻. "Recenti scavi e scoperte in Tripolitania." *LA*, suppl. 2 (1965): 65–111.
Lepcis Magna amphitheater and circus; triangular Punic mausoleum at Sabratha.

⸻. "La villa della Gara delle Nereidi presso Tagiura." *LA*, suppl. 2 (1965): 13–62.

⸻. "Diffusione del Cristianesimo nell'interno di Tripolitania." *CorsCultRavBiz* 13 (1966): 135–37.
Nine churches, including Donatist at Henchir Taglissi. See also his work by the same title, *QAL* 5 (1967): 121–42.

⸻. "Influences grecques et tradition orientale dans l'art punique en Tripolitanie." *MEFR* 80 (1968): 7–80.
Sabratha Punic mausoleum.

⸻. "Le date di fondazione di Leptis e di Sabratha, sulla base dell'indagine archeologica e l'eparchia cartaginese d'Africa." *HommRen* (1969): 196–202.

⸻. "La villa et la course des Néréides à Tadjura." *Archeologia*, no. 31 (November–December 1969): 60–67.
Good photographs.

⸻. "Gheriat el Gharbia." *EAAC*, suppl. (1970).

⸻. "Les Emporia de Tripolitania dans le rayonnement de Carthage

et d'Alexandrie: mausolées punico-hellénistiques de Sabratha."
LinH (1971): 172–80.

———. "Leggendo *Topografia dell'Africa romana* di P. Romanelli: considerazioni, note, segnalazioni." *QAL* 7 (1973): 165–87.
Review of a general book not in this bibliography. Emphasis on persistence of Punic cult.

———. "Il mausoleo punico-ellenistico B di Sabratha." *RM* 83 (1976): 273–85.

———. *Tripolitania ellenistica e romana alla luce delle più recenti indagini archeologiche.* MAL, 12 (Rome, 1976).
Not seen.

Vita-Finzi, Claudio, and Brogan, O. "Roman Dams on the Wadi Megenin." *LA* 2 (1965): 65–71.
Irrigation behind Oea.

Volkmann, Hans. "Limes." *KP* (1969).
Convenient survey of the course of Limes Tripolitanus, with bibliography.

Ward Perkins, John B. "Severan Art and Architecture at Lepcis Magna." *JRS* 38 (1948): 59–80.

———. "Gasr el Suk el Oti: A Desert Settlement in Central Tripolitania." *Archaeology* 3 (1950): 25–31.
Four fortified farms and a three-aisled basilica, about 125 kilometers south of Lepcis Magna. Perhaps Donatist. Deforestation caused abandonment.

———. "The Arch of Septimius Severus at Lepcis Magna." *Archaeology* 4 (1951): 226–31.
Popular summary, with photographs.

———. "The Art of the Severan Age in the Light of Tripolitanian Discoveries." *PBA* 37 (1951): 268–92.

———. "Excavations in the Severan Basilica at Lepcis Magna, 1951." *PBSR* 20 (1952): 111–21.

———. "Pre-Roman Elements in the Architecture of Roman Tripolitania." *LinH* (1971): 101–10.

———. "Lepcis Magna" and "Sabratha." *PECS* (1976).
Authoritative summaries.

Ward Perkins, John B., and Goodchild, R. G. "The Christian Antiquities of Tripolitania." *Archaeologia* 95 (1953): 1–80.

Ward Perkins, John B.; Toynbee, J. M. C.; and Frazer, R. "The Hunting Baths of Lepcis Magna." *Archaeologia* 93 (1949): 165–95.

Yorke, Richard A. "Les ports engloutis de Tripolitaine et de Tunisie."

Archeologia, no. 17 (July–August 1967): 18–24.
Sabratha, Gigthis, Acholla, Sullecthu, Thapsus, Lepcis Minor,
Mahdia.

7. Algeria: From Prehistoric Times through the Jugurthine War

Astruc, Miriam. "Nouvelles fouilles à Djidjelli." *RAfr* 80 (1937):
199–253.
————. "Supplément aux fouilles de Gouraya." *Libyca* 2 (1954):
9–48.
Balout, Louis. *Les hommes préhistoriques du Maghreb et du Sahara.*
Algiers, 1955.
Together with Camps (1974; see chapter 1), the standard works.
Berthier, André. *L'Algérie et son passé.* Paris, 1951.
Berthier, André, and Charlier, R. *Le sanctuaire punique d'El Hofra
(Constantine).* 2 vols. Paris, 1952–55.
Bonnell. "Monument gréco-punique de la Souma." *RecConst* 49 (1915):
167–78.
Early description of El Khroub mausoleum.
Bouchenaki, Mounir. *Le mausolée royale de la Maurétanie.* Algiers,
1970.
A guidebook.
————. "Les recherches puniques en Algérie." In F. Barreca et al.,
eds. *Ricerche puniche nel Mediterraneo centrale*, pp. 59–83.
Studi Semitici, 36. Rome, 1970.
————. "Algérie." In F. Barreca et al., eds. *Espansione fenicia nel
Mediterraneo*, pp. 47–63. Studi Semitici, 38. Rome, 1971.
Brahimi, Claude. "Encore des fouilles à Columnata." *RevHCMaghr* 9
(1970): 7–12.
Brunon, Colonel. "Mémoire sur les fouilles executées au Medras'en."
RevConst 16 (1873): 309–50.
Camps, Gabriel. *Aux origines de la Berbérie: monuments et rites
funéraires préhistoriques.* Paris, 1961.
————. "Nouvelles observations sur l'architecture et l'âge du Med-
racen." *CRAI* (1973): 470–517.
————. "Medracen." *PECS* (1976).
Camps-Fabrer, Henriette. *Un gisement capsien de faciès sétifien Medjez
II (El Eulma).* Etudes d'Antiquités Africaines [a supplement to
AntsAfrs]. Paris, 1975.
Escargotière 4850 ± 150 B.C. Painting with ocher; tattooing.

Carcopino, Jérôme. "Le culte des Cereres et les Numides." In his *Aspects mystiques de la Rome païenne*, pp. 13–37. Paris, 1942.
Controversial emendation of Sallust *Jugurthine War* 66.2.

Chabot, Jean-Baptiste. "Sur deux inscriptions puniques et une inscription latine d'Algérie." *CRAI* (1916): 242–50.
At El Hofra, a game-board and dedication to Ba'al Hammon; at Calama, a funerary inscription in Latin and Punic.

Christofle, Maurice. *Tombeau de la Chrétienne*. Paris, 1951.
A guidebook.

Cintas, Pierre. "Fouilles puniques à Tipasa." *RAfr* 92 (1948): 262–316.

Colozier-Boucher, Etiennette. "Une statuette grecque d'orante au Musée d'Alger." *MonsPiot* 47 (1953): 71–75.
Guelta bronze, oldest dated Greek object in Maghreb.

Desanges, Jehan. *Catalogue des tribus africaines de l'antiquité classique à l'ouest du Nil*. Université de Dakar, Faculté des lettres et des sciences humaines, Publications, section d'histoire, 4. Dakar, 1962.
Standard.

Février, James G. "L'inscription funéraire de Micipsa." *Revue d'Assyriologie* 45 (1951): 139–50.

Février, Paul Albert. *L'art de l'Algérie antique*. Paris, 1971.
Exemplary photographs.
———. "Siga" and "Tipasa." *PECS* (1976).
Including Beni Rhenane and the Tomb of the "Christian Woman."

Gautier, Emile F. *Le passé de l'Afrique du Nord*. Paris, 1952.
Good on cave paintings.

Grimal, Pierre. "Les fouilles de Siga." *MEFR* 54 (1937): 108–41.

Gsell, Stéphane. *Les monuments antiques de l'Algérie*. 2 vols. Paris, 1901.
Still fundamental, as is his *Atlas archéologique de l'Algérie* (Paris, 1911), for plans, maps, and succinct descriptions. Volume 2 has a useful topographical index, listing all monuments then known on a given site. His *HAAN*, vols. 6 (1929) and 7 (1928), treat mausolea and the Jugurthine War.

Holroyd, Michael. "The Jugurthine War: Was Marius or Metellus the Real Victor?" *JRS* 18 (1928): 1–20.

Lancel, Serge. "Tipasitana III: nécropole préromaine de Tipasa." *BAA* 3 (1968): 85–166.

Lefebvre, Gilette, and Lefebvre, Louis. *Corpus des gravures et des peintures rupestres de la région de Constantine*. Paris, 1967.

Leglay, Marcel. "A la recherche d'Icosium." *AntsAfrs* 2 (1968): 7–54.
On ancient Algiers.

Leschi, Louis. *Etudes d'épigraphie, d'archéologie, et d'histoire africaines.*
Paris, 1957.
Collected essays. Pages 325–28 record a hoard of Punic coins
from Algiers.

Lhote, Henri. "La route des chars de guerre libyens, Tripoli-Gao."
Archeologia, no. 9 (March–April 1966): 28–36.
Camps (1974) says chariot routes are imaginary.

———. "Problèmes sahariens: l'outre, la marmite, le chameau, le délou,
l'agriculture, le nègre, le palmier." *BAM* 7 (1967): 57–90.

———. *Les gravures rupestres du Sud oranais.* Paris, 1970.
Inter alia, on Thyout elephant, which he dates in the Bovidian
period (3550–3070 B.C., ±300 years).

———. *The Search for the Tassili Frescoes.* 2nd ed. London, 1973.
Popular treatment of cliff and cave art.

———. *Vers d'autres Tassilis.* Paris, 1976.

Mascarello, Anna. Various articles on Rusuccuru (Dellys), in *Rev-
HCMaghr* 9 (1970): 13–17; 10 (1973): 9–19; 13 (1976): 7–21.
To be used with caution; see P.-A. Février, "Rusucurru," *PECS*
(1976).

Missioner, François. "Fouilles dans la nécropole punique de Gouraya."
MEFR 50 (1933): 87–119.

———. "Stèles et inscriptions de Gouraya." *RAfr* 74 (1933): 54–74.

Pflaum, Hans-Georg. "Nordafrika und die Römer." *Annales Universi-
tatis Saravensis,* phil.-lettr., 5 (1956): 37–49.
Authoritative survey by the editor of *ILAlg.* These *Annales*
usually Marxist.

Poyto, Robert, and Musso, J. C. *Corpus des gravures et des peintures
rupestres de Grande Kabylie.* Paris, 1969.
To be used with caution.

Romanelli, Pietro. "Ancora sull'età della Tomba della Cristiana in
Algeria." *ArchClass* 24 (1972): 109–11.
Idiosyncratic proposed date, later than Hadrian's mausoleum
in Rome. Carbon 14 dates (between 220 and 320) could be of
additions to original structure.

Roubet, Colette. "Premières datations par le C14 obtenues à Alger."
L'anthropologie 74 (1970): 640–41.
Wood from Medracen, 2170 before present, ±155 years; Tipasa
necropolis (Lancel 1968), 2060 before present, ±140.

Saumagne, Charles. *La Numidie et Rome: Masinissa et Jugurtha.*

PublUTunFacLettr, 4th ser., histoire, 4. Paris, 1966.
To be supplemented from Camps (1960; see chapter 1).
Vuillemot, Gustave. "Fouilles du mausolée de Beni Rhenane en Oranie."
   CRAI (1964): 71–95.
   See also his "Siga et son port fluvial," *AntsAfrs* 5 (1971): 39–86.
———. *Reconnaissances aux échelles puniques d'Oranie.* Autun, 1965.
   Authoritative.
Walsh, Patrick J. "Masinissa." *JRS* 55 (1965): 149–60.

8. Algeria from Jugurtha to Trajan, 105 B.C.–A.D. 98

Alföldi, Marie R. "Die Schatzfund von Tipasa." In *Atti del Congresso
   Internazionale di Numismatica, 1961*, vol. 2, p. 421. Rome, 1965.
Allais, Yvonne. "Djemila: le quartier à l'est du Forum des Sévères."
   RAfr 97 (1953): 48–65.
———. "Une basilique cimitériale à Djemila." *BAA* 1 (1962–65):
   189–205.
   Saint's grave in west quarter.
Aupert, Pierre. *Le nymphée de Tipasa.* CollEFR, 16 (1974).
Aymard, Jacques. "La légende de Bellérophon sur un sarcophage du
   Musée d'Alger." *MEFR* 52 (1935): 143–84.
Baradez, Jean. "Les nouvelles fouilles de Tipasa et les opérations
   d'Antonin le Pieux en Maurétanie." *Libyca* 2 (1954): 89–139.
———. "Les fours à chaux des constructeurs de l'enceinte." *Libyca* 5
   (1957): 277–94.
———. "Nouvelles fouilles à Tipasa dans une nécropole païenne."
   Libyca 5 (1957): 159–220.
———. "Survivances du culte de Ba'al et Tanit au premier siècle de l'ère
   chrétienne." *Libyca* 5 (1957): 221–75.
———. "La maison des fresques et les voies le limitant." *Libyca* 9
   (1961): 49–129.
———. "Nouvelles fouilles à Tipasa: nécropole païenne occidentale
   sous la Maison des Fresques." *Libyca* 9 (1961): 7–48.
———. "Monnaies africaines anciennes découvertes dans les tombes
   du premier siècle après J.-C." *HommGren* (1962): 216–227.
———. "L'enceinte de Tipasa et ses portes." *MélPig* (1966): 1133–52.
———. "Nécropoles de Tipasa: tombes du cimetière occidental côtier."
   AntsAfrs 2 (1968): 79–93.
———. "Nécropole orientale côtière de Tipasa." *AntsAfrs* 3 (1969):
   83–114.

Benario, Herbert W. "L. Paccius Africanus." *Historia* 8 (1959): 496–98.
Inscription inset into Hippo forum is of proconsul of Africa,
A.D. 77/78.

Bérard, Jean. "Mosaïques inédites de Cherchel." *MEFR* 52 (1935):
113–45.
Especially on plowman mosaic.

Berthier, André. *Tiddis, antique Castellum Tidditanorum*. Algiers, 1972.
An official guidebook.

Berthier, André, and Leglay, M. "Le sanctuaire du sommet et les stèles
de Ba'al-Saturne de Tiddis." *Libyca* 6 (1958): 23–58.

——. "Colonia Cirta Sittianorum." *RecConst* 70 (1957–59):
91–118.
Argues, unconvincingly, that Cirta Regia was Sicca (Le Kef,
in Tunisia).

——. "Monnaies de Cirta." *Libyca* 7 (1959): 297.
Coins of L. Sittius.

Besnier, Maurice. "Les *scholae* des sous-officiers dans le camp romain
de Lambèse." *MEFR* 19 (1899): 199–258.

Blanchard-Lemée, Michèle. *Maisons à mosaïque du quartier central de
Djemila (Cuicul)*. Etudes d'Antiquités Africaines. Paris, 1975.
Exhaustive and fundamental.

Bouchenaki, Mounir. "A propos du port antique de Tipasa." *RevHC-
Maghr* 8 (1970): 22–40.

Boucher-Colozier, Etiennette. "Recherches sur la statuaire de Chercel."
MEFR 66 (1954): 101–45.
Juba's collection of copies.

Cagnat, René. *L'armée romaine de l'Afrique*. 2nd ed. Paris, 1913.
A classic.

Carcopino, Jérôme. "Une mosaïque récemment découverte à Tipasa."
BCTH (1914): 571–89.
Captives from civil basilica, called Domitianic. Actually
Antonine.

Chamoux, François. "Un nouveau portrait de Ptolemée de Maurétanie
découvert à Cherchel." *MélPig* (1966): 395–406.

Charbonneaux, Jean. "Un portrait de Cléopatra VII au Musée de
Cherchel." *Libyca* 2 (1954): 49–63.
Or possibly her daughter, married to Juba II.

Clauss, Manfred. "Probleme der Lebensalterstatistiken aufgrund
römischer Grabinschriften." *Chiron* 3 (1973): 416–17.
See caveat by Hopkins (1966/67; chapter 3).

Crook, John A. "Suetonius ab epistulis." *PCPS*, n.s. 4 (1956/57):
18–22.

Suetonius may have come from Pisaurum and have gone with Hadrian on tour in 128. Benefaction to Hippo might account for inscription. Contrast Townend (1961). Pflaum, *CRAI* (1952): 76–85, does not doubt that Suetonius was a native of Hippo.

Dahmani, Said. *Hippo Regius.* Algiers, 1973.
Guide, mostly borrowed from Marec (see below).

Deman, Albert. "Virgile et la colonisation romaine en Afrique du Nord." *HommGren* (1962): 514–28.
Possible pun on Sittius in *Ecl.* 1.64.

Desanges, Jehan. "Les territoires gétules de Juba II." *REA* 66 (1964): 33–47.

Durry, Marcel. "Valeur de Cherchel." In Jérôme Carcopino et al., eds., *Etudes d'archéologie romaine*, pp. 111–23. Ghent, 1937.
On statuary in Museum.

Duval, Paul-Marie. *Cherchel et Tipasa: deux villes fortes de l'Afrique romaine.* Bibliothèque archéologique et historique de l'Institut français d'archéologie de Beirut. Beirut, 1946.

d'Esturac-Doisy, Henriette. "Trophée de bronze découverte à Cherchel." *Libyca* 6 (1958): 75–88.

———. "Lambèse et les vétérans de la Legio III Augusta." *HommGren* (1962): 571–83.
They grew vines, as *possessores*.

Février, Paul-Albert. "Développement urbaine en Afrique du Nord." *CahsArchs* 14 (1964): 1–47.
Dates phases of Djemila.

———. "Nécropole orientale de Tiddis." *BAA* 4 (1970): 41–100.

———. *Djemila.* Algiers, 1971.
Official guidebook.

Grosso, Fulvio. "L'inscription d'Hippone et la vie de Suétone." *Rend-Linc*, ser. 8, 14 (1959): 263–96.

Gsell, Stéphane. *Atlas archéologique d'Algérie.* Paris, 1911.
Authoritative maps, plans, text.

———. *Inscriptions latines d'Algérie*, vol. 1. Paris, 1922.
See Pflaum (1957) for volume 2.

———. *Promenades archéologiques aux environs d'Alger.* Paris, 1926.
Cherchel, pp. 68–71; Gsell's authoritative guide to the site was published posthumously in 1952. Much excavation since.

———. *Histoire antique de l'Afrique du Nord*, vol. 8. Paris, 1930.
Juba II. Authoritative map, plans, text.

Gsell, Stéphane, and Joly, C. A. *Khamissa, Mdaourouch, Announa.* Algiers and Paris, 1918.

Heurgon, Jacques. "Les origines campaniennes de la Conféderation cirtéenne." *Libyca* 5 (1957): 7–24.

Janon, Marcel. "Recherches à Lambèse." *AntsAfrs* 7 (1973): 193–254. Important updating.

———. "Lambaesis: ein Überblick." *AntWelt* 8 (1977): 3–20. Good air views, plans, maps, reconstructions.

Kolbe, Hans-Georg. "Die Inschrift am Torbau der Principia im Legionslager von Lambaesis." *RM* 81 (1974): 281–300.

Lancel, Serge. "Suburbures et Nicives: une inscription de Tigisis." *Libyca* 3 (1955): 289–98. Flavian boundary stone of territorium of Cirta.

———. *Tipasa de Maurétanie.* Algiers, 1966. A guidebook.

Lassère, Jean-Marie. "Recherches récentes sur Hippo Regius." *CahTun* 19 (1971): 245–50. Numidian sea-wall; Suetonius.

———. "La chronologie des épitaphes païennes de l'Afrique." *AntsAfrs* 7 (1973): 7–151. Fundamental redating of inscriptions in *CIL* 8.

Lassus, Jean. "Fouilles de Mila." *Libyca* 4 (1956): 199–239.

———. "Cherchel—la mosaïque de Thétis et Pélée." *BAA* 1 (1962–65): 75–105.

———. "Venus marine." In *La mosaïque gréco-romaine*, vol. 1, pp. 175–96. Paris, 1965.

———. "La salle à sept absides de Djemila." *AntsAfrs* 5 (1971): 193–208.

Leglay, Marcel. "Le Mithraeum de Lambèse." *CRAI* (1954): 269–78.

———. "Taxation et autonomie municipale d'après une nouvelle inscription de Cuicul." In *Akten des IVten internationalen Kongresses der griechischen und lateinischen Epigraphik*, pp. 224–33. Vienna, 1964.

———. "Une dédicace à Vénus offerte à Caesarea par le futur empéreur Galba." *MélCarc* (1966): 629–39. Thanking the goddess for help against Tacfarinas.

———. "Les Flaviens et l'Afrique." *MEFR* 80 (1968): 201–46.

Leschi, Louis. "Inscriptions latines de Lambèse et de Zaria." *Libyca* 1 (1953): 189–205. The camp of A.D. 81.

———. *Etudes* (see chapter 7). Pages 50–84, viticulture; 145–62, inscriptions of Tiddis; 172–78, inscription from Chasseurs' Baths, Lambaesis; 189–200, Hadrian's speech.

Leveau, Philippe, and Paillet, Jean-Louis. *L'alimentation en eau de Caesarea de Maurétanie et l'aquéduct de Cherchell*. Paris, 1976. Heavily illustrated popular account appears in *Archeologia*, no. 105 (April 1977): 28–37.

————. "Les hypogées de la rive gauche de l'Oued Nsara et la nécropole orientale de Caesarea." *AntsAfrs* 11 (1977): 209–56. Underlines importance of both African and Roman elements in Christianity to the end of antiquity.

Logeart, François. "Bornes délimitatives dans le sud du territoire de Cirta." *RAfr* 83 (1939): 161–81.

Lucas, Christian. "Notes on the curatores r. p. of Roman Africa." *JRS* 30 (1940): 56–74.

Lugand, René. "Inventaire des objets conservés au Musée de Lambèse." *RecConst* 58 (1927): 117–98.

Marcillet-Joubert, Jean. "Lambaesis." *PECS* (1976).

Marec, Erwan. "Les fouilles d'Hippone." *CRAI* (1948): 558–63. Vespasian head; trophy.

————. "Le forum d'Hippone." *Libyca* 2 (1954): 365–402.

————. *Hippone la Royale*. Algiers, 1956. Best guidebook.

————. *Monuments chrétiens d'Hippone*. Paris, 1958.

————. "Une maison à étage à Hippone, la villa dite du Procurateur." *AntsAfrs* 3 (1969): 157–72.

————. "Une mosaïque originale d'Hippone: l'enfant vainqueur de la course au canard." *HommRen* (1969): 397–402.

Marec, Erwan, and Pflaum, H.-G. "Nouvelle inscription sur la carrière de Suétone l'historien." *CRAI* (1952): 176–85. Suetonius a native of Hippo.

Mazard, Jean. "Nouvel apport à la numismatique de la Numidie et de la Maurétanie." *Libyca* 4 (1956): 57–67. Additions to corpus of non-Roman coins from Cherchel, Cirta.

Mercer, Charles. *The Foreign Legion*. London, 1964.

Morel, Jean-Paul. "Céramique d'Hippone." *BAA* 1 (1962–65): 107–37.

————. "Rapport préliminaire sur une campagne de fouilles à Hippone, 1964." *BCTH*, n.s. 1/2 (1965/66): 191–94. Breakwater dated 90–80 B.C.: seafront mosaic A.D. 250.

————. "Recherches stratigraphiques à Hippone." *BAA* 3 (1968): 35–84. New dating for mosaics.

Nakli, A. "Essai de topographie maghrébine." *RevHCMaghr* 8 (1970): 42–62.

By-product of his translation of Sallust into Arabic; strongly nationalistic.

Pflaum, Hans-Georg. "L'onomastique de Castellum Celtianum." *Carnuntina* 3 (1956): 126–51.
Notes that of 1,271 names 107 are Libyan; there are 172 Punico-Roman cognomina. He concludes that Romanization was very superficial.

————. *Inscriptions latines d'Algérie*, vol. 2, part 1. Paris, 1957.
Updates *CIL* 8; lists 4,187 items. Volume 2, part 2 not seen.

————. "Remarques sur l'onomastique de Cirta." In *Limes-Studien: Vorträge des 3. internationalen Limes-Kongresses*, pp. 96–133. Basel, 1959.

Philolenko, Maximilien. "Les collèges des officiales tabularii legionis dans le camp de Lambèse." *RAfr* 69 (1928): 429–85.

Picard, Gilbert Charles. "Tigisis." *EAAC*, suppl. (1970).
Flavian terminus.

————. "Date du théâtre de Cherchel et les débuts de l'architecture théâtrale dans les provinces romaines d'Occident." *CRAI* (1975): 386–97.
Dated 19 B.C.

Rakob, Friedrich, and Storz, Sebastian. "Die Principia des römischen Legionslagers in Lambaesis." *RM* 81 (1974): 253–80.
Authoritative; appendix on inscription.

Romanelli, Pietro. "Ippone" and "Lambesi." *EAAC* (1961).

Salama, Pierre. "Les bornes milliaires de Djemila-Cuicul et leur interêt pour l'histoire de la ville." *RAfr* 95 (1951): 213–72.

Schulz-Falkenthal, Heinz. "Die Unterstützungstätigkeit in einem Militärcollegium der Legio III Augusta in Lambaesis und das Problem der Sozialleistigungen im römischen Vereinswesen." In H.-J. Diesner, ed., *Afrika und Rom*, pp. 155–71. Halle, 1968.

Souville, Georges. "Thibilis" and "Thubursicu Numidarum." *PECS* (1976).

Temple, Sir Grenville, and Chevalier Falbe. *Relation d'une excursion de Bône à Guelma et à Constantine*. Paris, 1838.

Thieling, Walter. *Der Hellenismus in Kleinafrika*. Leipzig, 1911.
Good on Juba II.

Townend, Gavin B. "The Hippo Inscription and the Career of Suetonius." *Historia* 10 (1961): 99–109.
Suetonius held office under Hadrian only till 121/22; perhaps with Pliny in Bithynia in 112; probably native of Hippo.

Troussel, Marcel. "Le trésor monétaire de Tiddis." *RecConst* 66 (1948): 129–76.

Turcan, Robert. "Une trouvaille monétaire à Announa." *Latomus* 31 (1972): 130–45.

Veyne, Paul. "Contributio: Beneventum, Capoue, Cirta." *Latomus* 18 (1959): 568–92.
Subordination of Collo, Milev, Skikda.

Wilmanns, Gustav, ed. *Corpus Inscriptionum Latinarum (CIL)*, vol. 8. Berlin, 1881; suppls. 1–5, 1891–1942.

9. The High Empire in Algeria, A.D. 98–238

Albertini, Eugène. "Un témoignage épigraphique sur l'évêque donatiste Optatus de Timgad." *CRAI* (1939): 100–103.

Alquier, Jane, and Alquier, Prosper. "Les thermes romains du Val d'Or." *RecConst* 59 (1928/29): 289–318.
On Oued Athménia villa and mosaics.

Ballu, Albert, and Cagnat, René. *Musée de Timgad*. Paris, 1903.
Describes Hermaphrodite and Diana-Actaeon mosaics.

———. *Les ruines de Timgad, antique Thamugadi: nouvelles découvertes*. Paris, 1903.

Baradez, Jean. "Organisation militaire romaine d'Algérie antique et évolution du concept défensif de ses frontières." *Revue inter-internationale d'histoire militaire* 4 (1935): 25–41.
Excellent advance summary of his *Fossatum Africae* (1949).

———. "Gemellae: camp d'Hadrien et ville des confins sahariens." *CRAI* (1948): 390–95.

———. *Fossatum Africae: Recherches aériennes sur l'organisation des confins sahariens*. Paris, 1949.
A classic.

———. "Inscriptions de la région du limes de Numidie de Biskra à Tobna." *Libyca* 1 (1953): 151–65.
Return of Legio III to Gemellae.

———. "Réseau routier de commandement, d'administration, et d'exploitation de la zone arrière du limes de Numidie." In *Limes-Studien: Vorträge des 3. internationalen Limes-Kongresses*, pp. 19–33. Basel, 1959.

———. "Deux amphithéâtres inédits du limes de Numidie: Gemellae et Mesarfelta." *MélCarc* (1966): 55–69.

———. "Les thermes légionnaires de Gemellae." In *Corolla memoriae E. Swoboda dedicata*, pp. 14–22. Graz and Cologne, 1966.

———. "Compléments inédits du Fossatum Africae." In *Studien zu den Militärgrenzen Roms*, pp. 200–210. Bonner Beihefte, 19. Bonn, 1967.

Baxter, James H. "The Martyrs of Madauros." *JThS* 26 (1924): 21–37.

Bayet, Jean. "Un bas-relief de Sour-Djouab et l'iconographie des provinces romaines sous l'Empire." *MEFR* 48 (1931): 40–74.
Goddess Africa at Rapidum.

————. "Les vertus du pantomime Vincentius." *Libyca* 3 (1955): 103–21.

Berthier, André. "Etablissements agricoles antiques à Oued-Athménia." *BAA* (1962–65): 7–20.

Birebent, Jean. *Aquae Romanae: recherches d'hydraulique romaine dans l'est algérien.* Algiers, 1962.
Standard work, by a government engineer.

Bloch, Raymond. "Un campagne de fouilles dans la vallée du Chéliff: les Tigava Castra." *MEFR* 58 (1941): 9–42.

Boethius, Axel, and Ward Perkins, J. B. *Etruscan and Roman Architecture* (see chapter 6), pp. 458–94.

Cagnat, René. *Les villes d'art célèbres: Carthage, Timgad, Tébessa.* Paris, 1912.
Still not outdated.

Carcopino, Jérôme. "La table de patronat de Timgad." *RAfr* 57 (1913): 163–72.

————. "Trois inscriptions de Madauros récemment découvertes." *RAfr* 60 (1919): 241–57.
Includes dedication to Apuleius.

————. "Les inscriptions de Doucen et l'occupation romaine dans le Sud-Algérien." *REA* 25 (1923): 35–48.

————. "Sur l'extension de la domination romaine dans le Sahara de Numidie." *RevArch* 20 (1924): 316–25.

Courtois, Christian. *Timgad.* Algiers, 1951.
An authoritative guidebook.

Courtot, Paul. "Essai historique sur Altava d'après l'épigraphie." *RAfr* 79 (1936): 401–29.

————. "Epitaphe d'un princeps d'Altava." *BAA* 3 (1968): 337–41.

Darmon, Jean-Philippe. "Note sur le tarif de Zaraï." *CahTun* 12 (1964): 7–23.

DeLaet, Sigfried J. *Portorium.* Bruges, 1949.
Zaraï tariff, pp. 263–71.

d'Esturac-Doisy, Henriette. "Inscriptions latines de Timgad." *MEFR* 65 (1953): 99–137.

————. "Inscriptions funéraires de Timgad." *Libyca* 4 (1956): 102–32.

_____. "Un soulèvement en Maurétanie Césarienne sous Sévère-Alexandre." *MélPig* (1966): 1191–1204.

_____. "Verrérie antique et collections du Musée National des Antiquités." *BAA* 2 (1966/67): 129–57.
Includes Donatist area of Timgad.

Etienne, Robert. "Rome eut-elle une politique douanière?" *AnnalesESC* 7 (1952): 371–77.
Review of DeLaet (1949): discusses Zaraï tariff.

Février, Paul-Albert. "Remarques sur la céramique romaine d'Afrique du Nord (Sétif)." *RivStLig* 29 (1963): 125–36.
When pottery import ceases, rupture of Roman unity is implied.

_____. "Notes sur le développement urbain en Afrique: Djemila et Sétif." *CahsArchs* 14 (1964): 1–47.
Sétif moribund A.D. 250–284; slow recovery 305–361; revival under Valentinian and Valens, 364–375.

_____. "Un art local méconnu: la sculpture antique de Sétif." *Archeologia*, no. 3 (March–April 1965): 61–65.
Beni Fouda Saturn uses elongated lion for throne.

_____. *Fouilles de Sétif: basiliques chrétiennes du quartier nordouest.* Paris, 1965.

_____. "Inscriptions inédites relatives aux domaines de la région de Sétif." *MélPig* (1966): 217–28.

_____. "Aux origines de l'occupation romaine dans les hautes plaines de Sétif." *CahTun* 15 (1967): 52–64.

_____. "La nécropole orientale de Sétif, rapport préliminaire (1959–64)." *BAA* 2 (1966/67): 11–93.

_____. "Inscriptions de Sétif et de la région." *BAA* 4 (1970): 319–410.

_____. "Sitifis." *EAAC*, suppl. (1970).

_____. "Rusguniae." *PECS* (1976).

Février, Paul-Albert, and Gaspary, A. "L'Hippodrome de Sétif." *Archeologia*, no. 8 (January–February 1966): 28–31.

Février, Paul-Albert; Gaspary, A.; and Guéry, R. *Fouilles de Sétif, quartier nordouest. BAA*, suppl. 1 (1970).

Frézouls, Edmond. "Teatri romani dell'Africa." *Dioniso* 15 (1952): 90–101.
Tipasa, Guelma.

Germain, Suzanne. *Les mosaïques de Timgad.* Paris, 1969.
A major work.

_____. "Mosaïques florales de Lambèse." *AntsAfrs* 11 (1977): 137–48.
From unpublished journal of excavations at temple of Aescu-

lapius, 1948–49. Parallels from Ostia, Schola Traiani; and Hippo, A.D. 200–250. Temple is of 162.

Graillot, Henri. "Ruines romaines au nord de l'Aurès." *MEFR* 13 (1893): 461–541.
A study of Mascula.

Gsell, Stéphane. *Monuments* (see chapter 7).
Pages 172–85, arches; 211–41, Timgad, South and Central Baths.

Guéry, Roger. "Notes de céramique." *BAA* 3 (1968): 271–81.
Saturn motifs, Sétif necropolis.

Guey, Julien. "Le limes romain de Numidie et le Sahara au IVe siècle." *MEFR* 56 (1939): 178–248.
Pioneering work, earlier than Baradez and Salama.

Hammond, Mason. "The Composition of the Roman Senate, A.D. 68–235." *JRS* 47 (1957): table, p. 77.

Heurgon, Jacques. "Fronton de Cirta." *RecConst* 70 (1957–59): 141–53.

Janon, Michel. "Lambèse et l'occupation militaire de la Numidie méridionale." In *Akten des 10ten internationalen Limeskongresses*, pp. 473–85. Bonn, 1976.
Maps; reconstruction of column recording Hadrian's visit.

Jarrett, Michael G. "The African Contribution to the Imperial Equestrian Service." *Historia* 12 (1963): 209–26.

————. "An Album of the Equites from North Africa in the Emperor's Service." *EpigStud* 9 (1972): 146–232.

Kennedy, George A. *The Art of Rhetoric in the Roman World.* Princeton, 1972.
Up-to-date and favorable account of Fronto, pp. 592–602.

Lassus, Jean. "Le site de St.-Leu (Portus Magnus)." *CRAI* (1956): 285–93.
See also his plan of St.-Leu in "L'archéologie algérienne en 1956," *Libyca* 5 (1957): 126.

————. "Le rinceau d'acanthes dans les mosaïques de Timgad." *HommGren* (1962): 948–60.

————. "Adaption à l'Afrique de l'urbanisme romain." In *Le rayonnement des civilisations grecque et romaine sur les cultures périphériques: actes du 8e congrès international d'archéologie classique*, pp. 245–59. Paris, 1963.
On Timgad and Djemila.

————. "Fouilles de Sétif, 1958–62." *BCTH* 55 (1964): 95–107.

————. "Une opération immobilière à Timgad." *MélPig* (1966): 1221–32.

On Timgad bursting its bounds, with Sertius as entrepreneur.

————. *Visite à Timgad*. Paris, 1969.

Good guidebook; good photographs.

————. "Mascula" and "Thamugadi." *PECS* (1976).

Lebel, P. "Voies romaines d'Afrique et de Gaule." *RevArchEst* 2 (1951): 192–94.

Review of Salama (1951). Gives names of inns.

Leglay, Marcel. "La vie intellectuelle d'une cité romaine des confins de l'Aurès." In *Hommages à Leon Hermann*, pp. 485–91. CollLat, 44 (1960).

Timgad library; pantomime Vincentius.

————. "La déesse Afrique à Timgad." In *Hommages à J. Bayet*, ed. Marcel Renard and Robert Schilling, pp. 374–82. CollLat, 70 (1964).

————. "Rapidum" and "Saldae." *PECS* (1976).

Leschi, Louis. "Centenarium quod Aqua Viva appellatur." *CRAI* (1941): 163–76.

See also his article by the same title in *RAfr* 87 (1943): 5–22.

————. "Découvertes récentes à Timgad: Aqua Septimiana Felix." *CRAI* (1947): 87–99.

————. *FA* 6 (1951): no. 5873.

On Rapidum praetorium.

————. *Etudes* (1957; see chapter 7).

Pages 38–41, on defenses between Thubunae and Gemellae; 258–66, Timgad "album," with facsimiles; 275–76, Mascula, dedication of infant to Saturn; 318–22, Gemellae, inscription; 329–32, Sétif milestones; 349–60, Saldae *iuvenes*.

Leveau, Philippe. "Un nouveau témoignage sur la résistance maure en Maurétanie Césarienne centrale." *AntsAfrs* 8 (1964): 103–10.

Alleges unrest at a new time, but undated.

Lewis, Naphtali, and Reinhold, Meyer. *Roman Civilization*, vol. 2 (1955; see chapter 3).

Zaraï tariff translated, pp. 146–47.

Lézine, Alexandre. "L'arc dit de Trajan à Timgad." *BAA* 2 (1966/67): 123–27.

Loriot, Xavier. "Les premières années de la grande crise du IIIe siècle." *ANRW* 2, part 2 (1975): 745–53.

Severan forts prompted by sense of menace to "useful" Africa.

Cashiering of the Legio III Augusta led to abandonment of Limes forts and growth of fortified farms around Sétif.

MacMullen, Ramsay. "Roman Imperial Building in the Provinces." *HSCP* 64 (1959): 207–35.
Translates Saldae aqueduct inscription.

Marcillet-Joubert, Jean. "Mosaïque tombale chrétienne de Port Romaine." *Libyca* 3 (1955): 281–86.

———. "Inscriptions de Tubusuctu." *BAA* 1 (1962–65): 163–70.
Reference to Saldae aqueduct as "incredibilis labor."

———. *Les inscriptions d'Altava*. Publications annuelles de la Faculté des Lettres de l'Université d'Aix-en-Provence, n.s., no. 65. Aix, 1968.
A major work.

———. "Ad Maiores" and "Altava." *PECS* (1976).

Marrou, Henri-Irénée. "La collection Gaston de Vulpillières à El Kantara." *MEFR* 50 (1933): 42–86.
A thousand objects, amassed by a solitary amateur, on Limes. Includes Saturn stelae.

———. "Survivances païennes dans les rites funéraires des Donatistes." In *Hommages à Joseph Bidez et Franz Cumont*, vol. 2, pp. 193–203. CollLat, 2 (1949).
Libation tube from Donatist quarter, Timgad.

———. "Sur une inscription commémorant Optat de Timgad." *BAA* 1 (1962/65): 235–38.

Oliver, James H. "Significance of the Municipal Album of Timgad." *RIDA* 5 (1958): 537–38.
Intended to assure upper class of privilege; not punitive. Contrast Piganiol (1954).

Pachtère, Felix de. "Le règlement d'irrigation à Lamasba." *MEFR* 28 (1908): 373–405.

Pallottino, Massimo. "Arco Onorario." *EAAC* (1958).
Convenient list of North African arches. See also Heinz Kähler, "Triumphbogen," *RE* (1939): col. 373–493.

Pekary, Thomas. "Untersuchungen zu den römischen Reichsstrassen." *Antiquitas* 17 (1968): 159–64.
Abutters levy tolls for upkeep.

Petitmengin, Pierre. "Inscriptions de la région de Milev." *MEFR* 79 (1967): 165–205.

Pfeiffer, Homer F. "The Roman Library at Timgad." *MAAR* 9 (1931): 157–66, Pls. 16–18.

Pflaum, Hans-Georg. *Les procurateurs équestres sous la haut-empire romaine.* Paris, 1950.

———. "Deux carrières equestres de Lambèse et de Zana." *Libyca* 3 (1955): 123–54.
Patron of Djemila, donor of Lambaesis arch and Mithraeum, Timgad waterworks.

———. "Une inscription de Castellum Arsalicanum." *RecConst* 69 (1955/56): 147–72.
Inscriptions from here now total 320. Roman knight "insidiis Bavarum deceptus," ca. 235; served also in Dacia and Britain.

———. "Une inscription de Madaure." *RecConst* 69 (1955/56): 121–27.
A procurator of a tractus and *flamen perpetuus*, Diocletianic.

———. "Les correspondants de l'orateur M. Cornelius Fronto de Cirta." In *Hommages à J. Bayet*, pp. 544–60. CollLat, 70 (1964): 544–60.

———. "Inscriptions impériales de Sila." *AntsAfrs* 3 (1969): 133–44.
Site southeast of Cirta; Septimius Severus as "propagator imperii."

———. *L'Afrique romaine: Scripta Varia*, vol. 1. Paris, 1978.
Collection of his articles, mostly epigraphic, mostly previously published.

Picard, Gilbert C. *Castellum Dimmidi.* Paris, 1947.
A model site-report. Pflaum, in a review in *Journal des savants* (1949): 55–62, emphasizes the Syrian detachment here and argues that Legio III favored Maximinus because the Palmyrenes, whom they regarded as rivals, were for Gordian.

Piganiol, André. "La signification de l'Album municipal de Timgad." *MemSocAntFr* (1954): 97–101.
Some evaded municipal duties. Contrast Oliver (1958).

Poulle, Joseph-Alexandre. "Les bains de Pompéianus." *RecConst* 19 (1878): 431–54.
Oued Athménia villa and mosaics.

Pouthier, Pierre. "L'évolution municipale d'Altava." *MEFR* 68 (1956): 205–45.
Berber menace greater than Vandal.

Salama, Pierre. *Les voies romaines.* Algiers, 1951.
The standard work.

———. "Nouveaux témoignages de l'oeuvre des Sévères dans la Maurétanie Césarienne," parts 1 and 2. *Libyca* 1 (1953): 231–61; 3 (1955): 329–67.

Part 1 discusses the Sétif-Auzia road; part 2, the immense network of forts, A.D. 198–205, built to deny nomads access to the Sahara.

————. "La colonie de Rusguniae d'après les inscriptions." *RAfr* 99 (1955): 5–52.

————. "La voie romaine de la vallée de la Tafna." *BAA* 2 (1966–67): 183–217.

Possibility of passing into Morocco across plain without metalled road.

Salama, Pierre, and Aline A. Boyce. "La trouvaille de sesterces de Rusguniae." *RAfr* 101 (1957): 205–45.

On hoard of 273 sesterces.

Saumagne, Charles. "Note sur la cadastration de Thamugadi." *RevTun*, n.s., no. 5 (1931): 97–104.

————. "Le plan de Timgad." *RevTun*, n.s., no. 13–14 (1933): 35–56.

Believes camp wall preceded grid; Lézine (1966/67) denies.

Seston, William. "Le secteur de Rapidum sur le limes de Maurétanie Césarienne." *MEFR* 45 (1928): 150–83.

Sherwin-White, Adrian N. "Geographical Factors in Roman Algeria." *JRS* 34 (1944): 1–10.

Good map.

Souville, Georges. "Statues impériales du Musée de Guelma." *Libyca* 2 (1954): 149–59.

————. "Madauros." *PECS* (1976).

Speidel, Michael. "The singulares of Africa and the Establishment of Numidia as a Province." *Historia* 22 (1973): 125–27.

Province of Numidia perhaps as late as 208.

————. "Continuous resistance? A Vexillatio of the Norican Ala Augusta in Mauretania." *ProcACA* 13 (1975): 36–38.

Argues that Marxists tend to spread dating of inscriptions to bolster hypothesis of constant revolt.

Strzelecka, Barbara. "Camps romains en Afrique du Nord." *Africana Bulletin* (Warsaw) 14 (1971): 9–32.

Tabular view with dates; map.

Syme, Ronald. "Tacitus, the Musulamii, and Thubursicu." In *Studies in Roman Economic and Social History in Honor of A. C. Johnson*, ed. Paul R. Coleman Norton, pp. 113–30. Princeton, 1951.

Outlines Roman policy: to found colony (Timgad), encircle Aurès, delimit Musulamii territory, establish municipia at Guelma and Khamissa. Useful distinction between "colonial aristocrats" and "Romanized Africans."

Tourrenc, Serge. "La dédicace du Temple du Génie de la Colonie à Timgad." *AntsAfrs* 2 (1968): 197–220.
Cost 64,500 sesterces; dedicator a great builder in area.

Turcan, Robert. *Le trésor de Guelma.* Paris, 1963.

Whittaker, C. Richard, ed. and trans. *Herodian.* 2 vols. Loeb Classical Library. New York, 1969–70.

10. Algeria from the Gordians to the Arab Invasion

Accame, Silvio. "Il testamento di C. Cornelio Egriliano e l'arco di Caracalla in Tébessa." *Epigraphica* 3 (1941): 237–43.

Arnheim, Michael T. W. *Senatorial Aristocracy in the Late Roman Empire.* Oxford, 1972.
Lists for years 284–395.

Baradez, Jean. "Le castellum de Mazafran et la colonia Aelia Augusta Tipasensium." *Libyca* 4 (1956): 265–90.

――――. "La basilique de Pierre et Paul à Tipasa et sa memoria." In *Akten des VIIten internationalen Kongresses für christliche Archäologie 1965*, pp. 341–56. Studi di antichità cristiana, 27. Seville and Berlin, 1969.

Berthier, André. "Edifices chrétiennes de Bou Tahrematen." *RAfr* 76 (1935): 137–51.
One of the buildings is a martyrium.

――――. "La sépulture du lecteur Georges à Sila." *BAA* 3 (1968): 283–92.

――――. "Du mot Numidia accolé aux noms antiques de Constantine." *AntsAfrs* 3 (1969): 55–67.

――――, ed. *Les vestiges du Christianisme antique dans la Numidie centrale.* Algiers and Paris, 1943.

Bonnal, Jean-Philippe, and Février, P.-A. "Ostraka de la région de Bir Troueh." *BAA* 2 (1966/67): 239–49.
Register of grain measures; related to Albertini tablets.

Bouchenaki, Mounir. "Nouvelle inscription à Tipasa." *RM* 81 (1974): 301–11.
In west zone, salvage archaeology unearthed a mid–fourth century seascape mosaic with unique inscription: PAX ET CONCORDIA SIT CONVIVIO NOSTRO.

――――. *Fouilles de la nécropole occidentale de Tipasa, 1969–1972.* Publications de la Bibliothèque nationale, histoire et civilisation, 1. Algiers, 1975.

Salvage archaeology. Examples of inhumation, in amphoras, under tiles, in cupulae, sarcophagi. Plots enclosed. Mensae for funeral banquets. Mosaic inscribed CONVIVIO NOSTRO, dated 381, with Christian symbols (fish, peacock).

Boucher, J.-Ph. "Nouvelles recherches à Tébessa Khalia." *MEFR* 66 (1954): 165–87.

———. "Le temple rond de Tébessa Khalia." *Libyca* 4 (1956): 7–31.

Brisson, Jean-Paul. *Autonomisme et Christianisme dans l'Afrique romaine*. Paris, 1958.
Marxist analysis.

Brown, Peter R. L. "Religious Dissent in the Later Roman Empire: The Case of North Africa." *History* 46 (1961): 83–101.

———. "Religious Coercion in the Later Roman Empire: The Case of North Africa." *History* 48 (1963): 283–305.

———. *Augustine of Hippo*. London, 1967.

———. "The Later Roman Empire." *Economic History Review*, ser. 2, 20 (1967): 327–43.
Review of A. H. M. Jones's *Later Roman Empire*, 3 vols. (Oxford, 1964).

———. "Approaches to the Religious Crisis of the Third Century A.D.' *EHR* 63 (1968): 542–58.

———. "Christianity and Local Culture in the Late Roman Empire." *JRS* 58 (1968): 85–95.

———. *The World of Late Antiquity*. London, 1971.

Burian, Jan. "Die einheimische Bevölkerung Nord-Afrikas in der Spätantike bis zur Einwanderung der Wandalen." In Franz Altheim and R. Stiehl, eds., *Die Araber in der Alten Welt*, vol. 5, part 1, pp. 170–304. Berlin, 1964.

Cadenat, Pierre. "La villa berbère-romaine de Aïn-Sarb (Tiaret)." *AntsAfrs* 8 (1974): 73–88.

Calderone, Salvatore. "Circumcelliones." *PdP*, fasc. 113 (1967): 94–109.

Callu, Jean-Pierre. "Le trésor de N'gaous." *MélPig* (1966): 303–20.

Camps, Gabriel. "Les Bavares, peuple de Maurétanie Césarienne." *RAfr* 99 (1955): 241–88.

Carcopino, Jérôme. "Le tombeau de Lambiridi et l'hermétisme africain." *RevArch* (1922): 211–301.

———. "Sur les traces de l'hermétisme africain." In his *Aspects mystiques de la Rome païenne*, pp. 207–314. Paris, 1942.
Lambiridi mosaic.

_____. "Un empéreur maure inconnu." *REA* 46 (1944): 94–120.

_____. "Encore Masties, l'empéreur maure inconnu." *RAfr* 100 (1956): 339–48.

Cayrel, Pierre. "Une basilique donatiste de Numidie." *MEFR* 50/51 (1934): 114–42.
Vegesala.

Chardon, Lieutenant. "Fouilles de Rusguniae." *BCTH* (1900): 129–49.

Chastagnol, André. "Le sénateur Volusien et la conversion d'une famille de l'aristocratie romaine au Bas-Empire." *REA* 58 (1956): 241–53.

Chastagnol, André, and Duval, N. "Les survivances du culte impérial dans l'Afrique du Nord à l'époque vandale." In *Mélanges d'histoire ancienne offerts à William Seston*, pp. 87–118. Publications de la Sorbonne, Série Etudes, 9. Paris, 1974.

Christern, Jürgen. "Basilika und Memorie der Heiligen Salsa in Tipasa." *BAA* 3 (1968): 193–258.

_____. "Il complesso cristiano di Tebessa: architettura e decorazione." *CorsCultRavBiz* 17 (1970): 103–17.
Important.

_____. *Das frühchristliche Pilgerheiligtum von Tebessa: Architektur und Ornamentik einer spätantiken Bauhütte in Nordafrika.* Wiesbaden, 1976.
Important synthesis. Argues that alleged temple of Aesculapius at Tebessa Khalia was a luxurious private reception room.

Christol, Michel. "La prosopographie de Numidie 253–260 et la chronologie des révoltes africaines sous Valérien et Gallien." *AntsAfrs* 10 (1976): 69–78.
Faraxen's capture, 269/70.

Courcelle, Pierre. "Une seconde campagne de fouilles à Ksar el-Kelb." *MEFR* 53 (1936): 166–94.
Vegesala.

Courtois, Christian. *Les Vandales et l'Afrique.* Paris, 1955.
The standard work. The Vandals precipitated Roman downfall in Africa but are not responsible for it. Romans themselves never bothered to occupy infertile areas; this proved a tactical mistake. The Vandals simply extended the area of "abandoned Africa."

Courtois, Christian; Leschi, L.; Perrat, Ch.; and Saumagne, Ch. *Les tablettes Albertini.* Paris, 1952.
The *editio princeps*.

Démandt, Alexandre. "Die afrikanischen Unruhen unter Valentinian I."

In H.-J. Diesner, ed., *Afrika und Rom*, pp. 277–92. Halle, 1968.

Diehl, Charles. "Deux missions archéologiques dans l'Afrique du Nord." *NouvArchMissSc* 4 (1893): 285–374.
Byzantine Algeria.

Diesner, Hans-Joachim. "Gildos Herrschaft und die Niederlage bei Theveste." *Klio* 40 (1962): 178–86.

Duval, Yvette, and Février, P.-A. "Procès-verbal de déposition de reliques de Telergma." *MEFR* 81 (1969): 259–320.
Evidence for Christianity, A.D. 636.

d'Esturac-Doisy, Henriette. "M. Cornelius Octavianus et les révoltes indigènes du 3e siècle." *Libyca* 1 (1953): 181–87.
On Faraxen, 259/60.

Ferguson, John. "Aspects of Early Christianity in North Africa." *Tarikh* (Ibadan, Nigeria) 2 (1976): 16–27.
List of reasons for Christian and Donatist expansion, especially appeal of martyr cult.

Février, Paul-Albert. "Mosaïques funéraires datées d'Afrique du Nord." In *Atti del 6⁰ congresso internazionale di archeologia cristiana*, pp. 433–56. Ravenna, 1962.
For example, at Theveste, A.D. 508.

————. "Toujours le Donatisme: à quand l'Afrique?" *RivStLettRel* 2 (1966): 228–40.
Review of Tengström (1964), whom Février thinks stronger in philology than in archaeology or topography. No olives in Donatist area; cities not in decline in fourth century A.D.

————. "Nouvelles recherches dans la salle tréflée de la basilique de Tébessa." *BAA* 3 (1968): 166–91.
Important.

————. "La recherche archéologique en Algérie et l'histoire ancienne du Maghrib." *RevHCMaghr* 5 (1968): 16–36.
Includes Tébessa amphitheater.

————. "Conditions économiques et sociales de la création artistique en Afrique à la fin de l'antiquité." *CorsCultRavBiz* 17 (1970): 161–89.

————. "Le culte des martyrs en Afrique et ses plus anciens monuments." *CorsCultRavBiz* 17 (1970): 191–215.
On Tipasa, Theveste, Vegesala.

————. "Les sources épigraphiques et archéologiques et l'histoire réligieuse des provinces orientales de l'Afrique antique." *CorsCultRavBiz* 19 (1972): 131–58.

On Vegesala, Tigisis, Augustine's Carthage, Hippo.

Février, Paul-Albert, and Marcillet-Joubert, A. "Pierre sculptée et écrite de Ksar Sbahi (Algérie)." *MEFR* 88 (1966): 178–79.
Late date for Abizar stele.

Frend, William H. C. "The Revival of Berber Art." *Antiquity* 16 (1942): 342–52.
Attempt to connect Donatist dissent with alleged artistic revival.

———. "The Roman Empire in the Eyes of Western Schismatics." *MiscHistEccles*, vol. 1, pp. 5–22. Bibliothèque de la Revue d'histoire ecclésiastique, 38. Louvain, 1961.

———. *Martyrdom and Persecution in the Early Church.* Oxford, 1966.
Important.

———. "Circumcellions and Monks." *JThS* 20 (1969): 542–49.
Circumcellions not monks. Archaeological evidence for chapels with grain stores (*cellae*).

———. "The Failure of Persecutions in the Roman Empire." *Past and Present*, no. 16 (November 1969): 10–29.

———. *The Donatist Church.* 2nd ed. Oxford, 1971.
Very important, but overemphasizes Donatism as sociopolitical movement. Tengström (1964) is corrective. Useful but inaccurate maps.

———. "Heresy and Schism as Social and National Movements." In Derek Baker, ed., *Schism, Heresy, and Religious Protest*, pp. 37–56. Cambridge, 1971.
Firmus' revolt allegedly spurred by overtaxation. Circumcellions as revolutionary zealots.

———. "The Christian Period in Mediterranean Africa, c. A.D. 200 to 700." *CHistAfr* 2 (1978): 410–12; 451–78.
Useful survey; still thinks Circumcellions were both religious and revolutionary.

Gagé, Jean. "Nouveaux aspects de l'Afrique chrétienne." *Annales de l'Ecole des Hautes Etudes de Gand* 1 (1937): 151–236.
On Vegesala.

Galand, Lionel. "Les Quinquegentanei." *BAA* 4 (1971): 277–79.
They revolt in A.D. 260, 290, 304, then disappear.

Gsell, Stéphane, and Graillot, H. "Ruines romaines au nord de l'Aurès." *MEFR* 14 (1894): 17–86.
Bagai, pp. 43–46.

Guénin, Commandant. "Inventaire archéologique du cercle de Tébessa."

NouvArchMissSc 17 (1908): 75–134, with index and map.
Anticipates Gsell, *AAA*, and Baradez, *Fossatum*. Good on
oil-works.

Guéry, Roger. "Les thermes d'Ad Sava municipium (Hammam Guer-
gour)." *BAA* 2 (1966/67): 95–106.

Hands, Arthur R. *Charities* (1968; see chapter 3).
Benefactions on Theveste arch, document 72, p. 206.

Heurgon, Jacques. *Le trésor de Ténès*. Paris, 1958.

Jacquot, Commandant L. "Le bénétier de l'église de Lemellef." *RecConst*
49 (1915): 129–34.
On Donatist violence.

Janier, Emile. "Inscriptions latines du Musée de Tlemcen." *Libyca* 4
(1956): 71–84.
Evidence for Judaism, A.D. 505.

Jaubert, Canon H. "Anciens évêchés et ruines chrétiennes de la Numidie
et de la Sitifienne." *RecConst* 46 (1912): 1–218.
Anticipates Frend (1971).

Jones, Arnold H. M. "Were the Ancient Heresies National or Social
Movements in Disguise?" *JThS*, n.s., 10–12 (1959): 280–98.
Answer is no.

Kohns, Hans P. "Versorgungskrisen und Hungerrevolten in spätantiken
Rom." *Antiquitas* 6 (1961): 219.
Tabular view of shortages in Rome, under thirty-six different
prefects.

Kolb, Frank. "Der Aufstand der Provinz Africa Proconsularis im Jahr
338 n. Chr." *Historia* 28 (1977): 440–77.
Denies that uprising was a class struggle.

Kolbe, Hans-Georg. *Die Statthalter Numidiens von Gallien bis Con-
stantin*. Vestigia, 4. Munich, 1962.

Kotula, Thadeusz. "Les principes gentis et les principes civitatis en
Afrique romaine." *Eos* 55 (1963): 347–65.
No principes gentis after 247: the Berbers exhibited "prideful
separateness."

———. "Die Aufstand des Afrikaners Gildo und seine Nachwirkungen."
Das Altertum 33 (1972): 167–76.

———. "Culte provincial et romanisation: le cas des deux Mauré-
tanies." *Eos* 63 (1973): 389–407.
Imperial cult in Mauretania dates from Claudius, broadened
under Vespasian. Volubilis assumed to be new capital, a center
of loyalty on the fringe of the civilized world.

_____. "Les Africains et la domination de Rome." *AnnsLittsUBes* 186
(1976): 337–52.
Copious footnotes. Stresses Faraxen. Berbers adopted Roman
culture while continuing to resist. Warning against hasty conclusions from native names. Equates Romanization with progress
for natives.

Lancel, Serge. "Architecture et décoration de la grande basilique à
Tigzirt." *MEFR* 68 (1956): 299–333.
Possibly Donatist. Identifies Tigzirt with Rusuccuru, not
Iomnium.

_____. "Aux origines du Donatisme et des circoncellions." *CahTun* 15
(1967): 183–88.
Circumcellions first appear ca. 340.

Lassus, Jean. "Les mosaïques d'un sarcophage de Tipasa." *Libyca* 3
(1955): 265–79.

_____. "Edifices de culte autour de la basilique." *Atti VI Congresso
di archeologia cristiana, Ravenna*, pp. 581–610. Rome, 1965.

_____. "La basilique africaine." *CorsCultRavBiz* 17 (1970): 217–34.
Orleansville (el Asnam), Vegesala. Vandal tombs in Hippo
cathedral. Warns against taking double-apsed churches as *ipso
facto* Donatist.

_____. "La forteresse byzantine de Thamugadi." In *Actes du 14e
congrès international des études byzantines*, vol. 2, pp. 463–74.
Bucharest, 1975.
Chapel was bigger than baths; chapel, baths, and headquarters
formed three sides of a quadrangle. Hasty but majestic: a show
of force.

Léquement, Robert. "Fouilles à l'amphithéâtre de Tébessa." *BAA* 2
(1966/67): 107–22.

Leschi, Louis. "Rome et les nomades du Sahara central." *Travaux de
l'Institut des Recherches Sahariennes* 1 (1942): 47–62.
Possible camel-nomad burials in Djedar necropoleis.

_____. *Etudes* (1957; see chapter 7).
Pages 85–110, Christian basilicas; 333–38, archaeology of the
Grande Kabylie; 371–88, Tipasa; 411–20, Saint Salsa.

_____. *Algérie antique*. Paris, 1962.
Good photographs of Theveste and Tipasa.

Leveau, Philippe. "Paysans maures et villes romaines en Maurétanie
césarienne: la résistance des populations indigènes à la romanisation dans l'arrière-pays de Caesarea." *MEFR* 82 (1975): 857–71.

Peasants and Romans coexisted rather than coalesced.

———. "Recherches historiques sur une région montagneuse de Maurétanie Césarienne: des Tigava Castra à la mer." *MEFR* 89 (1977): 257–311.
Fourteen new sites in river valley west of Gunugu. New plan of Tigava Castra, founded against the Mazices.

Logeart, F., and Berthier, A. "Deux basiliques chrétiennes de Sila." *RecConst* 63 (1935/36): 236–84.

MacMullen, Ramsay. *Enemies of the Roman Order.* Cambridge, Mass., 1966.
Pages 353ff. on Circumcellions.

Mandouze, André. "Encore le Donatisme! Problèmes de méthode posés par le thèse de J.-P. Brisson." *AntClass* 29 (1960): 61–107.
The movement was from nationalism to schism, not the reverse. Brisson weak in chronology, statistics, archaeology, epigraphy, and knowledge of Saint Augustine.

———. "Le donatisme représente-t-il la résistance à Rome de l'Afrique tardive?" *Assim et résist* (1976): 357–66.
Equivocal. Though Donatists saw themselves as primarily defending the true faith, to Rome they were a problem, behaving as though emperors had never made the Peace of the Church. Marxist and colonial approaches both anachronistic; evidence mostly anti-Donatist. He thinks that Courtois (1955) goes too far in saying bitter fruit of colonization was fraudulent bankruptcy at expense of provincials.

Marcillet-Joubert, Jean. "Mosaïques tombales de Tébessa." *RAfr* 104 (1960): 413–23.

Markus, Ralph A. "Christianity and Dissent in Roman North Africa: Changing Perspectives in Recent Work." In Derek Baker, ed., *Schism, Heresy, and Religious Protest,* pp. 21–36. Cambridge, 1972.
Eminently sane overview.

Marrou, Henri-Irénée. "Inscription martyrologue de Tipasa." *BCTH,* n.s. 7 (1961): 219–23.
On desire of faithful to be buried as close as possible to Saint Salsa.

Meunier, Jean. "L'arc de Caracalla à Theveste." *RAfr* 82 (1938): 84–107.

Millar, Fergus. Critical review of the first edition of Frend, *Donatist Church* (1965) in *JRS* 56 (1966): 232–34.

Frend overschematic on town-country dichotomy. Useful corrective: Picard (1959).

Monceaux, Paul. "L'épigraphie donatiste." *RevPhil* 33 (1909): 112–61.
Useful compilation.

Overbeck, Machteld. "Augustin und die Circumcellionen seiner Zeit." *Chiron* 3 (1973): 457–63.

――――. *Untersuchungen zum afrikanischen Senatsadel in der Spätantike.* Kollmünz, 1973.
W. Eck's review, *Gymnasium* 81 (1974): 333–35, criticizes lack of prosopography. Lists in Arnheim (1972).

Picard, Gilbert C. *Les réligions de l'Afrique antique.* Paris, 1954.
Denies that Salsa was Christian, virgin, iconoclast, or saint!

――――. *La civilisation de l'Afrique romaine.* Paris, 1959.
Dependable survey.

――――. "Tigisis." *EAAC*, suppl. (1970).

Poulle, Joseph-Alexandre. "Nouvelles inscriptions d'Announa." *RevConst* 27 (1892): 250–76.
Julian as *restitutor sacrorum*.

Reygasse, Maurice. *Monuments funéraires préislamiques de l'Afrique du Nord.* Paris, 1950.
Tin Hinan.

Roesch, Paul. "Une tablette de malédiction de Tébessa." *BAA* 2 (1966/67): 231–37.

Salama, Pierre. "Les déplacements successifs du *limes* en Maurétanie césarienne." In *Actes des XIten Kongress der Limeskunde.* Bonn, 1976.
Not seen.

Saumagne, Charles. "La caste sociale des circoncellions." *AnnalesESC* (1934); reprinted in *CahTun* 10 (1962): 279–93.
Uses scale of fines to show Circumcellions lower than plebs, above slaves and coloni.

Saxer, Robert. "Untersuchungen zu den Vexillationen des römischen Kaiserheeres (Augustus bis Diocletian)." *EpigStud* 9 (1967): 30–31, 100–110.
Important study of reinforcements to Legio III Augusta; for example, Austuriani at Auzia, responsible for Faraxen *cum satellitibus captus et interfectus*.

Schwartz, J. "Hoggar: note numismatique à propos du tombeau de Tin-Hinan." *Libyca* 3 (1955): 179–81.
Dates Tin Hinan A.D. 308–324.

Sérée de Roche, Etienne J. J. *Tébessa, antique Theveste.* Algiers, 1952.
Guidebook, to be supplemented from Christern (1976).

Seston, William. "Le monastère d'Aïn Tamda et les origines de l'architecture monastique en Afrique du Nord." *MEFR* 51 (1934):
79–113.
Catholic monastery between 474 and 533. Notes others: Tours,
Milan; Thagaste, Hippo (both Augustinian), Ruspe.

Simon, Marcel. "Fouilles dans la basilique de Henchir el Ateuch." *MEFR*
51 (1934): 143–177.
Very like Vegesala.

————. "Le judaïsme berbère dans l'Afrique ancienne." In his *Recherches d'histoire judéo-chrétienne,* pp. 30–87. Paris, 1962.

Soden, Hans von. *Urkunden zur Entstehungsgeschichte des Donatismus.*
Berlin, 1913.
Source-book; largely letters from Constantine.

Soyer, Jacqueline. "Les cadastres anciens de la région de St.-Donat."
AntsAfrs 7 (1973): 275–96.
Site southwest of Constantine. Deficient in dates.

————. "Les centuriations romaines en Algérie orientale." *AntsAfrs*
10 (1976): 107–80.
Area from Ras el-Oued to Constantine and southward. Again
no dates.

Szilégyi, Janos. "Die Sterblichkeit in den nordafrikanischen Provinzen."
AAHung 17 (1965): 309–34; 18 (1966): 235–377; 19 (1967):
25–59.
See caveat in Hopkins (1965; see chapter 3). Also on inflation,
see Szilégy, "Prices and Wages in the Western Provinces of the
Roman Empire," *Acta Antiqua Hungarica* 10 (1963): 325–90;
see also Werner Krenkel, "Währungen, Preise, und Löhne in
Rom," *Das Altertum* 7 (1961): 167–78.

Tengström, Emin. *Donatisten und Katholiken.* Göteborg, 1964.
Cool, careful, scholarly critique of Frend.

Thomasson, Bengt. *Statthalter der römischen Provinzen Nord-Afrikas
von Augustus bis Diocletian.* Lund, 1960.
Summarized by him in "Praesides provinciarum Africae Proconsularis, Numidiae, Mauretaniae," *OpuscRom* 7 (1963): 163–
211; updated by him in "Mauretania" and "Numidia," RE
supplbd. 13 (1973). Adverse review by Eric Birley, *JRS* 52 (1962):
219–27.

Trouillot, Alexis. "Autour de la basilique de Tébessa." *RecConst* 62
(1934): 115–99.
Pioneering.

Warmington, Brian H. *The North African Provinces from Diocletian to the Vandal Conquest.* Cambridge, 1954.

West, Rebecca. *St. Augustine.* London, 1933.
> Slight, impressionistic. Comparison with Tolstoy.

Wuilleumier, Pierre. *Musée d'Alger.* Paris, 1928.
> Rare photograph of Lambiridi mosaic.

11. Mauretania Tingitana

Aymard, Jacques. "La mosaïque du chat à Volubilis." *Latomus* 20 (1961): 52–71.
> Mock hunt of a rat, from House of Venus.

Baradez, Jean. "Deux missions de recherche sur le limes de Tingitane." *CRAI* (1955): 288–98.
> The stretch of the Limes south of Sala.

Bekkari, Mehdi. "Maroc." In F. Barreca et al., eds., *Espansione fenicia nel Mediterraneo,* pp. 29–46. Studi Semitici, 38. Rome, 1971.

Boube, Jean. "Fouilles archéologiques à Sala." *HespTam* 7 (1966): 22–32.

———. "Un nouveau portrait de Juba II découvert à Sala." *BAM* 6 (1966): 91–107.

———. "Documents d'archéologie marocaine au Maroc." *BAM* (1967): 263–367.

———. "Rabat"; "Sala"; "Tangeri." *EAAC,* suppl. (1970).

———. "Marques d'amphores découvertes à Sala, Volubilis, et Banasa." *BAM* 9 (1973/75): 163–235.
> Mostly from Sala, imported from Baetica from first to fourth centuries A.D. Volubilis, amid olive groves, did not need to import.

Boube-Piccot, Christiane. "Trophée damasquiné sur une statue impériale de Volubilis." *BAM* 6 (1966): 189–278.

———. "Techniques de fabrication des bustes de bronze de Juba II et de Caton." *BAM* 7 (1967): 447–76.
> Splendid photographs.

———. "Les bronzes antiques du Maroc I: la statuaire." *EtTravArchMar* 4 (1969).

Callu, Jean-Pierre; Hallier, G.; Marion, J; Morel, J.-P.; and Rebuffat, R. "Thamusida I–II." *MEFR,* suppls. 1–2 (1965–70).
> Part III, by Rabuffat and Marion, appeared in 1977. It treats finds by categories, including those from areas where excavation is unfinished. Coins (latest of Claudius II) confirm occupation of

site ceased between A.D. 274 and 280.

Camps, Gabriel. "Le Gour, mausolée berbère du 7e siècle." *AntsAfrs* 8 (1974): 191–207.

Carcopino, Jérôme. *Maroc antique*. Paris, 1943.
Standard.

———. "Note sur les deux bustes trouvés à Volubilis." *RecConst* 68 (1953): 63–85.
Thinks "Hellenistic Prince" is Cleomenes III of Sparta.

Castagnoli, Ferdinando. "Capitolio." *EAAC* (1959).
Authoritative list, including Tingi, Volubilis.

Chapelle, F. de la. "L'expédition de Suétonius Paulinus dans le sud-est du Maroc." *Hesperis* 19 (1934): 107–24.

Chatelain, Louis. "Note sur les fouilles de Volubilis." *CRAI* (1916): 359–66.
Opened by Lyautey.

———. "Le Forum de Sala." *CRAI* (1930): 336–40.

———. *Le Maroc des romains*. BEFAR 160 and 160bis. Paris, 1942–45.
Standard.

Cintas, Pierre. *Contribution à l'étude de l'expansion carthaginoise au Maroc*. Paris, 1954.
Argues North African "factories" were Phoenician. Denied by Harden (1948; see chapter 1).

Cristofani, Mauro. "Tamuda." *EAAC* (1966).

Desanges, Jehan. "Recherches récentes sur le peuplement indigène et sur les structures traditionelles de l'Afrique antique." In H. Diesner, ed., *Afrika und Rom*, pp. 121–34. Halle, 1968.
No Romanization east of Volubilis.

Desjacques, Jean, and Koeberlé, Paul. "Mogador et les îles purpuraires." *Hesperis* 42 (1955): 193–202.

Domergue, Claude. "L'arc de triomphe de Caracalla à Volubilis." *BCTH*, n.s. 4 (1966): 201–29.

———. "La représentation des Saisons sur l'arc de Caracalla à Volubilis." *MélPig* (1966): 463–72.

Drouhot, J. "Trouvailles autour de Chellah." *BAM* 6 (1966): 145–87.
Sala pottery.

Etienne, Robert. "Une inscription sur bronze découverte à Volubilis." *CRAI* (1954): 126–30.
Severus and Bostar. See also his article of the same title in *Latomus* 14 (1955): 241–61.

———. "Maisons et hydraulique de Volubilis." *PSAM* 10 (1954): 55ff.

———. *Le quartier nord-est de Volubilis*. 2 vols. Paris, 1960.

————. "La mosaïque des fauves à Volubilis." *HommGren* (1962): 586–94.

Euzennat, Maurice. "Fouilles opérées à Banasa en 1955." *BCTH* 53 (1955/56): 223–40.
See also A. Luquet on Banasa, *BCTH* (1957): 54–56.

————. "Le Temple C de Volubilis et les origines de la cité." *BAM* 2 (1957): 41–64.

————. "Anoceur (Kasbah des Aït Khalifa), faux poste romain dans le moyen Atlas." *BAM* 4 (1960): 381–410.
No evidence of Roman military installations east of Volubilis.

————. "Les voies romaines du Maroc dans l'Itinéraire antonin." *HommGren* (1962): 595–610.

————. "L'héritage punique et influences gréco-romaines au Maroc à la veille de la conquête romaine." In *Le rayonnement des civilisations grecque et romaine sur les cultures périphériques: actes du 8e congrès international d'archéologie classique*, pp. 261–78. Paris, 1965.

————. "Jérôme Carcopino et le Maroc." *MélCarc* (1966): 81–89.
Notion that Volubilis was Juba II's capital and that "Hellenistic Prince" is Cleomenes III both wrong.

————. "Une mosaïque de Lixus." *MélPig* (1966): 473–80.
Cupids cock-fighting.

————. "Fragments inédits de bronzes épigraphiques marocains." *AntsAfrs* 3 (1969): 115–32.
Twenty-nine diplomata from Tingitana, and seven tabulae patronatus.

————. "Le limes de Volubilis." *BJ Beihefte* 16 (1969): 194–99.
Good map.

————. "Grecs et orientaux en Maurétanie tingitane." *AntsAfrs* 5 (1971): 161–78.
Only fifty known, of whom eleven were soldiers. From Syria, Phoenicia, Palestine, Cappadocia, Thrace.

————. "Les édifices du culte chrétiens en Mauretania Tingitana." *AntsAfrs* 8 (1974): 175–90.
None in Lixus, nor Volubilis; these are mosques. One in Tangier, larger than El Asnam.

————. "Les Zegrenses." In *Mélanges d'histoire ancienne offerts à William Seston*, pp. 175–86. Publications de la Sorbonne, Série Etudes, 9. Paris, 1974.
On Tabula Banasitana family.

————. Articles on Babba, Banasa, Jibila ("Cotta"), Mogador, Rirha,

Sala, Tamuda, Thamusida, Tocolosida, Tingi, Volubilis. *PECS* (1976).

———. "Une dédicace volubitaine à Apollon de Claros." *AntsAfrs* 10 (1976): 63–68.
Connected with murder of Geta, victory over Alemanni, and edict of citizenship.

———. "Les recherches sur la frontière romaine d'Afrique (1974–1976)." In *Akten des Xten internationalen Kongresses der Limeskunde*, pp. 533–43. Bonn, 1976.
Useful updating. Notes that Speidel (1977) cancels Marion (1960) and Rebuffat (1971) on abandonment of Tingitana by Diocletian. Dates Bir Oum Ali as Trajanic, Tillibari as Hadrianic.

Feray, Guy, and Paskoff, Roland. "Les carrières romaines des environs de Volubilis." *BAM* 6 (1966): 279–300.

Frézouls, Edmond. "Nouvelles inscriptions de Volubilis." *CRAI* (1952): 395–402. Continued in *MEFR* 65 (1953): 139–72; 68 (1956): 96–125.
Editiones principes of the "altars of peace."

———. "Les Baquates et la province romaine de Tingitana." *BAM* 2 (1957): 65–116.
On the "altars of peace."

Gascou, Jacques. "Municipia civium Romanorum." *Latomus* 30 (1971): 133–41.
Disagrees with Saumagne (1962) on *ius Latii* only in provinces.

———. "L'évidence du statut juridique de Tanger entre 38 av. J.-C. et le règne de Claude." *AntsAfrs* 8 (1974): 67–71.
Roman citizens, attached to Baetica, 25 B.C.–A.D. 42.

Gsell, Stéphane, and Carcopino, J. "La base de M. Sulpicius Felix et le décret des décurions de Sala." *MEFR* 48 (1931): 1–39.

Harmand, Louis. "Observations sur l'inscription de Sala." *MélPig* (1966): 1211–20.

Herodotus. *Histories* 4.96.
On silent trading, Atlantic coast.

Jodin, André. "L'établissement préromain de Mogador." *BAM* 2 (1957): 3–40.

———. "Le tombeau préromain de Mogogha es Srira (Tanger)." *BAM* 4 (1960): 22–46.
Not mentioned in chapter 11. Analogy with LeGour: see Camps (1974).

———. "L'enceinte hellénistique de Volubilis." *BCTH*, n.s. 1/2 (1965/66): 199–231.

————. "L'archéologie phénicienne au Maroc." *HespTam* 7 (1966): 9–16.
Identifies, implausibly, Mogador with Hanno's Cerne.

————. *Mogador, comptoir phénicien du Maroc atlantique.* EtTrav-ArchMar, 2 (1966).
A 211-page monograph.

————. "La tradition hellénistique dans l'urbanisme de Volubilis." *BAM* 6 (1966): 511–16.

————. "Un vase arétin de P. Cornelius à Mogador." *MélPig* (1966): 519–28.
From an Augustan villa. Handsome photographs.

————. "L'exploitation forestière du Maroc antique." In *Actes du 93e congrès archéologique, Tours 1968*, pp. 413–22. Paris, 1970.
From Gardens of Hesperides to three hundred thousand hectares of cedars today.

————. "Banasa et le limes méridional de la Mauretania Tingitana." In *Actes du 95e congrès archéologique, Reims 1970*, pp. 33–42. Paris, 1974.

Letan, R. "A propos de la disparition des gravures rupestres du pre-Sahara marocain." *BAM* 9 (1973–75): 157–59.
View in text overalarmist. Thousands of sites protected by difficulty of access. But brainless collectors destroy sites and bribe urchins to do so.

Luquet, Armand. "Prospection punique de la côte atlantique du Maroc." *Hespéris* 43 (1956): 117–32.

————. "La céramique préromaine de Banasa." *BAM* 5 (1964): 117–44.
Influence of Carthage and Baetica.

————. "Contribution à l'Atlas archéologique du Maroc: région de Volubilis." *BAM* 5 (1964): 291–300; 6 (1966): 365–75.
Deals with Rharb region: Banasa, Thamusida, Sidi Slimane (Rirha).

————. "Blé et meunerie à Volubilis." *BAM* 6 (1966): 301–15.
Eight villae rusticae in environs; adequate yield.

————. "La basilique judicaire de Volubilis." *BAM* 7 (1967): 407–45.
Photographs, restoration drawings, elevations.

————. *Volubilis: les travaux et les jours d'une cité de Maroc antique.* Tangier, 1972.
Illustrated guidebook.

————. "Contribution à l'Atlas archéologique du Maroc: le Maroc punique." *BAM* 9 (1973–75): 237–93.

Garum could be Punic. Ships could cover 215–240 kilometers per 24 hours. Seven sanctuaries now known at Merja Zerga; five pre-Roman levels under Decumanus Maximus at Banasa, sixth century to ca. 146 B.C. Punic Volubilis dates from third century B.C., may have taken in refugees from Carthage in 146. Thamusida and Sala date from seventh century B.C., Mogador from 650. Fifty hypogaea known from Tit (Jadida).

Malhomme, Jean. "Corpus des gravures rupestres du Grand Atlas." *PSAM* 13/14 (1960/61): entire issue.

Marion, Jean. "Le peuplement de Tanger à l'époque romaine." *Hespéris* 35 (1948): 125–41.
See also his similar studies on Banasa, *Hespéris* 37 (1950): 157–80, and on Volubilis, *BAM* 4 (1960): 133–87.

———. "Les ruines anciennes de la région d'Oujda." *BAM* 2 (1957): 117–63.
Important Berber sites; well illustrated.

———. "Notes sur les séries monétaires de la Mauretania Tingitana." *BAM* 4 (1960): 449–67.
Thinks coins prove Diocletian abandoned Tingitana.

———. "Les dépôts monétaires du quartier du macellum à Banasa." *BAM* 5 (1964): 201–33.

———. "Contribution de la numismatique à la connaissance de la Mauretanie Tingitana." *AntsAfrs* 1 (1967): 99–118.
Strong connection with Spain.

———. "Les monnaies de Shemesh et des villes autonomes de Mauretanie Tingitana du musée de Rabat." *AntsAfrs* 6 (1972): 59–127.
Equates Shemesh with Hercules-Melqart.

Mazard, Jean. *Corpus Nummorum Numidiae Mauretaniaeque.* Paris, 1955.
Standard.

Nesselhauf, Herbert. "Zur Militärgeschichte der Provinz Mauretania Tingitana." *Epigraphica* 12 (1950): 34–48.
On Banasa diplomata.

Nowak, Herbert; Ortner, Sigrid; and Ortner, Dieter. *Felsbilder der spanischen Sahara.* Graz, 1975.

Oliver, James H. "Text of the Tabula Banasitana, A.D. 177." *AJPh* 93 (1972): 336–40.

Petersen, Leiva. "Lusius Quietus, ein Reitergeneral Trajans aus Mauretanien." *Das Altertum* 14 (1968): 211–17.

Picard, Gilbert C. *A travers les musées et les sites de l'Afrique du Nord,* pp. 173–239. Recherches archéologiques, 1: Maroc. Paris, 1947.

Ponsich, Michel. "Les lampes romaines en terre cuite de la Mauretania Tingitana." *PSAM* 15 (1961): 77–119.

———. "Contribution à l'Atlas archéologique du Maroc: région de Tanger." *BAM* 5 (1964): 253–90.

See *BAM* 5 (1964): 375–457, for Lixus.

———. "Lixus, cité légendaire, entre dans l'histoire." *Archeologia*, no. 4 (May–June 1965): 23–27.

Good photographs: air views, temples, theater, garum-vats, Hercules-Antaeus statuette, Ocean mosaic.

———. "Fouilles puniques et romaines à Lixus." *HespTam* 7 (1966): 17–22.

———. "Une mosaïque du dieu Océan à Lixus." *BAM* 6 (1966): 323–28.

———. "Un théâtre grec au Maroc?" *BAM* 6 (1966): 317–22.

Lixus.

———. "La céramique estampée du Maroc romain." *BAA* 7 (1967): 499–546.

Rare gray Visigothic ware at Lixus, Sala, Tamuda, Ceuta.

———. "Kouass, port antique et carrefour." *BAM* 7 (1967): 369–406.

———. *Nécropoles phéniciennes de la région de Tanger.* Tangier, 1967. Color plates.

———. "Nouvel aspect de l'industrie préromaine en Tingitane." *BCTH*, n.s. 4 (1968): 226–35.

Consortium of garum-processors and potters at Kouass.

———. *Recherches archéologiques à Tanger et dans sa région.* Paris, 1970.

———. "Volubilis in Marokko." *AntWelt* 1, part 2 (1970): 3–21.

Good photographs. I have not seen his book on Volubilis (Zurich, 1974).

———. "Perennité des relations dans le circuit du Détroit de Gibraltar." *ANRW* 2, part 3 (1975): 655–84.

Cultural affinity of Morocco with Spain; geographic unity led to economic unity.

Poulsen, Frederik. "Caton et le jeune prince." *Acta Archaeologica* 18 (1947): 117–39.

Could the young prince be Juba I?

Puigaudeau, Odette. "L'art préhistorique du Maroc pre-saharien sera-t-il effacé?" *Archeologia*, no. 30 (September–October 1969): 26–32.

Rebuffat, René. "Les mosaïques du bain de Diane à Volubilis." In *La mosaïque gréco-romaine*, vol. 1, pp. 193–217. Paris, 1965.

————. "Bâtiment à bossages du quartier du fleuve à Thamusida." *BCTH*, n.s. 1/2 (1965/66): 169–86.

————. "Le développement urbain de Volubilis au 2e siècle de notre ère." *BCTH*, n.s. 1/2 (1965/66): 231–40.

————. "Bronzes antiques d'Hercule à Tanger et à Arzila." *AntsAfrs* 5 (1971): 179–92.

————. "Les confins de la Mauretania Tingitane et de la Mauretania Césarienne." *StudMagr* 4 (1971): 32–64.
Roman coins at Oujda.

————. "Les fouilles de Thamusida et leur contribution à l'histoire du Maroc." *BAM* 8 (1968–72): 51–65.
Excellent summary: plans and photographs.

————. "La maison à la disciplina à Volubilis." *BAM* 9 (1973–75): 329–57).
Penultimate house on north side of Decumanus Maximus. No portico, pebbled court, careless construction, above average number of shops. If altar inscribed DISCIPLINAE is in situ, building may have been barracks, later converted to civilian use. Two coin hoards date from Pius to Gallienus, peak in reign of Gallienus, an index to trouble at accession of Diocletian.

————. "Les principia du camp romain de Lalla Djilaliya (Tabernae)." *BAM* 9 (1973–75): 359–76.
Camp measures 86 by 78 meters. Parallels at Rapidum, and in Wales and Scotland. Pre-Severan, destroyed end of third century A.D. Lists, with dimensions, thirteen Mauretanian camps; four have principia: Benian (important, 183 by 140 meters overall), Sidi Moussa, Thamusida, and this one.

————. "Enceintes urbaines et insécurité en Mauretanie Tingitane." *MEFR* 86 (1974): 501–26.
Walls as signs of prosperity rather than military necessity.

————. "Vestiges antiques sur la côte occidentale de l'Afrique au sud de Rabat." *AntsAfrs* 8 (1974): 25–49.
Punic ports of call to Mogador and beyond.

Reine, Marcel. "Les gravures pariétales libyco-berbères de la haute vallée du Draa." *AntsAfrs* 3 (1969): 35–54.
Horsemen, camels; three thousand figures, ranging over two thousand years.

Romanelli, Pietro. "Le iscrizioni volubitani dei Baquati e i rapporti dei Romani con le tribù indigeni dell'Africa." *HommGren* (1962): 1347–66.
The "altars of peace."

Roxan, Margaret. "The auxilia of Mauretania Tingitana." *Latomus* 52 (1973): 838–55.
In disagreement with Euzennat (1960), thinks of Bou Hallou as Roman (Caracalla), but also in an unconquered wedge between Caesariensis and Tingitana. For the latter, cites evidence for seventeen regiments and fifteen forts. Method: grants of citizenship on diplomata mean battle honors, which in turn mean revolts.

Saumagne, Charles. "Volubilis, municipe latin." *Revue historique de droit français et étranger* (1952): 388ff; reprinted in *CahTun* 10 (1962): 533–48.

Seston, William. "Rémarques prosopographiques autour de la Tabula Banasitana." *BCTH*, n.s. 7 (1971): 323–31.

Seston, William, and Euzennat, M. "Un dossier de la chancéllerie impériale: la Tabula Banasitana." *CRAI*: 468–90.
Deliberate policy of Romanizing influential Berbers to reduce incursions.

Sherwin-White, Adrian N. "The Tabula Banasitana and the Constitutio Antoniniana." *JRS* 63 (1973): 86–98.
Against Saumagne (1952) on Latin rights.

Simon, Marcel. "Le judaïsme berbère dans l'Afrique ancienne." In his *Recherches d'histoire judéo-chrétienne*, pp. 30–87. Paris, 1962.

Smith, David S. *Report of an Expedition to French Morocco, 1952*. Durham, 1956.

Souville, Georges. *Atlas préhistorique du Maroc*, vol. 1: *Le Maroc atlantique*. Paris, 1973.

Speidel, Michael P. "A Thousand Thracian Recruits for Mauretania Tingitana." *AntsAfrs* 11 (1977): 167–73.
Uses Dessau 2763 as evidence for land route from Numerus Syrorum to Volubilis. But see Rebuffat (1971): very fragile hypothesis; no milestones; might have been a simple track leaving no vestiges.

Tarradell, Miguel. "Las excavaciones de Lixus, 1948–49." *Ampurias* 13 (1951): 186–90.

———. "Marruecos antiguo: nuevas perspectivas." *Zephyros* 5 (1954): 105–39.

———. *Lixus*. Tetuan, 1959.
Not seen.

———. *Marruecos punico*. Tetuan, 1960.
Important but inaccessible.

———. "Contribution à l'Atlas archéologique du Maroc: région de

Tetouan." *BAM* 6 (1966): 425–44.

————. "El impacto greco-fenicio en el extremo occidente: resistencia y asimilación." *Assim et résist* (1976): 343–55.
Mostly in Spain. There is Phoenician-Punic jewelry in Tangier necropolis of sixth-fourth century. Towns like Lixus and Tamuda keep personality and prosper from agriculture, as recorded on coins. There was "diffuse stimulus," leading not to slavish copying but to independent artistic creation, as in Iberian sculpture.

Terrasse, Henri. *Histoire du Maroc.* 2 vols. Paris, 1949–50.
Includes Islam.

Thouvenot, Raymond. "La maison d'Orphée à Volubilis." *PSAM* 6 (1941): 42–66.

————. "La maison du cavalier et de l'apse." *PSAM* 6 (1941): 67–81.

————. *Valentia Banasa.* Paris, 1941.
Fundamental; has been updated by Thouvenot and A. Luquet in *PSAM* 9 (1951) and 11 (1954): 7–140, on baths, southwest quarter, macellum, northeast quarter, and finds of statuettes.

————. "La maison du chien." *PSAM* 7 (1945): 105–13.
Pages 114–56 treat the Houses of the Ephebe, Twisted Columns, Cavalier, and the Baths.

————. "Deux nouveaux diplômes militaires trouvés au Maroc." *CRAI* (1948): 43–48.
Banasa and Volubilis, Hadrian and Antoninus Pius.

————. "La maison des Travaux d'Hercule." *PSAM* 8 (1948): 69–108.
Pages 109–43 treat the House of the Nereids, Half-Columns, Apse, and No Name.

————. "Buste-appliqué trouvé à Volubilis." *RevArch*, ser. 6, 32 (1949): 1000–1007.
A bacchante?

————. "Diplôme militaire délivré par l'empéreur Domitien." *CRAI* (1952): 192–98.
From Banasa.

————. "Le premier Banasa." *PSAM* 11 (1954): 7–140.

————. "Rome et les barbares africains." *PSAM* 7 (1945): 166–83.
"Altar of peace," from reign of Severus Alexander.

————. "Maisons de Volubilis." *PSAM* 12 (1958).
Palace of the Gordians, House of Venus mosaic. Important.

————. "Note sur les mosaïques du Maroc." In *La mosaïque gréco-romaine*, vol. 1, pp. 267–74. Paris, 1965.
Lixus: Mars and Rhea Silvia. Volubilis: Venus, Labors of

Hercules, Ganymede, Orpheus, Dionysus.

————. "Banasa." *EAAC*, suppl. (1970).

————. "L'aréa et les thermes du Capitole de Volubilis." *BAM* 8 (1968–72): 37–52.

————. "Au delà des camps romains." *BAM* 9 (1973–75): 377–408. Believes there was a road to Altava: cites Roman coins from Meknes, Bou Hellou, Taza—but see Euzennat (1960). Believes Romans withdrew, between Aurelian and Diocletian, from Thamusida, Banasa, and Volubilis.

Wharton, Edith. *In Morocco*. New York, 1920.

Wuilleumier, Pierre. "Le municipe de Volubilis." *REA* 28 (1936): 323–34.
Severus and Bostar.

Zehnacker, Hubert, and Hallier, G. "Les premiers thermes de Volubilis et la Maison de la Cîterne." *MEFR* 76 (1964): 343–417.

12. The Balance Sheet of Empire

Bénabou, Marcel. "Résistance et romanisation en Afrique du Nord sous le Haut Empire." *Assim et résist* (1976): 367–75.
Sweetly reasonable summary of his book (1976; see chapter 2). Praising resistance is fashionable, but Carcopino (1943) spoke of the Berber aptitude for civilization. Romanization a matter of transfers, of property, of population, of culture. It could be reward or discouragement to independence. Not all tribal wars were trivial: not Tacfarinas' revolt, nor those under Hadrian and Pius. Limes a surveillance net; Romans were after not extirpation but equilibrium. Cultural resistance could be religious, social, linguistic. Roman religion could be refused, selectively adopted, integrated, remodeled. Romanization and resistance not dichotomous; most natives could neither go the whole way to nor totally reject Roman influence.

Churchill, Winston. *The River War*. London, 1899.

Colin, Jean. *L'occupation romaine du Maroc*. Rabat, 1925.
A pamphlet with a strong French bias.

Deman, Albert. "Science marxiste et histoire romaine." *Latomus* 56 (1960): 781–91.

————. "Die Ausbeutung Nordafrikas durch Rom und ihre Folgen." *JWG*, part 2 (1968): 341–53.

————. "Développement et sous-développement dans les provinces de l'Empire romaine." *ANRW* 2, part 3 (1975): 3–97.

Dill, Sir Samuel. *Roman Society in the Last Century of the Western Empire*. London, 1899.

Dodds, Eric R. *Pagan and Christian in an Age of Anxiety*. Cambridge, 1965.

Dyson, Stephen L. "Native Revolts in the Roman Empire." *Historia* 20 (1971): 239–74.

Gacic, Pierre. "En Afrique romaine: classes et luttes sociales d'après les historiens soviétiques." *AnnalesESC* 12 (1957): 650–61.

————. "Les historiens soviétiques et la décadence des villes de l'Afrique romaine." In *Actes du 83e Congrès des sociétés savantes*, pp. 160–66. Aix-en-Provence, 1959.

Hammond, Mason. "Ancient Imperialism: Contemporary Justifications." *HSCP* 58/59 (1949): 105–61.

Harmand, Louis. *L'Occident romain*. Paris, 1960.
Roman Africa, pp. 263–89.

Jones, Arnold H. M. "The Roman Civil Service." *JRS* 39/40 (1949): 38–55.

Koch, Hajo. "Die Deutung des Untergangs des römischen Reiches im historischen Materialismus." In Karl Christ, ed., *Der Untergang des römischen Reiches*. WdF 269. Darmstadt, 1970.

Lassère, Jean-Marie. *Ubique populus: peuplement et mouvements de population dans l'Afrique romaine*. Paris, 1977.
A demographic study, soberly documented with maps and tables, of the brighter side of Romanization, sensitively described as "not feeling inferior." Romans improved agriculture, water supply, capital crops; supported large population. Africa *absorbed* foreigners. Quite different tone from Bénabou (1976; see chapter 2).

MacKendrick, Paul. Review of Romanelli, *Province* (see chapter 2), *AHR* 64, part 2 (1959): 913–14.

MacMullen, Ramsay. *Roman Government's Response to Crisis*. New Haven, 1976.

Mazzarino, Santo. "Si può parlare di rivoluzione sociale alla fine del mondo antico?" *Settimane di Studio del Centro italiano di studi sull'alto medioevo* 9 (1961): 410–25, 434–75.
His answer is no.

Percival, John. "Seigneurial Aspects of Late Roman Estate Management." *EHR* 84 (1969): 449–73.
Sees latifundia as anticipating medieval manor.

Petit, Paul. *La paix romaine*. Paris, 1967; English trans., Berkeley and Los Angeles, 1976.

Prachner, G. "Zur Bedeutung der antiken Sklaven- und Kolonen-
  wirtschaft." *Historia* 22 (1973): 732–56.
Rivière, Charles, and Lecq, H. *Traité pratique d'agriculture pour le nord
  de l'Afrique*, vol. 2. 2nd ed. Paris, 1929.
  Stark, objective assessment of French mistakes in Algeria, pp.
  351–67.
Rougé, Jean. *L'organisation du commerce maritime en Mediterranée
  sous l'Empire romaine*. Paris, 1966.
  Statistics on haulage costs.
Snowden, Frank. *Blacks in Antiquity*. Cambridge, Mass., 1970.
  Argues that the Romans were without color prejudice.
Tarradell, Miguel. "El impacto greco-fenicio en el extremo occidente:
  resistencia y asimilacion" (1976; see chapter 11).
Thébert, Yvon; Bénabou, Marcel; and Leveau, Philippe. "La romanisa-
  tion de l'Afrique: un débat." *AnnalesESC* 33 (1978): 64–92.
  Discussion of Bénabou's book (1976; see chapter 2). Thébert says
  Romans were civilizers, denies that there were two Africas, claims
  local élite were partners with Rome and *wanted* Romanization.
  Bénabou agrees that natives showed capacity to integrate, but
  argues that Africans need to be placed at the center of their own
  history. Leveau sees Romans as exploiters and brigands, cooping
  up natives in reservations; he compares Russia under the Czars;
  sees resistance as a "healthy" reaction to this state of affairs.
Thouvenot, Raymond. "Au delà des camps romains" (1976; see
  chapter 11).
Tillion, Germaine. "Dans l'Aurès: le drame des civilisations archaïques."
  AnnalesESC 12 (1959): 393–402.
  Plight of the mountain native in French Algeria.
Van Sickle, C. E. "Public Works of Africa in the Reign of Diocletian."
  CP 25 (1930): 173–79.
Vittinghoff, Friedrich. "Die Theorie des historischen Materialismus über
  den antiken Sklavenhalterstaat: Probleme der alten Geschichte bei
  den 'Klassikern' des Marxismus und in der modernen Forschung."
  Saeculum 11 (1960): 89–131.
———. "Die Sklavenfrage in der Forschung der Sowjetunion." *Gymna-
  sium* 69 (1962): 279–86.
Woolman, David. *Rebels in the Rif*. Stanford, 1968.
  Analogies with ancient Berber revolts. Army corrupt, inefficient,
  oppressive, undisciplined, brutal; landowners parasitic.

INDEX

DATE DUE

GAYLORD			PRINTED IN U.S.A.